INTRODUCTIONS TO ENGLISH LITERATURE

GENERAL EDITOR: BONAMY DOBRÉE

VOLUME IV

THE VICTORIANS AND AFTER
1830–1914

THE VICTORIANS
AND AFTER

1830–1914

By

EDITH C. BATHO

Principal of Royal Holloway College, University of London

and

BONAMY DOBRÉE

Professor of English Literature in the University of Leeds

With a Chapter on the Economic Background by

GUY CHAPMAN

Professor of History in the University of Leeds

THE CRESSET PRESS
LONDON

Published in Great Britain by
The Cresset Press 11 Fitzroy Square London W.1

First published 1938
Second edition, revised, 1950
Third edition, revised and reset, 1962

Printed in Great Britain by
Butler and Tanner Ltd., Frome and London

CONTENTS

Editor's Preface   ix

Preface   xix

Introduction

    I   The Background: 1830-1914   1
   II   Poetry   23
  III Fiction   58
  IV General Prose Writers   86
   V   Drama   106
  VI Conclusion   113
 VII The Economic Background   116

Bibliography   131

  The Background: General Reading   135
  Biography and Autobiography   138
  History   140
  Travel   159
  Science   166
  Theology   171
  Philosophy   187
  Poetry   208
  Drama   249
  Novels and Short Stories   261
  Children's Books   320
  Criticism and Essays   324
  Nonsense and Parody; Humour and Light Verse   346
  Sport   351

Index   353

CONTENTS

EDITOR'S PREFACE

IF there is a danger of literature becoming separated from life, and at times the danger becomes actuality, there is a still greater one of the same thing happening in the study of literature. For one thing, it is apt to become that most arid of studies, literary history, in which history is largely, and literature, in any real meaning of the word, entirely ignored. The literature of the past is only of value in so far as it has significance today, just as history is only of use if it can throw a light upon the contemporary scene. But in the same way as history becomes illuminating by study, by finding out not only what people did, but why they did it, what circumstances, thoughts and emotions brought them to act, so we enlarge the boundaries within which the literature of the past has value if we gain an insight into the circumstances, thoughts and feelings which produced not only the writers, but also the readers of any particular period.

People of different ages speak different languages; not that the words are necessarily different, but the implications are. We of the twentieth century mean very little when we speak of the 'social virtues', whereas to an eighteenth-century writer the phrase implied a whole philosophy of civilization. For us to understand what Donne meant when he wrote:

> *On man heaven's influence works not so,*
> *But that it first imprints the ayre,*
> *Soe soule into the soule may flow . . .*

we have to be at least aware of a whole body of philosophic thought, we might say of philosophic apprehension, to which most of us are likely to be strangers, but which was common at the beginning of the seventeenth century. Thus one of the objects of literary study should be to enable us to translate the language of another day into that of our own, which we can do only if we realize that these divergencies of expression are not merely a question of literary allusion, but of what entered the minds of educated people every day, coloured the spectacles through which they looked at life, and moulded the form in which they uttered their feelings. Thus it is not altogether idle to ponder why Ben Jonson should have written:

> *What gentle ghost, besprent with April dew,*
> *Hails me, so solemnly, to yonder yew.*
> (Elegy on Lady Jane Pawlett)

while Pope should have preferred:

> *What beck'ning ghost, along the moonlight shade*
> *Invites my step, and points to yonder glade?*
> (In Memory of an Unfortunate Lady)

for there is a reason which lies deeper than personal idiosyncrasy.

It has become a platitude to say that an age is reflected in its literature, and like all platitudes the saying has ceased to have any force. Moreover, an age is often much better represented by what is no longer read, than by the works which we still take from our shelves. If, for instance, we try to reconstruct the Restoration period from the plays of the time, we shall get a view which is, to say the least of it, misleading: the age is far better represented by the turgid flood of pamphlets which issued from the inkpots of Penn and Muggleton, Thomas Hicks, John Faldo, and a dozen other forgotten and vituperative sectarians. We tend to read Dryden's plays, or certain of the satires, in preference to his other work; but he is far nearer his age in *Religio Laici* and *The Hind and Panther* than in his now more popular writings. And if each age brings forth its own recognizable progeny, how is it that Milton and Etherege appeared together? or Thomas Hardy and Sir Max Beerbohm? Each age has so many facets, that it is difficult to pitch on any as being its outstanding mirror, though each age will have certain peculiarities not shared by the others. But these peculiarities are often merely the surface of fashion, accidental rather than essential, and until we know something of the age, we cannot tell which peculiarity, when explained, can have any significance for us.

Yet, if it is dangerous to regard literature as the looking-glass of its time, every age has certain problems which seem to it to be of major urgency. In the Shakespearian age it was to incorporate the 'new learning' into life; later in the seventeenth century, the politico-religious issue was the important one; the eighteenth century, again, was lured by a vision of civilized man. That is to say that each age has its philosophy, its scale of values. But philosophy, which to some extent conditions literature, is itself conditioned, partly by the way people live, and partly by the influx of thought from foreign countries, though it is as well to remember that such thought will only penetrate or take root in ground already prepared for it. Therefore, the way people live, their social and political grouping, their economic formation, to some extent determine the way they write. Much has lately been made of the influence of economics: too much, for Marx cannot account for Milton, and it is as easy to argue that the economic development of the eighteenth century was due to the idea of the universe as defined by Newton as that 'Dutch finance', commercialism, and the expansion of trade, gives a clue to the philosophy of history which runs through Gibbon's *Decline and Fall*. Yet economics have an effect on literature; we can see it to some extent in *Piers Plowman*, and without the rise of the middle classes at the end of the seventeenth century we could not have had Defoe, Steele, or Addison; the polite essayist could not have come into being, quite apart from whether or not he preached the bourgeois virtues.

The influence of foreign thought is a subject that has loomed too large, perhaps, in most histories of literature, mainly because literature has on the whole been treated as separate from life. The influence of something on somebody has been a favourite subject for theses, and the answers have been as dubious as the theme has been ill-defined. Because Chaucer, having read Dante's

> Quali i fioretti di notturno gelo
>   chinati e chiusi, poi che il sol gl'imbianca,
>   si drizzen tutti aperti in loro stelo;
>
> tal mi fec' io . . .
>
> (Inferno II, 127 . . .)

or, more probably, the corresponding lines in the *Filostrato* of Boccaccio, proceeded to sing

> *But right as floures, thorugh the colde of night*
> *Y-closed, stoupen on hir stalkes lowe,*
> *Redressen hem a-yein the sonne bright,*
> *And spreden on hir kinde cours by rowe;*
> *Right so gan . . .*
> *. . . Troilus . . .*
>
> (Troilus and Criseyde, II St. 139)

that is not to say that Chaucer was influenced by Dante or by Boccaccio; indeed no prettier contrast to the *Divina Commedia* could be found than *The Canterbury Tales*, though it is clear that there is some connection between them and the *Decameron*. No one really familiar with the comedy of France and England in the seventeenth century, with an understanding of what they were up to, can believe that the English were influenced by the French to more than a superficial degree. Nevertheless, the thought of one country, or of one individual, can very profoundly affect a period, and the scepticism of Montaigne is apparent throughout the seventeenth century from Shakespeare to Halifax. In the same way, German thought obscured the clarity of Coleridge, and puffed the thought and style of Carlyle to an almost intolerable smokiness.

The writer, therefore, besides being a unique individual, is the product of the forces of his time. However much we may regret it, we have to abandon Shelley's contention that 'poets are the unacknowledged legislators of the world', though we need not altogether throw over the position; for though, no doubt, thought does sometimes influence action, it is more usually the successor of deeds, and it will not be denied that Locke is a child of the Revolution just as Hobbes was of the Great Rebellion. It is truer to say with Arnold that poetry is a criticism of life, though not quite true, for literature is, rather, a growth from life itself, a part of life, not its harvest only. We can go further and say that it is so ravelled with life that it can be described also as the soil and the seed. But that a metaphor should lead to such confusion is enough to indicate how closely tangled with life literature is, how complex the relation between them, and how impossible it is to separate one from the other.

.   .   .   .

The object of the Introductions in this series is to give the student some idea of the soil out of which the works of literature grew, so as to be able to grasp with fuller understanding the books mentioned in the Bibliographies. This, then, is not yet another History of English Literature, but rather, to exaggerate a little, a History of England in which not kings, battles, diplomatic or constitutional struggles, nor even economic development, are given pride of place, but literature. As is suitable to our age in which economics have come to be given a high place as determinants not only of our lives, but of our manner of thinking and feeling, and even of our religion, economics will be given more stress than they have hitherto been allowed in books on literature, but not, as some would no doubt wish, to the exclusion of everything else. For instance, though the question of the control of money no doubt played a larger part in the Great Rebellion than we were most of us brought up to believe, it would be absurd to neglect the religious elements in the struggle: indeed, as Professor R. H. Tawney has shown, it was religion itself that largely determined the economic trend of the eighteenth century. The effect of religion on literature is more easily traceable; it begins with *Beowulf* and runs through the whole, most markedly in the periods where the Church to a large extent stamped the nature of society, or when controversy raged high, as it did from the Reformation—or at least from the time of the *Marprelate Tracts*—to the foundation of the Bank of England. Philosophy also plays an important part, not only as being the matter of much admirable writing, but also in the general attitude towards life exhibited by writers who unconsciously, rather than in full awareness, absorbed the ideas of their time. But philosophy again is affected by economics, for no one can doubt that the individualism of the nineteenth century was largely the result of the Industrial Revolution, and that Carlyle's Cromwell must own as forbears Adam Smith and James Watt. Science also can affect literature, and without Huxley there would probably have been a different Hardy.

Another addition to the view of literature is made in these volumes by giving due place to the sister arts where they rose to any height, or seem to have importance with respect to writing. Thus music had an effect on poetry in the seventeenth century, while painting and architecture affected the poetry, and perhaps the prose, of the eighteenth. Wherever, in short, the literary 'movement' of a time seems congruous with that of the other arts, they are included in the survey. Most important of all, however, is the social background, the changes of milieu indicated, say, by the decay of the guilds or the rise of nationalism; for these are the things which most affect the way people live, and therefore what they will most wish to write and to read about.

The Bibliographies which form the major part of each volume are designed to give the reader a detailed view of the literature of each period, and being classified and commented will enable him to study or to enjoy either any special branch, or the whole literature of the period. Only the specialist can read everything; but the aim of this series is to enable anyone who so wishes, to get a clear idea of any one period by reading with a certain degree of fervour for a year, a clear notion not only of what was written, but, so to speak, of why and how, from what impulses, with what objects, and in what conditions morally speaking. It is hoped by this method to integrate literature with life, and so give the writings of the past that meaning without which to read is to be baffled, and to miss that greatest of all pleasures, a sense of unity of feeling with the writer of any work. Lacking this, literature is too far separated from living, and can have but little value.

The manner in which English literature has been split up in this series no doubt demands an explanation. There are many ways in which it can be split up. This has been done variously, sometimes rather arbitrarily by centuries or other irrelevant measuring rods, more often by grouping it around great figures: The Age of Wordsworth and so on; or by literary movements: The Romantic Revival, for instance. These divisions have their uses, but for our purpose here they tend to subordinate life to literature. It is admitted that there is an element of arbitrariness in the present divisions also, but the object is to relate literature to life, disregarding movements, which may only be different aspects of the same thing. The divisions here correspond in the main with social sense; roughly indeed, with what reservations you will, and with contradictions of a rule which cannot be rigid, since human nature refuses to fit into compartments.

In the first period, after the Conquest, you can say with some plausibility (though it is in this period that our structure is weakest) that literature was much more diffused among different classes; it was written for no particular brand of person. Everyone would read *Piers Plowman*, or applaud the miracle plays. There is, it is true, much that is courtly about Chaucer, but there is much that is not. When we get to Spenser, say, we feel that literature is being written for an aristocracy: the drama still maintained its general appeal (though even as early as the moralities and interludes there is a shift away from the people), but it became more and more aristocratic, till under Charles II it was entirely courtly. This period, then, we can describe as the aristocratic period: Donne, Jeremy Taylor, Sir Thomas Browne, Milton, are writers for an aristocracy, and this social sense we may say was established by the Tudors, and exploited by the Stuarts, till it came to an end at the Revolution of 1688. Then, with great suddenness, there appeared a literature written by the middle class, of the middle class, and for the middle class: the pamphleteers, the essayists, and soon Defoe and the novelists. Even the drama changed with startling rapidity, with the anti-aristocratic satire of Farquhar, and the sentimental comedy of Steele.

The ideas of the middle class, with its strong sense, as it then had, of an organized society, gave place in the last century to the idea of individualism, due partly to the French, and partly to the Industrial Revolution. It had been begun by the romantic poets, with their break-away from the idea of 'society' so dear to the eighteenth century. It might grieve Shelley to think that he was the forerunner of the excellent Dr Smiles, but so it is. At all events, individualism dominated literature until 1914. But even before that it was breaking down (having somewhat oddly consorted with a blatant imperialism), as can be seen from the plays of Bernard Shaw, and still more, perhaps, from the novels of Mr E. M. Forster. The post-War period has its own characteristics; a new twist has been given to our view by the recent investigations into psychology, ethnology, physics, and by the Russian Revolution.

There are, of course, several objections to this sort of division: odd elements appear everywhere: you cannot, for instance, rank Bunyan among aristocratic writers. But some division has to be made along chronological lines. It may be objected that the first period needs at least two volumes; it is so long and so varied. That is true, but the number of works which remain which can be of interest to the general reader are comparatively few, and it was thought better to devote more space to our more recent heritages, as being both fuller of works we are likely to read, and as having a closer influence upon our present-day approach to living.

BONAMY DOBRÉE

PREFACE TO THE THIRD EDITION

IT is now nearly a quarter of a century since we wrote this —not history but—Introduction to the history of what, as 'literature', was written during the reign of Queen Victoria, and a few years after: but perhaps we may be allowed to repeat something of what we then said as to our general idea of what we were trying to do.

A history of literature is (or should be) a history of literature: not of social conditions, nor of science or philosophy; it is an account, rather, of the changes in form and content of works to which the name of art, in one respect, or another, can be given. But the form is dependent on, a function of, the content; and the content is not merely what the work is 'about', but also the mind of the man who wrote it. In an introduction to a phase of literature, therefore, we are concerned to follow the changes in content, in social conditions, and in philosophy, keeping in mind, however, that the object of our studies is the understanding and enjoyment of books as literature, and not as social documents.

The question naturally arises in our minds whether those twenty-five years have much altered the perspective of what we were then looking at. We would say, 'On the whole, no!' Here and there an author has increased in stature, been shown to be more revealing, more permanent, in fact has turned out to be greater, than we then thought: we might refer to Clough and to Bagehot among these. No one, we feel, has much shrunk. Of others we felt a little modification was to the point; something had been left out, or been over-emphasized. We have accordingly made a thorough revision of what we said, altering where we thought it necessary, but leaving the main picture much as it was.

We would like to repeat our thanks for the help we received in the first instance, though many of our helpers are, alas, dead. We feel that wherever we may have diverged from their views, they would not be averse from the change.

It may be added that the Bibliography has been brought up to date, to include works printed up till December 1960.

E.C.B.
B.D.

I

THE BACKGROUND

1830-1914

OUR period is probably no more complex than any other, but it seems so because it is closer to us than the previous ones. Time has not performed so much sifting for our benefit; the actual number of authors and of books written is enormously greater than before, so that it appears almost impossible to make any clear general statements, or to disengage the cross-currents. One is forced, therefore, within the limits of endurable space, to put forward statements which should instantly be qualified, while at the same time being acutely aware that the history and significance of these eighty-five years will not be the same for one type of mind as for another.

Yet it can be said, without much fear of contradiction, that the age represents the triumph of the middle classes, and what is significant about this particular 'rise' is that the new middle classes did not aspire after the culture of the aristocracy, as they did in, say, 1700-20, but insisted that their values were the right ones, their culture final.

The first Reform Bill of 1832 ushered them in vociferously to the halls of power: the second, of 1867, enthroned them there, as the Manhood Suffrage Bill of 1917 may have portended their doom. Throughout the period the dominating ideas—and the reactions against them—were those based on middle-class idealism, middle-class prosperity, the whole system reaching its height in the sixties and seventies, when Queen, Lords, and Commons showed a singular, unprecedented homogeneity of thought and feeling; a middle-class monarch, an aristocracy identifying itself with the middle class, the whole mass of *bons bourgeois* sailing forward on a glorious sea of confidence, wafted by an hitherto unimaginable breeze of prosperity, feeling that the secret of living had at last been discovered, and that all the major problems were solved, or in sight of solution. The cracks in the structure were to appear later. And in the main the literature of the period is literature about the middle class, for the middle class, by the middle class, even that written by the most violent critics of the edifice.

The Victorian age still stands for most people as one of smug complacency, of hypocritical piety, and of unhealthy prudery. But even a very superficial examination shows us something in the main far different, though certainly one aspect, especially at one period, lends support to the unveracious commonplace. At the beginning we find a society which, having survived the terrors aroused by the French Revolution, was bent upon building itself up so as to avoid such an event at home: it based itself upon the Industrial Revolution, and, while casting an uneasy eye upon Malthus, pinned its faith on Ricardian economics and Benthamism (the doctrine of Utilitarianism, 'the greatest happiness of the greatest number'), which the wide-spread and prevailing Evangelicalism of the period did little to temper. It weathered the famines of 'the hungry forties', and the Chartist and other disturbances, menaces which, alarming in the thirties, were not laid until 1848, a year which seemed to prove that however much the Continent might totter, England was solid. The Exhibition of 1851 was the herald of a new age, with the middle-class industrialist, supported by the country squire and an obedient parsonage, firmly in the saddle, an age which reached its height in the middle-class apogee referred to above. All was for the best in the best of all possible countries. It was, indeed, admitted that there were still some injustices, the poor needed bettering morally and physically, but all would be cleared up by science and sound religion. In short, many agreed with the Mr Roebuck, pilloried into fame by Arnold, that there had never been anything so glorious in all past history: 'I pray that our un-rivalled happiness may last.'

Whatever it may have been, happiness or anything else, it did not last. The insularity of the period gave place in the eighties and nineties to a form of imperialism, the best side of which was voiced by Kipling. This, however, was to be a comparatively short phase: the nasty taste which the Boer War and the commercial side of Rhodes's imperialism left in the mouths of many (see, for instance, Mr Belloc's *Emmanuel Burden*) gave a fillip to the socialism which was still, however, middle class, being sponsored by Shaw, the Webbs, Wells, and others; the hero of the Battle of Trafalgar Square in 1897 was even the aristocratic Cunninghame Graham, while the dockers, in their great strike of 1890, were successful owing to middle-class support. The nineties show themselves as a confused and seminal period. 'To some it is the heyday of British Imperialism, when the empire "found itself". To others, observing the early undergrowth of socialism and the memorable trade-union conflicts, it is the time when the British proletariat "found itself". Those again, concerned with the fashionable surface of life and letters in London are struck with the revulsion from puritanism to raffishness, and speak of the "naughty nineties" . . . If we look at the Press revolution, we may call it the age of vulgarisation; but if we note how much material was being accumulated for the great educational advances of the next century, we may think of it as the dawning-hour of a new popular enlightenment.'* By the Edwardian period, then, the old Victorian picture (though not necessarily all the old Victorian ideals) had been completely shattered; the middle class was criticizing itself furiously, not in mere matters of detail or sentiment as the novelists from the beginning had done, but in questions of fundamentals, of structure. The superb confidence, the sense of being right, had gone.

Socialism, one need hardly say, had been present all through the period. It begins, in this connection, with Owen's

* R. C. K. Ensor. *England, 1870-1914. Oxford History of England,* 1936.

*phalansteries,** but its nature was all the time changing. Yet, like so much in this age, it was curiously paradoxical. The revolutionary, or rather reformist ideas of the Chartists, such tame ideas they seem to us living in a time when virtually all have been carried out, became largely through the direction taken by the Trades Union movement, Fabianism, with its doctrine of the inevitability of gradualness. But the movement was throughout shot with individualistic, more clearly Benthamite ideas, strangely at variance with the doctrines of Marx, which only at the end of our period really began to affect socialistic thought. Morris, for all his 'communism', was a hero-worshipper, and Wells had his Samurai. Nevertheless the old Victorian ideal of individualistic effort was decaying; this central middle-class idea was being attacked at the root.

Perhaps, indeed, the most salient point about the age, apart from the idea of progress which began many generations earlier, and which is still a part of our outlook on life, is this individualism (different from the eighteenth-century idea of independence within a rigidly defined social scheme). It was impossible under an aristocracy, with its ordered hierarchy, but it fell in quite naturally with Utilitarianism, and the ideas of the French Revolution as found in Tom Paine's *The Rights of Man*. The greatest happiness of the greatest number was to be achieved by individual freedom and individual effort. It was comforting to think that the miseries of the poor were due to their defects of character; Samuel Smiles's *Self Help* showed every robust and honest man the way to prosperity: and if the poor perished, was not this according to the law of nature that Malthus had discovered?

But apart from that, the trend of imagination led to the hero. To Carlyle, hero-worship was 'a fact inexpressibly precious'; he himself largely lived on the idea, which

* Self-supporting, self-contained communities, run on a socialistic, even communistic, basis. They were tried in Ireland, the United States, and Hampshire, at Glasgow, and especially New Lanark. Though some were temporarily very successful, all ultimately failed.

although he declared it to be out of fashion when he wrote, became one of the later characteristics of the period. Many older people still living were brought up under the shadow of great heroes. Even Morris, though he wrote the socialistic *News From Nowhere*, often enough glorified the hero. So did Charles Kingsley, and even Stevenson: and it was this hero-worship, just as much as the political ideas of Empire Federation, or financial ideas such as tariffs, that was responsible for Imperialism. How the idea of the individual as the most important consideration was pursued to the vanishing point will be traced when we come to discuss the novel.

A preliminary glance at the literature of the period once again warns us that in collating an age with its literature it must always be kept in view that the best minds may very well be in reaction against their age. The mass of Victorians did not think like Carlyle or Matthew Arnold, they thought, rather, like Martin Tupper or Trollope; and it was for that reason that Carlyle and Arnold wrote. We cannot deduce the age from its great writers, except in obverse, though, of course, they too were of their age. The great prophets of the time were all, for one reason or another, against the characteristics we have come to regard as typical (possibly because of their invectives against them): Ruskin, Morris, Tennyson, in many ways Browning, to add to Carlyle and Arnold and such lesser lights as Ebenezer Elliott. Nothing is finer in the history of literature than the constant fight for righteousness against cruelty and smugness which was waged by the chief figures of the time; and their urgent protests are as indicative of the age as the complacent 'moral philosophies' of the far more representative Tupper. There were indeed men with minds better than Tupper's who were confident that all was at last well, such as Macaulay, who gladly trumpeted forth the glad tidings, or Trollope or Surtees who placidly accepted the supposition for fact: but there is hardly a writer of influence who shared the supposed Victorian self-gratulation. They were nearly all in rebellion against it, loudly indignant or tortured with doubt. Even

Browning's well-known and vociferous optimism has been analysed as a bellow to cover his distress.

Perhaps the thread of 'medievalism', the cry of 'back to the Middle Ages' which occurs so often, may be attributed to a more general reaction against the ideas and realities of the period. It began, no doubt, in the eighteenth century, with the ballad-cult, Ossian, and other manifestations, and it was encouraged by Scott; but with the Victorians it ceased to be merely literary. Architecturally also it had begun in the eighteenth century, largely as a joke; in the nineteenth, as early as Pugin, it became a moral principle. This thread permeated much of the thought of the period, through manifestations as different as the writings of Cobbett and the productions of the Oxford Movement, but always as a protest against actual conditions, intellectual or physical. We see it not only in Morris, strangely enough in a self-styled adherent of Marx, but in Tennyson, Ruskin, and Arnold, and in historians such as Freeman. It is lamentably evident in much of the architecture of the time, the pity of it being that its most lugubrious manifestations should have coincided with the growth of popular education, making schools unnecessarily repellent, and spoiling hundreds of charming villages with hideously gloomy structures. Medievalism continued on through the Guild Socialism of the Edwardian period, persisting to recent times in some economic reformers, in Mr Belloc, in G. K. Chesterton, and in the Thomist revivalists. It constitutes one of the back currents in opposition to the idea of progress.*

How far it owed its strength and persistence to the Oxford Movement it is difficult to judge. Known at first as the Tractarian movement, later as Puseyism, this internal revolution in the Church figures as the most important centre of intellectual ferment in the early Victorian age. It is difficult for us, over a hundred years later, to appreciate the heat engen-

* A possible view is, that faced with the horrors of the Industrial Revolution, and thinking the price paid for progress too high, some were panic-stricken, and tried to bolt backwards through history.

dered by the issues which later turned to questions of ritual
and vestments, this violent quarrel of surplices or no surplices, this partisanship over various differences of opinion.
We come to forget that 'Pusey was never a Puseyite'. It
produced little literature that we now read, except for what
Newman wrote; but in the days when tracts and sermons
were common mental food, it had great literary importance.
The reasons why it caused so much excitement become a
little clearer if we try to analyse its emotional ingredients. It
was partly an attempt to clarify the religious confusion of the
time, a crusade against somnolence and dogmatic indifference. The spur to this, possibly, was Catholic Emancipation
(1829): dogma had to stand against dogma, just as when,
after 1871, Nonconformist disabilities were removed, the
High Church party was driven to accentuate its difference
from Dissent. It was partly a reaction against the new
rationalisms—Godwinism, Benthamism, and the rest. It may
to some extent have gained strength by suggesting itself as a
good receptacle for a dwindling romantic movement. It was a
symptom of the 'back to the Middle Ages' trend, and it was
to some extent a purely Tory reaction against the growing
power of the middle classes. But in the main, certainly in the
eyes of those responsible for it, it was an assertion of authority,
of authority lying outside the scope of Parliament. As a religious movement it was of profound interest to the majority of
people at that time, who were for the most part passionately
earnest about religion, and in some of its aspects it received
the support of the Evangelicals: without them, indeed, it
would hardly have been possible. But it soon went too far for
general acceptance: it cast a doubt, now accepted as being
well grounded, upon the Protestantism of the Thirty-Nine
Articles, notably in Newman's famous, and to most people
abhorrent, *Tract XC*, which rang the tocsin in every loyally
Protestant heart in the country. It seemed that the only
logical end was Rome, and many of the more eager spirits
seceded. In the fifties, indeed, there was a violent Papist
scare, owing to the re-establishment of the Roman Catholic

hierarchy in England. This was what came of Catholic Emancipation!* The Englishman was up in arms (as he was again, more tepidly, in 1927-28). All his dread of religious authority was awakened; he remembered the tyranny of Laud, not to go back further, though he seemed forgetful of the still worse tyranny of the puritan Saints. But the scare died down, and gradually the movement ceased to have much spiritual significance except for its adherents, and the issue became a political one. The attempt of the Church to impose its discipline met with one defeat after another,† one of the best remembered being the failure of the ecclesiastical authorities to punish a clergyman who had denied the doctrine of eternal punishment; the lay courts would not uphold the judgment, 'and took away from orthodox members of the Church of England their last hope of everlasting damnation'. The Public Worship Act of 1874 reaffirmed the authority of the state, as did in a different way the struggle over the 'Deposited Book' in 1927-28.‡

After about 1850, indeed, following the secession of Newman and others, the Oxford Movement ceased to be of great importance in its original form. In theology it broadened through contact with other types of thought; its distinction from Church Evangelicalism came to be one rather of ritual than of principle; the impulse behind it turned largely into the channel of social work. Within Church doors the High Church throughout our period was fighting a losing battle against what came to be termed 'liberalism': it suffered from 'traitors', as we shall see later in another connection. But if ritualism is still disliked by the non-church-going public (by the end of our period the great majority of the

* When, a little before the Crimean War, Florence Nightingale started a hospital for nurses in Harley Street, her committee wished to exclude Roman Catholics. But Miss Nightingale was a practical woman.

† For greater detail in these matters see the less 'external' sketch of the religious movement in the Bibliography pp. 171 seq.

‡ Yet neither affirmation was effective: the Public Worship Regulation Act was a dead letter within a few years, and the 1928 Prayer-Book is in use in many places under episcopal authority.

nation), it has triumphed in the Church itself, and the bishops, once hostile to it, have rallied to its side in a modified form, which those who still go to church prefer to any other.

It is difficult to assess the literary weight of this movement. Its importance to the people of its time can be judged by its appearance in literature, not only by its own right, so to speak, in the works of Keble, Newman, and others, but also in the works of the novelists such as Shorthouse, and especially Charlotte Yonge, whose books did much to break down the barriers earnest people erected against novel-reading. It can also be seen clearly in the work of its attackers, such as, to take a minor instance, Marmion Savage. It is difficult to trace its effects in later work, though it is even clearer in the works of certain poets than it is in that of the novelists named, Christina Rossetti, Patmore and Dixon, and, some would claim, Francis Thompson and Alice Meynell. Coalescing as it largely did with the Christian Socialism of F. D. Maurice, its influence can be found in the school of literature which he influenced, and which will be referred to later. In the popular mind it is easily confused with the aesthetic movement, stained-glass windows and incense-loving oddities such as Dowson, who nevertheless made some poetic utterances which still have power to move.

To most of us now the Oxford Movement is a matter of old unhappy far-off things; but a battle fresher in the memory was that which waged between science and religion from about 1860 to 1890. It was, no doubt, a mistaken war, and it is seen today that there is no necessary conflict between the two; but very few people saw it at the time, though some on the Church side* stated calmly that no inquiry into truth could possibly injure Truth, while many on the scientific side recognized that their enemy was not religion, but narrow-minded theology. From our point of view, however, the history of this period can be regarded as a struggle, not between religious conceptions—such as was the struggle between the High, Low, and Broad Churches (roughly, between

* Dean Church especially.

Scholasticism and Liberalism)—but one between Christian belief and unbelief, or, at any rate, between belief and the right to free thought, which might include atheism; rationalism, in short. If Newman was a hero on one side, so was Bradlaugh on the other. From the beginning of the century there had been a thread of atheism, from Godwin through Bentham, James Mill, and Harriet Martineau; but this was another matter. Rationalism (to its enemies a gross and shallow materialism) warred with religion (regarded by the other side as a gross and blinding, anti-progressive superstition), and in the main rationalism won, though its enemies may now with delight see it in turn attacked by other 'superstitions', such as aberrant psychologies, or the Divinity of the Proletariat. And the centre round which the battle raged was science.

Work in technical fields, such as electro-magnetism, a field graced by Faraday, probably had little influence except in so far as it reinforced the utilitarian movement, and encouraged the idea of progress and the sense that the troubles of existence were being conquered. But advances in the field of biology created a minor revolution. It began with a work by an anonymous author, later revealed to be Robert Chambers: *Vestiges of the Natural History of Creation*, published in 1844. It was scientifically unsound, but it startled believers of all denominations by giving a different view of the creation from that contained in Genesis, and it first made widely known the idea of the descent of man from monkeys, or of both from some common ancestor. It caused a furore; but it was not until Darwin published *The Origin of Species* in 1859 that the battle really began, and a new epoch dawned. The theories of science seemed for once to become comprehensible to the great mass of people; the idea of evolution, till then little known to the public, strongly reinforced the agnostic element represented by such teachers as J. S. Mill.*
The idea in its purity can be said to have been liberating

* In that very year Bagehot wrote, 'To-day, when scepticism is in the air . . .'

to Church and laity alike; but the worst side of it was that a popular misconception of the notion of the survival of the fittest gave another argument to the extreme individualists who did not see that, though nature might be red in tooth and claw, this did not argue that society should be constructed on such a basis. Huxley, who in the end taught them better,* reached the popular ear more widely than anyone, thanks to his humanism and his lucid prose, and he was one of those writers who for the next decade or two made the literary and thoughtful world resound with the noise of battle.

In a sense, both sides were right to fight. The Church thought that the new vision of the universe and of humanity, besides being false, would empty the churches—as it did; while the scientists could with more than a little justice accuse the godly of obscurantism, of denying the truth because they did not like it. The new views, however, received some support from certain members of the Church, regarded as 'traitors', such as those who contributed to *Essays and Reviews* (1860); and they were assisted by Bishop Colenso's *The Pentateuch and the Book of Joshua Critically Examined* (1862), which seemed to many believers to be a deadly stab in the back. Whatever the justice of the quarrel may have been, the middle of the century is filled with people who were losing their faith, either from scientific conviction or, with J. A. Froude and Mark Pattison, in reaction against the Oxford Movement. Clough was plunged into a state of despairing worry; Mrs Browning sought support in Mr Sludge, the medium; many came to the conclusion with Tennyson, that

> *There lives more faith in honest doubt,*
> *Believe me, than in half the creeds.*

Later we find a more frank rejection of Christianity in certain

---

* In the Romanes Lecture: Prolegomena to Ethics. 1892. But as early as 1845, Matthew Arnold had said:

> *Man must begin, know this, where nature ends;*
> *Nature and man can never be fast friends.*

groups, as in the paganism of Swinburne, which was less marked in Meredith, and a more general loss of faith, though just at that time such poets as Patmore and Gerard Hopkins were writing the best religious poetry produced since the seventeenth century. Agnosticism, or atheism, rose to its height in Hardy's gloomy acceptance of a malign fate, in the grimly complacent attitude of Butler, and the more boisterous defiance of Bernard Shaw. The way orthodox religion had broken up may also be judged by the multiplicity of 'faiths' or cults that cropped up—Christian Science, Spiritualism, the schools that followed Madame Blavatsky, the extreme perhaps being marked by such groups as returned to black magic and flagellation.* But much of the religious impulse gathered itself together in the Edwardian period in the form of idealistic socialism, of dreaming after Utopias; it is this which is more characteristic than anything else of the first fourteen years of the twentieth century.

This was partly the product of another important thread of thought and feeling apparent from the very beginning of our period, a thread which can hardly be called a movement, and to which, if it were, it would be difficult to give a name. One might perhaps call it roughly the humanitarian re-forming movement, fighting urgently against the effects of the Industrial Revolution and the economic orthodoxy of the time, the *laisser faire* doctrine which entrenched itself behind the phrase 'the inexorable laws of economics'. Shaftesbury is the popular hero of that battle in its early stages, but the real instigator was Michael Sadler, who compelled the government to investigate factory conditions, and who deserves a place in the story. It was through him that the public became aware, by means of the commission's report, of the appalling conditions of work and child labour which profoundly shocked all reasonable and feeling men and women. Much of the literature of the earlier part of our period is an outcry against the hideousness of the new civili-

---

* A similar multiplication of sects occurred in the seventeenth century for much the same reason; dissatisfaction with orthodox religion.

zation, especially around the forties and fifties. Besides works which will be mentioned later there was Hood's 'Song of the Shirt', published in 1844 in the Christmas number of *Punch*; there is Mrs Browning's 'The Cry of the Children'. This aspect of thought or feeling was given invaluable support by the Christian Socialists, headed by F. D. Maurice, founder of the Working Men's College. Christian Socialism did not last long in its original form; to some extent the Tractarians merged with it, and it revived later, and is visible in its latest form in the work of Bishop Gore. It was under Maurice's banner that Charles Kingsley and others fought so bravely;* and it is largely owing to Maurice that socialism in this country has taken a form which distinguishes it from Continental socialism. There has always been a strong section of the intellectual middle class working strenuously for it, a section that increased enormously during the Edwardian period, not only amongst the Fabians, and which is represented in literature by such men as Galsworthy.

But, throughout, the period shows an inextricable weaving of threads, of factions which seem leagues apart in philosophy combining for some object or another, idealism often making strange bedfellows. Rationalism, evangelicalism, utilitarianism, the Oxford Movement, Christian Socialism, materialism, the Salvation Army, agnosticism, revolve round one another in an extraordinary dance, now setting to partners, now furiously attacking one another. Each can take credit for something in the achievements of this amazing period, which was one of enormous vitality—if literature is any indication—and of continual conflict. What binds the period into a whole is the moral sense, the social conscience, which animated the middle class: the need for self-justification, the strain of puritanism, ran through everything. If the English of our period believed in Mammon, they also believed, to as great an extent, in God; they worshipped both. The puritan virtues, with their abnegation of enjoyment, led, as has been so often pointed out, to the accumulation of wealth in the hands

* See the chapter on Fiction.

B

of those who practised them. What is typical of the beginning of the period can be traced, in varying forms, to the end. A manufacturer of the thirties might make cruel use of child labour, but he would insist upon his little slaves singing hymns if they sang at all.* God was strangely twisted into the service of Mammon, and the service of Mammon made to seem that of God. Even so delicate, contemplatively religious a poet as Aubrey de Vere could write, after, moreover, criticizing virtue built up on the clay foundation of self-respect:

> Grasp ye, with ampler aim, that good
>   His tragic creed o'erprizes:
> With loftier mind revere in him
>   The Will that energizes
> The strong right hand, the lion heart
>   The industrial truth and valour:
> When comes reverse, he too can die,
>   But not in dirt and squalor.
>
> . . . Be yours to act! To manhood born
>   Be men! 'Who worketh, prayeth:'

while even Ruskin spoke of 'the three great Angels of Conduct, Toil, and Thought'. There is, indeed, an aspect of horror in some manifestations of the Victorian mind, though other confusions are more charmingly naïve. It did not seem at all odd that in 1846 the Rochdale Pioneers, the founders of the co-operative movement, should put at the head of their articles:

> The objects of this Society are the moral and intellectual advancement of its members. It provides them with groceries, butchers' meat, drapery goods, clothes and clogs.

By much the same interweaving of motives, Evangelicalism contributed to the Imperialist movement; and though this queer partnership lays the British open to the common

---

* See G. M. Young in *Early Victorian England*. Vol. II. Printed separately, with additions, as *Portrait of an Age*.

charge of hypocrisy, no one can deny that the effects have been beneficial. Justice, social and moral betterment, have always gone hand in hand with exploitation; and if the force behind colonial expansion has been the need for foreign markets and foreign investments, the individuals who have carried it out have been largely ignorant of this, and have been devoted servants of the people whom they ruled. If the deeper forces have been sinister, their agents have been idealists.

Whatever the political or religious complexions that chiefly obtained at any moment, the age throughout was one of reform, often achieved in the teeth of the popular theories of the day. Just as Catholic Emancipation seemed to some a grave mistake, so the Factory Acts seemed outrageous heresy to the Utilitarians. Yet the later developments, down to Mr Lloyd George's Old Age Pensions, owed as much to materialism as they did to religion, and still more possibly to the humanitarianism which, born in the eighteenth century, permeated all shades of middle-class opinion in the nineteenth. Protection of the worker, the education of his children, care of the unemployed, these things came by rapid stages, sometimes from one motive, sometimes from another, with the philosophy of the day often, and religious opinion sometimes, against them. One is tempted to think that what brought them about was a strong sense of common humanity which overrode party, and even class distinctions. It is odd that by the end of our period the most individualistic country in the world, with the possible exception of the United States of America, had become one of the most socialistically advanced countries in either hemisphere.

Socialism is perhaps a word one should be careful in using; it would be safer, as Mr Somervell suggests,* to call it collectivism. But at all events, society had changed markedly in its structure. Our period covers the extinction of the country interest and the triumph of industrialism, and it carries us almost as far as the capture of the latter by finance. But apart

* *English Thought in the Nineteenth Century*, by D. C. Somervell.

from this, and in the face of the individualistic spirit of the period, it also covers an almost bewildering development of State, and especially municipal control, not only in industry, but outside it, in schools, colleges, libraries, trams, swimming baths, communications. It is another of the odd paradoxes of the time. It was the middle classes that decreed all this, and at the same time decreed, perhaps, its merging into another class; for our period covers the rise, if not to power, at least to political importance, of the workers, of what came to be called the 'proletariat'; and at the same time it covers the expansion to its utmost limit of the Empire from the maintenance of which the working classes would dissociate themselves.

Economically the period was in the main one of previously unthinkable progress. There are troubled times until 1848, for some people indescribably cruel times that called out the early revolutionary spirit. Then, until the late seventies, an unparalleled prosperity and an astonishing increase in population carried the nation forward; a profound optimism and complacency seems to have been the dominant sentiment; revolution was dead. The difficulties that arose after that period were overcome, or lived through, but the seed of doubt had been planted. Neither a new prosperity nor the songs of the Imperialists could hide the fact that something was wrong; it was this that made the middle class critical, or at least dubious of itself, and gave the solid basis to socialistic thought which, characteristic of the Edwardian period, has yet to work itself out. It is this fluctuation in prosperity which gives the divisions to our period; there are the Early Victorians; then the Victorians proper, the Victorians of the great, energetic, characteristic age to which we attach a definite flavour which smacks neither of the eighteenth century nor of the twentieth; and then the late Victorians, Edwardians, and neo-Georgians,* who foreshadowed and

* We are already forgetting the ethos of those years, and are apt to look back on them as a golden age. Those born after 1900 are hardly aware of the strikes, the constitutional struggle, the war scares, the suffragette movement which marked the period.

partly prepared the age in which we struggle and hope with scarcely a trace of complacency left.

.   .   .   .

After this all too brief preamble, we can examine a little more fully what literary fruit the period brought forth; but before looking at it in any detail, it may be as well to venture a few remarks which can be applied to the whole period, generalizations to which many exceptions can, of course, be found, and which are perhaps not wholly true of any one man, but which may nevertheless serve to mark certain characteristics that lend a colour to the whole period. Such generalizations need not carry conviction: it is enough if they suggest a plausible approach; for art, by its nature, refuses to lend itself to broad statements, seeing that it is the first business of every work of art to be different from all others. Yet in every age there are certain stylistic qualities which enable us to recognize a work as belonging to that age; and by style is meant not only craftsmanship in words, but the whole question of handling the material. In these realms certain qualities or their absence can be noted.

The most forcibly striking aspect of most of the Victorians is their voluminousness. It is not that they wrote on a large scale; others have done that: it is not, to put it bluntly, that they wrote much, but that they wrote too much. They did not stop when they had made their effect, they went on making it, and so weakened it. Take even Tennyson, who was less guilty than most; the effect of *In Memoriam* is made long before the close of the poem. One can think of scarcely any of the outstanding writers of the period who would not benefit by a generous use of the blue pencil, even in their short lyrics. Something, of course, must be allowed for exuberance, for a superabundant vitality; but a vitality more certain of itself would not have erred in that way. There is often the sense of a quality both in structure and style that can only be described as bulbousness. The giants of the age were undoubtedly giants, but they seem to us to be malformed. There is not one who can be accepted as a whole, as we accept Milton or Dryden, Swift or Johnson; with the possible exception of Hardy, we can accept a portion only. It is doubtful if there is one of the 'minor' writers of whom we can say, 'Ah! that is the man for me!', as we may, at varying times, say of Herbert, or Marvell, or Traherne, the possible exceptions being completely outside the main Victorian current, Emily Brontë, Newman,* Gerard Hopkins. The age seems to abound in potentially great men and women who for some reason or another remain frustrated as artists.

There are several possible explanations, though it would perhaps be better to regard them all as contributory causes. One of them, certainly, was the lack of any standard of criticism, especially of self-criticism. They (to use 'they' generally, for any suggestion will apply more to one writer than to another), they seldom seemed aware of their own limitations, and would try to handle realms of thought, emotion, or observation, with which they were not fitted to deal, though in other realms they were altogether competent. Lord David Cecil has noted this with respect to the novel, and it is true also of their poetry (Tennyson dealing with the slums), and sometimes also of their essay-writing (Matthew Arnold adventuring into theology). There is a horrifying lack of structure about their novels—Dickens is the worst offender here—as there is about their longer poems: few had a sense of what Arnold called 'architectonics': almost everywhere there is a distressing lack of compactness.

We feel the same unnecessary expansion when we come to the question of style in the handling of words, as distinct from style in the handling of material. In neither is there that sureness, that adaptation to the desired effect, that mastery of the medium which we associate with the works of the seventeenth century, from the small fry to the great

* In referring to him as a minor writer, I do not mean that he was a minor figure: he was one of the greatest of the age. The others scarcely existed for their contemporaries.

whales.* Think of the fuliginous artillery of Carlyle, the un-
shackled wordiness of Browning, the tidal rush of many of
Dickens's pages, and the verbiage of much of Swinburne.
One may suggest what is meant by one or two examples from
poetry. Take this from Tennyson:

> *O that 'twere possible*
> *After long grief and pain*
> *To find the arms of my true love*
> *Round me once again.*

Six lines follow, then:

> *A shadow flits before me,*
> *Not thou, but like to thee:*
> *Ah Christ, that it were possible*
> *For one short hour to see*
> *The souls we loved, that they might tell us*
> *What and where they be.*

and compare those lines with

> *Western wind, when wilt thou blow,*
> *The small rain down may rain?*
> *Christ, if my love were in my arms,*
> *And I in my bed again!*

Has not the fifteenth-century poet the advantage in both precision and poetic suggestion? Or contrast Tennyson's *Ulysses*
with the few tercets from Dante; yet Tennyson is one of the
most restrained. Chapman, again, could do in one speech in
a play what Browning took the pages of *Bishop Blougram's
Apology* to achieve. There are two possible reasons for this:
the first is indecision of thought, the second uncertainty of
language. As far as the first cause goes, what has already been
said will explain it: where the second is concerned the reason
is more technical. It has been suggested, and a good case

* Excepting, always, some of the religious controversialists, Prynne,
Penn (who, however, had his moments), Muggleton, Faldo, and a dozen
others. And there is, of course, Blackmore, but no competent person, even
in his own day, took him seriously.

made out for the suggestion, that the linguistic element the Victorians used was ill suited to what they wanted to say;* they were using a language the eighteenth century had forged for its own needs to express very different emotions and apprehensions. If this was so, it is not surprising that there was fumbling, false emphasis, tortuousness, and a reliance upon atmosphere rather than upon precision.

There was one other difficulty with which the early Victorian writers had to contend, namely, the brooding spirit of Mrs Grundy, Victorian prudery, the convention that life was what one would like it to appear (this is not exactly hypocrisy), the Great Taboo which is often, wrongly, regarded as the outstanding characteristic of the Victorian age. Some accepted it willingly, as Trollope, who objected to the smallest chink being made in the fence of 'as we would like it to be', and could write of Rhoda Broughton's novels that they were 'not so sweet-savoured as are those by Miss Thackeray, and are, therefore, less true to nature'. But both Dickens and Thackeray felt the limitation. Dickens complained of it in a letter to Forster,† and Thackeray expressed annoyance at the taboo both in *Vanity Fair* and *Pendennis*: 'Since Tom Jones it has been forbidden to draw a picture of a man.' Some, however, may prefer the interdiction to the swing in the other direction brought about by release from it.

But perhaps the main reason for the Victorian characteristics was the spiritual discomfort of the age; hardly anybody of clear vision or artistic sensibility could accept the implications of the odd God-Mammon worship which pervaded most of the century, the idea that to make money through industry was itself a virtue, and, together with the repression of natural enjoyment (which militated against amassing riches) the virtue most pleasing to God. Emotionally, perhaps, they would have liked to belong to the Church, but in all intellectual honesty, they could not. Materialism, how-

---

* F. W. Bateson, *English Poetry and the English Language*. 1935.
† August 15th, 1856.

ever, did not satisfy them. They really were living between two worlds unrealized, one dead, the other powerless to be born, as Matthew Arnold had the perspicacity to see. It was not an age of scepticism so much as an age of muddle. The Victorians and Edwardians were floundering along to something, valiantly, energetically, but they were floundering; they looked into their hearts and wrote, but what they found in that treacherous organ was a confusion which their heads could not clarify. It is significant that of the three minor authors named who are wholly satisfactory, Emily Brontë created a spiritual world of her own, Newman became a Catholic, and Hopkins became a Jesuit. The major one, Hardy, was completely atheistical.

However all these things may be, it remains true that we read none of the longer poetry of the time with delight in its structure (except, possibly, Arnold's), and very little of the prose for its style. Landor is a glorious exception, but he belongs largely to the eighteenth century, and Thackeray is again an exception because his prose also is that of the eighteenth century. Ruskin, certainly, achieved greatness in some of his descriptive word paintings, but with him it is often a question of purple patches, which we are suspicious of now. Arnold is apt to be flat, lacking in agreeable accidentation (compare him with Jeremy Taylor) and annoying in his reiterations.* Trollope has no recognizable style at all, George Eliot little, and with the exception of Thackeray and Emily Brontë there is not a novelist in the early period who gets his or her effects from the use of a word or the cadence of a phrase. Later in the century there is an improvement. Bagehot evolved a style which could combine volume with epigrammatic lucidity. The scientists, Huxley in particular, brought about a happy clarity, visible in the writers of the later romances, from Stevenson onward. Meredith, certainly, had a style of his own, as had Pater, but the former's was apt to be tortured, while Pater's manner is a little clogged, as

* It is noteworthy that both Ruskin and Morris achieved their most satisfactory prose when addressing working men.

though he were hampered by his medium. Wilde, however, for all his faults, re-introduced swiftness, which we find alone among the Early Victorians in Newman, who transcended the linguistic limitations of his age. With greater freedom of material came greater freedom in using the language. Perhaps the writers who show best in the matter of style throughout the period are the historians and philosophers, from Macaulay to Sir Richard Lodge, from Sir William Hamilton through Bradley to Bertrand Russell. These groups had, the one a clearly limited field, the other a determined intellectual intention.

The above suggestions will need amplification or restriction in dealing separately with individuals.

II

POETRY

TWO characteristics mark Victorian poetry. The first is the great freedom in form and prosody,* which extends to the end of the period, though one often feels that the new forms were the result of fancy, rather than a newness forced upon the poets by new material demanding an original mode of expression. The second, which began to change in, roughly, the eighties, and is no longer true of the Edwardians, is the sense poets felt that they had an immediate mission, ought to utter a message. The mantle of the prophet had descended upon the poet with Wordsworth, so that his later contemporaries and his successors felt that they too ought to assume it. Dowden, writing on Shakespeare in 1875 said, 'He needed not, as each of our poets at the present time needs, to have a doctrine, or a revelation, or an interpretation,' and there can be little doubt but that readers of poetry looked for one or all of these things in the poetry that they read. They did not mind, it would appear, whether poetry was present or not, so long as they got the doctrine, the revelation, or the interpretation; they could swallow Tupper in enormous draughts. They would read Bailey's now unconscionably turgid *Festus* and quote:

> *We live in deeds, not years,*
> *In feelings, not in figures on a dial,*
> *We should count time by heart-throbs,*

while ignoring the 'diaphanous' lyrics of Landor. It was not, one would think, poetry itself that the Victorians asked for, but certain sensations they could remember having found in some of the poetry they had read. This was not altogether to

* For a good description of this aspect see Saintsbury's chapter in the *Cambridge History of English Literature*. Vol. XIII.

the bad. It enlarged the scope of poetry, which, together with the means (as regards diction and prosody) had been unduly restricted towards the end of the eighteenth century, and really continued the new freedom achieved by the Romantics. But it also introduced an alien element into poetry, which sometimes distorted it, sometimes weighed it down, occasionally allowed impostors to creep or bluster into the halls of fame, and at all events made the practitioners themselves uneasy. At its best it revealed itself in a sense of 'nobility': at its worst it introduced humdrum sermonizing or deliquescent sentimentality. It caused the poets to forget that the method of art is indirect, that poetry acts through the subconscious rather than the conscious (a fact perfectly understood in the seventeenth century, though differently phrased); it hoisted them, so to speak, from the fields or out of their studies on to the lecture platform or into the pulpit.

That it made some of them misuse or misunderstand their talents can be illustrated by the fact that Tennyson was shy of his superb lyrical gift, and did not until the third edition, 1853, introduce into *The Princess* the songs that make it live. It caused him to include passages critical of the times into the two *Locksley Hall* poems, passages which are quite out of place, and which insult his genius. It is right for a poet to be aware of the facts and emotions of his time, but he deals with the facts at his peril. What seems to vitiate a good deal of Victorian poetry is that the poets were not resolving their own inner struggles, but were trying to resolve problems alien to them as poets; and this led them into fields where their emotions and a superimposed intellectual structure were at variance.

Tennyson, with his perfect ear and his immediate mastery of versification, was born, one would think, to produce the effects of poetry by his music; even his unrhymed songs give the impression of being rhymed, so deft is his vowel variation. The music is almost always perfect with him, but the word is not always appropriate to the sound. It is rarely too arousing, but it is often too trivial:

Your mother is mute in her grave as her image in marble above,
Your father is ever in London, *you wander about at your*
will.

Sometimes, however, it is splendidly arresting:

> *As when it seemed far better to be born*
> *To labour and the mattock-hardened hand,*
> *Than nursed at ease and brought to understand*
> A sad astrology, *the boundless plan . . .*

Sometimes it is incongruous:

> *And the vitriol madness flushes up in the ruffian's head,*
> *Till the filthy by-lane rings to the yell of a trampled wife.**

It was not within his scope to deal with such matters as the
last, nor within the scope of any writer of that time. That Mr
Masefield in his day could integrate such things into his
poetry indicates not only a difference in talent, but a change
in the view of what poetry can do.

Such blunders—one is justified in calling them such—were
nevertheless merely the price Tennyson had to pay for one of
his great qualities, his attempt to apprehend his own time, a
quality lacking in many Victorian poets, who often denied
its implications, withdrew from it,† or simply ignored it.‡

An artist need not use his own time as subject matter, he can
deal with eternal things: but it is curious that artists, especially in literature, who are not aware of the implications of
their own age, as for instance Milton was, and Wordsworth in
his best period, do not outlive their own day. For it is likely
that if a man does not apprehend his own time, he does not
understand humanity, and so apprehends no other time, for
the historical imagination can only work through equating
the present in some measure with the past. To live without
being aware, in the full sense of feeling as well as of thought,
of the climate of one's age, is only half to live, and half-livers

---

* All the quotations are from *Maud*: I have emphasized phrases.
† To Arthurian or Greek legends, as Tennyson himself, Matthew
Arnold, Morris, and others: also to the Celts or Scandinavians.
‡ e.g., D. G. Rossetti in most of his work.

have never been complete poets. Tennyson was alive to the necessity of sharing the climate of his age; his ambition was to be its poetic mirror, and he used all his efforts to connect what he saw and understood with what he felt. But it is fair to say that his interests were not primarily in intellectual development. He was far from being the stupid man he has sometimes been said to have been: the man who met Manning and Huxley for discussion could hardly have been that; but he did not appreciate his own limits. His genius was for the lyric, or lyric elegiac, and he tried to interpret his age. Instead of being content to sing, he was bent on being oracular.

That is not to deny his achievement; his poetry is often exquisite, sometimes very fine, and at moments indubitably great. To enjoy Tennyson one must read *Ulysses*, the lines to Virgil, the songs in *The Princess*, a number of things in the earlier poems, and *Maud*. To understand him one must read him all—he is of that stature—to find some shockingly bad poetry, some of it due to his post as Poet Laureate, some intolerably mawkish; one must read also his plays and his experiments in classical metres, for he was a first-rate technician, and that implies something more than cleverness: but to find him at his most characteristic and often at his best, to see what he was after and where he stood in relation to his age and to his own work, it is enough to read *In Memoriam*, though one's reading should be glossed by reference to *The Two Voices*, *The Vision of Sea*, *Vastness*, and, especially, *The Ancient Sage*.

It is a fascinating, in a curious way compelling, and in patches great, poem. If it has no form, one all-pervading mood dictates it. It is not 'a medley' as *The Princess* is, but a collection of thoughts subservient to the mood of poignant regret, thoughts which include all Tennyson's philosophy, of which there was perhaps more than is necessary to a poet, and not enough to make up the minimum essential for a philosopher. Yet a philosophy he felt bound by the temper of his age to profess—a 'doctrine, a revelation, or an interpretation'—and in trying to formulate one he found he had

none to offer. As 'a weight of nerves without a mind' he could
only say

> Oh yet we trust that somehow good
> Will be the final goal of ill,

and sum up the passage with

> I stretch lame hands of faith, and grope,
> And gather dust and chaff, and call
> To what I feel is Lord of all,
> And faintly trust the larger hope,

a rather fainter trust, however, than he was to express in *The
Higher Pantheism.*

In Memoriam is in intention a reminiscent, elegiac poem; it
was actually a self-comforting one:

> I sometimes hold it half a sin
> To put in words the grief I feel;
> For words, like nature, half reveal
> And half conceal the Soul within.

> But for the unquiet heart and brain
> A use in measured language lies;
> The sad mechanic exercise,
> Like dull narcotics, numbing pain.

> In words, like weeds, I'll wrap me o'er,
> Like coarsest clothes against the cold:
> But that large grief which these enfold
> Is given in outline and no more.

That is very revealing. Imagine Donne making statements of
that kind, or Blake! It is, in a way, a representative passage;
but there is no passage in the poem which is wholly representative. It is a miraculously varied work, in which Tennyson employed most of his lyrical faculties, which continually
flash out to diversify the stately elegiac measure, and all his
power of dramatic imagery.

It is difficult for us, who regard Tennyson as the smoothest
of metrists, to understand how Coleridge, judging even the

early poems alone, could have found him so rough as not to be able to scan a line of him. This, no doubt, is because he contributed something new to poetry, and that is always enough to render a poet unreadable to those who have ceased to develop those sensibilities after a certain age. But he was not always so smooth; he could sometimes be dramatically swift and tense, as in *The Princess*:

> Out I sprang from glow to gloom:
> There whirl'd her white robe like a blossom'd branch
> Rapt to the horrible fall: a glance I gave,
> No more; but woman-vested as I was
> Plunged; and the flood drew; yet I caught her; then
> Oaring one arm, and bearing in my left
> The weight of all the hopes of half the world,
> Strove to buffet to land in vain . . .

There is some rougher verse still, and for Tennyson, very strangely intuitional thought, in the last section of the second part of *Maud*, in some ways his most interesting poem, except, perhaps, *The Ancient Sage*.

At the present day one is not easy in reading *Idylls of the King*, though here and there are some delightful passages: they, and his by no means unreadable plays, suffer from a certain archaism of language, that sham antiquarianism, the 'escape' looking-back to the Middle Ages, which did so much harm throughout the century. If to the real student of Tennyson they are indispensable, the general reader can be excused for omitting them.

Tennyson has been accused of inheriting the poetry of Keats and letting the inheritance go to ruin. This is an unfair accusation, since to have maintained the demesne he would have had to inherit the age also. There is no really great poet, of the stature of Milton or Wordsworth, in our period, and it seems almost impossible that there should have been one. The early impulse of the romantic movement had subsided; the splendid human hope of the French Revolution had perished. The appalling chemical resultant of the industrial revolution and the evangelical movement lay like a slime over the spirit of the age, to use a handy if indefinite phrase. Some poets struggled bravely for a while, and Tennyson was one of them: but in the end he gave up the struggle, and was content to croon, beautifully indeed, but a little dolefully.*

The next great figure in the main current of Victorian poetry is Robert Browning. His is a curious 'case'. He was, and is, fervently read by people who do not much care for poetry, and among those who do care for poetry he is admired chiefly by the few who are sufficiently trained to appreciate his boldness in versification. There is very little sensuous attraction in his verse, hardly a line, perhaps not a line at all, which one repeats to oneself as one may Tennyson's

> *The moan of doves in immemorial elms,*
> *And murmur of innumerable bees*

or

> *A livelier emerald twinkles in the grass,*
> *A purer sapphire melts into the sea,*

or a hundred others. Nor is there any flashing imagery, hardly anything to free the poetic imagination, nothing like the

> *When the hounds of Spring are on Winter's traces*

of Swinburne. The imagery is mainly photographic, of the sort supplied by

> *Oh, to be in England now that April's there,*

which tells us that the tiny leaf is out round the elm tree bole; so it is not, one suspects, for poetic reasons that the majority of Browning readers read him, but for the spirited emphasis put on thoughts or beliefs they share, or would like to share, as

> *God's in His heaven,*
> *All's right with the world,*

* But see *Merlin and the Gleam.*

a sentiment wrongly attributed to Browning himself; or:

> *Ah, but a man's reach should exceed his grasp,*
> *Or what's a heaven for?*

for those things, and for the flowing, swelling, bursting, outrageous rhythms (which, to be sure, are poetic qualities) in which they are expressed. He has all the vitality of a great poet, seldom the graces. His rhythms compel the reader to his thoughts, hurl them into the arena where his vigorous people clash, gesticulate, and talk, talk excessively. He is read, one thinks, for his thoughts, not for his rhyme, for his dramatic qualities, not for his music, though the last does occasionally undeniably exist, as when he describes Florence as 'washed in the morning's water gold', and in *Pippa Passes*. Sometimes, too, there is a sensuous element.

His dramatic qualities, however, were such in a limited sense, for he had little real turn for the drama, as his failures go to prove. He himself, however, called his pieces dramatic, and indeed, his poems are largely so, in form and in diction. *In a Balcony*, *In a Gondola* are dramatic dialogues, as dramatic as *Pippa Passes*; *Mr Sludge the Medium*, *Bishop Blougram's Apology*, *Fra Lippo Lippi*, *Andrea del Sarto* and dozens of others are dramatic monologues; they are to be uttered with the stress on the meaning rather than on the sound, which is often ungainly. The difference in his intention from that of Tennyson is clear from what Rossetti noticed when he heard them both read their work, Tennyson 'mouthing out the hollow o's and a's', while Browning laid stress on the conversational tones, on the dramatic element. This was where his genius lay, and his manner with its plunging, ploughing, energetic phrasing, his violent prosody—a fellow-poet called it grotesque—is just the manner which would suffer least from the Victorian vice of diffuseness. Whatever Browning may be, he is never flat; and as he gives voice to his characters, expands their casuistry (he can never be accused of contracting it!), we feel that his language follows their passionate thought.

In this respect Browning can be called a metaphysical poet,

but he was not a great thinker. There is no reason why a poet should be, in the sense that he resolves the problems of his age. Yet he did to some extent dwell in its intellectual climate; he joined in the disturbed search after God—a different God that is from the one who brooded Moloch-like over the age of industrial progress—and he sought for Him in a world which seemed to have in it as much as, if not more of, evil as of good. He himself, beginning as an Independent, passed through a period of atheism, to which he added vegetarianism, as a consequence of reading Shelley, and he emerged with a kind of unattached Christianity which postulated a personal God, a life after death to make this life in any way tolerable, and depended largely upon a love of human kind, a justifying love of one person for another. What emerges from his poetry is the sense that he was a great giver, as befits a man of superabundant energy, of genial robustness. He was intensely interested in his fellow-men; he loved them, but he hated evil and the evil in men. As his curious, vivid, muscular creations justify themselves—to themselves as much as to the world—in their long, rough monologues or dialogues, you feel all the while that Browning is concerned with what is ultimately the concern of all great art, the struggle between good and evil: and it was not always the good that won. It is true that as a sane, robust man, he loathed evil, but the creator in him could not always hate the evil man. The philosopher in him might stand aghast, the chameleon poet was delighted.

Perhaps the best poem through which to approach Browning, after the comparatively easy *Rabbi Ben Ezra*, is *Saul*. Written in smooth, for him unusually smooth, anapaestic measure, it contains more delightful imagery than is common with him, is as dramatic as anything that he wrote, and reveals as clearly as any of his work his conception of the spiritual values attained by the perpetual warring in life. The idea is, no doubt, commonplace; but it is the intensity of the emotion, the sense of revelation that it carries with it, that are important. David's return home after he has restored

Saul to sanity by his harp playing, and has himself become aware of the spiritual life, is one of the most moving and dignified passages in the whole of Browning:

> *I know not too well how I found my way home in the night.*
> *There were witnesses, cohorts about me, to left and to right,*
> *Angels, powers, the unuttered, unseen, the alive, the aware:*
> *I repressed, I got through them as hardly, as strugglingly there,*
> *As a runner beset by the populace famished for news—*
> *Life or death. The whole earth was awakened, hell loosed with her*
> *   crews;*
> *And the stars of night beat with emotion, and tingled and shot*
> *Out in fire the strong pain of pent knowledge: but I fainted not,*
> *For the Hand still impelled me at once and supported, suppressed*
> *All the tumult, and quenched it with quiet, and holy behest,*
> *Till the rapture was shut in itself, and the earth sank to rest . . .*

There the urgency of the emotion gave birth to poetry worthy of it, and it is with something of a shock that one turns to lines like these from *Waring*:

> *He was prouder than the devil:*
> *How he must have cursed our revel!*
> *Ay, and many other meetings,*
> *Indoor visits, outdoor greetings,*
> *As up and down he paced this London*
> *With no work done but great works undone . . .*

and that is by no means the worst Browning can do.

His work can conveniently be divided into three periods. The first is the least approachable, but in some ways the most interesting; it is the period of *Paracelsus* and *Sordello*, where he is engaged in a tremendous but hopeless struggle to get the world in order in his mind, to establish values, especially those of love and power, of knowledge and the ambition for knowledge; and in *Paracelsus* he seems to have been consciously aware of the intellectual currents of his time. Then followed the plays, including *Pippa Passes*. In about 1845, a year before his marriage, there opens the period in which he wrote his most characteristic work, from *The Flight of the Duchess* to *The Ring and the Book* (1868-69) a period which contains the fiery monologues, in which the characters seem to lend Browning a power of speculative thought which he was denied when he spoke as from his own person, as Lascelles Abercrombie noted, a period which produced the amazing gallery of portraits to be found in *Men and Women* and *Dramatis Personae*. But after 1869 Browning seems to have lost grip; his poems lack coherent driving-power, which in default of form, is what had held them together. A superb energy of being, rather than a directive energy of thought, had previously sustained his powers, and the first is apt to fail with years, especially when combined with an inveterate habit of dining out. For a time what was held to be his 'thought' maintained him in his hard-won popular esteem, but this seems to have fallen into the hands of the wrong people, sentimentalists who found the courage they lacked in some of Browning's rather too strident asseverations, and of those who like to think they could live by vicarious thinking. There is more than a little truth in Sir Max Beerbohm's witty vision of Browning Taking Tea with the Browning Society, where the rosily eupeptic poet is fawned upon by a number of pale, peaky-faced individuals of the earnestly spinsterish variety. The admiration of such did his reputation much damage in the minds of healthy younger generations. But his work exists apart from his thought: he did create, and moreover he helped to forge new instruments, so that his influence is becoming apparent in the work of some of the younger writers of the present day, possibly through the medium of Ezra Pound.

Of Mrs Browning it is not necessary to speak at length. Highly applauded in her day, suggested for the laureateship together with Tennyson on Wordsworth's death in 1850, there is little of hers that can now be read with more than vague suggestions of pleasure, even the once famous lyrics, such as the one that begins

> *What was he doing, the great god Pan,*
> *Down in the reeds by the river?*

which pleased one's later infancy. *The Mask*, however, with its suggestion of Christina Rossetti, stands up better. How little she was a poetess one can judge by taking something that she wrote in prose, and seeing what became of it when she turned it into poetry.

Whilst I was writing these last sentences, I heard her [the nurse] calling me—Wilson was out and Robert at the Post Office—'Signora—Signora—*ecco i Tedeschi!*' The Austrians had arrived. We ran out on the terrace together —and up from the end of the street and close under our windows came the artillery, and baggage wagons—the soldiers sitting upon the cannons motionless. Slowly the hateful procession filed under our windows. The people shrank back to let them pass, in the deepest silence—not a word spoken, scarcely a breath drawn.

'*Ah, signora,*' said our nurse, '*fa male di vedere questi. Sono brutti questi Tedeschi.*'

That is vivid and to the point. It became:

> *From Casa Guidi windows, gazing, then,*
> *I saw and witness how the Duke came back.*
> *The regular tramp of horse and tread of men*
> *Did smite the silence like an anvil black*
> *And sparkless. With her wide eyes at full strain,*
> *Our Tuscan nurse exclaimed, 'Alack, alack,*
> *Signora! these shall be the Austrians.' 'Nay,*
> *Be still,' I answered, 'do not wake the child!'*
> *For so my two-months baby sleeping lay*
> *In milky dreams upon the bed and smiled,*
> *And I thought, 'He shall sleep on while he may,*
> *Through the world's baseness. Not being yet defiled,*
> *Why should he be disturbed by what is done?'*
> *Then, gazing, I beheld the long-drawn street*
> *Live out from end to end, full in the sun*
> *With Austria's thousands. Sword and bayonet,*
> *Horse, foot, artillery—cannons rolling on,*
> *Like blind slow storm-clouds gestant with the heat*
> *Of undeveloped lightnings, each bestrode*

> *By a single man, dust-white from head to heel,*
> *Indifferent as the dreadful thing he rode,*
> *Like a sculptured Fate serene and terrible.*

Elizabeth Barrett seems here to have abandoned the virtues of prose for all the minor horrors of poetry. *Aurora Leigh* is not so bad as this, and her love poems to Browning, *Sonnets from the Portuguese*, will always possess a certain value, not so much as poetry, for as such they are not very good, but as the revelation of an adoring love, and a confident integrity of emotion.

Matthew Arnold brought to poetry qualities quite other than those which Browning possessed; and if he lacked something that Browning had, namely an effulgent imagination in certain directions, he possessed, or at least aimed at, 'sweetness and light' as opposed to Browning's wordy struggles and his often murky atmosphere. He also brought to poetry a notion of form rare throughout the age, experimenting in the lyric, especially the rhymeless variety, as Tennyson also did, and, vaguely, in classical metres. He was essentially a meditative poet, not an impulsive one. He thought about his poetry rather too much as something to be formed on a model, as opposed to an utterance which would imperiously demand its own form. Saintsbury remarks on his 'elaborate assumption of the singing robe', and it can be argued that he strove too much after elegance. Yet there is power in his poetry, the power of a thinking man deeply concerned for civilization. This concern appeared, however, more clearly in his essays, of which more will be said in another section, while in his poetry he expressed much of his love for the countryside, and the emotion, the emotion for himself, which he felt in living in a civilization which seemed to him largely pointless, as a slack period between two worlds, in which

> *The Kings of modern thought are dumb.*

His age was

> *an iron time*
> *Of doubts, disputes, distractions, fears,*

filled with men and women

> *Who fluctuate idly without term or scope,*
> *Of whom each strives, nor knows for what he strives*

and have nowhere to turn amid

> *this strange disease of modern life*
> *With its sick hurry, its divided aims.*

He himself, certainly, was in travail with the problems of his time, but he never brought forth a solution; and since he laboured under the Victorian curse of supposing that a poet ought to bring forth a solution, a feeling of melancholy and frustration pervades nearly all his verse. He could take no delight in the material glories of his age, nor care for the religion and dogmas offered him. Man, he was convinced could be moral, and if morality could only exist side by side with belief in revelation

> *For God's sake, believe it then!*

Yet in 'Mycerinus' he questions whether morality was really worth while, and whether he, at any rate, would not have done better to live by his impulses.* Certainly one may think that he would have done better to write by his impulses, and there is splendour and poetic movement in the free verse rhythms that might have come from the Greeks but may have come from Goethe, especially in what is in many ways his best poem, *The Strayed Reveller*. Much of his work reads a little dully to us now, but every once in a while it quickens to vivid life, or deepens to a profound sense of the need to go on in spite of the apparent futility of existence, an idea expressed almost as often as that of the directive nullity of his age. The 'On to the City of God' of *Rugby Chapel* is a strange and perhaps slightly false note for him to strike: more often it is:

> *The world in which we live and move*
> *Outlasts aversion, outlasts love,*
> *Outlasts each effort, interest, hope,*

* Morris brought this out much more clearly in the words of Sir Galahad in *The Chapel in Lyonesse* (*Defence of Guenevere*).

Remorse, grief, joy—and were the scope
Of these affections wider made
Man still would see, and see dismay'd
Beyond his passions' widest range
Far regions of eternal change,

or an expression that nature 'seems to bear rather than rejoice'.

It is unlikely that his short lyrics will ever again meet with glowing approval. 'Strew on her roses, roses' can safely be relegated to the schoolroom; but there are others with a real lyric quality. It is probable also that his longer poems, and his tragedy *Merope*, will be of delight chiefly to the curious scholar, except for the far more living *Sohrab and Rustum*, which, in spite of its long Miltonic similes, and equally Miltonic use of resounding proper names, is a moving story well told, with an undeniably fine ending. But his medium length poems, such as *The Strayed Reveller* with its fascinating rhythms, *The Forsaken Merman* with its swinging measures, and the highly individual *Scholar Gipsy* and *Thyrsis* always have a place in the story. There are others which will be found attractive.* He does, indeed, use 'Ah!' more often than any other poet, and, perhaps owing to his deliberate avoidance of the stresses proper to his native language, the syncopation of which with the metrical stresses forms much of the charm of our prosody, he employs the italics unforgivable in a poet: but he repays reading, if only because he was a capable man who took poetry seriously.

Arthur Hugh Clough, to whom *Thyrsis* is a memorial, had been Thomas Arnold's favourite pupil at Rugby, where he was something of a prig. For a time he adhered to the Oxford Movement, but fell from that pinnacle of mixed emotions into a gloomy agnosticism bitterer than Arnold's own. Yet behind his despair there was hope, as in his most popular, but by no means his best poem, 'Say not the struggle naught availeth'. He broke away from this somewhat pompous attitude, and its outworn diction, in his 'hurry-scurry anapaests',

---

* And even more: *Dover Beach* is deeply felt.

the lively and colloquial 'Bothie of Tober-na-Vuolich' and 'Amours de Voyage'. His extremely interesting 'Dipsychus', in all sorts of metres, faces the struggle central to Victorian attitudes, between the natural man and the social unit. It is relevant today, and Clough, after a period of neglect, is acquiring a very particular, if minor place, in the poetry of our period. The satirically inclined will always appreciate his 'The Modern Decalogue'.

It is usual to append James Thomson to Clough, though there is no especial connection, except that they both express the doubt which balanced the Oxford Movement in importance, though Thomson's disbelief went beyond agnosticism into out-and-out atheism. He was a critic of some force, but of little influence, since his work appeared in journals of limited scope, such as *The Secularist* and an organ devoted to the tobacco trade. His admirers rightly claim that he was a poet of some variety, and could express joy, but his masterpiece is undoubtedly *The City of Dreadful Night*, which gives voice to his melancholy despair with almost terrifying force, which for gloomy terror can only be matched by his *Insomnia*. Thomson was an able metrist, as happily in command of rhyme as Byron; but he was inclined to be slovenly, and occasionally fell into poetic verbiage—again that lack of discipline, of respect for the medium, which Arnold saw was the weakness of his age: but when he is really moved there is a fleeting grandeur in his verse, as in the last section of his famous poem where he describes Melancolia:

> The moving moon and stars from east to west
>   Circle before her in the sea of air;
> Shadows and gleams glide round her solemn rest.
>   Her subjects often gaze up to her there:
> The strong to drink new strength of iron endurance,
> The weak new terrors; all, renewed assurance
>   And confirmation of the old despair.

The quality is too diffuse to be given in a single stanza; but the moon is more enduring than the happier one of *Sunday up*

the River which contains the well-known 'Give a man a horse
he can ride.'

.   .   .   .

Emily Brontë must be taken separately, out of the main
current: it is as impossible to 'place' her poetry as it is to
pigeon-hole *Wuthering Heights*. Both are highly individual, indubitably the work of a great artist, but perhaps the poetry
suffers more from Emily Brontë's inexperience in writing than
the novel does. It is a commonplace to attach the word 'rare'
to its quality, and the adjective, though vague, serves as an
approach. But 'rare' must not be taken to mean any tenu-
ousness of quality; it implies, rather, in her best work, a
purification down to essentials. She seems to have striven all
the time to express some mystic experience in the simplest
possible terms, an experience which coloured life for her. All
three sisters seem in their work to have behind them this unusual illumination, but it comes out clearly in Emily's poems
alone, though by no means consistently. She is the reverse of
sensuous, but she is not ascetic; and though she was not a
master of vowel sounds, and sometimes stumbles in her
rhythms, there is about her best work the stamp of greatness,
the greatness that can bear to relate inner contemplation
to the outward vision, the greatness that finds calm in the
storm, and which though it by no means calls for pity, is yet
touched with pathos. She is the greatest poetess England has
produced, with the possible exception of Christina Rossetti;
but one feels that if she had lived, she would have held the
first place unrivalled.

Another poet somewhat out of the main track is Edward
FitzGerald. It has been suggested that Thomson succeeded
him as a poet of pessimism, but that is to misunderstand the
main theme of *The Rubáiyát of Omar Khayyám*, the poem by
which FitzGerald lives. It is true that FitzGerald shared as
little as Thomson in the optimism of the great bulk of the
mid-Victorian middle class, but his importance and his
popularity are due, not only to the skill and charm of his

verse, but to his reaction against the gospel of toil. Bourgeois political economy, as Marx remarked, was the most moral of sciences; its ideal was 'an ascetic but usurious miser, an ascetic but productive slave'. FitzGerald called loudly for wine, for roses, for love, for some of that impulsive enjoyment of life which the puritan, even the atheistical puritan (perhaps the latter especially), regarded with suspicion. Victorian morality at its strictest left out something essential to the fulness of life: FitzGerald tried to replace it, and it is not surprising that when his poem became known it was very widely read. Besides, it was easy to read; the verse was smooth and full of exotic imagery, the surface meaning easily grasped, the pessimism delightfully romantic. What the great public did not grasp, however, was that for FitzGerald the wine and the love were merely symbolic, though the roses had their actual counterpart, and it did not perceive that Fitz-Gerald had a sense of humour. But it did feel obscurely that he was spokesman for certain humane values which were in danger of being ignored. Toil and duty were no doubt very well, but there was also impulse, beauty, leisure, and, if not wine, at least the wine of life. It was prepared to accept determinism, especially when so nicely put and so charmingly palliated, so long as it was not the determinism of 'the inexorable laws of economics', that blasphemy which blackened a century, and against which Ruskin cried in vain. It felt that this life also was worth living, especially as the claims of the next were beginning to grow a trifle dim. Its instinct was right, even though it largely misunderstood the poem, and was, possibly, unable to appreciate its poetic qualities.

Yet FitzGerald's poem did not constitute a poetical revolution, as did those of the pre-Raphaelites (some of which preceded the *Rubáiyát*). It was a protest, not a new conception of the poetic idea. But here one must be careful: it is not altogether easy to say who the pre-Raphaelite poets were, and their conceptions of poetry varied a good deal. Dante Gabriel Rossetti is the only pattern poet of the school, but one must include his brother William Michael, and his sister

Christina, though she had other affinities. Morris, Swinburne, Patmore, for various reasons and in different senses, are part of the movement, and so, naturally, are such minor figures as the sculptor Woolner. But certain things can be said at least about their beginnings, as published in their magazine, *The Germ*, which appeared in 1850,* and lasted for four numbers. It is easier to describe what the school did not stand for than to say what it maintained, or, rather, in what way it differed from the current of the time. It did not regard poetry as being prophetic, as being mainly philosophical in intent; it was not on the whole going to concern itself with intellectual complications after the manner of Browning, nor with social conditions. Thus it divided itself sharply from the great writers of the time, Tennyson, Browning, Arnold. As an intellectual movement, judged in retrospect, it is something of a backwater; it smacks too much of the ivory tower. But it brought back into the idea of poetry something that was in danger of being lost, the idea of its indirect effect, the idea that it deals with modes of thought and feeling that cannot be expressed in prose, and it reintroduced the notion of the primacy of personal feeling. It went further—and this is its positive achievement—it introduced what, if not entirely lacking in English poetry up to that date, was very rare— symbolism; and it insisted on simplicity of expression and directness of sensation. Rossetti's own passionate, erotic symbolism was unlucky with reference to the period, still evangelical and largely prudish. It need not surprise us that he should have been regarded as belonging to the 'fleshly' school.

> *Lady, I fain would tell how evermore*
> *Thy soul I know not from thy body, nor*
> *Thee from thyself, neither our love from God,*

is the kind of utterance open to misinterpretation. But the attack surprised and hurt Rossetti, just as in our own century

* The Pre-Raphaelite Brotherhood (P.R.B.) was founded in 1848. Its first pictures were exhibited in 1849, and much derided till Ruskin flew to the rescue.

it surprised and hurt the essentially puritan D. H. Lawrence to be attacked as an immoralist and regarded as a satyr. Both represent a curious vein which seems to run peculiarly through English poetry, a kind of fleshly mysticism which has never been investigated as a tradition, but which deserves attention. It is not to be confused with the sensuousness leading to something else which Keats illustrates; it is something that you get in one other pre-Raphaelite, Coventry Patmore; you get it in Blake, you get it in Milton. But it shocked the Victorians.*

What it symbolized for Rossetti was a curious state of being, half sensuous, which gave him not very clear apprehensions of the Infinite: it was not visionary, as with Blake, nor intellectually clear-cut as with Milton: it was not so profoundly emotional, nor so deeply religious as with Patmore, nor was it a protest as it was with Lawrence: but it had an effect of reality strong enough to be compelling. With him it was inseparable from an idea of beauty; and it is here that we come upon the beginnings of the aesthetic movement. Rossetti wrote poetry of considerable intellectual force; he gave new life to the ballad, in a modified, cultured form; and if he had no very strong rhythmic gift, he had a fine sense of vowel sounds. He could write narrative; he was happy in his imagery, he could 'paint' extremely well in words, as you would expect; and like many painters, he had an extraordinary faculty for seeing unexpected likenesses. But the unique quality of his poetry, the quality which makes him important, and which adds something to the body of English poetry which it would not otherwise have, is the amazing sense of silence he can produce. With him you can hear the silence, not only when he is describing it, as he sometimes does, but even when he does not seem to be thinking about it. It is a mystic silence, a rapt silence. He can therefore give an astonishing effect of the cessation of all movement, almost of time itself, the sense of 'I have been here before' with the whole attention concentrated on one thing, preferably a

* Blake, Rossetti, and Patmore, were influenced by Swedenborg.

thing to be seen. The symbolism and the imagery are both splendidly illustrated in 'The Blessed Damozel', but there he did not quite attain the motionless quality of some of his later work.

This kind of emotion, somewhat removed from the ordinary sphere of existence, was something new to the average Victorian reader, and it roused Browning to furious remonstrance:

'Yes, [he wrote to Isa Blagden] I have read Rossetti's poems—and poetical they are—scented with poetry, as it were—like trifles of various sorts you take out of a cedar or sandal-wood box: you know I hate the effeminacy of his school,—the men that dress up like women,—that use obsolete forms, too, and archaic accentuations to seem soft—fancy a man calling it a lilý—lilíes and so on; Swinburne started this, with other like Belialisms—witness his harp-playér, etc.: it is quite different when the object is to *imitate* old ballad-writing, when the thing might be; then how I hate "Love" as a lubberly naked young man putting his arms here and his wings there, about a pair of lovers—a fellow they would kick away in the reality. . . .'

Rossetti, on his part, admired Browning and tried his hand, not very successfully, at the monologue in 'Jenny' and in 'A Last Confession'; and he may have admitted some bite in the criticism, if ever he heard it, especially as regards the medieval affectations of the school. We certainly admit it:

> *The air blows pure for twenty miles*
> *Over this vast countrié;*
> *Over hill and wood and dale it goeth,*
> *Over steeple and stack and tree:*
> *And there's not a bird on the wing that knoweth*
> *How sweet the meadows be*

is a production by John L. Tupper, which we may call typical of the school, since W. M. Rossetti's sooth is almost as silly, even though his manner is not quite so bad. Nor was it so much D. G. Rossetti as others of the school who exhibited

what they called 'an entire adherence to the simplicity of art'.
This is what it led to in the hands of Thomas Woolner in his
once famous poem 'My Beautiful Lady':

> *I love my lady; she is very fair*
> *Her brow is white, and bound by simple hair;*
> *Her spirit sits aloof and high,*
> *Although it looks through her soft eye*
> *Sweetly and tenderly . . .*

and so on until we get

> *My lady's voice, altho' so very mild,*
> *Maketh me feel as strong wine would a child,*

a not very happy simplicity when you consider that strong
wine would most likely make a child feel sick. The naked
lubberly young man is better than this, especially as Rossetti's personifications were natural to him, and by no means
a convention. It is true that 'The House of Life' sonnet collection is a trifle 'scented with poetry', and that the scent is
that of hothouse flowers; but some of the sonnets are very
good indeed, and they deal with a range of emotions which
were a closed book to Browning.

But it is Christina Rossetti's achievement which is the
highest. 'Goblin Market', written in 'dedoggerelized Skel-
tonic', has something of earth in it, of earth mysteriously
apprehended as it was in her brother's work; but for the rest
her poems breathe an extraordinarily pure spirituality. Her
range is narrow, but within that range she reaches perfection,
a perfection in subject, in feeling, in treatment, which places
her nearly on a level with George Herbert, of whom one is
often reminded when reading her, especially in such things as
'Uphill', with its typically Herbertian conclusion:

> *Shall I find comfort, travel-sore and weak?*
> *Of labour you shall find the sum.*
> *Will there be beds for me and all who seek?*
> *Yea, beds for all who come.*

Pre-Raphaelite though she was in her beginnings, she is the

finest flower of the Oxford Movement, to which she intellectually and emotionally belonged. Swinburne, who was a fine if too ecstatic judge, said of her 'New Year Hymn' that 'it was touched as with the fire and bathed as in the light of sunbeams, tuned as the chords and cadence of refluent sea-music beyond reach of harp and organ, large echoes of the serene and sonorous tides of heaven'. There is, perhaps, too much of the pathos of renunciation felt between the lines of her poetry, its very perfection adding to the pathos, so much so that Sir Walter Raleigh declared, when he had to hold forth about her, 'The only thing that Christina makes me want to do is cry, not lecture.' For in the clear quality of her verse, the renunciation, though strong, has not forgotten the pain, nor the price paid; it is a little nostalgic:

> *The irresponsive silence of the land,*
>   *The irresponsive sounding of the sea,*
>   *Speak both one message and one sense to me:—*
> *Aloof, aloof, we stand aloof, so stand*
> *Thou too aloof, bound with the flawless band*
>   *Of inner solitude: we bind not thee*
>   *But who from thy self-chain shall set thee free?*
> *What heart shall touch thy heart? What hand thy hand?*

There is silence there, too, but it is an intellectual, not a physical one.

It is the most violent change imaginable to turn from her cool atmosphere to the fervour of Swinburne, from her quietude to his rushing verse, to his renouncing of all renunciations, to his cry for liberty, for libertinage, to the somewhat adolescent yelp for freedom which he retained to the end. Nobody can suggest that his eroticism is symbolic; the complaint is, rather, that it is not very actual. He was a strange phenomenon for that time, one to make puritanical flesh creep; and his acceptance, if not without some resistance, by the Victorians, is an illuminating guide to what was happening to the Victorian moral sense. It was the beginning (with Ouida's novels) of the breakdown of evangelical

c

rigidity. But that, of course, is not Swinburne's title to fame; nor is that why his contemporaries read him, nor why he is read now. His triumph is that he created poems, objects of delight, almost solely by the glory of the word, by the music which often is, literally, stunning. He seemed, and seems, possessed by the instrument he played on; he was superbly intoxicated by it, and his drunkenness is infectious. At first, however, he seems to have been more in control. If from the beginning he juggled (using the expression in no belittling sense) with words and their sounds, and showed himself the most consummate wizard in prosody, one feels that in the first two series of *Poems and Ballads* and in the ever-fresh *Atalanta in Calydon,* he had had something to say, at once as a man and as an artist. It is not so much that he immediately established himself as a 'pagan' poet (in the common acceptance of the epithet), as that as a man he stood for every kind of freedom, personal and political, fearing no liberty, hating all restraint, and as an artist for something less didactic than the public had become accustomed to. There is, no doubt, a good deal in *Poems and Ballads* which now strikes us as false, poetically rather cheap, in the manner of:

> Could you hurt me, sweet lips, though I hurt you?
>   Men touch them, and change in a trice,
> The lilies and languors of virtue
>   For the raptures and roses of vice;

but how easy they were to say! How they stuck in the memory! They were deliriously exciting. It was glorious to walk along country lanes and shout out the splendid chorus of *Atalanta*:

> When the hounds of spring are on winter's traces,
>   The mother of months in meadow or plain
> Fills the shadows and windy places
>   With lisp of leaves and ripple of rain;
> And the brown bright nightingale amorous
>   Is half assuaged for Itylus,
> For the Thracian ships and the foreign faces
>   The tongueless vigil, and all the pain.

There is a suggestion of meaning, of profound meaning even, in those lines and the ones that follow; there is dignity too in the play, and real tragedy, combined with a sense of rebellion against God (which possibly is the theme of tragedy). There was also in those days a sense of thrilling wickedness in the lines which Christina Rossetti expunged from her copy: 'The supreme evil, God.' Some of the other choruses are as good:

> Before the beginning of years
>   There came to the making of man
> Time, with a gift of tears;
>   Grief, with a glass that ran . . .

and it is not true to say, as is sometimes said, that time and grief might well, had better even, be transposed. Swinburne was fond of the sort of transposition he here employed, and it had a real point; partly the surprise of the transposition, partly the exactness of the statement when the attributes have been changed about.

It is too often said that Swinburne's immense fluency ran away with him and destroyed the poet;* this is to beg the whole unresolved question of matter and manner, to use a phrase of those days. It is true that he did not much care to exercise self-criticism (that he was capable of it is proved by his admirable parodies of himself),† but then, any restraint would have been fatal. The streams of varied sensation within him were bound to pour themselves out in a tumultuous torrent of words; the only discipline it was safe to apply was that of prosody. We may wonder at several poems of politically naïve content, when as in *Songs Before Sunrise* he was inspired by European revolutionary movements, but he had not the advantage of our own disillusions. And he could build up on a solid basis of thought and argument, as in 'Hertha'. But he was not the sort of man who could divide himself. He soon broke away from the pre-Raphaelites, under

* Another theory is that the prudery of his age, reinforced by Watts-Dunton, inhibited the expression of his most profound emotion.
† e.g., *Nephelidia* (Collected edition, Vol. V).

whose wing he began to write, and his output is extremely varied. Not only was he master of many forms, but he could produce poems of large scope, such as 'The Hymn of Man', very complex, or such simple things as 'The Jacobite's Lament', and poems on children. His three plays on the theme of Mary Stuart are too bulky to tempt the ordinary reader; they contain some fine passages, and some dramatic moments, but they cannot be ranked as successes. A minor triumph, however, is his fragment on Cesare Borgia, *The Duke of Gandia*, in which, for once, the staggering verbal felicity was tamed, and acted under the control of a directive intellectual force. It not only reads well, but plays with great effect.*

More typical, perhaps, of the movement as a whole is William Morris. *The Defence of Guenevere* contains his best, most concentrated verse, and his medieval reconstructions have a reality which most of the similar work of the century lacks. He could not produce the effect of tension that Rossetti did, but a robuster blood flows in the veins of his people, a more generous joy exists in their songs. His energy and his capacity are shown to the full in *Sigurd* and *The Life and Death of Jason*. But more popular and, on the whole, more characteristic of Morris is *The Earthly Paradise* in which Norsemen and ancient Greeks alternately recount the stories or myths, heroic or romantic, of their respective climes. Just as Morris wrote these tales in various Chaucerian metres, from a sense that these were fitting for what he wanted to say, so he seems to have had the same sort of interest in his people as Chaucer had; but he is at his best when adapting or translating the northern sagas, for there he could indulge both his romantic temper and his leaning towards the epic. His tales are all extremely readable as tales, but Morris wrote verse too easily to be always a satisfactory poet, and there is sometimes a monotony in his verse which Swinburne at his most impulsive would have known how to avoid. He appears too truly to have felt that he was 'the idle singer of an empty

* Swinburne's prose is touched on in the Bibliography.

day', and that his poetry was not worth troubling over. He gives the impression, therefore, of going on and on interminably, and is sometimes in danger of becoming prosy. He has, too, some irritating tricks, and one can be almost sure that whenever a line ends with 'man' or 'swan' or some similar conclusion, the rhyme will be achieved or approximated with 'waters wan'. The tales, in fact, seem to express, not intensity of experience, but width of knowledge and variety of sympathy, though the dominating feeling is often one of melancholy, due to the brevity of life and the bitterness of love. But he is never languorous, and whatever reservations one may make as to the poetry, one will freely admit that the stories in *The Earthly Paradise* are undoubtedly charming, and make very agreeable reading. They add to the general impression of Morris's immense and genial stature.

Very different from Morris and Swinburne, comparable rather with Christina Rossetti, is that unduly neglected poet Coventry Patmore. One might say that he is pre-Raphaelite only where he is weak ('the simplicity of art' theory did him a good deal of damage), and that when he really expresses his own developed nature he is as little pre-Raphaelite as Christina herself. His long, and once very popular poem, *The Angel in the House,* is held by his admirers to contain some very fine things; to the average reader it will appear insufferably silly, 'garrulous and prattling'. Crabbe become sloppy, or, as Gosse said, 'humdrum stories of girls who smell of bread and butter'. The theme, when discovered, is splendid, the treatment is deplorable. One can hardly believe that the great Odes were written by the same person. This group of poems, covered by the title *The Unknown Eros* (which includes 'The Victories of Love') conveys, in beautifully controlled free verse, the mysticism of love combined with an intense religious feeling as no other poems in the language do. They are not all, strictly speaking, odes, though they are all written in the irregular metre often associated with odes in the history of English poetry. When these have been read it is easy to see that the ideas to a great extent lie swaddled in *The*

Angel in the House; but Patmore deliberately turned from what was easy and popular to forms which, though difficult, satisfied his intellectual integrity and his high artistic conscience. He was a visionary, a seer, not afraid of the flesh, essentially intuitive, original but not impeccable in prosody, inventive in form. What he thought and felt about religion and poetry he expressed in the title-essay of the volume *Religio Poetae*, and he had the courage to carry out his precepts in his odes. The 'transfiguration of the senses', which he found in love, carried him forward to the mystic love of the Roman Catholic church, and it is to be eternally regretted that he took the advice of Gerard Hopkins and destroyed the essay *Sponsa Dei* which most clearly expressed this. It was, Hopkins told him, 'telling secrets'. Nevertheless it would seem that the main idea of the poem, 'an interpretation of the love between the soul and God by an analogy of the love between a woman and a man' is implied in the odes. Such notions may be repellent to some, but that does not prevent the odes from being great poetry. Nor are they all transcendental; some of them, especially when his children are the subject, express his great tenderness and delicacy in a perfectly simple manner, a deceptive simplicity if you like, but giving much for ordinary minds to grasp. It seems likely that Patmore's reputation will grow, while that of others, more regarded during our period, will dwindle.*

Meredith also can be loosely linked with the pre-Raphaelites; at least he once shared a house with Rossetti and Swinburne—an entertainingly varied trio. But there is little else to attach him to this group; there was nothing 'aesthetic' about him, he did not hanker after the past, and though not so riotously 'pagan' as Swinburne, there is nothing specifically Christian about him. Yet he has this in common with the group, the determination that art should not, in Ruskin's phrase, be the handmaiden of morality; it was not the busi-

---

* Other religious poets, who attach themselves to this line of tradition, such as Alice Meynell and Francis Thompson, are briefly treated in the Bibliography.

ness of poetry to purvey an ethic, and there is nothing about his poetry of 'the perpetual coxcombry of our moral pretensions'. Life was what mattered; it was glorious, unceasingly exciting, and always worth while. So long as the poet stuck to this belief, he was fulfilling his function, revealing life to those that lived it:

> And you shall hear the herb and tree,
> The better heart of man shall see,
> Shall feel celestially as long
> As you crave nothing but the song;

and the song, it should be noted, was to be 'seraphically free of taint of personality'. The tremendous vigour, the metrical skill (the measure possibly a little too marked) of his long lyrics (possibly a little too long), such as 'The Lark Ascending' and 'Love in the Valley', remind one of Swinburne, but rather as a flight of birds may remind one of a torrent. There is hard thinking in Meredith's poems; such pieces as 'The Woods of Westermain' and 'Earth and Man' grapple with the Darwinian problem of those days. His great work, though often pedantically stigmatized as being of 'that bastard form' a novel in verse, is probably *Modern Love*, written in 'sonnets' of sixteen lines. Some of the sonnets are excellent in themselves, apart from their context, and it would not be extravagant to hold that *Modern Love* is the most successful long poem in the period. It is moving in the whole, it expresses an attitude—much the attitude of Meredith's novels, with a heightened sense of tragedy—and its half-seen things, its 'half-images', give it an intellectually exciting quality different in kind from that given by the exactness of *In Memoriam*; the feeling, though as poignant, is less personal, and so more immediately present.

Yet having hazarded the suggestion that *Modern Love* may be the greatest long poem in the period, *The Dynasts* at once springs to the mind: but then Hardy's masterpiece is largely in prose, and depends to a great extent for its effect upon the reader's power to translate the printed word into dramatic action. But *The Dynasts* does not lend itself to classification. It has no predecessors, and is probably too grandiose to have imitators. The immense Napoleonic struggle unrolls itself as drama, novel, tragedy, comedy, but especially perhaps epic. And Hardy exists otherwise as a poet. His verse, as does his prose, exhibits a certain woodenness which all the more reveals Hardy's genius when it is overcome. He can sometimes be as prosaic as Wordsworth, but then he can sometimes produce an effect of illumination, of penetration, which if not quite so dazzling as Wordsworth's, is comparable with it. As the years go by he increases in stature. Some of his best work is 'pessimistic' enough, full of his fatal acceptance (take 'Only a man harrowing clods'), but sometimes, with extraordinary simplicity, he gives a twist to a moment of human experience which conveys just that queer sense of super-reality which such moments in real life actually have. *Moments of Vision*, the title of one of his volumes, would be an apt description of his poems as a whole, visions of emotional moments charged with the inheritance of past ages of emotion, bringing into play irrational, half-conscious feelings, which the contemplative mind must recognize as being part of everyday experience.

Hardy was not a master of versification as Bridges was; and indeed Bridges was a useful influence in bringing back a certain scholarly quality which it is necessary should occasionally be injected into English poetry as a call to order. To say that he was too much of a scholar to be a great poet—a common criticism—is, of course, nonsense. Good scholarship never spoilt a good poet; and Bridges, though a good poet, lacked the imaginative leap, the ability to transform experience, which makes a great poet. Yet his earlier work has a fine lyrical spring, and Bridges can rank as a lyric poet somewhere in the neighbourhood of Arnold. Later, a somewhat crabbed philosophy rusted the spring. His *Shorter Poems* show him at his best. There are, indeed, some good passages in the stanzaic narrative *Eros and Psyche*, and work of some magnificence in the sonnet sequence *The Growth of Love*; but it is in the shorter lyrics, where he could express an intense joy in the mere fact of existence, and the emotions of love, that he is most surely a poet. Besides, the prosodic complexity of such things as 'Whither O splendid ship', 'Awake my heart to be loved, awake, awake', and the superb 'London Snow', contain delights which lovers of verse will always savour. His archaisms are irritating; and his defence that they were not affectations but grammatical necessities to him does not make them any less so.

Bridges was not a very original poet; he added little that was new to the tradition; but he very remarkably summed up in his work many strands of the tradition up to his own day, and carried the result forward through the breakdown in the nineties and the Edwardian period. He carried it, in fact, beyond the birth of a new formulation which itself went back to the old, but to different aspects of the old, reacting against 'Georgian Poetry', the final flicker of Victorian romanticism, including pre-Raphaelite romanticism. Georgian poetry is scarcely a distinct brand, and it takes its name merely from the anthologies with that title published at the beginning of King George V's reign. Yet there is some excuse for the name, since the poems written at that period reveal a definite revival of the lyric impulse. There had been a distinct lull. The Victorian tradition had faded out in the religious verse of Alice Meynell and Francis Thompson, or in the lighter verse of Austin Dobson, Andrew Lang and others. The age had broken up; its assumptions had collapsed, and there was no grand current of thought or feeling to carry poets along, or for them to crystallize. Its later poets, even while rebelling against it, had been carried forward by its momentum, but in the Edwardian period it was a dead weight. The waters were lifeless, but for directionless eddies. Here and there some good work was done by such men as Blunt, Lord Alfred Douglas, and Arthur Symons, but nothing decisive emerged. Kipling, from the first, struck a much more original note; but he had the bad luck to offend the aesthetes, and, quite wrongly, to be accused of the jingo

Imperialism which was rapidly becoming the preserve of a clique. It is a thousand pities that he should have been judged by, and rejected for, his popular banjo jingles. He was a master craftsman, with seventeenth-century affinities, and great boldness of metrical invention and adaptation. There is nothing quite like 'M'Andrew's Hymn' or 'The Mary Gloster' in our literature, though they owe something to Browning. He can attain great and touching simplicity, as in 'My Boy Jack', inspired by the loss of his son in the first Great War, and a starkness about some of his later poetry as in the 'Hymn of Breaking Strain' approached only by Wallace Stevens. He was a real poet, whom only the foolish or the prejudiced will ignore. Newbolt, with an irritating monotony of subject, scarcely disguised by a variety of metres, and a great appearance of nobility, celebrated the worst side of Imperialism. Hewlett was a good poet spoilt by living in a day when there was nothing much that a poet could do, and few to listen to him; poetical conventions, of a bad kind, clogged his manner, and he was often forced back to classical themes. One of the best poets of the period, John Davidson, voiced a black despair in verse which was exquisite: 'Thirty Bob a Week' is a great and powerful poem.

Masefield found new metres and new matter; *Sea Pieces* promised a new poet of strength and originality. His narrative poems, *The Everlasting Mercy*, *The Widow in the Bye Street*, and *Dauber*, took the public by storm. There was nothing highfalutin' about them, and they were so readable that they were said to be 'not poetry', which implies a criticism not of Masefield, but of what other poets were writing. These narratives were full of life and realism; they were rattling good yarns, novels in verse which anyone could understand. They certainly shook a good deal of the stiffness out of poetry, the sort of stiffness exhibited by such poets as the derivative William Watson on the one hand, and on the other the far better, more original, Wilfred Scawen Blunt. They brought poetry appreciably nearer life, in the sense that the readers of H. G. Wells's novels understood it; but that is not the sort of life poetry can remain embedded in except at its peril. Chaucer's could survive it, but Mr Masefield, though a poet of distinction, is not Chaucer, even if there is something Chaucerian about *Reynard the Fox*.

But in the four years before the War there was a distinct if rather yeasty ferment agitating English society, more perceptible from a distance than it was at the time. There had been a certain amount of political agitation in the previous decade, and a change in the constitution: a collapse of the monarchy did not seem beyond the bounds of possibility. After 1910 there was a series of strikes; the suffragettes broke windows in Regent Street, chained themselves to the gallery in the House of Commons, and one threw herself under the King's horse at the Derby. The tension over Ireland was so great that at the beginning of 1914 there was grave danger of civil war, and actually a military rebellion. There was, indeed, a sense of rebellion in the air, against convention, against accepted codes of morals, and, with Bernard Shaw in the van, against almost every accepted idea.

And in this ferment a new kind of singing made itself heard, and was conveniently gathered into anthologies known as *Georgian Poetry*. Harold Monro's Poetry Bookshop formed a centre and, less in the public eye, a group of young poets gathered round T. E. Hulme were forging out new conceptions of the way in which poetry should be written. Hulme's influence, however, was not much felt within our period, and we can confine ourselves to the better known writers of the time. They were young men, and some of the most distinguished are still living: some will be treated in the next volume. The work of these poets*—they cannot be called a group—was lyrical, it was disciplined, and sometimes the impulse behind it was thoughtful. The best of these writers have developed so markedly since those days, and so diversely, that it is now impossible to speak of them as a school; but we can here, perhaps, repeat the criticisms born

* e.g., Lascelles Abercrombie, D. H. Lawrence, Walter de la Mare, Æ., Sturge Moore, Harold Monro, W. J. Turner, etc.

of the reaction against the movement, and which apply to it as a whole. These poets, it is said with some justice, were too consciously 'lyrical', too innocently lyrical, we might say. They sang only of surface experiences, and their work was 'scented with poetry'. Some too readily withdrew themselves into worlds of birds and flowers, and crooned about them; or into worlds of their own sensations; or into worlds of meaningless antiquity. But not all were cut off from the major emotions of their age, and they did something towards clarifying the intellectual and emotional muddles of their time. At all events, whatever their faults, they did reintroduce a freshness; there is no sense of exhaustion about their work; and even if you argue that it did not in itself constitute a revival, you have to admit that though it may have been the last flicker of a dying romantic flame, it was also the herald of a new era in writing poetry.

Three of them may be dealt with here; two because they died during the War, the third and best because he has, apparently, ceased to write, to the regret of all lovers of poetry.* Ralph Hodgson's slim volumes, however, make up in quality what they lack in bulk. He is, one feels, a poet of complete integrity, who would only write when he had something he urgently wished to say; and who takes care to say it in the best possible way. His 'Song of Honour', a hymn of praise, may be too reminiscent of Smart's 'Song to David'; but 'The Bull' is a rock-like piece of work conveying tragic acceptance: others of his poems express a deep humanitarianism. Rupert Brooke is the darling of adolescents and of anthologists, but he deserves better than that. What he did he did extremely well. His verse, really, is light verse; there is rarely any profundity of emotion, little complexity of experience, but there is a certain curious wonder and some very real unsentimental sentiment. It is very melodious, and goes with a run; it is easy, pleasant and, at first, refreshing. Brooke really sang, and sang with a clearer, more tuneful note than any of his contemporaries. Flecker exhibits all the

* He did, however, produce another slim volume in 1959.

faults of the Georgian chorus, and few of the virtues. *Hassan*, in part redeemed by a fine nostalgic song, is a piece of horrible romanticism and sham orientalism. His verse is ill-designed, soft, and meretricious, and consists largely of vapid rhetoric; but he had a certain tunefulness, that tunefulness which the Georgian poets did much to restore.*

Ephemeral, but important in its results, was the school of Imagistes, of which the chief ornaments were H.D., Richard Aldington, and F. S. Flint. To them should be added Ezra Pound, who at this stage at least can be considered an English poet. Their name expresses their object, encouraged by Hulme, which was to gain their effect not by suggesting thoughts, or expressing emotions, but by showing things. They were, especially Flint, exponents of free verse, but some of their work, especially with H.D. (Hilda Doolittle, also an American), exhibits a sense of form in a more rigorously disciplined manner, often in adaptation of classical forms, but not of classical metres. They were for gem-like rather than flower-like poetry. Their presence was a healthy element at the time, and their influence made itself felt for some years.

It is hardly necessary to say that the greatest poet of this latter part of the period was W. B. Yeats, who was gradually forging his way through from beginnings of pre-Raphaelite affinities to a firm grasp of other essentials; he was gathering together the shattered shards of a collapsed culture and building them up again into a new shape with the necessary additions. He is of such stature that discussion of his work cannot be split up; it is a coherent, progressive whole, and will be dwelt upon in the next volume.†

---

* Many consider this view too harsh, even unjust; they can point to his highly competent adaptation of Persian metres. No one can claim to be a 'perfect witness', and the reader must decide for himself.

† For reasons given in the Bibliography, Gerard Manley Hopkins will also be discussed in the next volume.

III

FICTION

POETRY in the Victorian era was widely read by those who considered themselves in the least degree educated. It was worthy matter, as worthy of serious reading as history, philosophy, or possibly sermons. The novel was read by the masses of the great new middle class, for entertainment; the educated regarded it as frivolous reading. In the course of our period this changed. Two figures largely helped to break down the barriers the evangelicals had erected against the novel—the heir of Redclyffe with his noble nature, and Mr Pickwick with his goodness and the inextinguishable laughter that accompanied him: but whatever the cause poetry came to be less read, sermons hardly at all (though devotional literature in other forms was still read), while the novel increased in importance till it became the medium of cultured expression that poetry had been. The transition can perhaps be illustrated by the doubt that still exists in some minds as to whether Meredith and Hardy will survive as poets or as novelists; both would rather have devoted their best energies to poetry, both were compelled to adopt the novel form as the chief vehicle of their attitudes, since they knew that their poetry would neither be widely read nor earn them a livelihood. At the beginning of the period nobody thought of regarding a novel as a work of art, except possibly Thackeray, while at the end of the period it was the most important art form. It had become penetrating with Meredith and James, tragic with Hardy, ideological with Wells. It was the novel, and not the poem, that came to be read for spiritual nourishment. This is not to say, however, that the bulk of novels are not still written for the idle entertainment of the poor in spirit and weak in mind.

This, of course, has had a considerable effect on the way

novels have been written. At the beginning of the period they were composed in the main for the great mass of *bons bourgeois*, often in parts for serial publication: the episodes, therefore, had to be exciting, the pathos tear-compelling, the melodrama beautifully thrilling. Form went by the board, the construction was often chaotic, and when the public was offered a masterpiece of tense concentration in *Wuthering Heights* it ignored it, the critics, Tennyson's 'indolent reviewers', being largely as impercipient as the flocks they were supposed to lead. Dickens, naturally, was this public's darling. Whereas today we enjoy his genius in spite of his incoherence, in his own day the incoherence was a positive aid to popularity. The others, except Thackeray, to a great extent exhibit the same lack of organization: Dickens's unequalness, his masterly handling of certain aspects, his doleful declension in the treatment of others. One of the reasons, no doubt, is the one noted by Lord David Cecil, namely that they wrote about everything whether they knew about any special thing or not, about every emotion, apart from the Great Taboo of sex, whether or not it was the sort of emotion they were competent to deal with. A novel had to be, not a slice of life, but the whole pudding. Yet what a pudding it was, stuffed full of plums; and if there was a good deal of dough about it, this was easily swallowed. To abandon the metaphor, what made these novels so palatable was not only the drama or the comedy, the thrill or the laughter, but the expectation of finding them all there combined with the terrific zest of the narrative which caught you up at the beginning and hurled you through to the end.

Consciousness of form, the acceptance of organization as a necessity, seems therefore foreign to the conception of the novel at the beginning of our period. It appeared gradually, first with Wilkie Collins; it was developed by Meredith, and became dominant in George Moore and especially in Henry James. Thus the novelists of the Edwardian period were all aware of it though they often flouted it. Form, of course, is inseparable from unity of theme. There is no theme in

Dickens; the theme in Thackeray is for most readers concealed by the dominant ironic mood; it is impossible to find one in Trollope, even in the Barsetshire series. But Meredith built his novels round a theme,* and we find a progressive development in this respect, through Moore, James, Conrad, and E. M. Forster. It is true that quite early in the period there were novels with a purpose, social reform novels with a thesis, but that is not the same thing; a theme is more philosophical. The ultimate subject-matter of Hardy's novels illustrate the difference.

The novel, moreover, passed through several phases. Apart from the thesis novel, which can adapt itself to any form, there were various kinds of novel at different periods, dovetailing chronologically in a way that is the despair of anyone who wishes to docket periods and forms. But on the whole we can say that the period began with a development of the picaresque novel, the novel, that is, of amusing, adventurous incidents loosely strung together. *Pickwick* is a perfect example. Thackeray, however, who had a sense of structure, saw that something more than mere stringing together had to be done; he saw what Fielding had accomplished and developed, and he completed the tradition. He took it as far as it would go, but that was not far enough. The picaresque novel, however, tends to become the character novel, and this is largely what the novels of our period were in its early and middle phases. But Eliot and Meredith led towards the psychological novel, while, towards the end of the century, a movement parallel with this one led with George Moore to realism and with Gissing to the 'slice of life' novel. At the same time Stevenson re-established the romance, to be followed by a host of writers, of whom the most distinguished was Arthur Quiller-Couch.

Yet perhaps a more important change is the change in the idea of the function of the novel. It is dangerous to try to define what a novel is, or what its function may be, beyond

---

* George Eliot, to be sure, had a theme; but it did not succeed in imposing a form, and her work remained largely episodic.

that of entertaining, which is merely a primary condition. The point is to discover what sort of entertainment it provides. We shall make a definition, realizing that such definitions, such theories, are not eternal verities, but merely useful scaffoldings; and shall suggest that the function of the novel, as distinct from that of poetry, or drama, or romance, is to reveal society to itself. That is what Defoe and Fielding had done; that is what Thackeray did and, in the main, Trollope. One can say that Disraeli's object was the same, as it was certainly not that of Dickens except when he was attacking certain aspects or institutions. Gradually, however, the character in his relation to society became the important thing, as it had been with Richardson and Jane Austen; the development is clear in the work of George Eliot, clearer still in that of Meredith; we are on the edge of the psychological novel, where the interest is entirely centred on the minds of the personages, where the individual exists for his own sake. This novel of the 'individual' is quite different from the 'character' novel: the character is a type or 'humour', the individual might be you or me. So the supremely important thing in the novel came to be what happened to people; the individual was what mattered and society largely disappeared; it vanished almost entirely in Hardy. *Tom Jones* and *Vanity Fair* are about society; what happens to Tom Jones or Rawdon Crawley is interesting, but does not much matter: but it does matter what happens to Dr Lydgate in *Middlemarch*, to Clym Yeobright in *The Return of the Native*, to Beauchamp in *Beauchamp's Career*. The person became a symbol.

It was all a complex process, this movement from depicting society to concentrating on the inner struggles of men and women, and one can hazard a guess as to how it came about. Since the form of society seemed fairly fixed* and God was rapidly vanishing, man's private emotions and thoughts came to seem the supremely important thing. With Meredith a man

* Now, however, that the form seems far from fixed, interest in the psychological novel is waning, and we are returning to the social form (1938). We seem now to have passed beyond this—to what? (1949).

is still struggling with society, but later it was the 'personal relation' that took the field, a subject perfectly treated by E. M. Forster; this led still a step further, to the isolation of man from everything but his own divine impulsion, as exemplified in the work of D. H. Lawrence. Such a scheme must not be pressed too closely (we shall come upon some contradictions later), but it does on the whole present a not very distorted picture of what happened to the form and content of the novel. Part of the content was, of course, influenced by the breakdown of the Great Taboo; from Ouida onward, blameless as her novels appear to us now, it became gradually more and more possible to take into account the physical side of sex; George Moore loosened the bands almost completely. In the present century the results of the breakdown have been to give exaggerated importance to this aspect of human life, but it is ultimately a gain to an art to be able to handle any material that offers itself, and the distortion in the present direction is perhaps not so vicious as distortion in the other.

It is not that one directly misses the sensual erotic motive in the earlier novelists: Thackeray, as Professor Hamilton Thompson noted, suffers the most, since his subject-matter was largely human pretensions in the face of human weakness and folly. But the absence of this element makes itself felt in the falsity which reveals itself as sentimentality. It does not perhaps affect the men so much, since a good deal was left to be inferred on the 'wild oats' principle, but it is a commonplace that most of the ideal young ladies of the early Victorian novelists are intolerable. But Thackeray did not admire Amelia Sedley, as can be seen when Becky Sharp upbraids her; and Dobbin's final refuge from her is in writing his History of India. Disraeli's heroines certainly think, as do Meredith's. The worst side of the Victorian respect for feminine chastity and refinement, apart from the horrible punishment inflicted upon those who slipped (one has only to think of Little Em'ly or Mrs Gaskell's Ruth), was their segregation from the intellectual currents of the time. Up till the triumph of the new middle class, every educated woman spoke Italian, French, and possibly German or Spanish; she had a grounding in the classics, and some musical culture; she could meet man conversationally on equal terms. By the mid-Victorian period her highest functions were to mind the baby, or distribute soup to cottagers;* her musical education extended to playing the family hymns on Sunday evenings. The Victorians are guilty of having tried to diminish woman to the lowest level she had reached for centuries. Yet there are splendid examples of magnificently individual women, such as Mary Kingsley; and Florence Nightingale's outburst, which Jowett thought it 'wiser' not to publish, has considerable significance. 'Women must have no passions . . . the system dooms some minds to incurable infancy, others to silent misery . . . marriage being their only outlet in life, many women spend their lives in asking men to marry them, in a refined way . . . the woman who has sold herself for an establishment, in what way is she superior to those one may not name?'† Women died, she suggested, from starvation, that is, their moral activity expired. This attempted murder was the first accomplishment of the middle classes in the realm of culture. This, even more than the limitation with respect to drawing a man whole, injured the presentation of life in their novels; women in most fiction conformed not so much to life, as to what the Victorians wanted life to be.

Yet in spite of these grave, and with respect to European literature fatal, faults, the accomplishment was tremendous. It is too often vitiated by sentimentality; there is a good deal of pity-mongering, and the number of satisfactory death-bed scenes is inordinate; but still the result is frequently glorious, so much so that it is not necessary to praise the giants,

* It is shocking to think that Keats may be partly responsible for this ministering angel attitude. But the higher ideal did persist: see Charlotte Yonge's *The Daisy Chain*. Also social work was often undertaken by the most cultivated.

† You might not name them, because if you did not name a thing it did not exist: prostitution ought not to exist, therefore it did not exist: the proof of its non-existence was that you never named it. Admirable logic!

Dickens and Thackeray; it will serve to draw a few distinctions, and to re-state, with a perhaps slightly different stress, what has often been stated before.

It will be as well to begin with Thackeray, though his great work did not begin to appear till after Dickens had made his name. As already suggested, he was a delineator of society as such, his range, where he is at all secure, being limited to the upper middle classes. He had a better sense of various ways of living than any of his contemporaries, but it is only in *Vanity Fair* that this is fully exhibited. He had greater narrative power over long stretches than any of them, and his dramatic moments can be strong and subtly delicate. His chief interest was the actions of human beings within society; to that extent he was interested in his characters, who are in the main admirably realized. Thackeray knew his middle classes thoroughly well and he has been accused of cynicism because he was always concerned to prick their pretensions and especially to expose their snobbery, their 'mean admiration of mean things', money, titles, position. His most frequent target was the marriage-market. He never entered into possession of the hearts of the people because they were always a little suspicious of what he meant: some little barb might be concealed in the most innocent-looking statement of honest feeling. Yet many found, and still find, something fascinating in his brilliant delineation of the society of his day, in all the varieties of men—and of women too when we think of Becky Sharp—who haunt, not only the pages of *Pendennis*, *The Newcomes*, and *Vanity Fair*, but even at this date the streets of London. Besides there are few who have an ear who are not seduced by his admirable, lucid, flowing prose, eighteenth-century prose at its most graceful, and excellently suited to his slightly mocking attitude. As a craftsman in words he is at his best as an essayist: the *Roundabout Papers* are a model. Yet the earnest in every period feel a little uneasy in his presence: they would prefer the round trouncing of satire to the ironic tone which is apt to seem 'superior'. But then, Thackeray was not a satirist: he in no way disliked humanity, nor did he love it so much as to be crushed or infuriated by its failure to live up to its ideals. He was a cultivated humanist, a little dubious of human progress, an artist who rejoiced in the pageant. It is not just to blame him for not being what it was not in his nature to become, for the qualities his detractors demand of him would have been inimical to those which enabled him to create so solid a simulacrum of the society which moved around him.

On the other hand he had certain qualities which Dickens lacked, and which would have done the latter no harm had they had been added to his genius. A sense of form, an ability to use the blue pencil, a certain discipline in his emotions, especially the lachrymatory ones, would perhaps have made Dickens the outstanding master of a form which he handled with the infuriating carelessness of a giant. His creative capacity, his imagination of physical things, exceeds that of any writer of our period, perhaps of all English literature except for Shakespeare. The pity is that this giant never grew up intellectually; he could not enter into the minds of grown men as Browning could; but he could, and most brilliantly did, into the minds of youths up to about twenty. David Copperfield as a boy is without a possible rival. But where Dickens touched upon social reform, anywhere in fact where he began to think, he falls below the level of the second-rate, though the generous indignation that he shows is worthy of a full and complete man. He is on anybody's level when he describes places, especially places in London, and the opening pages of *Bleak House* with its description of foggy London in a *locus classicus*, and hardly less so is the picture of dreary marsh country in *Great Expectations*: but where he excels, where he tops imagination, where he is on the level of Shakespeare, is in his fantastic comic creations. His great glory consists in the fact there never were, and never could have been till he gave them birth, such persons as Mrs Gamp, Pecksniff, Chadband, Micawber, Pickwick, and Sam Weller. They are outside life, but still they are part of humanity.

His books are nearly always unpardonably confused. *Pickwick* is an exception, because, being a purely picaresque novel, it need be nothing but a succession of incidents loosely strung together; and at the end he began to learn something from Wilkie Collins. What is worse is the entire lack of emotional structure. At one moment you are carried along on a glorious sea of the most outrageously tempestuous fun, at the next you want to hurl the book across the room in supreme irritation. He has spoilt it all, or nearly, by some relapse into sententiousness, some hideous infelicity of style, or a bad joke, or pitiless sentimentality. In the end you forgive all for the enormous creative vitality, the fun sometimes rising to comedy, though not the same kind of high comedy as Thackeray touched and Meredith revelled in, and above all for his immortal additions to the number of our fellow-beings. There is nothing like them in life, but life is the poorer for being without them. If Providence did not create Mrs Gamp, Chadband, and the rest of them, it ought, we feel, to have done so.

Like Thackeray, Dickens in the main described the class from which he sprang, in his case the lower middle class. The moment he strays outside it he is at fault. He has been blamed for beginning 'the cult of the lower classes', but whether or not blame attaches to that, it is not true. He hated the fact that the lower class existed, and often either reviled them or made fun of them; as far as they were concerned he is by no means sentimental. He had, at one time, perilously belonged to them himself. He understood little of the workings of the mind, and was entirely uninterested in general thinking; but he hated everything that was mean and cruel, and loved everything that was generous and of good report; it was these qualities that endeared him to the masses, but it is his capacity for creating his tremendous figures of fantasy that gives him his high place among those who care for literature as such. These figures were not always first-rate; his 'good' fantasies, his Cheeryble brothers and so on, are a trifle painful; but at his best, at his most vivid, when he is not trying to represent virtue, he is unsurpassable.

There is only one man who can be said to belong to the same race, and that is Surtees; many others have tried to imitate Dickens, all of them unsuccessfully, but Surtees is a lesser example of the same breed. He is much more restricted; his creative fantasies belong almost entirely to the hunting-field and they are nearer reality (see Bibliography, p. 277). But they have a life of their own. Not only James Pigg and the immortal Jorrocks*—who surely reached the level of the high comic when, floundering along upon Arterxerxes he cried 'How I wish I was a heagle!'—but a dozen others: Lord Scamperdale, who while regretting that a Lord might not swear enlarged the invective scope of the language; wheezy Mr Jogglebury Crowdey whose passion was for cutting sticks and carving heads on them; Facey Romford, Soapey Sponge, Lucy Glitters, all the riff-raff of the hunting-field and the small watering place, most of them, however, though ignoble, redeemed by a selfless passion for the chase. There is acute observation too, gusto, a certain amount of anti-snobbish satire (Surtees was a friend of Thackeray), and above all a great enjoyment of racy idiom. There is no great structure in his novels, and his comic figures belong to the species of fantasy known as the 'humour'; but there is in them a vast interest in the doings of men and their idiosyncrasies.

And there is another interest in Surtees. He was as little interested as Dickens in the thought of his day, but he was really concerned for the countryside. He is an index to many of the changes that were going on, such as the opening of the new middle-class watering places, the coming of the railways and the decay of the turnpike, the birth of the London residential club which should do much to civilize the country squire, and the extension of land drainage. He inveighs against bad farmers, turf gamblers, and anything likely to spoil the country. It is this aspect which gives his absurd

* *Pickwick*, by the way, was started as a rival to *Jorrocks's Jaunts and Jollities*. This is a poor work, but it was to gallop off into *Handley Cross*, as *Pickwick*, after the opening scenes, was to take wing to Parnassus. Both Pickwick and Jorrocks have trouble with the law, into the clutches of which they are each introduced by a woman.

creations solidity; they are attached to something bigger than themselves: this, and a real knowledge of hunting and of the law, in which he was brought up, enable Surtees to give the illusion of reality to his figures. His hunting scenes are worth all those in Trollope, Kingsley, Lever, and Whyte-Melville put together.

Thackeray also had his pendent, in Trollope, 'the little Thackeray' as he was at one time called. His reputation stands higher now than it ever did, perhaps a little too high. He is admired by novelists who have no particular point of view, and who think it artistically meritorious to have no special attitude towards life. Trollope can draw figures he dislikes—he cannot be said to have had any affection for Mrs Proudie except such as an artist has for his creations—but he is never ironical. He seems to have accepted with complete complacency the world of ideas in which the majority of his fellow Victorians so prosperously existed. He was one of the very few writers of the period who did not rebel against the philosophy which it lived. His style is not so plodding as the careless reader may think, and he gave a fairly comprehensive and wholly comprehensible picture of the society in which he moved, and he created the county of Barsetshire, which is entirely livable. Whether or not his pictures of ecclesiastical life are true to ecclesiastical life or not does not matter; they are true to life. Live in Barsetshire for a month or so, and you live in an England which is very like the England Trollope lived in, within the sphere of his social circle. He may be a small figure among the giants, but he is a permanent one. He was a good honest workman, steady in his application, and he understood what he wrote about within the limits he set himself. He is rarely supremely vivid, he rends no veil, but he is comfortingly solid. If his comedy never rises to sublime heights, you know exactly where you are with him. If you do not like Trollope you are not worthy to admire Thackeray.*

* To adapt a phrase of Sainte Beuve: *Quiconque n'aime pas Regnard, n'est pas digne d'admirer Molière.*

If neither Thackeray nor Trollope nor Surtees ever wrote a *roman à thèse*, Dickens did, in *Hard Times*, for example,* and this links him with another group, of writers who wrote for a purpose. The chief one among them is Disraeli, and with him may be put Mrs Gaskell, Charles and Henry Kingsley and, in a different sense, George Eliot. Disraeli in his best novels, those he wrote in the forties, used the form for expressing the Tory ideas which he developed from Bolingbroke and Burke, and used it with some effect. He had a curiously oriental sense of style, in the use of gaudy words rather than in the phrase: he loved the grandeur and the glitter of riches either in Jerusalem or in the ducal home: here and there we may detect a little tawdriness. But he had the glimmerings of a sense of structure. His main motive was to oppose benevolent aristocracy to the materialistic ideas which accompanied the industrial revolution. *Sybil* is concerned with 'the two nations', and in it Disraeli draws a terrible picture of the poor in contrast with the rich in a capitalist society. In *Coningsby* and *Tancred*, and later in *Lothair* and *Endymion* (but in the last two with a recognizable loss of vivacity due partly to failing vigour and partly to the braking effect of experience) he expressed his ideas with less insistence on the immediate actuality of the distressing state of the country;† and all through his characters are interesting not so much for what they do as for what they think. They are the most thoughtful people before George Eliot, one might say before Meredith. They live by the energy of the mind rather than by the energy of the body. There is indeed movement in Disraeli's novels, and a clash of personality, and there is enough story to carry them on; but their main interest lies in the ideas expressed in them, ideas profound enough to be still of value at the present day since they are based on a knowledge, which is at least adequate, of the historical development of England. The early *Ixion* and *The Infernal Marriage* are good fun, and

* There are passages in other novels, of course: *Bleak House* and *Little Dorrit*.

† In *Tancred*, for instance, making great play with *Vestiges of Creation*.

artistically successful as witty extravaganzas; the early novels
are amusing and romantic, but in the later novels Disraeli
combined his qualities—the conversations are often brilliant
—with a profounder knowledge of what he wanted to say.

It seems at first sight odd to connect the fantastic, clever,
intensely self-conscious Jew with Charles Kingsley, the disciple of F. D. Maurice, the author of *The Water Babies*, who
came, somewhat to his annoyance, to stand for 'muscular
Christianity'. But his first two novels, written at the turn of
the forties and fifties, link him with Disraeli, whose cry *sanitas
sanitatum, omnia sanitas* he thoroughly endorsed. He was profoundly, and rightly, disturbed at the horrors of the slums,
and made exposures which caused the more complacent
Victorians to regard his morals as immoral. (You ought not
to mention the thing that ought not to be.) His muscular
Christianity was shared by Hughes, of *Tom Brown's School
Days* fame (does anyone read that decayed classic today?), a
form of piety particularly distasteful to us now. It was, of
course, part of the same thing as the public school system
which Thomas Arnold gave to an admiring world, a system
in which games are played not for fun but because of the
moral training they are supposed to inculcate, and in which
young prigs, known as prefects, beat the bottoms of smaller
boys to the greater glory of God and the British Empire. But
Yeast, a Problem and *Alton Locke, Tailor and Poet*, were generous
outbursts against the conditions of the working classes.
Kingsley sympathized with the Chartists—*Yeast* began to
appear in the year of their collapse, 1848—but he thought
the workers too rigorously bound by the Charter. They must
discipline themselves, they must imbibe the principles of self-
help. *Yeast*, a study of the country labourer, is full of passages
of exhortation mingled with the narrative (it is odd that the
most vigorous and famous passage should be an account of a
run with hounds), and *Alton Locke*, a picture of sweated
tailoring, is a queer mixture of sympathy with the worker and
'be good' doctrine: it has odd flashes of understanding of
the economic trouble, but beseeches the workers to abjure

political action in favour of a kind of Co-operation, so that they could get goods 'very little above cost'. Neither can be accounted works of art, but they were useful books, still very readable, based on a first-hand knowledge of conditions, and they are finely indignant. *Hypatia,* his most successful work, deals with the problem of faith and civilization as worked out in Alexandria; it is, in parts, brilliantly descriptive. *Westward Ho!* is probably his most famous book; its appeal is to the adolescent mind rather than to the mature one, and in many ways it foreshadows one side of the imperialist feeling which became manifest towards the end of the century.

Mrs Gaskell was as outspoken on social evils as Kingsley was; she also belonged to the school of 'interventionists' as they were called, who believed that *laisser-faire* would not do. In *Mary Barton* she deals with the distresses in Manchester in the early forties; her outraged sympathies are with the poor, and her remedy is that employers should treat their men as 'brethren and friends'. *North and South* treats the problem from a slightly different angle: it gives perfectly the ladies' school gentility that shudders at trade, dissent, or a northern accent. Trades-unionism had begun to make progress, factory legislation had begun to take effect,* and this development began to colour her idea of the remedy. Both novels received a good deal of abuse; her theories, they said, were all wrong. Perhaps they were, but her facts were right, and that was the important and unforgivable thing. She referred to immediate problems in others of her books, mainly however, moral problems, as in *Ruth,* which roused a storm of protest, since it preached Christian forgiveness for sins for which the Victorians thought there should be no forgiveness; she was supported, however, by Maurice, Kingsley, and Florence Nightingale. But her chief claim to fame, whether justified or

* Note these dates: 1844, *Coningsby.* 1845, *Sybil.* 1847, *Mary Barton, Tancred.* 1848, *Yeast.* 1851, *Alton Locke.* 1854, *Hard Times.* 1855, *North and South* (which appeared in *Household Words* as the immediate successor of Dickens's book). It was in 1844 that Engels wrote his account of the condition of the English working classes. Reade should also appear in this connection.

not, is undoubtedly *Cranford*, probably the only one of her books considerably read now. Her other books do not lack vivacity or character-drawing, but they may excusably be found dull in long stretches. *Cranford*, however, is, in spite of certain 'humorous' lapses, delightful reading, an immense improvement on Miss Mitford's *Our Village*, though it has none of the genius of Jane Austen. It can best be related to Crabbe's poems, which Mrs Gaskell admired. The prose is beautifully adapted to the personalities and the slight movement. Others, however, would plead for *Wives and Daughters* or the pastoral *Cousin Phillis*.

One has to put in the Brontës where one can; they are, both in their novels and in their poetry, rather out of the main current, Emily completely so: but their name attaches itself to Mrs Gaskell, whose greatest work, it is coming to be seen, is her *Life* of Charlotte, attacked, when it first appeared, for telling too much of the truth. Anne's work is the weakest, yet about *Agnes Grey*, the bitter record of a governess's life, there is a certain strength and dignity, while *The Tenant of Wildfell Hall* is easy reading, if not wholly convincing. Charlotte was a very considerable artist, Emily a supreme one. The personages that both create are animated by the flame within; all that matters to either authoress is the inner life; they are not concerned with society or social criticism, or with generalities; they create personages spun out of their imaginations and are intent to describe not actions but emotions. For them the world of sense in persons or in landscape, however glorious or enthralling, was only a door opening to a more rapturous world. Charlotte shows herself to have been a potentially greater artist than she actually was; there are scenes in *Shirley* and *Villette* as well as in *Jane Eyre*, that are masterly; they do what she wanted them to do. But she is spoilt partly by the usual Victorian lack of any standard of art, and one feels sometimes that she is placating her public. It is not that her studies are melodramatic—a number of the greatest stories or novels are that—but that she attempts to force our emotions in much the same way that Dickens does. Nevertheless she

was a fine artist, and her prose often achieves splendid directness. But it was in Emily's *Wuthering Heights* that the miracle
was achieved. Except for a certain hesitation at the beginning, a touch of clumsy humour which has been attributed
to their brother Branwell, and in spite of a somewhat awkward construction, the book is a remarkably unified whole,
a thing able to stand completely by itself, so integral are the
passionate striving after the absolute, the fearlessness, the
lack of sentimentality, the emotion which sweeps through
the whole tortured scene, and somehow, by a still greater
miracle, achieves serenity at the end, a feeling of reconciliation. It has been said that 'it is not desirable to read; to take
Wuthering Heights from the shelf is to prepare for oneself no
pleasure'.* No easy pleasure, certainly, but a pleasure that
has to be fought for and won, a difficult pleasure that is all
the more worth achieving, for once seized hold of it is held
for ever. It is permissible to think that *Wuthering Heights* and
Vanity Fair are the only great masterpieces of the early
Victorians in the realm of fiction.

To turn from *Wuthering Heights* to the novels of George
Eliot is to descend from the tops to comparatively mundane
levels. George Eliot's work belongs to the school of solid
novels, to the problem novel school, but she brought to the
form a deeper intelligence, a more pervasive imagination,
and a better instructed philosophy than the Kingsleys or Mrs
Gaskell. At this distance we can avert our eyes from *Romola*
(for some reason most Victorian novelists thought it their
duty to assault the historical novel: it was Scott's fault and
they none of them got near Scott's achievement); but *Adam
Bede, Felix Holt the Radical,* and especially *Middlemarch* and
The Mill on the Floss are still extremely interesting, while the
early *Scenes of Clerical Life* have the freshness which comes
from lively observation at first hand.† She is at times rather
heavy reading, she was certainly not economical, and it is the

---

* One might say the same of *Lear*!
† And *Silas Marner*? Well, it may be psychologically valid, but the
moral atmosphere is too thick: in form it has virtues the others lack.

has 9

seriousness of ~~her~~ intent rather than the briskness of her narrative that carries the reader on. Her work is full of comment; not that she stands aside as Thackeray does, following Fielding, to give us her own opinions at length, but the sententious remark, of a moralistic or philosophic character, is every now and again inserted, extending sometimes to a dangerous length.

George Eliot is not so amusing nor so tense, nor so enthralling perhaps, as any of the writers so far named, though all her work is shot with a delightful and essentially feminine sense of humour; she created no inimitable figures (except perhaps those in *The Mill on the Floss*), and her countryside is viewed through the eyes of a farmer and the movement of her novels is not very swift; nor has she any particular grace of phrase or felicity in her choice of words. She is not at the moment as much read as her predecessors. In her own day, however, she was acclaimed as the equal of Sophocles, and her contemporaries were in a sense right, because earliest among English novelists she introduced the idea of retribution; for her each individual act had its consequence, every evil action carried its nemesis with it. Historically she is of the greatest importance; artistically she is basically sound; not so much for this idea, but because on account of it she was the first to trace the development of character, how it changed according to social pressure and according to the personal act; 'character too is a process and an unfolding'— a great discovery in the realm of fiction. Moreover, she built up her novels round an idea. The idea is the novel, which is to say more than that the novel illustrates the idea. Her books scarcely have the form which the idea compels, and it must be admitted that the moral idea is sometimes a little too compulsive, since George Eliot was a puritanical rationalist, and when morality takes the place of God in an age when the name of God is loudly shouted (to cover up less pleasant sounds) it is apt to be Procrustean, and distort life. But in doing what she did, George Eliot broke with the old tradition, and began that of George Meredith and Henry James,

Developed characters. - George Eliot.

and, in another way, that of Hardy. Before her time the characters had not developed; they had performed to specification, and often acted quite inconsistently without any reason being suggested. Before her day characters had not thought, they had only felt. Disraeli's, it is true, had uttered thoughts, but their lives were not troubled by their thoughts as the lives of George Eliot's were.

Her people are of interest to us now because we can easily identify ourselves with them: we can be, because we can understand, Maggie Tulliver in *The Mill on the Floss* or Dr Lydgate in *Middlemarch*: we cannot be Micawber, Becky Sharp, or Heathcliff. We understand all about George Eliot's characters because they reveal ourselves to ourselves. This had never happened before in the English novel, at any rate not in that way. So if we can once let ourselves go in her novels and refrain from pressing those grim moral premises which deny all irresponsible joy, we can live their dramas—and they are searching enough dramas, they cover a large range of human emotions—with feelings which if not of the highest intensity, are solid enough. George Eliot did one more thing that was not normally done by her contemporaries: she criticized society as a whole, the thoughts by which society lived; she criticized its failure to live up to its ideals: and all the time she kept her eye on society, alert to note all its changes. Thackeray, it is true, criticized society, but he did not so much criticize either its mechanism or its ideals as its working within those ideals, while sometimes revealing their earthy basis. George Eliot took the process a stage further, into the realm of psychology, while never relaxing her hold on society.

Thus it is but a step from George Eliot to George Meredith. This brilliant, and linguistically sometimes too effervescent genius, was able to a large extent to maintain the variety of the early Victorian novel while making it the vehicle of a theme. After *Richard Feverel* he abjured the easy way—'fiddling harmonics on the sensual strings'—and tried always to inculcate, but in no way didactically, his keenly intellectual attitude towards life. He steered a perilous way between realism and romance, borne onward all the time by the fervour of his thought. His almost constant point of attack was 'the conscience residing in thoughtfulness', and he always firmly believed that humanity could rise above its animal limitations. Life for him was a perpetual process of affirmation; to live was to be judged, and so throughout his work he insists upon a judgment of values. One can almost say that with him an idea, rising and struggling, defeated or victorious, was the hero of each book. Some of his limitations occasionally spoil his work: he had undue admiration for a life to which he was not born—the public schools, the fighting services—and he is a little apt to fall prone before major-generals. But these are small flaws in the living reality he created, in a series of beings who are essentially living. He managed to make his people matter, or, to phrase it differently, he made them significant as symbols: and over the whole of his world, even in the tragic pieces, there plays the brilliant lightning of a gloriously sharp sense of the comic. His laughter is illuminating and spiritual, far from the physical laughter of Dickens. If in his gallery of people his women are the more fascinating—Diana of the Crossways, Cecilia Halkett, and others—his men, in their striving thought, which is never divorced from their bodily activity, are as admirably convincing. 'Meredith is a prose Browning,' Wilde remarked; and if he added 'and so is Browning', the error in criticism does not invalidate the justice of the first part of the phrase. He can hardly be called a political novelist, but all through his work and especially in *Beauchamp's Career*, we are conscious of a liberating trend of thought; he did much to promote the emancipation of women. His prose often suffered from being over-poetized, especially in the earlier version of *Richard Feverel*, and sometimes it is so packed as to seem distorted, so that his most brilliant work, *The Egoist*, is not to be approached unawares; his conversationalists are often so quick-witted that they omit steps usually trodden by slower mortals. But he could achieve a high level of artistic purity, and his errors are largely due to his determination to keep the reader's mind alert.

His religious scepticism, more apparent in his poetry than in his novels, was carried a step further by Hardy, who offered an at first somewhat timid public a complete disbelief in Christian dogma. There is much to be said against his novels from the point of view of the craftsman; they are often lumbering in construction, and his prose is at some times wooden, though at others it achieves great beauty; but what his novels transmit is his integrity, the urgency of his tragic vision, and his complete acceptance of it. It is this which makes his successful novels wholly satisfying as such, however much we may disagree with his standpoint and, although his structure is of a simple kind which hardly rises above the mere handling of the narrative, too often directed to an irony of accident. But no doubts strike across his line of sight. For him man was a creature doomed by an inexorable destiny, an idea he rams home by nearly always choosing to portray people of the peasant or yeoman classes, bound as such people are by the conditions of their lives. It was for precisely the opposite reason, that they had to be able to move freely under the spur of their thought, that Meredith chose people of the upper middle class. But the patterns Hardy's dignified and, in their restricted way, thoughtful victims make while working out the design, are full of pathos, sometimes serene, at others grimly comic, sometimes invested with an extraordinary grandeur, even with a radiant beauty. He is George Eliot developed with a ruthless logic. His characters are even more than hers formed by their circumstances, however much they may rebel against them. He is the first great tragedian in novel form, depicting man as the creature of an utterly indifferent Immanent Will; and he makes his reader share his profound sympathy with, his touching love of, the essentially human beings he portrays. He was even less than Meredith concerned with the politics, the social conditions of his day, and from these two begins the severance of the novel as an art form from immediacies, a severance in some ways beneficial, but which has also been injurious. The artist need not be concerned with the activities of his time: but in the novel at least (since the novel is a picture of society), he must deal with the emotions arising out of these activities: otherwise he will not be read. George Eliot was the last of the great novelists to be read by the mass of readers, and it is with Meredith and Hardy that begins the decline of the novel as an intellectual force acting on the great body of public opinion. Neither was as close to the common life of the people he portrayed as his great predecessors were.

The removal went on progressively with George Moore and Henry James, the former a considerable artist, the latter a supreme master of form. It is sometimes said that they thought too much about their art, which is nonsense. An artist cannot think too much about his art, but he can think too exclusively about certain aspects of life. Moore, rightly impressed by the achievement of Flaubert, tried to paint in Flaubert's manner with far less general colours, and on a smaller canvas. He is sometimes exquisite, but he mistook the nature of Flaubert's realism. There is a certain morbidity about *The Mummer's Wife*, too petty a sensuality about *Evelyn Innes*, to make them sufficiently universal as works of art. He lacked Flaubert's robustness and is at times 'ninetyish'. He had, however, an accurate sense of form, so that his novels do precisely what he wanted them to do; but in his praiseworthy effort to exclude, he left out too much. The same may be said of his prose. It is often lovely chamber music (though the modulations sustained by 'and' tend to become wearisome), but it is not the full orchestra of Meredith.* The atmosphere is often 'boudoir' as opposed to the moorland breeze of the creator of Cecilia Halkett and Beauchamp. His later work, however, is on a larger and profounder scale. *The Brook Kerith*, an agnostic but sympathetic imaginary life of Christ, and *Héloïse and Abelard*, are not only monuments of delightful craftsmanship, but also probe into human emotions and motives; they betray deeper sympathies than his

* G. M. Young called it 'ribbon development'.

earlier work, and have an atmosphere of mellowness. His appeal will never be to a very wide audience, but he will never lack admirers among those who care for fiction as an art.

It is likely that Henry James will for ever have a still smaller audience, but his admirers will be enthusiastic. Combining as he did a supersensitive feeling for the surface of things, a remarkable sense of nuance in matters spiritual and physical, and a profound capacity to gather implications together with a pervading sense of the macabre, he depicted with an artist's joy in phenomena, and a civilized man's horror at what it all meant, the decay of a society which he at once admired and abominated. The complexity is obvious, shade upon shade of delight and fear. Yet however much he may have been aware of the imminent collapse of the society which he studied and in which he moved, he cannot be claimed as a prophet by the communists; he saw the merits of each of the doomed societies he confronted. He was intensely aware of his time, but he did not think of things in political or economic terms. However much he may have loathed 'the black and merciless things that are behind great possessions', he had a very clear sense of the values latent in those possessions. To see exactly what he was at demands an application of psycho-analysis which is not to the purpose here. What is to the purpose is to notice his treatment of the novel as a form, one which in his hands tended more and more to the dramatic. Within him factual narrative is of minor importance; what counts is the way he builds up the structure of his readers' emotions. This, in the last analysis, is what structure means; but James seems to have approached the problem in a more open-eyed fashion than any novelist before or since. In his earlier, more popular writings, many of which appeared in *The Yellow Book*, such as *The Death of a Lion*, *The Coxon Fund*, *The Aspern Papers*, or even in *A Turn of the Screw*, his method is fairly straightforward; but he was always concerned to 'present reality', the reality registered by the nerves. It is in his later work, pellucid though in a sense it is, that he demands an attention, exacts a sensibility, which few novel-readers are willing, or indeed able, to give. Besides his being a great master of form his prose is a continual fascination in its oblique method of bringing the emphasis on exactly the right point. He is a symbol and a portent: a symbol of the state of society in which the artist cannot happily move, a portent of an art having reached a point in certain directions beyond which it cannot go.

The only important figure within our period who can claim descent in the legitimate line from James, as a conscious artist, is Joseph Conrad. To a large proportion of readers he seems too strange to be acceptable, but his work must always have a profound appeal for those who can joyfully palate a slightly peculiar prose, a treatment of English which has a freshness sometimes given to foreigners to discover. His life as an officer of marine gave him a distinctive, and in some of his works an epic, vision. Many of his figures are monumental, some seem to flame with a quality of endurance. The theme of a number of his novels is a combined one of solitude and betrayal (the theme of betrayal often occurs with James also) and behind the human beings who move, almost predestined one sometimes feels, across his scenes, there is often a symbol of some compelling power— the sea, a volcano, a silver mine—a symbol of something with which his people grapple and to which in the end they usually rise superior, but profoundly altered. He and James, foreigners both, stand a little outside the main current of English novel-writing, and provide a sorely needed influence. How much they contributed to clarifying the consciousness of their time, how much they revealed society to itself, is a difficult question to answer; but they did to some extent affect man's vision of man, which is, perhaps, a greater achievement.

The strands, we see, ravel out from the nineties onward; it has been impossible to be consecutive, but we can now go back to Gissing. This somewhat lugubrious author can be linked with George Moore on the naturalistic side, but

Gissing was not concerned to explore the emotions and intellectual sensations of groups of beings so much as to reveal the physical and cultural impoverishment of the lower middle classes. His main object was to depict certain things rather than to create works of art, and he did it in a severely devastating manner. Thus his novels are an indictment, detached enough, of a certain aspect of civilization, done in a relentlessly prosaic manner, in a tight, inexorable narrative form, through the medium of a pitilessly prosaic prose. He plods desperately and firmly on; he seldom runs, never skips, and one cannot conceive inviting him to take wing. His novels are pathetic in that they expose a sore, the deadness of the lower middle-class mind, as in *Thyrza*, *Demos*, and *New Grub Street*, whereas in *Lonely Lives* he dilated upon the miseries of loveless women. He was no social reformer; he was simply and purely a presenter, and not always of squalor. *The Private Papers of Henry Ryecroft* will live longer than his other works, one imagines, by the sole reason of its sunniness and sense of contentment.

But if the great mass of novel-readers was no longer getting enrichment from, and forming its ideas on, the works of the novelists, and was no longer swept away by the gusto, the genial acceptance of life as such which had made the earlier novelists best-sellers as well as important figures, a new sort of writing in the form of the romance was springing up to enliven the dull hours. This was due to the inventive talent of Stevenson. His works have little to do with life as ordinarily lived; they attack no problems; they excite and move the emotions, more usually the gentler ones, and constitute a respite from life rather than an illumination of it. They have, it is true, that relation to life which is essential to all art, but it is no longer an immediate relation. They depend for their charm mainly on the narrative; their appeal is vicarious action and adventure. Stevenson, moreover, had a literary gift which though minor, as he himself recognized, is far from commonplace. He used words with a sure sense, his phrasing is often delightful, and he could evoke a scene, give a sense of the humorous, the strained, or the macabre, in a wholly convincing manner. His long-short stories are far more complete and satisfying than his full-length romances; he could endow those with form, could keep up the illusion by methods which failed him in longer work. 'Ollala', 'The Merry Men', 'A Lodging for the Night', have a freshness and a charm which have not yet faded. He had a style. He was followed by a host of other writers, Conan Doyle, Seton Merriman, Rider Haggard, Stanley Weyman, Anthony Hope (Hawkins), all very readable, but with so little contact with reality that they led inevitably to some Ruritania or other. The only one among his successors with a sense of literary values was Sir Arthur Quiller-Couch, who, always aware that literature must mean something, displayed his wise human-ism in his novels as clearly as in his criticism. Nevertheless the modern romance is a form which does not much matter, and never did. In the old days it had been important to read the last production of Dickens, or Thackeray, or Charlotte Brontë, or George Eliot; they were significant works. The romances had no significance, except, indeed, the not unimportant one of giving pleasure and refreshment.

But while the romances were, on the whole, displacing the novel, which was itself losing importance, one man arose who, besides being an admirable artist, had something to say, and was as significant of the thought of his time as Hardy: Rudyard Kipling. It is a mistake to regard him as a trumpet of Imperialism. With him, Imperialism was an accident; it gave him scope for expressing his philosophy of action. Action (since thought without action is incomplete) was for him the only means man has for combating the nothing-ness that surrounds him; and action is supported by the sense of romance inherent in all action, purified by the virtues of loyalty and self-abnegation which can only be called out by something greater than the individual. This something the empire lay happily at hand to provide, yet it is to be noticed that his stories or poems about the Empire are often severe criticisms of a failure in sense of responsibility to a trust. Devotion and abnegation, work and laughter, those were Kipling's anodynes against despair; and with that philosophy to move him he created a gallery of figures which can take their place beside any born in our period, figures purged by suffering, cleansed of self-love, sustained by their manhood and their sense of humour. He rarely deals with men's 'insides', but again and again he stresses the individual's sense of isolation, and the necessity of facing loneliness, of standing by one's own self by virtue of what one has inside. His weak point was a sentimental adoration for men of action who in actuality had none of the qualities he would have wished to find in them, and some may feel an equal hesitation in accepting his 'psychic' stories. His supernatural apologues are tremendous inventions, in which he was best able to express that profound intuition of the need of compassion, and his urgent sense of the need for healing, themes which dominate his later work. But on his proper ground he was a superb craftsman in words and in form. His prose was based on seventeenth-century English, and he is the greatest master of the short story in the language, developing it from one of crisp simplicity to one of immense complexity. He represents, as already suggested, all that is best in Imperialism, and seems to have been innocent of its squalid side. He was acclaimed largely for the wrong reasons, and the grounds of his fame will change; but his wide sympathies, his intense love of life and of the humbler people who live it and do its work, his respect for virtues without which society cannot exist, and his comic sense, combined with the virility and vividness of his prose, are likely to make his work enduring.

Wholly different in character and in approach, in method and in matter, is the work of E. M. Forster. In his novels and short stories we find the deepest reaction against the things that Kipling stood for. Each has a distinct scale of values, but they are values in different worlds. Both, however, are typical of the Edwardian period. For Mr Forster, Kipling's world is the useless outer world, a scene of telegrams and anger, of futile efficiency, of misdirected effort. For him the things of importance are the inner things, the quiet things, and particularly important are those emotions which spring from what we have come to call 'the personal relation'. His is a world of introspection, Kipling's an extrovert world. The delicacy of his prose, as accurate and precise in its own way as Kipling's, matches the delicacy of the sentiments of Mr Forster's characters. These beings, so jealous of their integrity, would hate all Kipling's characters, who, in turn, would despise Mr Forster's. Kipling's would willingly risk their souls for The Thing; Mr Forster is anxious that empire and efficiency should not destroy men's souls, since they only have one life in which to enjoy them. Forster's novels made no great noise at their first appearance* (his post-War novel, *A Passage to India*, was a different matter), and indeed the structure of the earlier ones is halting and clumsy, as though their author were a little uncertain of what he wanted to convey; but they took an increasingly firm hold on a generation of novelists, and gradually became more widely known. Most of Mr Forster's work has an intimately moving quality, and he is not afraid to apply his values to a broader sphere than that suggested by his earlier work.

If Kipling and Mr Forster represent two of the most important aspects of the Edwardian period—the responsibilities of national power and the reaction against such involvement —a third aspect, equally important, is that represented in the novels of H. G. Wells, the 'ideological' aspect. Wells was a writer who, in spite of his loose prose and his often loose thought, produced work which by its sheer vitality has tremendous persuasive power. From the purely literary point of view his early imaginative stories, and his early novels, are by far the most satisfactory. Acutely conscious, as few of his contemporaries at that time were, of the implication of the social changes gradually transforming the country, and of the enormous strides made in technology, his vision was turned away from the fascination of the present to the possibilities of

---

* Except *Howard's End*; but the war swamped all literary considerations.

the future. It was an age of ideologues, 'those mortal enemies of experience', of rationalists, 'mortal enemies of those reasons the reason knows nothing of', to adopt a phrase of critics unjustly inimical to such aspirations.

But an element of propaganda spoils Wells's later work; we all the time feel that he is forcing us to share his view, and this makes us suspicious of the validity of his characters. In his earlier work, in the stories, in *Kipps* and *Tono Bungay*, and books of that kind, he takes high rank as a creative and interpretative artist. His delight in existence, in the oddity of human beings, so immensely various; his knack of portraying personalities, and his joy at the magnificent adventure and research that life is, gave him a tremendous influence for good or ill on a whole generation; not on writers, for his influence there is small, but on people, especially the young, eager to gratify their desires for expansion and self-expression. His misty theology—a vague vitalistic Deism—was extremely welcome to a generation that had lost its faith in Christianity, and could not face the responsibilities of agnosticism. This is to speak only of his work within our period; his further development belongs to a later period, as do the novels of Galsworthy, G. K. Chesterton, and Belloc. The two last, it may be noted here, are representative of the growth of Roman Catholicism during the first fourteen years of the new century.

IV

GENERAL PROSE WRITERS

ARTISTS, PROPHETS, PRIESTS AND ESSAYISTS

WALTER SAVAGE LANDOR belongs to no Victorian movement; he was born too early, and besides, living so much abroad, he was hardly influenced by any English 'climate of opinion'. Intellectually he was a mid-eighteenth-century rationalist, emotionally a late eighteenth-century republican, and the thoughts and feelings proper to such animated him to the end. But he had an independent mind; he would not follow even his admirations blindly, and his memory was stocked with a great store of classical and historical knowledge which enabled him to make illuminating statements, and strike out those clear generalizations which make his *Imaginary Conservations* of direct applicability even now. His great gift was that of making the past seem like the present, its difficulties and its delights the same as ours. He was full of violent prejudices, it is true, but he earned the right to them, for he was the only one of the young romantic poets who actually fought for republicanism, and who, living to be old, did not renounce his earlier enthusiasms.

Yet it is not for his political opinions that he is read now so much as for his general sentiments, his admirable criticism, his very living reconstructions of the past, which range over a great variety of countries, times, and personages, from the early Greek age to the mid-Victorian. Above all he is to be read for his prose, of which he was an outstanding master. He has the splendid tread of Dryden together with the delicious modulations of Congreve, and he can move to scorn, to tenderness, to indignation, to laughter, and to love. It is possible to maintain a charge of sentimentality against him by the quotation of extracts; but his energy, his capacity to

86

order abundant material, his succinctness, outweigh his lapses a hundredfold. He was never popular, for he is too intellectually aristocratic to appeal to large numbers, and it was his proud boast, 'I shall dine late, but the dining-room will be well lighted, the guests few and select.' He was a great and noble writer, moved especially by an enthusiasm for justice, and a profound feeling of pity for all that is oppressed; and above everything he was generous. He stands apart from his age, but not to be acquainted with him is to be a great deal the poorer.

If Landor is a writer whose influence can never be calculated—it is possibly quite powerful though invisible—Macaulay's more clangorous prose and shallower thoughts moulded men's ideas for three-quarters of a century. He stamped the Whig idea on three generations. It is not our business here to discuss the rightness or wrongness of his doctrine, nor to examine his historical accuracy, but to discuss his literary claims and his place in the story of our era. His literary merits are obvious, they even advertise themselves. His prose flows along vigorously, it is well balanced, and free from any ambiguity; but indeed there is no excuse for a man not to be clear when he has no doubts as to the rightness of his thoughts. His essays are robust, full of common sense and crammed with information; he was always able to bring an amazing amount of knowledge to bear upon any point that occurred to him. His judgment of persons is never subtle, and his appraisal of literary points is so 'sound' as often to be almost meaningless; yet he is not always trite, and though he is so often wrong about the details of people's lives, he has an uncanny trick of getting the general perspective right; time has reversed the 'soundness' of his literary views, yet they have acquired a meaning as representing something of his age. He was the first to write history that everybody could read; he had a most unusual talent for narrative, and besides could bring his readers into close touch with the daily lives of people in the past. His description of England at the end of the seventeenth century is an acknowledged masterpiece which combines movement and vividness with compression. But he could never see anything except through the eyes of a thoroughly representative and highly successful early nineteenth-century bureaucrat; his prose, for all its skill, is a machine-made product of the industrial revolution; it works beautifully, like a well-oiled engine; it glitters magnificently as the pistons work smoothly and relentlessly up and down. No one can help admiring Macaulay. He was as near being an artist as a man can be who has nothing of the artist in him. The *Essays* are overwhelmingly brilliant; the *History* is a shattering achievement; but they are just not the real thing, in the same way as *Lays of Ancient Rome* are just not real poetry. But Macaulay exists as an immaculately representative figure.

What he represented was a very important, perhaps the dominant, side of early Victorianism. He shared the opacity of vision combined with a certain grandeur, a certain nobility even. He shared also the complacency, but with him it was hard, not soft. He believed in God and he believed in the British Constitution; both were perfect, and existed for the sake of Britons; but the Constitution had been created by good Whigs in a hundred hard-fought battles. He represented, in fact, just those sides of the early-Victorian mind, which, enormously useful as they undoubtedly were, we have come to hate, though perhaps we might be grateful if we could share its certitude. The curious thing about Macaulay is that, distinguished man of letters that he was, he was the only one who thought as he did and still remains great. The others have sunk into derision, or maintain a lesser place by reason of other qualities (Sir James Stephen, for example). Everybody who still retains eminence fought hard against those very things for which he stood so placidly, and, it would seem, unconsciously. Opposed to him on all the grand points are the great men who, in the sphere of literature, walked as giants in those and immediately succeeding days: Carlyle, Ruskin, Arnold, Morris.

They make an odd quartette; the dyspeptic Scotch peasant,

the neurotic rich wine-merchant's son, the correct product of Rugby and Oxford, and the giant who radiated health from his heart, his hands, and his head. They were all tremendous—yes, even Arnold—they were temperamentally antagonistic on many points, and they drew quite different results from similar causes. Nobody would think from reading what Carlyle and Arnold had to say, or listening to the way they said it, that both drew much of their inspiration from Goethe. Nobody comparing Ruskin's views on art with Carlyle's would imagine that Ruskin would whole-heartedly acknowledge Carlyle as his teacher in anything. Morris and Ruskin seem poles apart, yet both were affected by the medievalism which with some became a hampering disease. But there is no end to the curiosities we discover if we try to unravel the threads of cultural heredity in this exciting and confused age. The important thing to notice is that all four of these men hated as the thing above all things accurst the prevalent philosophy of economics which the industrial revolution, together with Adam Smith, Bentham, the Mills and others had brought about. They all fought it tooth and nail, for different reasons, and with different remedies in view; they fought it in various ways, by screaming, by preaching, by reasoning, by doing; and though they do not seem to have had any great immediate effect, their efforts probably prevented things from being as bad as they might have been, and they planted seeds which are only now, it would seem, beginning to sprout. Arnold is the exception; his seed came up too soon, and the visible harvest is over; yet what he stood for will necessarily remain as an element in any civilized consciousness.

We must begin with Carlyle, the sage of Chelsea who never ceased to be the obstinate peasant of Ecclefechan. His nature was as tortured and 'impossible' as his grotesque prose. With his violently puritan, pleasure-hating nature, akin to that of John Knox, he tried to absorb German romanticism, and even the monstrous transcendentalism of Novalis. He longed to be what he was utterly incapable of being, a man of action.

'Brave young friend . . . you are, what I am not, in the happy case to learn to *be* something and to *do* something, instead of eloquently talking about what has been and was done and may be!' The sort of man of action he would have liked to be was a mixture of Frederick the Great and Jeremiah. He loved denunciation, one is bound to think, for its own sake; he would have wished today,* perhaps, to be Hitler (their utterances are not unlike), a dictator with a torrent of words at his command. A dictator was what he called aloud for, in an anguished rush of rhetoric.† His hatreds were many and manifest; it is hard to discover his loves. He believed that nothing could prosper which was not founded upon what he called veracity, the will of nature, or the commands of God: but everything that he personally disliked was what he meant by unveracious, or contrary to the will of God— Parliaments, Popery, Progress—and if he maintained that men were Godlike individuals, he also asserted that they were mostly fools. His ideas usually came out in a fury of sound which makes him nearly unreadable; his strange concatenations of words and phrases, his jibes and jeers and capital letters, his Germanic constructions, his smokiness, his thunderousness (with its occasional lightning flashes), make it intolerable to read him. 'Clotted nonsense'? Clotted, yes, but by no means nonsense. 'A sort of Babylonish dialect . . . at times a sort of singular felicity of expression': the contemporary criticisms of *Sartor Resartus* still hold. At first the tremendous nervous vigour appeals; for a few paragraphs one feels an accession of strength: but soon the effect is numbing; it is like the mad rantings of Nathaniel Lee. The storm goes on raging, but one ceases to take any notice.

Yet with all his vociferations Carlyle was an artist. It is not only that he occasionally struck out a memorable phrase, but that he could create a vision of the past. He is not, we

---

* In 1937, perhaps, but hardly in 1940, though he would in that year have stood a strong chance of internment under 18B.

† Landor could have told him something about dictatorships which might have disturbed him: e.g., in the conversation between Solon and Pisistratus.

are told, to be trusted as a historian, for though he went through enormous travail in seeking out original documents, he distorted history to suit his own arguments. No doubt every historian necessarily does this to some extent; but Carlyle seems to have made no attempt to guard against it; the lower veracity must make way for the higher. For him history was a moral weapon with which to bludgeon his opponents, and in the process of using history to this end he painted the most magnificent series of wildly Turnerian landscapes, filled with figures as active and diverse, as multitudinous and immediate, as those of Peter Breughel, and as strange as those of Hieronymus Bosch. *The French Revolution* is a superb phantasmagoria; the Abbot in *Past and Present* an eternally great imaginary portrait. What they are meant to convey need no longer matter. And there are, it is true, certain qualities in the prose which make for the effects; the vigour in the soil which made the brambles into such scratchy hedges also made the corn sprout luxuriantly.

And if he was wrong-headed and perverse in a dozen ways, in one respect, in his greatest hatred and contempt, he was right. He loathed Mammon and his works with all his heart. He hated orthodox economics, 'the dismal science' with its 'inexorable laws', its *laisser-faire*, its reduction of men to hopeless slavery. He could not analyse what the horror and the blasphemy were due to, and laid the charge to the door of democracy ('physical-force Chartism' seems to have inspired him with a terror which never left him), but he knew in his deepest part that the whole thing was fundamentally wrong. And it was in this realm that Ruskin became his disciple, a disciple who surpassed him in clearheadedness, and had a far more balanced sense of values. Ruskin never believed, as Carlyle did, that the only happiness lay in nerve-racking, back-breaking toil. He was far too sensible to accept the view that work was the sole aim of man's existence on earth: some time at least should be given to the contemplation of God's handiwork, and the enjoyment of beautiful things. He hated industrialism at least as much for creating the Black Country as for starving people by the operation of 'over-production'. If Carlyle cursed bishops for discussing prevenient grace while three thousand sempstresses were being sweated into starvation, Ruskin saw that there might be some point in discussing prevenient grace, though he would not waste his own time in doing so. His earlier works were devoted to art, to the attempt to make people see things. He went forth bravely to attack the dull clods who mocked at Turner or the pre-Raphaelite painters (for which we must forgive the crassness of his attack on Whistler); and if nobody now pays much attention to his art criticism, and still less to his goody-goody effusions, his art criticism, curiously confused with morality, medievalism, and a dislike of the Renaissance and all its works, was the fount of most art criticism for at least a generation. What was most important, however, was his insistence that art is necessary, that it matters extremely, and that a nation neglects it at its peril. In details he may have been absurd, and often was, but in essentials he was right.

Himself something of an artist—a delicate draughtsman and to some extent a poet—he turned from art to economics. He felt that the landscape and the society brought about by industrialism, and supported by orthodox economics (too often the apologist for the *status quo*), was mortally inimical to art, which could not exist without human life having some decency, some idea other than that of Mammon. It was Carlyle who first convinced him of the horror of industrial economics, and he acknowledged him handsomely as his teacher. But he was more acute than Carlyle: he learnt that ranting and raving was no good; he saw that dictators were no good; he did not believe with Kingsley and Mrs Gaskell that all that was needed was a change of heart among the employers, and nicely behaved employees; he was too realistic for that. He saw that the whole basis of the economic system would have to be changed, and he set himself to learn economics. The discipline bettered his prose considerably. Before, it had been too uncontrolled, a little spongy, redeemed by purple passages which he later strove to excise.

His prose is rarely beautiful in itself, as Landor's is; it is a little too drawn out, always a trifle school-ma'amish: but it became in the end a lucid instrument. His incursion into economics caused an uproar. *Unto This Last* began to appear in *The Cornhill Magazine* in 1860 under Thackeray's editorship: but the essays 'were reprobated in a violent manner', and he was not allowed to continue them. The same happened with *Munera Pulveris*, the mere outline of a work, which began to appear in *Frazer's Magazine*, and was promptly quashed. In details he may have been absurd (his road-making adventures with Oxford under-graduates certainly were), but in essentials he was right. His proposals were 'lunatic', but many of them have achieved the stamp of sanity between the sober covers of the statute-book, and it is possible that even his more thorough-going principles may some day be adopted.

Unlike Carlyle and Ruskin, Matthew Arnold made no plea for a return to the Middle or any other Ages. He did, it is true, write the stimulating if ill-informed *On the Study of Celtic Literature*, rather, one feels, because many people around him were interested in such things than because he himself was attracted towards them. He disliked his own age as much, possibly, as the bearded prophets did, but his remedy was not 'go back'. For him the cure was to go forward, and the way to do this was not to stir up religious feelings which he himself did not share, but to throw open the doors to the 'sweetness and light'* of the reason. He was in many ways a true disciple of Goethe. His range of interests was unusually wide, as a surprised public discovered when the first series of *Essays in Criticism* was published, and though for us today his examples are not very well chosen (we are apt to find the journals of Amiel a bore, while Maurice de Guérin has faded out of the picture) it is the two series of these criticisms that still remain the important things. The titles of his books, *Culture and Anarchy*, *Literature and Dogma*, in themselves

* The phrase came originally from Swift's *Battle of the Books*. For him sweetness and light were the qualities that distinguished 'the ancients'.

indicate his trend towards a new humanism, which to a large extent he succeeded in founding as an island of refuge in the religious *débâcle* which took place in the last half of the century. He has been much blamed for his incursions into theology, and for the levity of his tone when dealing with religion, but it is scarcely fair to take this sort of exception. If theology is not the preserve of a clique, if it really is important to every intelligent and cultured man, then surely an intelligent and cultured man has a right to give his views about it. 'Levity' is an attitude of mind allowable to a man who wishes to attack something he feels to be dangerous; it is a more effective weapon than solemnity. It was only natural that an unbelieving but temperamentally religious humanist should anger the believers of his age, as he appears to irritate the believers of this. These, naturally, cannot approve of a man who describes religion as 'morality touched by emotion', who defines God as 'a stream of tendency, not ourselves, that makes for righteousness'; these definitions do not correspond with their experience. But they did, and do, correspond with the experience of thousands of other people who are ready with him (as a disciple of Renan) to adore 'the sweet reasonableness of Christ'. Carlyle appeared more tremendous to his contemporaries; it was Arnold who had the most effect.

For this European-minded man, for ever fighting against insularity, upholding the Mediterranean as well as the Nordic tradition then so fashionable, the mental attitude of his contemporaries, and of Englishmen in general throughout history, lacked 'sanity'. Its 'fantastic' nature revealed itself in 'incredible vagaries', in literature, art, religion, and morals. England was—and here he borrowed his sharpest arrow from Heine—Philistine. He battled continuously against provincialism, smugness, narrowness of view, and continually criticized the 'Thyestian banquet* of claptrap' which, as he saw it, constituted English public life. It was essential to see life clearly and to see it whole. Basing his style on French

* At which Thyestes unwittingly ate the flesh of his two sons.

prose, of which he never caught the subtle music (just as he was deaf to French poetry), he was always lucid and sometimes incisive; but towards the end he developed a mannerism of repetition; a sense of fatigue dimly pervades his later writings. As a publicist he is no longer of direct importance, but he permanently affected the thought of this country: much of what is best in our present-day attitude is traceable to Arnold, chiefly in an insistence upon values which are neither materialistic nor religious. His literary criticism still endures. He said much that can be combated; his own favourite phrases, by dint of being repeated by himself and others, have come to seem silly: but his approach was the right approach. He insisted that literature was something important, and that it must finally be judged by a quality of utterance peculiar to itself. That is a commonplace now, but was not so in his own day. It is difficult for those who now deride Arnold to realize how much they owe him on several grounds.

There remains Morris, in some way the greatest, the fullest, the most complete of the Victorians. We may now dislike his wallpaper and his furnishings, tire of his printing, and resent the affected prose of some of his romances; but the vibrations of his tremendous vitality are still felt. He was not a great anything—painter, poet, romancer, or philosopher—but he was a very great man. As a prose-writer he has two distinct sides; the one as a creative writer, which no longer appeals to us; the other in his socialistic work where he was, in the end, far more creative. The pseudo-medieval style of his romances is intolerable; but there is this to be said for Morris's medieval stigmata—he really felt and understood certain sides of the Middle Ages. He did not use them as a bludgeon to beat his enemies with, as Carlyle did; he did not flee to them as an escape, after the manner of Ruskin; they were more to him than picturesque material, and in a sense he lived them. But the prose* makes it seem as though this

* It was once known as 'Wardour Street' because antiques, and sham antiques, were sold there; the phrase has gone out now that Wardour

love had been an affectation, which it was not. In a more leisured age people may return to *The Well at the World's End* and *The Water of the Wondrous Isles*, but in this hurried age it is the detective novel, however badly written, that will provide the escape, while Morris's dreamlike fairy-stories, beautifully written as they are in their own manner, will remain undisturbed in the tomb-like glory of the collected edition.

But *A Dream of John Ball* and the Utopian *News from Nowhere* are written with a keen eye on actuality, and in that clear, decisive, unmannered prose which a sense of actuality brings. Like the three men already discussed, Morris hated the smutching of beauty and the degradation of the individual which was the price paid for commerical supremacy. Once he had become aware of the process he never ceased to battle against 'that ocean of half-conscious hypocrisy which is called cultivated society'; and being acute enough to see that the hypocrisy was only half conscious, he realized that the teachings of his predecessors did not cut deep enough. It was no use treating the symptoms; you had to attack the cause, which was not only the economic structure, but the whole framework of society. He had read Marx, with what degree of understanding is uncertain; he became a stump orator; and knowing that art could not flourish in the conditions he lived in, he set himself to 'make socialists'. If socialism became his religion, he never let his enthusiasm cloud his vision. He was intensely realistic, and forecast the abortive course of the English socialist movement with extraordinary accuracy. He was what we now call a communist, but always because he was first and foremost an artist, and he was willing to sacrifice himself as an artist, and even art itself in the revolution, so that art might ultimately live. He was convinced that under the regime into which he was born art would perish, and on the whole he was right. He held

Street consists mainly of restaurants. But Morris's is very different from the pastiche horror of Hewlett's in *The Forest Lovers* or Butcher and Lang's in their *Odyssey*.

his opinions firmly, and had the courage of those opinions to their logical end; thus his lectures to working men contain better prose than any of his other work, or than the work of Carlyle, Ruskin, and Arnold.

Cutting across this line of intellectual development, acting in a more general sphere, and each of them of more importance as far as results go than the men previously discussed, are two of the most brilliant minds of the century, standing for opposed truths:—Newman and Huxley. They had certain things in common: a fundamental scepticism which they resolved differently, a passionate honesty and love of truth for its own sake whatever the consequences might be. Huxley wrote very good prose indeed, Newman was a great artist in the medium, Newman first attracted public attention by his poems, and then achieved notoriety by his famous *Tract XC*; he dropped out of the general view on his conversion to Romanism, so that the public did not take much notice of his inspiring *Idea of a University*, nor of the more difficult *Grammar of Assent*. He soared suddenly into permanent fame through the magnificent *Apologia*, which he wrote in a storm of sublime indignation when Charles Kingsley was foolish enough to attack the veracity of the Roman Church through Newman himself. His extreme, almost neurotic sensibility, combined with a hard core which never flinched, reveal themselves in this astonishing confession, in prose which is swift and sinewy, and carries the reader on in a tremendous surge of intellectual excitement which breaks through into the emotional. It is one of the great documents of the century, and stands for all that is best in the Victorian religious mind. Newman has affinities with Pascal, and even with Augustine, but he is strongly streaked with English puritanism. It is difficult to assess his influence, which is possibly stronger outside his community than within it; we are given to understand that he was not always quite sound on certain points of scholastic doctrine. The purity of his life and his thought, revealed in the purity of his prose, have always reminded people that a point of view exists that may be very different from their own, but may yet be valid and of equal value with theirs.

Huxley, on the other hand, stands for all that is best in the Victorian agnostic mind, and he also is streaked with English puritanism. His influence was, and to some extent still is, enormous. Himself a scientist of high distinction, after the publication of *The Origin of Species* he devoted himself largely to maintaining Darwin's doctrine against all comers, and to combating Christian dogma. His prose, even if a little over-punctuated, is a model in both the controversial and the expository styles; and, thanks to his sense of humour, his tussles with Gladstone and others still make excellent reading. A man of wide knowledge and interests (he wrote on Hume and Berkeley), and of deep human sympathies, he became a great popular figure, standing for the new enlightenment. He undoubtedly enjoyed his function of 'smiting the Amalek-ite', and the sharp clear weapon of his thought, his sterling honesty, his firm prose, probably did more execution among believers than any other agent. But it is a mistake to think that he represented and defended the 'red in tooth and claw' theory as regards society; there is no excuse for this common error, since his views are pellucidly expressed in his *Evolution and Ethics*, in the Romanes lecture which gives the book its title, and in the 'Prolegomena' which precedes the lecture. The cosmic process was, in the main, one of relent-less struggle, but not necessarily of individual struggle; there are insect and animal polities as well as human ones. But beyond this, in man, there was the ethical process, opposed to the cosmic process, and always making inroads upon it. Man must subdue, in society, the qualities of the ape and tiger which originally made for his survival. Huxley, in fact, was a humanist; but he accepted Rousseauish doctrines of noble savagery as little as he did those of original sin and the fall of man. He derives from Hobbes and Descartes through Hartley. Sentimentalists always hate Huxley; anti-intellec-tualists despise him. But the Newmans and Huxleys of this world honour each other as foes strangely fighting in the same cause, the happiness, the dignity, and the mental integrity of mankind.

Neither Newman nor Huxley was primarily concerned with 'literature'; they emerged from their spheres to take their place as artists, and we can now return to those who figure as professional men of letters. Pater is the most significant of the later ones, and stands in the popular eye as the great exponent of the 'aesthetic' doctrine, the 'art for art's sake' school. The movement is now regarded with tolerant contempt, but fundamentally it was sound, though its slogan, like most slogans, overstated the case. The doctrine merely is that though art may be ultimately concerned with morals, religion, and politics, and is finally to be judged in relation to a manner of living, it is itself autonomous, deals with a different grouping of emotions and has a different approach. The movement, however, became somewhat flabby and sickly; it became too much a yearning after 'beauty' (Rossetti is perhaps a little to blame for this); it was fascinated by malady in both the physical and the moral sense. There is a good deal of the greenery-yallery about it, the somewhat verdigrised languor of certain pre-Raphaelite windows, and it ended in the macabre of Aubrey Beardsley. It became distorted by the amoralists and, flaunted in the nineties, died out in the first decade of the new century, except perhaps in the more enduring person of Mr Arthur Symons, who, endowed with considerable intellectual force, bravely kept flying the flag of a cause already decayed.

Pater himself, however, was a moralist, in the direct line of descent from Arnold. Though he wished life to be treated 'in the spirit of art', this itself was 'moral significancy of art and poetry'. He was afraid of his own view that life must be caught as a series of intensely appreciative moments and that none of the moments should be sacrificed to any system or abstract morality, so he expunged from the conclusion of *The Renaissance* the essay in which he brilliantly stated his theory. For him art largely replaced religion; and even when, after a period of flagrant antagonism to the Church he returned to the fold, what attracted him was the artistry of it. 'You seem to think, Mr Pater,' Jowett said to him, 'that religion is all ritual.' It was, if the conclusion of *Marius the Epicurean* is any indication. Pater no doubt had a considerable influence, and by no means a bad one, in educating people to a finer perception of the arts, and a realization of their value. He continued Arnold's battle for culture, and if the result was not quite what he would have wished, that was not altogether his fault.

Good as his essays are, and admirable as much of his criticism is, especially his essays on style, on Wordsworth and on Coleridge, where he ceases to be impressionistic and becomes analytical, his great achievement was the *Imaginary Portraits*, with which we may include *Gaston de Latour*. The *Renaissance* was a fine piece of pioneer work, but the *Imaginary Portraits* are living re-creations of personalities, in a peculiar form, half short story and half essay, which owe a good deal of their effect to the careful modulations of the prose. It is the fashion now to look down on Pater and to abominate his prose; but his interpretation and his criticism have illuminating moments; and if his prose is sometimes languorous, it is with the languor of an athlete at rest. He is the conscious prose-artist of the period; he had a good ear, and a respect for words; and though he is not a model to be followed, there is much to be learnt from him.

Wilde certainly learnt a good deal from him, and moreover endowed his style with speed, a clear swiftness which he shared with Landor and Newman alone in the Victorian era. His prose is over-adjectived, but it is firm and concise as well as rippling. His short stories and novels have about them a somewhat disagreeable sentimentality, but his essays and his criticism are free from this taint. He is extremely witty, and his paradoxes, though they often seem outrageous, are as often based on keen observation, if not at a very profound level. His dialogues on art, *Intentions*, are possibly his best work outside his plays; and if *De Profundis* contains his plainest prose, it is the outcry of a broken man. Wilde is not a good advertisement for humanism: his pride of intellect, his devotion to the flesh, are neither Attic, as he thought, nor humanistic, as he probably supposed. His amorality was a symptom of the timc, but he was not so shallow as is now generally assumed; and though you may not agree with the conclusions of *The Soul of Man under Socialism*, you have to admit that it was written by a thoughtful man.

After Wilde, except possibly for Symons, the line of writers who wrote large books to which the public paid attention died out, to be replaced by publicists who preferred to manoeuvre as essayists in the columns of the weeklies, which gradually ousted the quarterlies and monthlies as organs of opinion. They also returned to the Kingsley-Mrs Gaskell tradition, and wrote novels. The most explosive among them all was Samuel Butler; he loved to drop bombs and crackers in any nest which he thought harboured the fledglings of cant, but he prided himself a little too much on being paradoxical. He has been described as the typical English eccentric who delights in standing everything on its head; and it has been suggested that he may be compared with Peacock, who had he lived earlier might have found something constructive to say, but who, living when he did, found it all said already, and had to resort to paradoxical opposition to give his individuality scope. Scientifically, Butler was opposed to the Darwinian view, and it was he who inculcated Shaw with the idea of Creative Evolution (the Lamarck-Bergson 'vitalism'). His *Note-Books*, his *Alps and Sanctuaries* and such like, are his most characteristic work, but his most famous is *Erewhon*, in which he described an imaginary society living by the values of his day startlingly reversed. It is crammed with amusing critical *aperçus* of our society, some of which are severe and justified. It might, at a stretch, be considered a successor of Johnson's *Rasselas*, and the irony is often admirable. More truly a novel, however, is *The Way of All Flesh*, still more excitingly destructive of the values current in his day, a book in which he shrewdly exploded much of the cant upon which middle-class society rested.

Most of the 'names' of the Edwardian period are those of men who belong more properly to the next volume— H. G. Wells, Hilaire Belloc, G. K. Chesterton, and G. B. Shaw in his prefaces. The prose of all, except Wells, is good, and even he has vigour. The curse of Victorian prolixity had been lifted, the solemnity, the prophetic objurgation had departed. Shaw's prose is particularly admirable, sinewy, direct, with a buoyancy, a conciseness of phrasing, and a modelling, which take us back to Dryden and Swift. These writers belong to different schools of religious thought, Wells and Shaw to the agnostic school, flirting occasionally with a vague transcendentalism, Belloc and Chesterton to the Roman Catholics. All of them, from various angles, attacked the social structure, having no hope of bettering the human being until the conditions of his life are bettered. The bourgeoisie was rapidly becoming conscious that its castle was built upon the sandy foundations of intolerable injustice and a decaying economic system. It was the heyday of Fabianism; eager young men dropped their Herbert Spencer and took up the volumes of the Webbs. There was a new sense of marching on towards better things, not on the old industrial-evangelical basis, but, in the main, on a non-revolutionary Marxism (if that is not too contradictory an expression), which would not altogether abolish religion, though it would break free from its trammels. The political troubles of the early Georgian years lent hope to the movement; forces were gathering for a great change which the war interrupted, and the Russian revolution re-directed.

Standing rather apart from all this were the minor essayists, of whom the most distinguished was Augustine Birrell, who in elegant prose dealt with literature in the spirit of Liberalism. He lived to be the last of a great line of literary statesmen, and dealt in a way which did not matter with things that did. The other essayists were engaged in bringing the form to a state of degraded futility, believing they were continuing the tradition of Charles Lamb.

Alone, possibly, among the essayists, stands the figure of

Sir Max Beerbohm, whose fame as a caricaturist has a little obscured his merits as a writer. Beerbohm was a real critic of literature, and his own style is exquisitely chiselled. His pen is as keen and hard as his intellect. *Zuleika Dobson* is a superb piece of fantastic fooling with a sharp critical point, and Beerbohm had a rigorous artistic conscience. His work exemplifies a kind of writing which seems ephemeral, but which has in it the quality of endurance.

.   .   .   .

Difficult to include in a short survey of this kind are a number of men who, not primarily men of letters, but economists, philosophers, bankers, historians, psychologists, yet reached the general public in their works and are of some literary importance. J. S. Mill, for instance, though his philosophy was not much read by the generality, yet reached the public not only through his work on economics, but especially through his *Liberty* and his *Representative Government*, both of which are worth pondering today. Froude, who was very much an artist, is well known through his still charming *Short Studies on Great Subjects*. Bagehot was an extraordinary man, who made his mark as a philosopher and a banker, but whose interest to us here is chiefly in his *Critical Studies*; he is always worth reading, not only as representing the best informed criticism of his day, but as being illuminating now. In always relating literature to a broad experience of life, he exhibits a common sense amounting to genius, all couched in a vigorous, living prose which has even today the accents of the interested voice. Never portentous, with 'no fangs for recondite research', he always delights because he is always humane. Among popular historians again there is J. R. Green, whose fantastic view of the early and some of the later history of England may be neglected, but who made excellent story of the rest, not however, so free of the 'drum and trumpet' aspect as he wished his readers to suppose; still, as a history of the English people it was a pioneer work. Dowden remains, especially as a Shakesperian critic, though his work has

largely been superseded by A. C. Bradley's brilliant book on
the tragedies. Morley and Stephen stand out as biographers
in an age of biographies; Morley's *Gladstone* and his *Voltaire*
are especially good of their kind.

Towards the end of our period we find men who link up
more readily with the present day. J. M. Robertson's
rationalistic books are perhaps not much read now, but they
were very symptomatic of the agnosticism of the Edwardian
period. A larger figure is that of Edward Carpenter. Not
only his *Towards Democracy*, a curiously Whitmanesque book
of poetry, but *Love's Coming of Age* and *Civilisation, Its Cause
and Cure* had a considerable effect in their day. Not only the
form of his poetry, but the message of his books, in their idea
of an all-embracing redeeming love, derives largely from
Whitman. He was symptomatic also of the complete breakdown of the Great Taboo of sex, for though he aimed at a
high idealism, he discussed sexual matters with the greatest
freedom. So also did Havelock Ellis, a much greater artist,
who strays over a wide literary field, and seems only inci-
dentally to have been a pioneer in sexual psychology. His
Impressions and Comments are books of distinctive grace and
charm; his free inquiring mind, happily allied with a sense
of beauty, has forged out a set of values which many find
inspiring.

Bertrand Russell's main popular work falls outside the
period but he may be mentioned here as one of the liberators
in all fields of thought of whom Lowes Dickinson was the
centre and the popularizer. Dickinson was perhaps the last
and finest flower of Liberalism, a Liberalism based not on
any system of economics, but on the Greek view of life. In
his exquisite prose he commented in various forms—imaginary letters, dialogues, and even a play—on every aspect of
our civilization that made for or against culture in the fundamental sense of the term and not as a varnish spread over
ignorance. His delicate agnosticism is in marked contrast to
the blatant cudgelling of Robertson; if he thought that all
our guesses as to what 'It' was about were terribly wide of

the mark, he had a firm conviction that 'It' was about something. His work is always penetrating and charming; one feels in reading him, that one is in contact with a sage, endeavouring to brush away all the cobwebs that interfere with mankind's vision of itself and its destiny.

V

DRAMA

THERE is little to be said about the drama in our period until its revival in the eighties. To all intents and purposes there was none, and we might be led to conclude from the history of this and the previous period that the literary value of the drama is in inverse ratio to the dominance of the actor-manager. The drama is essentially a form of literature, and to be of any value it must carry the weight of contemporary ideas as much as any other branch of literature. The actor in the main, especially the great actor-manager, cares only for plays which give him resounding parts; and in the early years of the century the actors' parts had literally to be resounding, for officially there were still only two theatres in London, and thus to accommodate theatre-goers, they had to be vast and high. Also, public taste had been thoroughly debauched with pantomimes and farces, with shoddy tragedies and ranting melodramas, while the comedies, instead of representing life, gave shadowy imitations of old comedies, and copies of them again; the public had also been largely regaled with spectacles and scenic contraptions of all kinds. Later in the century there was small chance for the native writer, since, owing to the non-existence of copyright agreements with France, it was cheaper for the manager to get translations of bad Parisian farces than to employ English talent. Matters went to such a length that in one play we see an English valet learning French so as to read 'English' plays in the original. This state of affairs was ultimately remedied by the efforts of Charles Reade, Dion Boucicault, and Bulwer Lytton.

Yet the poor state of the drama was not altogether the fault of the actors: the men of letters were producing nothing for them of any value for the theatre. The poets, from Coleridge to Swinburne, even to Stephen Phillips, and including Tennyson and Browning, offered them material which was utterly unsuitable. It was imitation Elizabethan, which brought into being a certain amount of good poetry when good poets wrote it, but not good poetic drama. In the hands of lesser men such as Sheridan Knowles (who ultimately left the stage for the pulpit), Talfourd, Sir Henry Taylor, and sometimes Tom Taylor, the result was, and is, dreary in the extreme. There were some good dramatic ideas in these plays, but the characters were given words to speak such as were never uttered on sea or land, the authors being under the impression that tragedy demanded this fustian. Comedy was slightly better; the language was appallingly stilted, but some of the plays, such as Lytton's *Money*, had a faint reference to life, and the glimmerings of an idea; but on the whole the only works which had any success were the diversions of Planché, such farces as Morton's *Box and Cox* (from the French), and the now to us appalling *facéties* of Douglas Jerrold, Mark Lemon, and Gilbert à Beckett.

The work of Tom Taylor is still readable, however; his people do not speak badly, and he had some notion of dramatic movement. Dion Boucicault is an interesting figure. He wrote nothing of any permanent value, but he broke down many of the dead traditions that were cumbering the stage, and began to accustom the public to a small degree of originality: but he had no ideas to impart. His Irish dramas are his best work. But a more important herald of what was to come was T. W. Robertson. His comedies seem to us now rather gawky and obvious; the moral is platitudinous and the machinery creaks, but at least he brought a breath of air into the theatre, dealt with human beings, and tackled what the people of his day were talking about. His plays are just readable and just actable, for at last here was a man working neither in an out-worn stage tradition, nor a threadbare literary mode.

There was a gap of ten years between Robertson's last play in 1869 and the first play of Henry Arthur Jones, which was followed nine years later by the first play of Arthur Wing Pinero. Neither of them was a great playwright, but both deserve credit as pioneers, especially Jones, who though not so accomplished as Pinero and with rather a slighter capacity for creating character, is historically more important. *The Silver King* created a furore. Matthew Arnold, who very sensibly had not been to the theatre for twenty years, broke his habit, sat in the stalls and wrote an astonishingly commendatory report on it. Jones had introduced naturalism; it was a bad play, but the people in it spoke as people do speak. Naturalism is not all, and there was soon to be a rebellion against it, especially in Ireland, but it was just the element the drama then needed. Moreover, Jones went on to deal with the real problems of real people, who always, however, nobly renounce their happiness when Mrs Grundy tells them they ought, a curious state of affairs in a man who was always girding at Mrs Grundy. Shaw hit the nail on the head when criticizing him: 'And now comes the oddity of the situation. Mr Jones, with a wide and clear vision of society, is content with theories of it that have really no relation to his observation.' He wrote comedy without having a comic conception of society. His three best plays are *The Case of Rebellious Susan*, *The Liars*, and *Mrs Dane's Defence*; *The Dancing Girl* is ridiculous, *Carnac Sahib* full of falsity and claptrap, while *The Tempter* is a ghastly symbolic play in still more ghastly blank verse. But whatever his defects or his merits, Jones did restore the drama to a place of dignity in letters and insisted that the author was a more important person in the theatre than the actor-manager. He knew the stage well, and though he loathed Ibsen he had learnt from Sardou, Scribe, and d'Ennery, and thus was in a strong position. Pinero can be regarded as his successor.

Wilde is next in date, but he does not belong to the movement of which Jones and Pinero were the harbingers. His only attempt at tragedy, *Salome*, is a brilliant exercise in Maeterlinckian idiom, but is not more than that; his genius lay in the direction of farcical comedy of which *The Impor-*

tance of Being Earnest is an almost perfect example. His world resembles that of Etherege, in which there are no values, so that the ridiculous and startling paradoxes can be wholly enjoyed as a pyrotechnic display. His great mastery, however, is shown in his phrasing, a matter in which all his successors except Shaw have been deficient. There he was really an artist. He realized that stage speech was a special kind of speech, a truth which never penetrated to the naturalists. He has no social significance, but his best comedy is likely to be read so long as men are aware of the comic spirit and can appreciate a virtuoso use of language.

It was at the end of the nineties that the great period began, a period which will possibly rank as high as that of the Restoration, but which falls below the highest standard because, though it concerned itself as drama should do with what men are thinking and feeling, it did not relate these thoughts and feelings to the eternal, what we may call the metaphysical, thoughts and feelings of mankind. It represented more clearly than any other form the bourgeois revolt against bourgeois conceptions which indicated the break-up of the Victorian view of life. It consistently attacked the basic assumptions of society, but it stood for reform rather than revolution. One might say that this drama was by Ibsen out of English puritanism. From 1898 to 1914 there was a succession of plays, many of them of a very high standard, probably as high a standard as can be reached within the limits of naturalism, dealing with the urgent political and moral problems of the day. Shaw and Galsworthy were the leaders; Granville-Barker made rather profounder contributions which were a little too subtle for the public; Hankin skirmished over ground a little removed from the great mass of playgoers; St John Ervine removed the setting to northern Ireland (he is to be classed with the English, not the Irish dramatists). There were many lesser playwrights who added at least one good play to the canon: Elizabeth Baker with *Chains*; Stanley Houghton with *Hindle Wakes*; Githa Sowerby with *Rutherford and Son*; Allan Monkhouse with *Mary Broome*;

E

all these and others tended to a new liberation and a fresh illumination, and it seemed for the moment as though the drama would oust the novel from its place as the chief literary vehicle of the period.

Shaw is the greatest and the most brilliant of them all; he never adhered to naturalism, and his phrasing was in itself a delight. Like his countryman Farquhar, two hundred years earlier, he wrote the comedy of rationalism, but a rationalism more and more tinged with the mysticism of vitalism, of the Life Force, which, with a number of other things, he learnt from Samuel Butler. He is a rationalist lured by metaphysics; he cannot bear the idea of a world of which he cannot see the purpose: but in the period with which we are concerned, the rationalist was uppermost. He made it his business to expose the cant and hypocrisy, not to mention the muddled thinking, which lay behind most of our social assumptions, and he exposed them brilliantly owing to his inexhaustible capacity for invention, his sense of comedy and fun, and his uncanny knowledge of the stage. He is far from being the mountebank and the farceur which those who found his criticism unpalatable attempted to make people believe. He always meant what he said with all the urgency of his vigorous intellect, and he reinforced his meaning in the prefaces, which are the finest pamphleteering since Swift. His plays probably had as much effect on the thought of the succeeding generation as the novels of Wells. In religion agnostico-mystic, in politics Fabian Socialist, in art anti-aesthetic, he stands as the most typical advanced product of the Edwardian era.

Galsworthy was less militant; his plays are pervaded, not by the common sense which animates those of Shaw, but by a sense of pity and an overwhelming desire for social justice. *The Silver Box* is probably his best play, since there a sense of comedy rams the lesson home, but *Strife* did a good deal to humanize the class conflict. It can be objected that his plays are too obviously didactic, but that did not prevent them from being extremely telling on the stage. Granville-

Barker was a far greater artist, concerned mainly with the conflict between public morality and private morality, which he treated in different ways, tentatively but charmingly in *The Marrying of Ann Leete*, powerfully in *Waste*, but most successfully and subtly in *The Voysey Inheritance*. There is blood-and-bone sympathy, a faith that life is worth living for its own sake in Granville-Barker's work, that is absent from Shaw's. Barker, as artist, was always intensely interested in production, and, at the time when Gordon Craig was conducting his fantastic but indirectly valuable experiments, did more than any other producer to improve the visual aspect of the drama. On ceasing to write plays he turned to writing Prefaces to Shakespeare's plays, invaluable to the producer, and showing that his interest in the drama was as keen as it had ever been, and more profound.

While the dramatic revival in England was at its height, it was paralleled in Ireland by what is known as the Abbey Theatre Movement, in which the great names are Synge, Yeats, and Lady Gregory. Unlike their English counterparts, and unlike such successors as Sean O'Casey, they had no political axe to grind, though there hovers over some of their plays a ghostly presence somewhat irritating to outsiders, namely that of Kathleen ni Houlihan. Synge was a poet, and tried to restore to the theatre the power of the word. For him, as for John Davidson, who failed in his task in England, the object of the drama was to give delight, and he hated 'the joyless and pallid words of Ibsen'. The special dialect he invented was admirably adapted to what he wanted to do, and his tragedies and his comedies alike are by its means steeped in an atmosphere which gives a curious sense of permanence and reality. He had a fine sense of high comedy, but his tragedy is a little too 'poetic' to be altogether satisfactory. He was a 'pure' artist of the best type, and his plays have a significance beyond the problems of any particular time. His work should endure, though it is possible that his diction, in spite of its admirable phrasing, may come to seem an affectation, and 'date' his plays to their detriment.

Yeats's plays can hardly be dealt with apart from his poetry as a whole; they are part of his earlier manner, his earlier mysticism, and are full of his early Irish symbolism. *The Countess Cathleen* and *The Land of the Heart's Desire* contain some of his most musical, moving, and characteristic poetry (of that period), but the plays depend too much on their poetry, which is an addition to, rather than an integral part of, the structure. In great poetic drama you do not notice the poetry as poetry, in Yeats's plays you do. Lady Gregory, one may say, is complementary to Synge and Yeats; her prose comedies are Molièresque, and are excellent and entertaining examples of their kind: *The Workhouse Ward* is typical. All three dealt with Irish life, chiefly as it is lived by the peasantry.

A symptom of, and an incentive to, the dramatic revival in England was the work done by the repertory theatres, particularly those of Manchester and Birmingham; they attempted, with some success at the time, to break down the vicious tyranny of the 'star' actor and actress, and the deadening effects of the long run. They did much to encourage not only young playwrights, such as Stanley Houghton, but also the poetic drama, and gave opportunities for presentation to such good work as was being written at the time, notably by Lascelles Abercrombie and Gordon Bottomley. But the poetic drama movement died; it did not tune in with an age of political excitement and social struggle, and the War interrupted its use as a stage instrument. It was re-born later in a rather different form, and, we might think a more important one, as being more exploratory of means; but this does not fall within the scope of this volume.

VI

CONCLUSION

THIS introduction has been too brief to do more than sketch the bare outlines of English literature in a period which, beginning with an age of evangelical thought and keen religious excitement, ended in one of agnosticism or indifference, though, naturally, there were agnostics at the beginning of the period, and profoundly religious believers at the end. Socially, England changed from a period in which the upper middle classes were dominant to one in which the working classes were beginning to show their power. Economically, the period reveals the increasing decay of agriculture, and the changeover from industrial capitalism to finance capitalism with its accompaniment of oversea expansion.

It is by no means easy to see how these changes affected literary forms. One can see, however, how they affected the subject-matter of literature, and the attitude taken up by writers, who were all, with scarcely an exception, of the middle class. Take, for one example, the change between such critics of the social structure as Kingsley at one end, and Shaw at the other. Under industrial capitalism and in an age of faith, it was possible to suppose that the inculcation of Christian virtues into the hearts of employers might bring about a satisfactory state of affairs; in the later age, under finance capitalism, it was quite clear that a change of heart, however Christian, would be powerless; the machinery itself would have to be altered, and the whole class structure revised; it was believed also that a faith more in accordance with the discoveries of science would have to be evolved.

Such an analysis might be applied to other forms, but we may here draw a picture from another aspect. One can say that our period began with moralizing literature, such as that of Carlyle and Tennyson, passed through a phase of cultural ambitions with Arnold, a phase which developed into the art for art's sake or aesthetic movement, to be replaced in its turn by a period of didacticism. Although throughout the age under consideration the great writers were all opposed to the orthodox economic theories, in the realm of social theory the earlier writers were solidly in support of the then structure, whereas the later writers were determined to alter it.

One lesson, however, can be drawn from a study of the age, if lessons must be drawn from literature; and that is that the great writer is always concerned for the quality of life as it is lived in his day, and that he is intensely aware of the currents of thought and feeling which animate his fellows. Unless he deals with the immediate and actual he will have nothing to say of an eternal nature. The theatre in the nineteenth century, for example, did not begin to live, to call forth works of power or beauty until it began to deal with what mattered at the moment. There are occasional exceptions, especially in the realm of poetry, which can deal more directly with the universal and eternal by a profounder treatment of the personal; poetry also can give delight more directly than any other form.

There are, however, periods when the actual is too strident, too harsh, too uncertain, to allow of that quiet gestation which is essential to great works of art; and that is why the Edwardian and early Georgian periods, though they produced works of great energy, of brilliance even, and of impeccable earnestness, seem shallower than those of the Victorian period. Great art cannot be produced in an age when the artists feel that it is more important to attack the crude disharmonies of life than to work upon what is subtler and more profound; when they feel that neither the conditions of work, nor the appreciation their work is likely to meet with, make for art. Morris already found it more urgent to make socialists than to create works of art.

So in the literature of the present century there is little

real joy. Now and again we hear a protest against the failure
of art to produce joy, and some writers in their youth produced work which aimed at pure delight; but once they saw
that life was ugly, they abandoned the attempt. Thus Wells,
a born novelist if ever there was one, took to writing tracts;
Galsworthy, though he became more humane, became more
bitter; others, such as Granville-Barker, gave up 'creative'
writing altogether. In the main, therefore, the best literature
of the century within our period, at any rate the most powerful literature, was didactic; prolific entertainers abounded,
but they are mostly negligible. Instead of being buoyed up
by a sentiment of glorious advance, as the mid-Victorians
were, even when they criticized, the ideologues were served
only by a feeling of hope, which was somewhat naïve. The
interest of this part of the period is enthralling, the achievement dubious; what followed will be discussed in the next
volume.

VII

THE ECONOMIC BACKGROUND

By Guy Chapman

THE epoch between 1839 and 1914 is conventionally divided into four periods, corresponding with the movement of the price-level. The first period runs to about 1850; it is the last decade of a price fall which has been going on since 1815. The second period, 1850-73, is one of rising prices. The third to about 1896 once more shows falling prices, while the general trend is upward until 1914. But the divisions are conventional, and not clean cut: elements of one survive in the next, and while the years of rising prosperity are marred by crises, the years of decline are relieved by short spasms of recovery. Moreover, no generalization will fit the whole of England, let alone the whole United Kingdom. Conditions in one area contradict those in another; and while one trade is flourishing, another may appear at the point of death. With these reservations, the following pages will attempt to show the economic background of the times.

i. 1839-50

The fact which was most apparent to the average man in the years 1839-42 was the revolt of an exasperated proletariat against intolerable conditions of life, a revolt formulated under the general title of Chartism. He saw, as he thought, an insurgent movement of 'the masses' (note that the words first become part of popular speech in 1837) directed to a single objective, the Six Points of the Charter, which would make them the dominant power in the State. What he did not perceive was that the political formula covered divergent aims of divergent economic groups, some progressive, some reactionary.

The working population had, as a whole, fought as strenuously for the Reform Bill of 1832 as had their middle-class allies. Their reward, they found, was the disfranchisement of such of them as had been voters in favour of a richer class: and, on top of this, they felt themselves to be the victims of the new centralization of government under the influence of the Radical disciples of Jeremy Bentham: the symbol of this policy was the new workhouse, 'The Poor's Bastille' built for the purpose of economy in local administration. Their dissatisfaction was further increased by four years of bad trade, unemployment, a succession of bad harvests, by the incidence of disease, in particular cholera, in the rapidly growing and wholly unsanitary towns. Perhaps worst, the high birth-rate of the past twenty years was now flooding the industrial market with cheap labour. The dissatisfaction found its expression in the demand for a completely democratic constitution. In consequence the years from 1839 to 1842 are marked by a series of strikes and riots, forcibly suppressed by an insensible magistrature backed by a far from intelligent government. The Potteries, Lancashire, Yorkshire, and South Wales (the Newport affair of 1839 is the bloodiest episode) all experienced violent conflicts. The movement failed, but it had one consequence. It quickened the interest of the middle and governing classes in what was to be known as the 'Condition of the People'. It brought home the fact that there was a real question, and although the Chartists drawn by Disraeli are pure grotesques—the exotic creatures of *Sybil* should be compared with the real figures shown in the autobiographies of Lovett and Cooper —the phrase, 'The Two Nations', kindled imaginations. For the first time, there was an impetus towards sociological discovery; and the recent Blue Books were at hand to chart unprofessional investigators. The Report on the Handloom Weavers of 1841 and the report (with crude and horrifying cuts) on the Coal Mines raised a wave of disgust at the conditions under which women and children were forced to labour, while the several reports on 'The Sanitary Condition of the Labouring Population', including a fantastically grim essay on the disposal of the bodies of the dead in the poorer quarters of the towns, sent a shudder through their readers.

The Chartist movement, although five of its once notorious Six Points are today part and parcel of our electoral system, failed. By 1848, although a march on London was that year staged, it once more frightened Whitehall out of its wits, and the town houses of the great were barricaded and abandoned to the care of the servants, Chartism was dead; it was only its corpse which passed along the streets.

The reasons for the disintegration of the movement are to be found in its divergent elements. On the one side were the skilled craftsmen of the London Workingmen's Association, and the textile workers of the northern factories. On another stood the semi-socialist pioneers of Robert Owen's New Model World, who would find their panacea in the Co-operative movement. On another were the representatives of the obsolescent trades, asking nothing better than to return to the eighteenth century, the domestic craftsmen, hand-loom weavers and stocking-frame knitters, earning, maybe, as low as 4s. 6d. or 5s. a week a family, doomed to vanish from the economic field. Or, other reactionaries, the disciples of Cobbett, who looked to refound an idyllic patriarchal peasant society. Such were some of the diverse elements temporarily allied in a movement of the working classes as a whole.

Alone this diversity of aim would not have caused the failure. But after 1844 conditions changed. The boom in the new-fangled railways relieved the pressure of unemployment; skilled and unskilled labour was in demand. Some progressive groups abandoned politics for self-improvement in the Mechanics' Institutes, while others involved themselves in the more material Ten Hour Movement. Both deserted the adherents of a bygone age to political disappointment and slow death.

Moreover, at least some sections were distracted by

preachers no less vociferous and infinitely more materialist than the leaders of the Chartists. The Anti-Corn Law League, under Cobden and Bright, from 1838 to 1846, the date of the Repeal of the Corn Laws, was at least as energetic in propaganda as the Chartists, and, what is more to the point, offered to the industrial worker an easily intelligible means to the improvement of his existence.

The Repeal movement is, however, only part of a wider advance towards the freeing of trade and the enshrining of the doctrines of *laisser-faire*, which had been slowly illuminating the minds of industrialists and politicians since the country's exporting power had become apparent at the end of the Napoleonic Wars. Over some thirty or forty years the tariff schedules, based on the prices of the days of William III, were gradually pared away. England was now ready to offer herself as the world's workshop, conscious that no other country could compete. And to achieve that position, she was prepared to sacrifice (as they said) the farmers of the country. Since the greater number of the arable farmers depended on the home-market for wheat, the Anti-Corn Law League appeared as much closer kin to the Devil than the Chartists (*Hillingdon Hall* runs the whole gamut of the farmer's attitude to innovations with its constant references to the League, drainage and guano: 'Muck's your man!'); but they could not withstand the new economic doctrines, and in spite of the country gentlemen, Repeal was passed.

The 1830's and 1840's are thus in some measure the liquidation of the past, of the political-industrial system, based on status, of the Tudors. On the other hand, they revive the Tudor centralization which had been allowed to lapse into parochialism after 1640. Whereas the Tudor system had been directed to the preservation of a static society, the Victorian was directed to the enhancement of the health and morals of a dynamic community. Bentham is perhaps the one person in English history who has moulded the future, and not been merely the representative figure of his age. Although he was dead before his suggestions were implemented, yet under the ruthless drive of his disciple, Edwin Chadwick, the governance of England was transformed.

In 1830, Local Government resembled an abandoned garden over which plants, trees, and shrubs have grown as best they may, a pushing, jostling, greedy mass of vegetation.

In the boroughs incompetence reigned beside corruption. The Report on Municipal Corporations of 1835 reads like a hilarious nightmare. With towns rapidly growing (Leeds, for instance, trebled its population between 1801 and 1841), without water, without drainage (sewers were still controlled by an act of Henry VIII, which contemplated only surface drainage), without lighting, paving, or police, with duties divided between various *ad hoc* committees, with rising death-rates (e.g., Glasgow, per 1,000: 1821, 28; 1838, 38; 1843, 48) there was no exaggeration in Chadwick's comparison of their state to that of 'an encamped horde or an undisciplined soldiery'. Mr Boffin's dust-heaps had their counterparts in every city; and the Royal Borough of Windsor was found by the inspector 'the worst beyond all comparison'. From 1835 to 1854, under the energy of Chadwick and his aides, England and Scotland were shaken, reproved, dusted, and washed. Volumes of reports were issued, committees formed, Acts passed. The Bentham principles, classification, centralization, specialization, and inspectability, were forcibly introduced in spite of the opposition of vested interests, in the face of the criticisms of Mr Podsnap ('I knew it. Centralization! No, sir. Never with my consent. Not English!') and of Toulmin Smith.

Further, Benthamism, coupled with Cabinet necessity, led to the reorganization of the Civil Service in the fifties and sixties, the Civil Service which had been the squirrel's hoard of Privilege, in which a Grenville could find sinecures for thirty-eight dependants, including two maiden aunts.

Finally, the binding together of England and Scotland into a single economic unit was completed by the railways.

It must be remembered that in 1840, owing to slowness of transport, local markets were on the whole still predominant, that different weights and measures survived in different areas, and in spite of the freedom of trade, trade was still hampered by tradition. The railway began to open up a countryside which had depended on roads, 'nationalized' too late to retard steam, on canals, slow and subject to internecine rivalry, and on coast-wise trading vessels. The rapid extension of the railway in the forties broke down provincialism, slowly but effectively. It linked up localities and created a national market.

No less important, it created a national market for the investment of money. The railway boom of 1845-46 drew from the hoards of the small tradesman and 'the frugal operative' the pent-up savings of years. In the speculative flurry of those years men (such as Thackeray's Jeames) learned to become millionaires overnight and paupers in a week. In the long run, the railway mania taught investment to the poorer classes. It accumulated idle capital, while it inoculated even the poorest with the itch for acquisition. Those effects would only become apparent at a later date.

ii. 1850-73

There is a change in tempo as the fifties arrive; a kind of busy serenity comes over the country. The new age was appropriately registered by the International Exhibition of 1851, and Tennyson caught the note in his Choral Ode:

> *Is the goal so far away?*
> *Far, how far, no tongue can say.*
> *Let us dream our dream today.*

As Mr G. M. Young has pointed out, 'Victorians saw the endless new world which Bacon had sighted or imagined, where nothing need remain unknown.' And as if to guarantee the genuineness of the dream, the new mines of California and Australia sent their gold to the world's financial centre. There was indeed nothing that seemed impossible;

in Dr Clapham's phrase: 'It is easy to develop a world with money at 2 per cent.' What the Englishman did not observe were the as yet puny figures of Germans, Frenchmen, Dutchmen, and Americans rapidly growing in the new sunlight.

The fifties and sixties might be called the Era of Technical Learning, both in commerce and industry. For the first time, empiricism began to give way to scientific reason, and the laboratory was yoked to the workshop. While Darwin and Huxley shocked the faithful, Whitworth was tracing his way towards standardization and the perfection of machine tools, Armstrong was developing hydraulic machinery and the rifled bore, Bessemer, Siemens, and Gilchrist Thomas were experimenting in the production of cheap steel. The telegraph, the potentialities of which were scarcely discussed in 1851, became of such social importance that in 1870 the Government, in spite of *laisser-faire*, acquired control. There followed the deep-sea cable, at first a failure owing to imperfect knowledge of the ocean-bed, but pushed on furiously after the Indian Mutiny. The system of domestic industry was safely liquidated; handicrafts died year by year; the labour-saving machine, the time- and cost-cutting factory, were now permanent features of the economic landscape.

While the population of England rose from 18 millions in 1851 to 32½ millions in 1901, the numbers of employed in various industries changed too. Makers of lace, linen, and silk fell away rapidly, while coal miners trebled, those employed in iron and steel doubled, in machine-making and ship-building nearly quadrupled. The exports of the United Kingdom were expanding at a pace hitherto unknown and not to be known again. The value of exports more than doubled between 1855 and 1874; and so too did imports. Average imports of cotton rose from 9·2 million cwts. to 13·6; of wool from 118 million lbs. to 307: the output of coal climbed from 66·1 million tons to 120·7; of pig-iron from 3·5 millions to 6·4.

It was prodigious, amazing. The prosperity was obvious; and the pace was too good for the average man to inquire.

True, there were uncomfortable matters, which obtruded themselves, the prisons, the asylums, the coffin-ships, which furnished backgrounds to Charles Reade. There were the curiosities of City finance, the crisis of 1857, the Overend and Gurney scandal of 1866, the perpetual and unsavoury bankruptcies, odd little episodes such as that in which the financial editor of *The Times* became involved in the meshes of 'Baron' Grant, and the Thunderer found itself the catspaw of a shady financier. In so golden an age, these things passed censured but rarely amended. Free trade and light taxation were the *mots d'ordre*, and only 'the Cassandras of Political Economy' sounded occasional warnings.

Even Labour had become almost tranquil. The Unions, not yet legitimized, were re-forming. The Associated Society of Engineers, founded in 1851, with a hierarchy of officials, became the new model; and the other skilled trades followed them. After the first wave of panic, employers found that they were very different metal from Cromwell's Ironsides, that their leaders were well informed, well disciplined, and full of the *tact des choses possibles*, who prevented more strikes than they promoted, and who had accepted the economic system as it stood. Their behaviour paved the way for their gradual recognition; and the election of working men to Parliament set the seal on the respectability of organized labour.

The Unions were, however, no more than a small proportion of the workers. Outside their ranks lay millions of partially or wholly unorganized workers, in textiles, in the mines, on the docks and in the factories, the sweeping children, the sweated tailors, furriers and sempstresses, the match girls. When they struck, their strikes were broken in detail. Their time was not yet, and they subsisted darkly and violently in the slums of the cities, which for all Chadwick's battles were still squalid and insanitary. One may note the rise of the death-rate between 1851 and 1871, and perceive little difference between the picture painted by Engels in 1843 and that by Taine in 1869.

In the country, agriculture, in spite of the prophecies of Bentinck and Disraeli, had taken a new lease of life. The Repeal of the Corn Laws had not hurt, but released, the farmer to experiment with new crops and new methods. The impetus given to industry after 1844, and the consequent rise in wages had increased the demand for foodstuffs, while the railways brought them more easily to the townsman's door. Agriculture flourished as it had not done since Waterloo. Nor did it fear rivals. From 1851 to 1871, war, or its rumours, kept Europe, still the world granary, from competition. It is the Indian Summer of the great landlord, who, until the passing of the Ballot Act, could suspend over Radical-minded tenants the threat of eviction. In the now settled hierarchy of landlord, tenant, and landless labourer, the last alone got little benefit from the rising prosperity. With wages at ten or twelve shillings a week, and the bye-industries as good as dead, he had no hopes, as his grandfather had had, of himself becoming a farmer. The energetic migrated or emigrated; the rural population fell from twenty to ten per cent of the whole between 1831 and 1871. The more inert remained docile until 1870, when Joseph Arch founded the Agricultural Labourers' Union. But Arch was fifteen years too late.

It was a fat age, during which the deeper social problems seemed almost to have been solved; and the novelists ignored them. To Meredith and Trollope the social scene is shut off below the upper middle class, although the Shaftesburys and Kingsleys are still fighting for the oppressed.

Only a few had misgivings. While Arnold denounced the Philistine, more materially-minded men caught some vision of the future at the Exhibition of 1867. The foreigner was coming along at a great pace; indeed in some lines he had already outstripped this country and threatened our supremacy. But their warnings fell on deaf ears. In 1871, *The Times* leader-writer said: 'We can look at the present with undisturbed satisfaction. . . . Turn where we may we find in our commerce no traces of decadence.'

iii. 1873-96

The economic frost which stole over England after 1873, and persisted with minor relaxations until the end of the nineties, was once known as the Great Depression. But except for the fall in prices and save in a few industries, it is doubtful if the name is appropriate. It might be nearer the mark to call it the age of Imperial Transformation.

For one thing, even in the most desperate periods, production on the whole was rising. If the output of iron rose no more than fourteen per cent, steel increased from half a million tons to over three million, while coal passed from an average 120 million tons to 180 millions. In textiles, too, the consumption of both wool and cotton went up by fifty per cent.

Unfortunately prices all round sagged and sank from the high level of 1873 year by year till 1879; then, after a brief upward turn, sank to a still lower level in 1886. Four years of slight recovery followed, only to be succeeded by a further slump to the lowest point in the nineteenth century, in 1895-96. By the middle of the eighties, a House of Commons, interested in higher matters, could resist no longer the complaints of industrialists. A Royal Commission produced three heavy folios on the theme of the Depression in Trade and Industry, and a couple of years later another inquired into the national failure in technical education.

Their findings were, on the whole, nebulous. Later comers have been able to see more clearly. England for half a century had enjoyed a monopoly position over other nations. She had partially perfected her industrial structure, and, out of the profits from her exports, she had exported it to other countries no whit behind her in adaptability, energy, and brains. With the resumption of peace, Europe and the United States leapt into competition. Whereas England's export figures were scarcely higher in 1895-99 than they had been in 1870-74, Germany's had increased by over fifty per cent, and those of the U.S.A. by more than 120 per cent.

The export of railways and their concomitants of railway iron and locomotives was finished. And what was to some eyes worse, the new overseas countries, through the opening up of virgin territory, were able to beat the English farmer out of the home market. America, thanks to the railway and the now punctual steamship, overwhelmed him with wheat from the Middle West. The Australian, with the new refrigerating process, could send his hitherto unexportable mutton to Smithfield. The intensive farming of the old country, with its high rent and high labour cost, could not compete with the colonial countries, their free land, their mechanization, and their unbroken soil. In England rents dropped; bankruptcies occurred by the thousand. East Anglia nearly gave up the struggle and went back to wilderness. But the farmer was not defeated. He wrested power from the landlord, and readapted himself to the changed conditions, to the growing demands of urban markets for milk, fruit, eggs, vegetables, and flowers, the stand-by of the small-scale farmer. The partial solution was at the expense of the labourer. It was no sudden madness that raised the emigration figure for this group from a normal 10,000 to 14,000 in 1883-4-5, to 21,000 in 1886, and to 30,000 in 1887-88.

The troubles of agriculture do not weigh heavily on an urban society, to whom the farmer's complaints are a standing joke. More important appeared the complaints of investors. Yet as Mr Beales has pointed out, the pessimism was overdone.* Many industries were flourishing; and Goschen, the Chancellor of the Exchequer, was able to show that the most striking phenomenon was the increase in the number of incomes between £150 and £500 a year. Capital was becoming more diffused. The middle classes were slowly, unrestingly, unhastily, accumulating wealth; and Samuel Smiles's *Self-Help* and *Thrift* remained in constant demand.

The Englishman, in his inner consciousness, is practical, if not far-sighted. The owner of capital is always seeking a more advantageous line of investment; it is, after all, his

* H. L. Beales, 'The Great Depression'. *Econ. History Review*, Oct. 1935.

speciality. The English had once possessed an empire, and had lost a great part of it. The pain of that loss they had soothed by a disbelief in colonies. Now in their believed extremity, they turned back to the scattered pieces of the world they owned, and began to reknit them and to extend their boundaries. In the last thirty years of the century, the new British Empire was formed. India was by now largely controlled; but in those thirty years many other areas were acquired. In 1880 our possessions in Africa, with the exception of Cape Colony, were negligible. By 1914, they had swollen to $3\frac{1}{2}$ million square miles. Malaya was federated and effectively protected. Capital was poured into Australia, Canada, and India. To amend an old catchword, 'the Flag followed Trade'—of a kind. And with the extension of the Empire, a new *mystique* came to life. 'The White Man's Burden', sanctified by Kipling, became a moral duty. Whereas in the eighteenth century our Clives, Hickeys, and Francises set out with the firm purpose of making fortunes out of the pagan, their grandchildren took posts, civil or military, under the British government; and carried the torch of civilization at the expense of the uncivilized. Their justification lay in the future. In 1874 our exports to British possessions formed only 25·5 per cent of our trade; in 1900-4 32·5 per cent; in 1929 it was 43 per cent.

The scramble for colonies which is the conspicuous element in international politics from 1880 onwards, was an effect, and not a cause. One cause, already indicated, was the competitive power of industrial rivals. The other was man's increased control over the forces of nature, his improved knowledge, the saving of time and labour, the discovery of and utilization of new materials, rubber, the light metals, electricity. The seventies, eighties, and nineties, for all their gloomy appearance, were in fact the decades of the final lifting of the Industrial Revolution from an empiric to a scientific base. The technological transformation which took place in these years, was too swift to grasp. Although control would become greater, it was by the end of the century fundamentally complete. If the man of 1848 had seen the mirage of the new Atlantis, the visionary of the nineties believed he could perceive 'the shape of things to come'.

iv. 1896-1914

After 1900, Englishmen viewed the future with satisfaction. London was the centre of the financial world. The Empire was being consolidated. An Englishman could travel the earth with no better passport than an English sovereign. True, the excess of imports over exports alarmed certain circles; but Tariff Reformers were regarded as interested parties by an electorate more than eighty per cent urban. And in answer it could be pointed out that our shipping and the income from our overseas investments were bringing in a handsome balance in our favour, handsome enough to top £200 millions by 1914. The first fourteen years of the nineteenth century show an ostentation of wealth and a vulgarity unknown since the days of James I.

But there were waking two movements which misgave critical observers. The first was the women's suffrage movement, the full implications of which would not be seen until after the War of 1914-18. The other had been apparent before the end of the eighties. As is usual, during the decline of prices after 1873, the value of real wages rose for those who remained in employment, while the uneven spread of the depression meant that unemployment, except in one year, 1879, was not general during the early years. Unemployment did not begin to be felt severely until the middle of the eighties (it is significant that the titular designation, 'the unemployed', appears for the first time in 1886), but during the whole of that decade a new insurgence was fermenting among the workers. It has been suggested that the responsibility for this awakening is due to Henry George's *Progress and Poverty*, published in 1880. But all revolts have a background of real discontent, usually inarticulate, before any movement takes place. People are indifferent to propaganda which does not touch their interests; and those who talk most glibly of agitation forget that agitation is only effective when indifference has prepared the ground. The background of the resurgence of Labour in 1889 may be found in the composition of the working class as a whole. The Unions were few, autocratic and restrictive, representing only the skilled workers (and perhaps not more than some thirty-five per cent of them), interested mainly in maintaining their wages by their exclusiveness. On the other hand, as mechanization improved, the half-skilled workers of the forties and fifties were degenerating into quarter-skilled, a lower grade, in whom the T.U.C. had little interest. These groups were thus least able to resist wage-cuts which industry after industry enforced as the depression deepened. Through the eighties discontent was simmering. It was perhaps not very apparent. Gissing perceived it, and certain intellectuals, Morris, for one, tried to do for the craftsman what Cobbett had tried to do for the peasant. Even the socialists and Fabians seem not very aware of the approaching storm. It began with a small and successful strike of the London match girls in 1888, but it was the impressive Dockers' Strike of 1889 which struck the public imagination. From that year Trade Unionism took on new life. Something of the Chartists' spirit flared up. New unions were formed; old unions increased their membership. In 1892, the Parliamentary Labour Party was formed. Members independent of the older political parties began to get into Parliament. Labour for the first time became a comparatively organized active party with a programme.

If, however, we look at the price-level during the next twenty years, we find it unsteadily rising, while real wages remained stationary: and it may be taken that, between 1900 and 1914, the average worker found himself not better but worse off. To this uneven discontent, which stings the worker as his particular industry suffers from increased competition, may be added the general uneasiness which prevailed from 1908 (the year of Aehrenthal's diplomatic *coup-de-main* in Bosnia), the tension induced by the Irish question, by the House of Lords imbroglio, and by the Women's Suffrage Movement. To these stresses should also be added the somewhat unwise counter-attack of the judicial bench on the Trade Unions through the Taff Vale and Osborne judgments. The last few years before the War are marked by successive large-scale strikes of railwaymen, of dockers, of miners. The pace set by the rapid accumulation of capital (and consequent higher capitalization) by the upper and middle classes was rendering more acute the strain between the secure and insecure groups. In 1914 Labour, to use a too general term, was approaching the zenith of its power. The outbreak of war may or may not have forestalled a sharper encounter than any earlier battle. Although it is as yet too early to judge, it may have marked the end of the historical period of the manual workers as a separate class ticketed 'Labour'.

The development of our present civilization has been through the growth of innumerable invisible seeds, broadcast with no prevision of their future. By 1914, the machine had become not only the tool, but also the master. Looking back less than a century, we see the difficulty of disciplining man to the machine. The hand-loom weaver asked no more than his subsistence; he preferred death by starvation to the rhythm and despatch of the factory. The hatters of Ashton-under-Lyne, a Blue Book tells us, kept a pack of hounds and hunted three days a week rather than grow rich by fashioning their beavers. In the expressive phrase of a German sociologist, they were 'whole men'. In 1914, they and their kind are dead; and a race of half men, stimulated to the regular toil which a materialistic civilization demands by the lust of possessions, had taken their place.

BIBLIOGRAPHY

THIS bibliography does not pretend to be a complete record either of the authors of the period or of the works of those who are included. It should be regarded rather as a list of suggestions which may be supplemented from the biographies of the older writers and from current books of reference such as the bibliographies of *The Cambridge History of English Literature* and *Who's Who*. It should also be particularly noted that no attempt has been made to deal with American literature, although certain American writers were as much read in this country as in their own, and some—e.g., Henry George and Edward Bellamy—had as much influence on thought here as there. A general reference must suffice to American literary criticism, which has also, especially of recent years, affected English criticism and practice; but in any bibliography of nineteenth-century literature and thought the names of George Santayana and Paul Elmer More should at least be mentioned, with a note that much of their work is easily accessible.

The versatility of the Victorians and some of their successors makes it difficult to compile any classified list without repetitions. To save space, cross-references are used here— e.g., C. M. Doughty is considered under TRAVEL with a cross-reference under POETRY.

It has proved impossible to make the division between this volume and those on each side of it strictly chronological, and several writers who did much of their work after 1830 have been left to the preceding volume, just as others who did much before 1914 have been left to the next volume. An obvious instance is Barrie. On the other hand, it has been convenient to fit Bernard Shaw into this volume.

Only special collected editions are noted in addition to first publication; but many, if not most, of the books named here are obtainable in such editions as *Everyman's Library* and *The World's Classics*.

CONTENTS

The Background   *page* 135

Biography and Autobiography   138

History   140

Travel   159

Science   166

Theology   171

Philosophy   187

Poetry   208

Drama   249

Novels and Short Stories   261

Children's Books   320

Criticism and Essays   324

Nonsense and Parody: Humour and
    Light Verse   346

Sport   351

Note: No arrangement of the classes of a bibliography is entirely satisfactory in logical sequence. It may, however, be observed that here the graver matters, which give the foundations of knowledge, thought, and belief, come first and are followed by those kinds of writing, largely growing out of them, which are sometimes, though mistakenly, regarded as more 'literary': poetry and drama, novels and short stories with children's books, and criticism, of which parody is a form.

THE BACKGROUND:

GENERAL READING

With a Note on Magazines

THE biographies mentioned here, as well as the biographies of other great Victorians—e.g., among statesmen, Lord Palmerston and Lord Salisbury; among reformers, Lord Shaftesbury and Dr Barnardo—will help to provide a background of social life and thought. They might be supplemented by such books as—

E. Halevy—*Histoire du peuple anglais au* xixe *siècle.*
> One of the best and fullest histories, carrying the story on to the twentieth century. It has been translated.

G. M. Young, ed.—*Early Victorian England.*
> The final chapter, *Portrait of an Age*, by the editor, is a brilliant résumé. It has been enlarged to cover the whole Victorian Age and published separately.

E. L. Woodward—*The Age of Reform, 1815-1870.*

R. C. K. Ensor—*England, 1870-1914.*

R. H. Gretton—*A Modern History of the English People, 1880-1922.*

G. P. Gooch—*History of our Time, 1885-1911.*

W. L. Davidson—*Political Thought in England: From Bentham to J. S. Mill.*

Ernest Barker—*Political Thought in England: From Herbert Spencer to To-day.*

Lytton Strachey's *Eminent Victorians* is brilliant and stimulating, but inaccurate in detail and often unjust in general impression. His *Queen Victoria* is a better book in every respect.

It should not be forgotten that Queen Victoria was herself in some ways the most eminent and characteristic Victorian, and her *Letters* and *Journals*, published during her lifetime and later, should be consulted.

D. C. SOMERVELL—*English Thought in the Nineteenth Century.*
A very able account, succinct and comprehensive.

ASA BRIGGS—*Victorian People* and *The Age of Improvement.*

JOHN HOLLOWAY—*The Victorian Sage.*

G. C. LE ROY—*Perplexed Prophets.*

JAMES LAVER—*Victorian Vista.*

BASIL WILLEY—*Nineteenth Century Studies. More Nineteenth Century Studies.*

E. E. KELLETT—*Religion and Life in the Early Victorian Age.*

To this list some more general studies of literature may be added—

HOLBROOK JACKSON—*The Eighteen Nineties.*

J. W. CUNLIFFE—*English Literature during the last Half-Century,* 1919.
A carefully-compiled manual of novelists and poets with bibliographies.

OSBERT BURDETT—*The Beardsley Period.*

JOHN DRINKWATER, ed.—*The Eighteen Sixties.*

H. GRANVILLE-BARKER, ed.—*The Eighteen Seventies.*

W. DE LA MARE, ed.—*The Eighteen Eighties.*

FREDERICK HARRISON—*Studies in Early Victorian Literature.*

The Cambridge History of English Literature, Vols. XII, XIII, XIV.

GEORGE SAMPSON—*The Concise Cambridge History of English Literature,* Ch. XII to end.

LEGOUIS and CAZAMIAN—*History of English Literature,* Vol. II.

Chambers's Cyclopaedia of English Literature, Vol. III.
This contains critical essays—many of them excellent—on the writers of the nineteenth century, with long illustrative quotations and some bibliographical information. An invaluable book of its kind, in spite of occasional inaccuracies.

CRAIK's *English Prose Writers* (Vol. V) and WARD's *English Poets* (Vols. IV and V) may also be noted; they are of the same critical and anthological type as *Chambers's Cyclopaedia,* but do not cover so wide a field.

The importance of the great magazines and reviews should be remembered, both for their influence on public opinion and for their reflection of it. *The Quarterly* and the *Edinburgh* were at their full strength at the beginning of the period, and they were presently joined by *The Nineteenth Century*, *The Contemporary Review*, *The National Review*, and others. *Blackwood's* printed George Eliot's *Scenes of Clerical Life*; the *Cornhill* had Thackeray for its first editor, and included Trollope among its contributors; Dickens edited, and largely wrote, *All the Year Round* and *Household Words*, which also contained work of Mrs Gaskell and Charles Reade. *The Germ* and *The Oxford and Cambridge Magazine* contained the early work of Rossetti and William Morris. Later in the century *The Athenaeum* had a great influence on literary opinion, and *The Hibbert Journal* showed movements in philosophical and religious thought. *The Yellow Book*, edited by Henry Harland, 1894-97, contains contributions by Max Beerbohm, Henry James, Baron Corvo, Henry Harland, Kenneth Grahame, W. B. Yeats, W. Watson, Saintsbury, A. Symons, Gosse, John Davidson, R. Garnett, 'John Oliver Hobbes', George Moore, Austin Dobson, E. Dowson, L. Johnson, E. Nesbit, H. D. Traill, Maurice Baring—to name only contributors who are included in this bibliography—as well as many of Beardsley's illustrations. *The Savoy*, edited by Arthur Symons, 1896, is more definitely 'decadent' in the impression it gives; it includes work by most of those mentioned above, and also by George Bernard Shaw, Havelock Ellis, Edward Carpenter, and Joseph Conrad, who are hardly decadent; the impression is probably due to the overweighting of the magazine by Beardsley's prose writing as well as his illustrations. These are only a few examples from the immense magazine literature of the time. A note on some of the children's magazines will be found under Children's Books.

BIOGRAPHY AND AUTOBIOGRAPHY

ONE of the greatest and most successful undertakings of the nineteenth century was the *Dictionary of National Biography* (*D.N.B.*), published under the direction first of Leslie Stephen and afterwards of Sidney Lee. With its supplements it now covers the whole of the historical period up to 1950, and a further supplement is being prepared. It should be consulted for all writers who died before 1950, but biographies of special interest are noted later under the names of their subjects or their authors.

A few outstanding biographies which would otherwise escape mention are added below—

JAMES SPEDDING—*Bacon*, 1861-74.
JOHN FORSTER—*Goldsmith*, 1848 (2nd edition, 1854).
DAVID MASSON—*Milton*, 1859-80.
F. S. OLIVER—*Alexander Hamilton*, 1906.
(Most of Oliver's work falls outside the period.)

Certain other biographies, although they are noted elsewhere, may be mentioned here also as of particular interest—

W. BAGEHOT—*Biographical Studies*.
S. BARING GOULD—*Hawker of Morwenstow*.
LADY BURNE-JONES—*Memorials of Edward Burne-Jones*.
THOMAS CARLYLE—*Life of John Sterling*.
JOHN FORSTER—*Life of Charles Dickens*.
MRS GASKELL—*Life of Charlotte Brontë*.
H. FESTING JONES—*Samuel Butler*.
J. W. MACKAIL—*Life of William Morris*.
JOHN MORLEY—*Life of Gladstone*.
A. P. STANLEY—*Life of Dr Arnold*.
LESLIE STEPHEN—*Studies of a Biographer*.
G. O. TREVELYAN—*Life of Lord Macaulay*.

It will be noticed that many of the authors considered here

have written full or partial autobiographies. Some of these are merely useful documents, but others have an individual value of one kind or another. Among these may be mentioned especially—

(Under *History*)—Carlyle, 'George Bourn', Beatrice Webb.

(Under *Travel*)—George Borrow, Edward John Trelawney.

(Under *Science*)—Hugh Miller.

(Under *Theology*)—Isaac Williams.

(Under *Philosophy*)—John Stuart Mill.

(Under *Poetry*)—Thomas Cooper, W. H. Davies, Alfred Noyes.

(Under *Drama*)—Sir Henry Taylor, Cicely Hamilton.

(Under *Novels*)—Meadows Taylor, Harriet Martineau, Henry James, Arthur Machen, Flora Annie Steel, Joseph Conrad, H. G. Wells.

(Under *Criticism*)—Leigh Hunt, Ruskin, Mark Pattison, Gosse, W. H. Hudson, Maurice Baring.

A reading of these autobiographies alone would give a fair view of most of the movements of thought and many of the social movements of the nineteenth and early twentieth centuries.

HISTORY

THE nineteenth century was as great an age of historical study and research as of science, but a general warning must be given that all but the most recent of the historians who are noted here must be used with caution as historical authorities. Thus, e.g., in the last sixty years archaeology has profoundly modified all our conceptions not only of the ancient world but of early English history, and it would be unwise to take Freeman or even Oman unquestioningly as a guide; the further study of documents has made much even of Stubbs's work obsolete; and the work of Thorold Rogers in the field of economics has been largely superseded. For the historical value of the work of English historians and their place in the wider field of European scholarship, it would be well to consult G. P. Gooch, *History and Historians in the Nineteenth Century*, especially Chapters I and XV-XX. See also Lytton Strachey, 'Six Historians' in *Portraits in Miniature*.

The list here is divided according to subjects and the authors are arranged roughly in chronological order.

A. ANCIENT, GREEK AND ROMAN HISTORY.

Milman, G. Grote, T. Arnold, Finlay, Merivale, T. Hodgkin, Bury, W. M. Ramsay, Flinders Petrie, Evans.

B. ENGLISH AND EUROPEAN HISTORY.

I. The older historians:

Napier, Palgrave, J. Stephen, Alison.

II. Carlyle to Trevelyan:

Carlyle, Macaulay, J. H. Burton, A. P. Stanley, J. A. Froude, Freeman, Stubbs, Gardiner, Acton, Seeley, J. R. Green, G. O. Trevelyan, Creighton, Rosebery, J. H. Ramsay, Plummer, Tout, Firth,

H. W. C. Davis, Oman, Fisher, A. F. Pollard, G. M. Trevelyan.

III. Law and Custom; Thought and Civilization:

Buckle, Maine, J. FitzJames Stephen, Leslie Stephen, Lecky, Dicey, Bryce, Anson, Maitland, Vinogradoff.

IV. Economic History, etc.:

Jessopp, Thorold Rogers, H. Mayhew, W. Booth, W. T. Stead, C. Booth, 'George Bourn', W. Cunningham, A. Toynbee, Beatrice and Sidney Webb.

C. MISCELLANEOUS.

Creasy, Curzon, J. A. Doyle, G. Adam Smith.

See also under—

Travel (Kinglake, Layard, Johnston).
Theology (Neale, Church, Bright, Lightfoot, Westcott).
Philosophy (Dickinson, Spencer, Westermarck, Hobhouse).
Poetry (R. W. Dixon, Lang, W. S. Blunt, Masefield, Drinkwater).
Novels (Meadows Taylor, Disraeli, Thackeray, T. A. Trollope, H. Martineau, C. Kingsley, C. M. Yonge, Conan Doyle, H. G. Wells).
Criticism and Essays (Helps, Hare, Symonds, Bagehot, Hutton, Morley, Traill, Whibley, Cunninghame Graham, Belloc).

A. ANCIENT HISTORY

MILMAN, HENRY HART (1791-1868)

History of the Jews, 1830.
History of Christianity to the Abolition of Paganism, 1840.
History of Latin Christianity, 1854-55.

A good deal of Milman's work is still valuable. He had also some reputation as a poet in his own time, but only a few hymns preserve their life.

F

GROTE, GEORGE (1794-1871)

History of Greece (1845-56).

Even Bury's work has not entirely superseded the books of Grote and Finlay (see below).

ARNOLD, THOMAS (1795-1842)

Arnold's influence was through character rather than writings, but his quality comes out in them, especially his sense of the moral values in history. He was also one of the first to realize the importance of the work being done by German scholars on half-legendary classical history.

History of Rome (3 vols. only), 1838-43.
Oxford Lectures on Modern History, 1842.
Life, by Arthur Penrhyn Stanley, 1844—an important book for the understanding of nineteenth-century public life. For a recent study of his influence see *The Doctor's Disciples*, by Frances J. Woodward.
Thomas Arnold, by T. W. Bamford, 1960.

FINLAY, GEORGE (1799-1875)

History of Greece from the Roman Conquest to the Present Time.

This was issued under various titles at dates from 1844 to 1861, and re-issued as one work in 1877.

See comment on Grote, above.

MERIVALE, CHARLES (1808-93)

History of the Romans under the Empire, 1850-64.
The Fall of the Roman Empire, 1853.

These also are not entirely superseded.

HODGKIN, THOMAS (1831-1913)

Italy and Her Invaders, 1879-99.

Excellent reading and in the main trustworthy.

BURY, JOHN B. (1861-1927)

History of the Later Roman Empire from Arcadius to Irene, 1889.
Student's History of the Roman Empire from Augustus to Marcus Aurelius, 1893.
History of Greece to the Death of Alexander the Great, 1900.
The Constitution of the later Roman Empire, 1910.
History of the Eastern Roman Empire from the Fall of Irene to the Accession of Basil I, 1912.
The Idea of Progress, 1920—a general essay which should be read.

Bury is the great authority of his period, and his predecessors, however readable in themselves, should be checked by him as well as by such later writers as Norman Baynes. His edition of Gibbon's *Decline and Fall* should also be noted, 1896-1900. His style is clear and direct, scientific rather than literary.

Three of the greatest of the archaeologists who have changed our conception of Ancient and New Testament history may be mentioned together.

RAMSAY, SIR WILLIAM MITCHELL (1851-1939)

The Church in the Roman Empire before A.D. 170 (5th ed. 1897).
Historical Commentary on St Paul's Epistle to the Galatians, 1899.
Pauline and Other Studies in Early Christian History, 1906.
(ed.) Studies in the History and Art of the Eastern Provinces of the Roman Empire, 1906.
The First Christian Century, 1911.
The Bearing of Recent Discoveries on the Trustworthiness of the New Testament, 1914.

PETRIE, SIR WILLIAM MATTHEW FLINDERS (1853-1942)

A History of Egypt (6 vols.), 1894-1905 (author of first 3 vols. and editor of series).
Syria and Egypt from the Tel-el-Amarna Letters, 1898.
Researches in Sinai, 1906.
Personal Religion in Egypt before Christianity, 1909.
The Arts and Crafts of Ancient Egypt, 1910.
Egypt and Israel, 1911 (new ed. 1923).
Some Sources of Human History, 1919.
Social Life in Ancient Egypt, 1923.
Religious Life in Ancient Egypt, 1924.
Palestine and Israel: Historical Notes, 1934.
Anthedon, 1938.
Egyptian Architecture, 1938.
The Funeral Furniture of Egypt, 1938.

EVANS, SIR ARTHUR (1851-1941)

From 1893 onwards Sir Arthur Evans was engaged in excavations, and from 1900 to 1908 in excavating the Palace of Knossos in Crete, thereby revealing a whole ancient and almost unsuspected civilization. The reports on this were issued at different dates. See especially—

Scripta Minoa, 1909.
The Palace of Minos, 1922, 1928, 1930.

Time and Chance (1943) by Joan Evans, his half-sister, tells of the archaeological work both of Sir Arthur and of his equally distinguished father, Sir John Evans.

B. ENGLISH AND EUROPEAN HISTORY

i. The Older Historians

NAPIER, SIR WILLIAM FRANCIS PATRICK (1785-1860)

History of the Peninsular War, 1828-40.

Still an authority, though prejudiced; it should be corrected by Oman (see below). But the spirited and vivid style—that of an eye-witness of many of the events—is likely to preserve the book for many years to come.

PALGRAVE, SIR FRANCIS (1788-1861)

History of Normandy and England, 1851-64.

Almost pioneer work and now superseded, but of importance in its time.

STEPHEN, SIR JAMES (1789-1859)

Essays in Ecclesiastical Biography, 1849 (1867 edition has a life by his son, James FitzJames Stephen).
Lectures on the History of France, 1852.

Stephen was one of the *Edinburgh* Reviewers, and his *Essays in Ecclesiastical Biography* show exactly their temper of superiority combined with a genuine desire to be fair.

ALISON, SIR ARCHIBALD (1792-1867)

Alison was not unprejudiced, but his books on almost contemporary history were of use in their time.

History of Europe from the Commencement of the French Revolution to the Restoration of the Bourbons, 1833-42.
History of Europe from the Fall of Napoleon to the Accession of Louis Napoleon, 1852-59.

ii. Carlyle to Trevelyan

CARLYLE, THOMAS (1795-1881)

Carlyle as an historian is considered by G. P. Gooch (see introduction to this section) and by G. M. Trevelyan (*The Two*

Carlyles, in *Recreations of an Historian*). Carlyle as a philosopher was described by Edward Caird as 'the author who exercised the most powerful charm on young men who were beginning to think'; and Muirhead considers that he influenced the course of philosophical thought in England by criticizing Reid's philosophy of Common Sense and by preparing the way for the study of Kant and post-Kantian philosophy in England; but on the whole the philosophers do not seem to have much respect for his philosophical powers. As a literary critic he is capricious and uncertain.

Most of Carlyle's earlier critical writings appeared in magazines, especially *The Edinburgh Review*, *The Foreign Quarterly*, *The Westminster Review* and *Fraser's Magazine*. They were first collected in 1840 and will be found in later collected editions.

Sartor Resartus, 1838 (in Fraser's, 1833-34).
The French Revolution, 1837.
Chartism, 1839.
On Heroes and Hero-Worship, 1841 (lectures in 1840).
Past and Present, 1843.
Oliver Cromwell, 1845.
Latter-Day Pamphlets, 1850.
Life of John Sterling, 1851.
Frederick the Great, 1858-65 (written 1851-65).
Reminiscences, 1881 (written 1867).

The centenary edition of 1896-1901 in 31 vols., edited with introductions by H. D. Traill, should be noted; and for serious study the editions of *The French Revolution* by J. Holland Rose, 1902, and of *Oliver Cromwell* by S. C. Lomas, with an introduction by C. H. Firth, 1904, should be used.

Carlyle's biographies are inseparably connected with those of his wife. The first and authorized biography was that by J. A. Froude (*Thomas Carlyle, a History of the First Forty Years of His Life*, 1882; *Thomas Carlyle, a History of His Life in London*, 1884), which was attacked at the time as treacherous to his memory. Very full information is contained in David A. Wilson's *Life of Carlyle* (*Carlyle till Marriage, Carlyle to the French Revolution, Carlyle on Cromwell and Others, Carlyle at His Zenith, Carlyle to Threescore and Ten, Carlyle in Old Age*)—the last volume with D. W. MacArthur. See also *Letters and Memorials of Jane Welsh Carlyle*, 1883; *Early Letters of Jane Welsh Carlyle*, ed. D. G. Ritchie, 1891; *New Letters and Memorials of Mrs Carlyle*, ed. A. Carlyle, 1903;

Correspondence between Carlyle and Emerson, 1883; *Early Letters of Thomas Carlyle*, 1886 and 1888; *Correspondence between Goethe and Carlyle*, 1887; all this correspondence of Carlyle was edited by C. E. Norton.

The study of Carlyle by John Nichol is rather harsh; a kinder estimate is that by G. M. Trevelyan, noted above. (The title does not refer to Mrs Carlyle.) See also Osbert Burdett, *The Two Carlyles*, 1930. (The title here refers to Mrs Carlyle.) From what is written above it will be seen that Mrs Carlyle's letters are worth reading; some would give most of her husband's works for them. More recent studies are by Julian Symons, *Thomas Carlyle: The Life and Ideas of a Prophet*, and by Lawrence and Elizabeth Hansen, *Necessary Evil: The Life of Jane Welsh Carlyle*.

MACAULAY, THOMAS BABINGTON, LORD (1800-1859)

Macaulay's most popular writings, his critical and historical essays, were written from 1825 onwards, and most of them appeared in *The Edinburgh Review*. There was a collected edition of these Edinburgh essays in 1843, and of his miscellaneous writings in 1860.

The History of England (never completed) was begun in 1839, and successive volumes appeared in 1848, 1855, 1861. It was intended to cover the period from the Exclusion Bill to the end of the eighteenth century or even later, to the death of George IV, but in fact it came down only to 1700. The best edition is by C. H. Firth (6 vols.), 1913-15, and Firth's *Commentary on Macaulay's History of England*, 1938, should also be consulted.

The *History* was immensely influential, not least because the brilliance of the writing in it and in the essays imposed that 'Whig view of history' which survives in many text-books: in spite of a strong effort to attain impartiality, it may be seen in the work of Macaulay's nephew and great-nephew—Sir George Otto Trevelyan and Professor G. M. Trevelyan (see below)—and it is noticeable in smaller men. In the last sixty years there has been also a reaction against it, which sometimes leads to equally prejudiced writing on the other side.

Lays of Ancient Rome, 1842 (with other poems, 1848).
The *Lays* may not be of the highest kind of poetry, but they have the same brilliance and colour as the prose of Macaulay.

Complete Works, 1866.
Sir G. O. Trevelyan: The Life and Letters of Lord Macaulay, 1876; one
of the best biographies in English.

BURTON, JOHN HILL (1809-81)

Burton is a minor figure, but he did useful work as an editor and his *History of Scotland* 1853, and *The Scot Abroad*, 1864, have a little value still. He was a great bibliophile, and his *Book-hunter*, 1860, is a classic of its kind.

STANLEY, ARTHUR PENRHYN (1815-81)

Stanley's best book is *The Life and Correspondence of Dr Arnold*, 1844 (enlarged in later edition). He was one of Arnold's pupils and in some ways a weaker Arnold, more of an amateur as a theologian and historian. It is perhaps a misuse of terms to apply either to him. But he had a quick sense of the lively and picturesque parts of history, especially of the historical associations of places, and for this reason his books may be read with pleasure.

Memorials of Canterbury, 1854.
Sinai and Palestine, 1856.
Lectures on the History of the Eastern Church, 1861.
Lectures on the History of the Jewish Church (three series), 1863, 1865,
    1876.
Memorials of Westminster Abbey, 1868.
R. E. Prothero: Life and Correspondence, 1893.
Hector Bolitho: *A Victorian Dean*, 1930.

FROUDE, JAMES ANTHONY (1818-94)

Froude's brilliance as a writer is equalled only by his bias: note especially that *The English in Ireland* provoked Lecky to write his history of the same period (see below), and that most of his work on the sixteenth century has been very severely handled in the last sixty years. He remains a great English writer, but as an historian he should be used with caution. His novels (e.g., the historical *The Two Chiefs of Dunboyne*) are less interesting than his histories.

See also Carlyle, above.

History of England from the Fall of Wolsey to the Defeat of the Spanish
    Armada, 1856-70.
The English in Ireland in the Eighteenth Century, 1872-74.
Short Studies on Great Subjects, 1867-83.

Life and Letters of Erasmus, 1894.
English Seamen in the Sixteenth Century, 1895.

A minor work of some interest is *The Nemesis of Faith*, 1849; J. A. Froude was the brother of Richard Hurrell Froude (see under Theology), and was himself at one time affected by the Oxford Movement, but reacted against it with violence.

FREEMAN, EDWARD AUGUSTUS (1823-92)

Freeman's excessively 'Germanic' views of early English history—and perhaps, too, his excessively violent methods of controversy—provoked a reaction; many of his conclusions have been modified by later workers, but he was a great historian.

History of the Norman Conquest, 1867-79.
Growth of the English Constitution, 1872.
Historical Geography of Europe, 1881-2 (ed. by Bury, 1903; of great utility).
History of Sicily, 1891-92.
Historical Essays, 1871, 1873, 1879, 1892—containing some of his best work.

STUBBS, WILLIAM (1825-1901)

Much of Bishop Stubbs's work lay in the editing of original documents and comment on them, and has been superseded by later work of the same sort, but he was one of the giants of the nineteenth century. The *Lectures* and *Introductory Essays* give examples of his power of exposition and his mastery of historical problems.

Constitutional History of England down to 1485, 1873-78.
Seventeen Lectures on the Study of Mediaeval and Modern History, 1886.
Introductory Essays to the 'Rolls' Series, 1902.
European History, 1904.
Letters, ed. W. H. Hutton, 1904.

GARDINER, SAMUEL RAWSON (1829-1902)

History of England 1603-42, 1863-82 (coll. ed., 1883-84).
The Great Civil War, 1886-91.
History of the Commonwealth and Protectorate, 1895-1901.
The Last Years of the Protectorate (unfinished; completed by Sir Charles Firth, 1909).

These volumes form a deliberately impartial history of a most controversial period. A shorter study is *The Puritan Revolution*,

1876. Gardiner's *Student's History of England*, 1890, is one of the best general text-books of English history.

ACTON, SIR JOHN EMERICH EDWARD DAL-BERG, BARON (1834-1902)

Lord Acton was one of the profoundest and most influential historians and political thinkers of his time. Apart from articles in reviews (*Home and Foreign Review, North British Review, English Historical Review*), his work is best represented in posthumously published volumes of lectures. He was the inspirer and first editor of *The Cambridge Modern History*.

Lectures on Modern History, 1906.
History of Freedom and other Essays, 1907.
Lectures on the French Revolution, 1910.

SEELEY, SIR JOHN ROBERT (1834-95)

Ecce Homo, 1865.

This was first published anonymously, and made considerable stir as a contribution to liberal theology.

Seeley's main importance as an historian was as one of the first to realize the meaning of the growing British Empire and to endeavour to impress it upon his countrymen; though it would scarcely be accurate to call him imperialistic, his writings undoubtedly influenced the growth of imperialist feeling at the end of the century.

The Expansion of England, 1883.
The Growth of British Policy, 1895.
Lectures on Political Science, 1895.

GREEN, JOHN RICHARD (1837-83)

A Short History of the English People, 1874.

One of the first books to consider social history and the development of the nation rather than purely political history. It remains the best introduction to English history written in the period, by virtue of its spirit and the vividness of its narrative, but many of its statements and interpretations are now known to be highly incorrect, especially as regards the earlier history. *The Making of England*, 1881, and *The Conquest of England*, 1883, should not be regarded as authoritative.

TREVELYAN, SIR GEORGE OTTO (1838-1928)

The Early History of Charles James Fox, 1880.
George III and Charles Fox, 1912, 1914.
The American Revolution (4 vols.), 1909 (published between 1899 and 1903).

See also under Macaulay, above.

Memoir, by G. M. Trevelyan, 1932.

CREIGHTON, MANDELL (1843-1901)

History of the Papacy, 1882, 1887, 1894.
The Age of Elizabeth, 1876.
Cardinal Wolsey, 1888.
Queen Elizabeth, 1896.

Bishop Creighton's quest of impartiality led him into unusual trouble: he was blamed by Acton for his lenient treatment of the Renaissance popes—Acton being a Roman Catholic and Creighton an Anglican.

ROSEBERY, ARCHIBALD PHILIP PRIMROSE, LORD (1847-1929)

Pitt, 1891.
Sir Robert Peel, 1899.
Napoleon: The Last Phase, 1900.
Oliver Cromwell, 1900.
Lord Randolph Churchill, 1906.
Chatham, 1910.
Miscellanies Literary and Historical, 1921.

Rosebery's political and historical studies have a special interest as coming, not from a professional historian, but from an experienced politician; cf. Curzon, below.

Life by Lord Crewe, 1931.

RAMSAY, SIR JAMES HENRY (1832-1925)

ed. The Scholar's History of England (55 B.C. to A.D. 1485) (8 vols.), 1892-1913; and contributed to it Lancaster and York, 1892.
Foundations of England; or Twelve Centuries of British History, 1898.
The Angevin Empire, 1903.
The Dawn of the Constitution, 1908.

PLUMMER, CHARLES (1851-1927)

The Life and Times of Alfred the Great, 1902.

This is still the best book on its subject.

TOUT, THOMAS FREDERICK (1855-1929)

History of England for Schools, with F. York Powell, Vol. II, 1890, III,
    1898. (Vol. I, by York Powell, appeared in 1885.)
Edward the First, 1893.
The Empire and the Papacy, 1898.
History of Great Britain (for schools), 1902, 1903, 1906.
History of England 1216-1377, 1905.
The Place of the Reign of Edward II in English History, 1914.
Chapters in the Administrative History of Mediaeval England, I and II,
    1920; III and IV, 1928; V, 1929.

FIRTH, SIR CHARLES HARDING (1857-1936)

Scotland and the Commonwealth, 1895.
Scotland and the Protectorate, 1899.
Oliver Cromwell, 1900 (new ed. 1923).
Cromwell's Army, 1901 (2nd ed. with illustrations 1912).
The Last Years of the Protectorate, 1909.
The House of Lords during the Civil War, 1910.

See also Carlyle and Macaulay, above; both must be corrected
by Firth.

DAVIS, HENRY WILLIAM CARLESS (1874-1928)

Charlemagne, 1900.
England Under the Normans and Angevins, 1905.
Mediaeval Europe, 1911.

OMAN, SIR CHARLES WILLIAM CHADWICK (1860-1946)

History of the Art of War in the Middle Ages, 1898.
History of the Peninsular War, 1902; now the acknowledged classic on
    the subject.
The Great Revolt of 1381, 1906.
History of England before the Norman Conquest, 1910.
History of the Art of War in the Sixteenth Century, 1937,

and other works.

Things I Have Seen, 1930.
Memories of Victorian Oxford, 1941.

FISHER, HERBERT ALBERT LAURENS (1865-1940)

The Mediaeval Empire, 1898.
Studies in Napoleonic Statesmanship, 1903.
A Political History of England, 1906.
Bonapartism, 1908.
Life of F. W. Maitland, 1910.
The Republican Tradition in Europe, 1911.

Political Unions, 1911.
Napoleon Bonaparte, 1913.
Studies in History and Politics, 1920.
The Common Weal, 1924.
Life of Lord Bryce, 1926.
Life of Sir Paul Vinogradoff, 1927.
The Whig Historians, 1928.
A History of Europe, 1935; rev. ed. 1938.
Pages from the Past, 1939.
An Unfinished Autobiography, 1940.

POLLARD, ALBERT FREDERICK (1869-1948)

England Under the Protector Somerset, 1900.
Henry VIII, 1902; new eds., 1905, 1913.
A Life of Thomas Cranmer, 1904.
Factors in Modern History, 1907.
A History of England, 1912.
The Reign of Henry VII, 1913-14.
The Evolution of Parliament, 1920.
Factors in American History, 1925.
Wolsey, 1929.
Parliament in the Wars of the Roses, 1937.

TREVELYAN, GEORGE MACAULAY (1876-1962)

In much of his historical work Trevelyan is the heir of his great-uncle Macaulay, though with a greater and far more successful attempt at impartiality; but in the choice of field and the liveliness of treatment the descent is obvious. There are two clearly marked divisions, as well as smaller categories, in his work —the Italian and the English.

Garibaldi's Defence of the Roman Republic, 1907.
Garibaldi and the Thousand, 1909.
Garibaldi's Making of Italy, 1911.

England under the Stuarts, 1904
England under Queen Anne: Blenheim, 1930; Ramillies and the Union
    with Scotland, 1932; The Peace and the Protestant Succession, 1934.

History of England, 1926—the best recent one-volume history.
English Social History, 1944.

BIOGRAPHIES:
Life of John Bright, 1913.
Lord Grey of the Reform Bill, 1920.
Sir George Otto Trevelyan, 1932.
Grey of Falloden, 1937.

CRITICISM:
The Poetry and Philosophy of George Meredith, 1906.
Recreations of an Historian, 1919.

III. Law and Custom; Thought and Civilization

BUCKLE, HENRY THOMAS (1821-62)

History of Civilization in England, 1857, 1861.

An important book of the difficult, generalizing kind.

Life by Giles St Aubyn, *A Victorian Eminence*.

MAINE, SIR HENRY JAMES SUMNER (1822-88)

Maine's studies in the genesis of law and institutions have affected all later research, though some of his conclusions have been seriously modified by his successors.

Ancient Law: Its Connection with the Early History of Society and its Relations to Modern Ideas, 1861.
Village Communities, 1871.
The Early History of Institutions, 1875.
Dissertations on Early Law and Customs, 1883.

STEPHEN, SIR JAMES FITZJAMES (1829-94)

Liberty, Equality, Fraternity, 1872-73.
History of the Criminal Law, 1883.
Horae Sabbaticae (collected articles, 3 series), 1892.
Life, by Leslie Stephen, 1895.

STEPHEN, SIR LESLIE (1832-1904)

Leslie Stephen was literary critic, philosopher, historian and biographer—he was the first editor of the *Dictionary of National Biography*—and in all capacities his work was remarkable. His style is easy and attractive.

History of English Thought in the Eighteenth Century, 1876, 1881.
The Science of Ethics, 1882.
An Agnostic's Apology, 1893.
The English Utilitarians, 1900.
English Literature and English Society in the Eighteenth Century, 1904.
Hours in a Library (several series), 1874-90.
Studies of a Biographer, 1899-1902.
Collected Essays, 1907 (10 vols.).
Life and Letters, by F. W. Maitland, 1906; Leslie Stephen by Noel Annan.

LECKY, WILLIAM EDWARD HARTPOLE (1838-1903)

History of the Rise and Influence of the Spirit of Rationalism in Europe, 1865.

History of European Morals from Augustus to Charlemagne, 1869.

History of England in the Eighteenth Century, 1878-90 (cabinet ed. 1892, separating the English and Irish sections).
This is the book which was provoked by Froude's *The English in Ireland* (see above).

Democracy and Liberty, 1896 (revised ed. 1899).

Historical and Political Essays, 1908.

Memoir, by Mrs Lecky, 1909.

DICEY, ALBERT VENN (1835-1922)

The Conflict of Laws, 1896 (revised later; the best edition is that of 1915).

The Law of the Constitution, 1885 (revised later; the best edition is that of 1922).

The Relation between Law and Public Opinion in England during the Nineteenth Century, 1905 (the best edition is that of 1914).

The title describes the book, which is of particular value for clearing up vague notions about the reform of laws by the pressure of public opinion.

The Statesmanship of Wordsworth, 1916.

An unusual war-book: from an examination of Wordsworth's political principles and ideals, Dicey proceeds to apply them to the situation in 1916 and to the nature of the peace which should be striven for. A good deal of trouble might have been saved if his conclusions had been generally accepted.

Memorials, ed. R. S. Rait, 1925.

BRYCE, JAMES, LORD (1838-1922)

The Holy Roman Empire, 1862 and 1884.

The American Commonwealth, 1888.

Studies in History and Jurisprudence, 1901.

Studies in Contemporary Biography, 1903.

University and Historical Addresses, 1913.

Bryce joins Rosebery and Curzon as a statesman who had practical experience of the working of historical principles and the government of men.

Life, by H. A. L. Fisher, 1926.

ANSON, SIR WILLIAM (1843-1914)

The Principles of the English Law of Contract, 1879.
The Law and Custom of the Constitution, 1886, 1892.
Memoir, ed. H. H. Henson, 1920.

MAITLAND, FREDERICK WILLIAM (1850-1906)

A History of English Law before the Time of Edward I (written in conjunction with Sir Frederick Pollock), 1895.
Doomsday Book and Beyond, 1897.
Township and Borough, 1898.
Roman Canon Law in the Church of England, 1898.
Constitutional History of England, 1908.
Collected Works, 1911 (essays, articles and reviews).
Selected Historical Essays, ed. H. M. Cam, 1957.
Life, by H. A. L. Fisher, 1910.

VINOGRADOFF, SIR PAUL (1854-1925)

Villeinage in England, 1892.
The Growth of the Manor, 1905.
English Society in the Eleventh Century, 1908.
Collected Papers, 1928.
Life, by H. A. L. Fisher, 1927.

iv. Economic History, etc.

JESSOPP, AUGUSTUS (1823-1914)

One Generation of a Norfolk House, 1878.
The Coming of the Friars, 1889.
Studies by a Recluse, 1893.
Before the Great Pillage, 1901.

And other studies and editions of MSS., especially from the side of economic history. His work now needs supplementing.

ROGERS, JAMES EDWIN THOROLD (1823-90)

A History of Agriculture and Prices in England, I and II, 1866; III and IV, 1882; V and VI, 1887; VII (2 parts), 1902.
Six Centuries of Work and Wages, 1884 (revised 1886).
The Relation of Economic Science to Social and Political Action, 1888.
The Economic Interpretation of History, 1888.

Thorold Rogers's work, like that of other pioneers, has undergone much revision in recent years.

MAYHEW, HENRY (1812-87)

London Labour and the London Poor, 1851 and 1864 (*Selections* by P. Quennell, well chosen).

Other works of social observation, some in collaboration, anticipating the Booths.

BOOTH, WILLIAM (1829-1912) and STEAD, W. T. (1849-1912)

In Darkest England and the Way Out, 1890.

The best of many lives of General Booth are those by Harold Begbie, 1920, and St John Ervine, 1935; the second is called *God's Soldier*.

BOOTH, CHARLES (1840-1916)

Life and Labour of the People in London, 1891-1903.
Poor Law Reform, 1910.

The first of these books gives a complete picture of the poorer classes in London within those years.

Charles Booth, a Memoir (by his widow), 1918.

'GEORGE BOURN' (George Sturt) (1863-1927)

The Bettesworth Book, 1901.
Memoirs of a Surrey Labourer, 1907.
Change in the Village, 1912.
The Wheelwright's Shop, 1923.

and others.

Sturt's books are mentioned specially because they are good examples of a kind of book of which there have been many in the last thirty years; studies from direct observation of changes in the life of the countryside due to economic causes.

CUNNINGHAM, WILLIAM (1849-1919)

Growth of English Industry and Commerce, 1882; revised in each of six subsequent editions, 1892-1910.

TOYNBEE, ARNOLD (1852-83)

The Industrial Revolution, 1884 (lectures with a memoir by Jowett. The 4th ed. 1894 includes two lectures on Henry George.

Toynbee and Cunningham are both important to the student of economics and economic history at the time. Toynbee was one of the first, if not the first, to coin the phrase 'industrial revolution'. Toynbee Hall, the first of the 'university settlements', was founded in memory of him.

WEBB, SIDNEY (1859-1947) and BEATRICE (1858-1943)

Fabian Essays (with other writers), 1889.
History of Trade-Unionism, 1894.
Industrial Democracy, 1897.
Problems of Modern Industry, 1898.
English Local Government (The Parish and the County, 1906; The
    Manor and the Borough, 1908; Statutory Authorities, 1922; The Story
    of the King's Highway, 1913; English Prisons, 1922).
Consumer's Co-operative Movement, 1921.
The Decay of Capitalist Civilization, 1923.
English Poor Law History, 1927-29.
Methods of Social Study, 1932.
Soviet Communism: A New Civilization, 1935.

And many other social and statistical works, written in
collaboration or separately.

Mrs Webb's autobiography of her early years—*My Apprentice-
ship*, 1926—explains how the partnership began. The temper
of those years is in some ways strikingly different from that of
the last book noted above.

The *History of Trade-Unionism* is the classic work on the subject,
and has probably done more than any other book to influence
the course of the Labour movement in this country.

C. MISCELLANEOUS

CREASY, SIR EDWARD SHEPHERD (1812-78)

Fifteen Decisive Battles of the World, 1852.

A book which still retains some reputation, particularly as a
school prize.

CURZON, GEORGE NATHANIEL, LORD (1859-1925)

Russia in Central Asia, 1889.
Persia and the Persian Question, 1892.
Problems of the Far East, 1894.
Lord Curzon in India, 1906.

See on Rosebery and Bryce, above.

The authoritative *Life* of Curzon is by Lord Zetland, 1928.
See also Harold Nicolson: *Curzon: the Last Phase, 1919-25*, 1934.

DOYLE, JOHN ANDREW (1844-1907)

The English in America, 1882.
The Puritan Colonies, 1887.

The Middle Colonies, 1907.
The Colonies under the House of Hanover, 1907.

These form part of a *History of the American Colonies down to the War of Independence*—much of it now superseded. But Doyle was a vigorous writer and still gives good reading.

Essays on Various Subjects, with a biographical introduction by W. P. Ker, 1911.

SMITH, SIR GEORGE ADAM (1856-1942)

Not in the strict sense an archaeologist, he might have been included among those named on pp. 161-3, but his travels in Egypt, Syria and what is now Jordan lie behind his textual and historical studies of Old Testament literature and thought.

The Book of Isaiah, 1888-90; rev. ed. 1927.
The Historical Geography of the Holy Land, 1894. The standard book on its subject, 25th ed. 1931.
The Twelve Prophets, 1896-97; rev. ed. 1928,

and many other works, historical and theological, which have deeply affected modern conceptions of the Old Testament.

TRAVEL

SINCE the nineteenth century was one of the great ages of travel and exploration, and most of the explorers could write well, this section might have been made much larger; but the entries here may serve as signposts to a rich and heroic literature.

A. EUROPE.
> Borrow, Ford, Trelawney, Dufferin, Kinglake, Whymper.

B. SOUTHERN HEMISPHERE.
> Waterton, G. H. Kingsley.

C. ASIA AND NORTHERN AFRICA.
> Joseph Wolff, Lane, Layard, Burton, E. H. Palmer, Doughty.

D. CENTRAL AND WEST AFRICA.
> Livingstone, Speke, H. M. Stanley, Mary Kingsley, Harry Johnston.

See also under

History (W. M. Ramsay, Flinders Petrie, Evans, A. P. Stanley, Curzon, G. Adam Smith).
Science (Darwin, A. R. Wallace, Huxley, Tyndall).
Poetry (W. Morris, W. S. Blunt).
Novels (Meadows Taylor, Dickens, H. Martineau, C. Kingsley, R. L. Stevenson, Kipling).

A. EUROPE

BORROW, GEORGE HENRY (1803-81)

The Zincali, or Gypsies of Spain, 1841.
The Bible in Spain, 1843.
Lavengro, 1851.
The Romany Rye, 1857.
Wild Wales, 1862.

Borrow's life may be seen in his works, but he sometimes improved the facts for artistic purposes. W. I. Knapp's *Life, Writings and Correspondence of George Borrow* (1899), is a trustworthy book; and the editions of *Lavengro*, by Knapp (1900), and F. Hindes Groome (1901), and of *The Romany Rye*, by John Sampson (1903), may also be consulted.

Borrow is one of the most picturesque figures as he is one of the most picturesque writers of the period—and, a philologist might add, one of the most picturesque philologists. *Lavengro* and *The Romany Rye* are fascinating and highly coloured accounts of gypsy life in England, with insistence on the romantic and eccentric. He was an out-and-out Bohemian, revelling in the company of gypsies and bruisers, and it was an odd fate which led him to sell Bibles in Spain on behalf of the Bible Society. His books, which are very readable, are a mine of information on the subjects which he loved.

FORD, RICHARD (1796-1858)
Handbook for Travellers in Spain, 1845.

This is still one of the recognized authorities on Spain.

TRELAWNEY, EDWARD JOHN (1792-1881)
Adventures of a Younger Son, 1831.
Records of Shelley, Byron and the Author, 1858.

The first of these books is far more a spirited autobiography than fiction, but must still be taken with caution as a record of fact. Trelawney's name survives by it and by his friendship with the great poets whom he commemorates in the second book.

DUFFERIN, LORD (1826-1902)
Letters from High Latitudes, 1856.
Life, by A. C. Lyall, 1905.

All the brilliance, charm and humanity of Lord Dufferin, which were afterwards displayed on a wider scene when he was Viceroy of India, are shown in these letters of a journey to Iceland and the Arctic Circle; they may be compared with William Morris's letters and journals of twenty years later.

KINGLAKE, ALEXANDER WILLIAM (1809-91)
Eothen, 1844.

Kinglake's lively account of his travels in the Levant is, both as a piece of brilliant writing and as an historical document, superior to his more ambitious *History of the Invasion of the Crimea* (1863-87).

WHYMPER, EDWARD (1840-1911)

Scrambles amongst the Alps, 1871—a classic and an admirable piece of undecorated prose.
Travels among the Great Andes of the Equator, 1892.

Whymper also wrote shorter guide-books to the Alps, and published a condensed account in 1879 of the first ascent of the Matterhorn. His style is admirable.

B. SOUTHERN HEMISPHERE

WATERTON, CHARLES (1782-1865)

Wanderings in South America, 1825.
Essays on Natural History . . . with an Autobiography, 1838, 1844, 1857.

Waterton's travels began rather early for inclusion here, but as the greatest English traveller in South America in the first half of the century he ought to find his place in a volume which later includes W. H. Hudson and R. B. Cunninghame Graham (v. *Essays*).

KINGSLEY, GEORGE HENRY (1827-92)

South Sea Bubbles, by the Earl and the Doctor, 1872.
Notes on Sport and Travel, 1900 (with a memoir by Mary Kingsley).

Only these books survive as a taste of George Kingsley's powers of writing, though he spent most of his life in travel. He was the brother of Charles and Henry Kingsley and the father of Mary Kingsley (q.v.), in whose *Life* some further notes of his may be found.

C. ASIA AND NORTHERN AFRICA

WOLFF, JOSEPH (1795-1862)

Narrative of a Mission to Bokhara to ascertain the Fate of Colonel Stoddart and Captain Conolly, 1845.
Sketch of the Life and Journal of Joseph Wolff, 1827; Missionary Journal and Memoir, 1824; Journal for 1831, 1832; Researches and Missionary Labours among the Jews, Mohammedans, and other Sects between 1831 and 1834, 1835; Journal of Joseph Wolff, containing an Account

of his Missionary Labours from 1827 to 1831 and from 1835 to 1838, 1839.
Travels and Adventures of Joseph Wolff, 1860.

Wolff—'Apostle of our Lord Jesus Christ for Palestine, Persia, Bokhara and Balkh', as he signed himself—was an extraordinary person in many ways. His life and character may be discerned in his own *Journals*, and are brought out in the studies by H. P. Palmer: *Joseph Wolff, his romantic life and travels*, 1935; and Fitzroy Maclean: *A Person from England*, 1958.

LANE, EDWARD WILLIAM (1801-76)

Account of the Manners and Customs of the Modern Egyptians, 1836.

This is still a standard authority, and is never likely to be superseded.

The Thousand and One Nights, 1838-40.

This was the first full and accurate translation of *The Arabian Nights* into English, and is still unrivalled. Lane was an admirable Arabic scholar and one of the best of English translators.

LAYARD, SIR AUSTEN (1817-94)

Nineveh and its Remains, 1849.
Discoveries in the Ruins of Nineveh and Babylon, 1853.

Layard's excavations were among the first which revealed the magnitude of the ancient civilizations; and D. G. Rossetti's poem, *The Burden of Nineveh*, shows the same kind of poetic reaction as a famous passage in Bridges's *Testament of Beauty* (Book IV) does to the discoveries at Ur eighty years later.

BURTON, SIR RICHARD FRANCIS (1821-90)

Personal Narrative of a Pilgrimage to El Medinah and Mecca, 1855, and many other works. Note especially his translation of *The Arabian Nights*, 1885-88, which does not, however, equal Lane's. A selection from this by P. H. Newby was published in 1950. He wrote one poem, The Kasidah, 1880.
Life, by Lady Burton, 1895 (re-edited 1898).

Burton was one of the first Christians to enter Mecca, though he did it in disguise as a Moslem: he had not the obstinacy of Doughty and Lawrence, who, however, did not attempt that adventure. He is among the most distinguished of the scholar-adventurer explorers who made the Middle East their own. He was a great Victorian figure, and his prose has all the dignity we associate with the solider writings of the period. His widow destroyed his memoirs.

PALMER, EDWARD HENRY (1840-82)

The Desert of the Exodus: Journeys on Foot in the Wilderness of the Forty Years' Wanderings, 1871.

Palmer wrote much besides, scholarly papers arising out of his expeditions, popular manuals on the Near East, and translations from Arabic and Persian, the most important being that of the *Koran* (*Sacred Books of the East*, Vols. VI and IX, *The Qurân*, 1880). He was murdered while on a diplomatic mission among the Bedouin.

DOUGHTY, CHARLES MONTAGU (1843-1926)

Travels in Arabia Deserta, 1888 (new ed., with introduction by T. E. Lawrence, 1921). There is also an abridged edition, Wanderings in Arabia, 1908.

The Dawn in Britain, 1906. A volume of selections from this, arranged by Barker Fairley, was published in 1935, and a full centenary edition, with critical essay by Ruth Robbins, in 1943.

Adam Cast Forth, 1908.
The Cliffs, 1909.
The Clouds, 1912.
The Titans, 1916.
Mansoul, 1920.

All but the first of these volumes are poems; but though in them Doughty was poet and prophet, it is probable that his great prose work, which to him was as much a poem as anything which he wrote in verse, will prove his chief title to memory.

Doughty's writings are entirely outside the tradition of Victorian prose or poetry. 'The verse is breathless and the style obscure,' Sir H. Grierson remarks, 'because the writer uses the English language as if he had found it lying about and was free of it without regard to any tradition of idiom or structure.' His great epic, *The Dawn in Britain*, has many strange constructions and obsolete words. Only enthusiasts can read Doughty's verse with real pleasure. But *Travels in Arabia Deserta* is a great prose classic: the style is superbly suited to its matter, hard and gaunt, but rich and with magnificent movement. The manner may repel for the first few pages, but after that will be found to be fully justified—an original discovery of genius.

Barker Fairley: Charles M. Doughty, 1927.
Anne Treneer: Doughty, A Study of his Prose and Verse, 1935.
Life, by D. G. Hogarth, 1928.

D. CENTRAL AND WEST AFRICA

LIVINGSTONE, DAVID (1813-73)

Missionary Travels and Researches in South Africa, 1857.
Narrative of an Expedition to the Zambesi and its Tributaries, 1865.
Last Journals, 1874.
Family Letters, ed. I. Schapera, 1960.
Private Journals, ed. I. Schapera, 1960.
Life, by Sir Harry Johnston, 1891.

There is a good short study by D. C. Somervell, 1936.

SPEKE, JOHN HANNING (1827-64)

Journal of the Discovery of the Source of the Nile, 1863.

STANLEY, SIR HENRY MORTON (John Rowlands) (1841-1904)

How I Found Livingstone, 1872.
Through the Dark Continent, 1878.
In Darkest Africa, 1890.
Autobiography, ed. by his widow, 1909.

KINGSLEY, MARY (1862-1900)

Travels in West Africa, 1897.
West African Studies, 1899.
Life, by Stephen Gwynn, 1932.

Mary Kingsley in her sympathetic understanding of other races was like Gertrude Bell, and her adventures not only in actual discovery but in the interpretation of the African peoples whom she encountered are told by her without ostentation in a style full of point and wit.

JOHNSTON, SIR HARRY HAMILTON (1858-1927)

The River Congo, 1884.
Kilimanjaro, 1885.
History of a Slave, 1889.
Life of Livingstone, 1891.
British Central Africa, 1897.
A History of the Colonisation of Africa by Alien Races, 1899-1913.
The Uganda Protectorate, 1902.
The Nile Quest, 1903.
Liberia, 1906.

George Grenfell and the Congo, 1908.
A History of the British Empire in Africa, 1910.
Comparative Study of the Bantu and Semi-Bantu Languages, 1919, 1922.
The Story of My Life, 1923.

Johnston also amused himself by writing novels which carried on the fortunes of the characters of Dickens and Shaw (*The Gay-Dombeys*, *The Veneerings*, *Mrs Warren's Daughter*), but though these are readable, he will be remembered as African administrator and historian.

SCIENCE

MOST of the scientific writing of the period is too technical for the general reader, but there remains a great deal which is not only comprehensible, but good literature. Its effect on the thought and belief of the time does not need further emphasis here; see the Introduction. But one point of interest may be noted: the chronological movement through the physical sciences and geology to biology and so to anthropology and eugenics.

A. Mary Somerville, Lyell, Hugh Miller, Faraday, Clerk Maxwell.
B. Darwin, Alfred Russel Wallace, Huxley, Tyndall, Ray Lankester.
C. E. B. Tylor, Sir James Frazer.
D. Francis Galton, Karl Pearson.

See also under—

Philosophy (Herschel, Romanes, Havelock Ellis, Westermarck, Lloyd Morgan, J. S. Haldane, S. Butler).
Poetry (Lang, Noyes).
Novels (C. Kingsley, H. G. Wells).
Criticism and Essays (R. Chambers, Smiles).

A

SOMERVILLE, MARY (1780-1872)

The Connection of the Physical Sciences, 1834. (A brilliant and original piece of popularization; the edition of 1842 should be noted for its anticipation of the discovery of Uranus.)
Physical Geography, 1848.
Molecular and Microscopic Science, 1869.
Personal Recollections of Mary Somerville by her daughter Martha Somerville, 1873.

LYELL, SIR CHARLES (1797-1875)

Principles of Geology, 1830-33.
The Elements of Geology, 1838 (later divided into The Principles of Geology and The Elements of Geology).

The Geological Evidences of the Antiquity of Man, 1863.
Life, Letters and Journals, ed. by his sisters-in-law, 1881.

MILLER, HUGH (1802-56)

The Old Red Sandstone, 1841.
The Testimony of the Rocks, 1857.
My Schools and Schoolmasters, 1852—one of the best autobiographies in English.

FARADAY, MICHAEL (1791-1867)

Experimental Researches in Electricity, 1839-55.
Researches in Chemistry and Physics, 1859.

The standard life is by Bence Jones, 1870; see also Sylvanus P. Thompson's *Faraday*, 1898.

Faraday wrote a singularly clear and pure prose, and Huxley called him the prince of lecturers.

MAXWELL, SIR JAMES CLERK (1831-79)

Collected Papers, 1890 (experimental physics, electricity and magnetism).
Life, by L. Campbell and R. T. Garnett, 1882.

B

DARWIN, CHARLES ROBERT (1809-82)

The Origin of Species, 1859.
The Descent of Man, 1871.

Darwin's journal of the voyage which set him on the researches which ended in the Darwinian hypothesis was published in 1833 —*The Voyage of the Beagle*—and in book form in 1839. His *Journal* and *Notebooks* have been edited by Sir Gavin de Beer, and his *Autobiography* was first published in full, edited by his granddaughter Nora Barlow, in 1958. His prose is good of its kind, but there is a tendency today to overrate it.

Life and Letters, ed. F. Darwin, 1887; More Letters, ed. F. Darwin and A. C. Seward, 1903. See also B. Willey's Darwin and Butler, and W. Irvine's Apes, Angels and Victorians and Gertrude Himmelfarb's Darwin and the Darwinian Revolution.

At the same time that Darwin was working out his hypothesis, Wallace was working on the same line of thought, and their collaboration is one of the most honourable stories in scientific research. Their joint paper was read to the Linnacan Society on July 1, 1858.

WALLACE, ALFRED RUSSEL (1823-1913)

Essay on the Law which has regulated the Introduction of New Species, 1855.
Contributions to the Theory of Natural Selection, 1870.
Darwinism, 1889.

A. R. Wallace's own travels and researches are described in—

Travels on the Amazon and Rio Negro, 1853.
The Malay Archipelago, 1869 (by some considered his most important book).
The Geographical Distribution of Animals, 1876.
Island Life, 1880.

He also wrote on social questions, and was convinced by experiment of the claims of spiritualism.

Land Nationalization, 1882.
Studies Scientific and Social, 1900.
Man's Place in the Universe, 1903.
Miracles and Modern Spiritualism, 1875.
My Life, an Autobiography, 1905.

HUXLEY, THOMAS HENRY (1825-95)

Zoological Evidences as to Man's Place in Nature, 1863.
On the Physical Basis of Life, 1868.
On the Hypothesis that Animals are Automata, 1874.
Lay Sermons, Essays and Reviews, 1877.
American Addresses, 1877.
David Hume, 1879.
Ethics and Evolution, 1893.
Collected Essays (9 vols.), 1893-95.
Scientific Memoirs (4 vols.), ed. Sir Michael Foster and Sir Ray Lankester, 1898-1903.
Diary of the Voyage of H.M.S. Rattlesnake, 1935.
Life and Letters, Leonard Huxley, 1900.

Among Huxley's collected essays are to be found those which reveal not only the philosophical basis of his thought, but also his wide range of interests: e.g., *Science and Education Method and Results* contains some of his clearest work: his controversial theological essays are to be found in *Science and Hebrew Tradition* and *Science and Christian Tradition*.

The two men whose names follow did perhaps their most valuable work as popularizers of science, though they were also original researchers.

TYNDALL, JOHN (1820-93)

The Glaciers of the Alps, 1860.
Fragments of Science for Unscientific People, 1871,
and many other works.

Life and Work of John Tyndall, by A. S. Eve and C. H. Creasey, 1945.

LANKESTER, SIR EDWIN RAY (1847-1929)

The Advancement of Science (coll. essays), 1889.
Zoological Articles, 1891.
Extinct Animals, 1905.
The Kingdom of Man, 1907.
From an Easy Chair, 1908.
Science from an Easy Chair, 1910; 2nd series, 1912.
The Diversions of a Naturalist, 1915.
Science and Education, 1919.
Secrets of Earth and Sea, 1920.
Great and Small Things, 1923.

Lankester was an admirable popularizer: his *Easy Chair* series are written in a beautifully lucid, plain prose, and are meant for everyone to read.

C

TYLOR, SIR EDWARD BURNETT (1832-1917)

Researches into the Early History of Mankind, 1865.
Primitive Culture, 1871.
Anthropology, 1881.

FRAZER, SIR JAMES GEORGE (1854-1941)

The Golden Bough, 1890 (2nd ed. 1900; enlarged by later studies to 12 vols., completed in 1915; there is an abridged edition, published in 1922).
The Belief in Immortality and the Worship of the Dead, 1913-24.
Folklore in the Old Testament, 1918 (abridged ed. 1923).
Man, God and Immortality, 1927.
Myths of the Origin of Fire, 1930.
Garnered Sheaves (essays, addresses and reviews), 1931.
The Fear of the Dead in Primitive Religion, I, 1933; II, 1934.
Creation and Evolution in Primitive Cosmogonies, 1935.

Sir James Frazer would hold a high place as a man of letters if he were not so dominating an anthropologist. He wrote excellent passages of emotive prose, and he brought a wide culture to anything that he considered.

D

GALTON, SIR FRANCIS (1822-1911)

Tropical South Africa, 1853.
The Art of Travel, 1855 (and later editions).
Meteorographica, 1863.

With the next book we come to Galton's lifework

Hereditary Genius, 1869.
English Men of Science, 1874.
Human Faculty, 1883.
Natural Inheritance, 1889.
Finger Prints, 1893.
Blurred Finger Prints, 1893.
Finger Print Directory, 1895.
Noteworthy Families, 1906.
Memories of My Life, 1908.
Life and Letters, by Karl Pearson, 1915, 1924, 1930.

Galton wrote good prose, but his claim to distinction is the impulse he gave to the study of heredity.

PEARSON, KARL (1857-1936)

The Ethic of Freethought, 1887, 1901.
The Chances of Death, and other Studies in Evolution, 1897.
The Grammar of Science, 1899, 1900, 1911.
National Life from the Standpoint of Science, 1901,

and many statistical works and tables, and other works.

Pearson was largely a disciple of Galton, and some of his work becomes incomprehensibly mathematical to the layman. But he was a great man in many fields: his *Grammar of Science* is a classic, and he exemplifies with a clearness for which the layman is grateful the scientific attitude which immediately preceded that which Whitehead, Eddington and Jeans are now making familiar.

THEOLOGY

EVANGELICALISM was dominant in the mid-nineteenth century, both within the Church of England and without, but though immensely influential on the life and thought of the time, it has left little of direct and immediate value in literature. Its adherents were notable for personal devotion and good works rather than for intellectual power—the good Lord Shaftesbury, a typical lay Evangelical, shows most of the characteristics of the clergy whom he approved of—and its product of theological literature has hardly even historic interest. Its indirect products, characters in novels, are often difficult to distinguish from the traditional portraits and caricatures of Methodists: Stiggins and Mr Slope are far more inheritances from the eighteenth century than strictly contemporary figures. As against Mr Tryan, George Eliot's respectful portrait of an Evangelical clergyman, there are Thackeray's Rev. Charles Honeyman and the unfavourable pictures of provincial Nonconformity in the novels of 'Mark Rutherford' and some of those of Mrs Oliphant, and its less lovely features provoked much of Matthew Arnold's social criticism. Mrs. Gaskell in *Ruth* and *Cousin Phillis* showed, on the other hand, the spiritual beauty and intellectual integrity of such 'Independent'—really Unitarian, not Evangelical—ministers as she herself knew, and the greatest name in Nonconformist thought in the century, that of James Martineau, is also that of one who called himself a Unitarian. With a few exceptions, such as R. W. Dale later, orthodox Nonconformists and orthodox Evangelicals within the Church of England had too little intellectual and philosophical power to leave lasting monuments, and before the century was much more than half over they were having to meet challenges which were exceedingly hard to meet on their own ground. Most of the literature of doubt or of disbelief came in the later nineteenth century, as it still comes, from men who had been bred in an Evangelical theory of the verbal inspiration of Scripture which could not honestly be made to square with scientific discoveries and the critical textual study of the Bible; much of the rest came from men who were at one time attracted by the Oxford Movement and, for one reason or other, experienced a reaction.

It will be noticed in the section of the Bibliography which follows that almost all the names are those of Anglicans, and these not of the Evangelical party; and the explanation of what looks like a disproportion lies partly in what has already been said, and partly in the fact that three great movements of religious thought affected the Church of England before they affected other religious bodies, and within the Church of England affected men of great intellectual and literary power. Two of these have been mentioned: the Oxford Movement and the critical study of the text of the Bible: the third was the growth of social conscience, as distinct from humanitarian sentiment, among religious people. The three strands of thought were not unconnected from the first, and it is interesting to notice how they became more closely intertwined during the century.

Chronologically, the critical study of the texts of the Old and New Testaments comes first. Dr Arnold was early aware of the work being done in Germany and realized that orthodoxy would have to reckon with it. Pusey was also aware of it, and though he himself was excessively cautious in accepting its conclusions, the fact that a man of his orthodoxy, authority, and influence accepted the necessity of an honest dealing with textual criticism was of considerable importance for the next and following generations of those who were affected by the Oxford Movement. The Tractarians in any case did not inherit or hold so rigid a theory of the authority of the actual word of Scripture as the Evangelicals, and were consequently better able to adjust themselves by degrees to new knowledge. There were degrees: it should not be forgotten that Liddon, who was of the second generation, was in 1890 shocked and distressed by the opinions expressed in

Lux Mundi by Gore who, without having changed his views, was looked upon forty years later as the champion of orthodoxy. But the fact remains that the Tractarians and their heirs, and the men of very varied opinions who were roughly and often incorrectly called Broad Church, were able to assimilate the results of textual criticism, as they were able to assimilate the results of scientific research, because they based their beliefs not on an infallible text but on theories of authority and reason.

The Oxford Movement was, in the first place, an assertion of authority in religion. Its immediate occasion—not its ultimate cause—was the obvious unfriendliness of the Reform Parliament of 1832 to the Church; and Newman and others have dated its beginning from that Assize Sermon on National Apostasy, preached in July 1833, in which Keble raised the whole question of authority: whence did the Church in fact derive its authority? Newman and others in the end found the answer in the Church of Rome, and with their reception into it the Oxford Movement, properly speaking, is usually supposed to end. But Keble and Pusey and others who remained in the Church of England were not spent forces: in the years which followed they and their disciples—some of whom were rather embarrassing in their methods—set themselves to restore what seemed to them wanting in its ordinary teaching and practice and in the ordinary public conception of it, and found themselves, it would now be generally admitted, opposed by prejudice far more than by reason. It proved useless to invoke the Judicial Committee of the Privy Council or any other secular authority against them: the Public Worship Regulation Act of 1874, which was intended 'to stamp out Ritualism', succeeded only in making enough martyrs to disturb the public conscience and fell into practical abeyance. The last serious attempt to prosecute 'ritual offences' was the attack on Edward King, the saintly Bishop of Lincoln, in the nineties, and Archbishop Benson's judgment on the points in dispute, which reversed on his own authority earlier decisions of the Judicial

G

Committee of the Privy Council, proved the effective victory of the principles of the Oxford Movement far more than the gradual raising of the standards of congregational worship and practice, of which the ordinary churchgoer was more conscious.

The third great movement of religious thought, that which insists on the connection between Christianity and social righteousness, may be taken back for our purpose to F. D. Maurice, though Maurice himself would have taken it back to the New Testament. Maurice, like his second master Coleridge, had a seminal mind, and inspiration derived through him may be seen in more than one school of theological thought and practical endeavour. In one line he is behind Charles Kingsley and others who were indignant at the wrongs which provoked Chartism; in another behind such a man as Bryan King, who was mobbed nominally for 'Ritualism', actually for his fight against sweat-shops and brothels; in a third behind Barnett, the founders of Toynbee Hall and the founders of the Workers' Educational Association—he was himself one of the founders of the Working Men's College; in a fourth behind Westcott and Gore, who were concerned with large industrial problems and the large question of the organization of society upon Christian principles, and equally with the problem of combining intellectual honesty with acceptance of the discoveries of critical scholarship. The last two names by themselves, especially that of Westcott, will indicate how, by the end of the century, the strands of religious thought had, in many minds, become united.

The separate notices which follow will modify some of these broad statements and deal with some other sides of religious thought.

For the study of the period see especially—

L. E. ELLIOTT-BINNS—*Religion in the Victorian Era.*

C. E. RAVEN—*Christian Socialism, 1848-54.*

S. C. CARPENTER—*Church and People, 1789-1889.*

V. F. STORR—*The Development of English Theology in the 19th Century*, 1913.

Some more detailed studies are mentioned below, especially in the introduction to Section A.

A. THE OXFORD MOVEMENT AND AFTER.
    Keble, R. H. Froude, Isaac Williams, Newman, W. G. Ward, Pusey, Neale, Liddon, R. W. Church, W. Bright.

B. MAURICE AND OTHERS.
    Maurice (with a note on Colenso and Farrar), F. W. Robertson, R. W. Dale.

C. THE CAMBRIDGE TEXTUAL CRITICS.
    Lightfoot, Westcott, Hort.

D. THE LAST GENERATION.
    Tyrrell, von Hügel, Gore.

Note: Some theologians are more than half philosophers, and some philosophers are mainly interested in theology. Certain names which might be looked for here will be found under *Philosophy*, e.g., Balfour, Inge, Martineau, Romanes. See also under *Philosophy*—
    Mansel, Morell, Stirling, Caird, T. H. Green, Seth (Pringle Pattison), Campbell Fraser, Sorley, Jowett, Westermarck, G. E. Moore, Schiller, Alexander, McTaggart, Reade, S. Butler, Carpenter.

(Under *History*)—J. A. Froude, Seeley, G. Adam Smith.
(Under *Science*)—Huxley, A. Wallace, Frazer, K. Pearson.
(Under *Poetry*)—C. Rossetti, R. W. Dixon, Hopkins, Patmore, Noyes (and the notes on some of those in the general Introduction).
(Under *Criticism*)—Myers, Pattison.

A. THE OXFORD MOVEMENT

The Oxford Movement and its sequels may be studied in the biographies of the leaders mentioned below and also in the biographies of Cardinal Manning, Archbishop Tait, Archbishop Benson, Archbishop Davidson, Bishop King, Lord Halifax and others whose names will be suggested by these books. Two histories may be specifically named—

R. W. CHURCH—*The Oxford Movement*, 1891.
WILFRID WARD—*William George Ward and the Oxford Movement*, 1889.

Both of these deal with the earlier stages of the Movement. To them should be added Geoffrey Faber's *Oxford Apostles*.

The influence of the Movement in poetry may be seen in Christina Rossetti and R. W. Dixon; in Coventry Patmore, Gerard Manley Hopkins, Dolben and, a little later, Alice Meynell and Francis Thompson; and a complete or partial reaction against it in Clough, J. A. Froude and Mark Pattison: to name only some who are included in this bibliography. See also the notes on Miss Yonge and J. H. Shorthouse (under *Novels*); and Joseph Ellis Baker, *The Novel and the Oxford Movement*, 1932.

Two famous co-operative works of the early days of the Movement should be specially mentioned here.

A. *Tracts for the Times* appeared from 1833 to 1841. Newman was the principal contributor, and his *Tract 90, Remarks on Certain Passages in the Thirty-Nine Articles*—which points out what is now commonly accepted, that these passages are susceptible of a Catholic interpretation—may be considered to have brought on the storm which ended the first phase of the Movement. Other famous *Tracts* are noted here under the names of Isaac Williams and Pusey. The *Tracts* were subsequently collected in volume form, and some selections are also obtainable.

B. *Lyra Apostolica*, 1832 and later, contains sacred poems by the leaders of the Movement in its early stages. The best known are Newman's *Lead, kindly Light*, and *Thou to wax fierce*, and Keble's translation from the Greek, *Hail, gladdening Light*.

KEBLE, JOHN (1792-1866)

The Christian Year, 1827.
Sermon on National Apostasy, July 1833 (printed in *Sermons Academical and Occasional*, 1847).
Contributions to *Lyra Apostolica*, 1832-33.
Contribution to *Tracts for the Times*, 1833-41.
Lyra Innocentium, 1846.
On Eucharistical Adoration, 1857.
Letters of Spiritual Counsel and Guidance, 1870.
Parochial Sermons, 1867-80 (these appeared under various titles).
Occasional Papers and Reviews, 1877 (including a letter on Keble from Newman).

Keble was Professor of Poetry at Oxford, and his lectures on poetry are important and original; they were delivered in Latin, but have been translated by E. K. Francis (1912). His sense that poetry is akin to prayer reappears in the now influential work of the Abbé Brémond.

The most authoritative biographies are those by Sir John Coleridge, 1869, and Walter Lock, 1895, but the general studies noted above should also be consulted. Keble's sermon on *National Apostasy* has been regarded as marking the beginning of the Oxford Movement (see introduction to this section); by his other writings and teaching he influenced not only his own generation but all the later history of the Church of England, and the minds of many outside his own communion.

FROUDE, RICHARD HURRELL (1803-36)

Contributions to *Lyra Apostolica*, 1832-33.
Remains, ed. J. B. Mozley, 1837 and 1839.

In spite of R. H. Froude's youth and the small bulk of his writings left to us, he was one of the most striking and influential figures of his time.

WILLIAMS, ISAAC (1802-65)

Williams also contributed to *Lyra Apostolica* and wrote other devotional poetry, of which some is familiar in hymn-books: *The Cathedral*, 1838; *Thoughts in Past Years*, 1838 and 1852; *The Baptistery*, 1842; *The Altar*, 1847, etc. His *Devotional Commentary on the Gospel Narrative* (reprinted in 1869-70 from earlier volumes), like his sermons and his *Autobiography* (written 1851, published 1892), shows his devout, gentle, inflexible and scrupulous temper. He too contributed to the *Tracts for the Times*, and his *Tract 80*, on *Reserve in Communicating Religious Knowledge*, was widely misrepresented and caused as much scandal as Newman's *Tract 90*.

NEWMAN, JOHN HENRY (1801-90)

Though Keble was, in a sense, the beginner of the Oxford Movement, Newman was, until his secession in 1845, looked upon as its leader. He contributed to *Lyra Apostolica* and to *Tracts for the Times* (see above). His greatest works, with the exception of the *Parochial Sermons* of 1837-42, were written after his submission to Rome.

As a poet he is to be classed among the minor poets. *The Dream of Gerontius*, however, has virtue, and Newman was too fine a critic ever to let anything bad appear from his pen. In his collected poems he never sinks below a certain level. If *Lead, kindly Light* (to which he himself gave the title of *The Pillar of the Cloud*) is his best known piece, his real best is often reminiscent of George Herbert.

An Essay on the Development of Christian Doctrine, 1845.
Loss and Gain, 1848 (novel).
Lectures on Certain Difficulties felt by Anglicans in Submitting to the Catholic Church, 1850.

With these three books should be classed the much greater *Apologia pro Vita Sua*, 1864, and *The Idea of a University*, 1852, and *An Essay in Aid of a Grammar of Assent*, 1870.

His other works include—

Discourses to Mixed Congregations, 1849.
Sermons Preached on Various Occasions, 1857.
The Dream of Gerontius, 1865.
Verses on Various Occasions, 1868.

There is an excellent volume of selections from the prose works, *A Newman Treasury*, chosen and edited by C. F. Harrold, 1943 and another of the Prose and Poetry edited by Geoffrey Tillotson, 1957. The standard *Life* is by Wilfrid Ward, 1912, and Sean O'Faolain's *Newman's Way* is an excellent study of the early life. Collected Works (36 vols.), 1868-81.

The earlier *Letters and Correspondence*, with a brief autobiography, were edited by Miss Mozley, 1891; *Catholic Life and Letters*, ed. W. Meynell (under the pseudonym of J. Oldcastle), 1887.

WARD, WILLIAM GEORGE (1812-82)

Ward is best known to most people, perhaps, through Tennyson's poem addressed to him—'most generous of all ultramontanes'. His *Ideal of a Christian Church*, 1844, written while he was still nominally an Anglican, was officially condemned by the authorities of the University of Oxford, and only the veto of the proctors prevented the attempt to deprive him of his degree. Even then he was in fact in his views what Tennyson called him. The most important of his later works is the *Essays on the Philosophy of Theism* (reprinted from *The Dublin Review*, 1884), but his influence on the thought of his time is not to be measured by his books, most of which are now little read.

Wilfrid Ward: *William George Ward and the Oxford Movement*, 1889; William George Ward and the Catholic Revival, 1893.

See also Maisie Ward's *Life of Wilfrid Ward*, the earlier chapters.

PUSEY, EDWARD BOUVERIE (1800-82)

After the secession of Newman (1845), Pusey was popularly looked upon as the leader of the Tractarians, his position in the University of Oxford and his learning giving him an authority which he accepted though he did not seek it. His life by Liddon and others (1893-94) tells the history of the later stages, as well as the earlier, of the Oxford Movement. His own writings have not the grace of Newman's, but there is a solid dignity and strength in them. Of those mentioned below, all but the second and fourth are sermons.

The Holy Eucharist: a Comfort to the Penitent, 1843.
The Doctrine of the Real Presence, 1856.
The Nature of Faith in relation to Reason, 1855.
Eirenicon, 1865; second, 1866; third, 1869. (These three pamphlets form one of the first serious attempts at suggesting a basis for reunion between the Churches of Rome and England.)
University Sermons, 1872.
Parochial and Cathedral Sermons, 1883.

Pusey contributed to the *Tracts for the Times* what was in effect a treatise on *Baptism*, Nos. 67-9; unlike other *Tracts*, these were signed.

NEALE, JOHN MASON (1818-66)

Neale's immense learning is shown in his church histories:

Introduction to the History of the Holy Eastern Church, 1850.
History of the Holy Eastern Church (5 vols., unfinished), 1873,

and other historical and theological works. He also wrote many tales and books for the young, mainly historical, from *Herbert Tresham*, 1842, to *Theodora Phranza*, 1857, most of them of considerable merit. To the ordinary reader he is best known as a hymn-writer and translator of more than considerable merit; he ranks, indeed, almost with Charles Wesley in the quality and the quantity of his work, though his hymns and translations alike are often sadly mangled by editors. (There is a shocking instance in the *Songs of Praise* version of the Easter hymn, *Come ye faithful, raise the strain.*) A few of the more familiar among his translations are *Jerusalem the Golden* (with the other parts of the same hymn— *Brief life is here our portion*, etc.); *All glory, laud and honour*; *Jesu, the very thought is sweet*; *Fierce was the wild billow*: among his original hymns, *Art thou weary, art thou languid*; *O happy band of pilgrims*. In the old edition of *Hymns Ancient and Modern* he was responsible, as author or translator, for about one-eighth of the entire number, and the proportion is still high in more recent collections. There is a collected edition of his *Hymns, Sequences and Carols*, 1914.

A brief *Life* by R. F. Littledale, himself one of the minor lights of the Movement and interesting for his influence on Christina Rossetti, was prefaced to the 2nd edition of Neale's *Essays*, 1867; and there is a longer *Life* by Mrs E. A. Towle, 1907.

LIDDON, HENRY PARRY (1829-90)

On the Divinity of Our Lord and Saviour Jesus Christ (Bampton Lectures), 1866.

Some Elements of Religion, 1870 (pub. 1872), and volumes of sermons. Liddon was one of the greatest preachers in an age of great preachers. He also wrote the first three volumes of the standard life of Pusey, but died before completing it.

CHURCH, RICHARD WILLIAM (1815-90)

Church's *History of the Oxford Movement* appeared in 1891, just after his death, and remains one of the major pieces of historical writing of the century. In his lifetime he was also known as a great preacher, and his sermons keep their life and intellectual value still, like those of F. W. Robertson; and also as a literary critic of power and subtlety, and here again his work is not outmoded. His *Anselm* 1843 (expanded 1870), and *Dante*, 1850, showed his understanding of medieval thought and history; his *Spenser*, 1879, and *Bacon*, 1884 keep their place among the most discerning and best balanced studies of Spenser and Bacon. He did much reviewing of the graver kind, and his *Essays and Reviews* were collected in 1854, his *Occasional Papers* in 1897. Among his sermons may be mentioned—

Human Life and its Conditions, 1878.
The Gifts of Civilization, 1880.
The Discipline of the Christian Character, 1885.
Cathedral and University Sermons, 1892.
Pascal and other Sermons, 1893.
Life and Letters, ed. M. C. Church, 1895.

BRIGHT, WILLIAM (1824-1901)

A History of the Church, A.D. 313-451, 1860.
The Age of the Fathers, 1903.

Also more definitely theological works, and some well-known hymns.

B. MAURICE AND OTHERS

MAURICE, FREDERICK DENISON (1805-72)

On one side Maurice marks the breakdown of theological opposition to German influence in philosophy; and he himself inaugurated a new philosophical criticism, especially in Kantian criticism. His expression of theological opinions was much misunderstood in his lifetime, partly through his own obscurity, and his *Theological Essays*, 1853, lost him his chair at King's College, London; but there was, in fact, no doubt of his orthodoxy. On the other side his passion for social justice had an equally wide influence, and can be traced through T. H. Green to Gore and later men.

Moral and Metaphysical Philosophy, 1871-72.
Subscription no Bondage, 1835.
The Kingdom of Christ, 1838.
Christmas Day and other Sermons, 1843,

and other volumes of sermons.

The Word Eternal and the Punishment of the Wicked, 1853.
What is Revelation?, 1859.

The Claims of the Bible and of Science, 1863.
Life by Sir F. Maurice, 1884.

The last three of Maurice's books mentioned above touch on some of the questions which most agitated the minds of men from the middle of the century onwards. Two more writers should be noted here, as having much importance in their time: Colenso and the very popular Farrar.

COLENSO, JOHN WILLIAM (1814-83)

Colenso was a mathematician, whose text-books are not entirely out of date. He was less successful, though he caused a remarkable sensation, when he applied mathematical methods to a *Critical Examination of the Pentateuch*, 1862-79. The importance of the book lies not in itself, but in its significance as a popular work which made the general public aware—to its great alarm —of the tendencies of modern criticism.

FARRAR, FREDERICK WILLIAM (1831-1903)

Farrar wrote popular books and stories on early Church history; he also, though it is perhaps unkind to mention them here, wrote school stories—*Eric, or Little by Little*, 1858; *St Winifred's, or the World of School*, 1862. More typical of one side of the thought of his time are—

Eternal Hope, 1878.
Mercy and Judgment, 1881.

ROBERTSON, FREDERICK WILLIAM (1816-53)

Address delivered at the Opening of the Working Men's Institute, Brighton, 1849.
Two Lectures on the Influence of Poetry on the Working Classes, 1852.
Lectures and Addresses on Literary and Social Topics, 1858.
Expository Lectures on St Paul's Epistle to the Corinthians, 1859.
Sermons preached at Trinity Chapel, Brighton, 5 series, 1855, 1857, 1859, 1890.
Literary Remains, 1876.
Letters, with a Life, ed. Stopford Brooke, 1865.

Some of Robertson's sermons, redistributed in their order, are obtainable in *Everyman's Library*.

'He testifies to what he himself has seen and known. . . . People weary of unreality find in Robertson a mind which is sure with-

out being insincere, forcible without being partisan, which is
brave as well as tender, strong as well as humble.'

Samuel Barnett.

DALE, ROBERT WILLIAM (1829-95)

Dale was one of the greatest, if not the greatest, of Nonconformist preachers and theologians of the period. Note especially:

The Atonement, 1875.
The Epistle to the Ephesians, 1882.
The Living Christ and the Four Gospels, 1890.
Fellowship with Christ, and other Discourses, 1891.
Christian Doctrine, 1894.
Essays and Addresses, 1899.

C. THE CAMBRIDGE TEXTUAL CRITICS

Three great textual critics—'the Cambridge three'—go together. By their labours the Greek text of the New Testament was, except for some details, established: Westcott and
Hort's *New Testament* appeared in 1881 and has been superseded only to a certain extent by later discoveries of early
texts; but they were far more even than great students. All
were notable preachers and theologians, and the first two
also distinguished themselves as bishops who were concerned
for the social as well as the spiritual welfare of their flocks.
Westcott succeeded Lightfoot as Bishop of Durham.

LIGHTFOOT, JOSEPH BARBER (1828-89)

Commentaries on Galatians, 1865, Philippians, 1868, Colossians and
Philemon, 1875.
A Fresh Revision of the New Testament, 1871.
Answer to an Article on Supernatural Religion (*Contemporary Review*, Dec.
1874 to May 1877; reprinted with additions, 1889),

and many works on early Church history, patristic and Biblical
subjects, as well as sermons.

Life, by B. F. Westcott, 1894.

WESTCOTT, BROOKE FOSS (1825-1901)

General Survey of the History of the Canon of the New Testament during
the first Four Centuries, 1855.
Characteristics of the Gospel Miracles, 1859.
Introduction to the Study of the Gospels, 1860.

The Bible in the Church, 1864.
The Gospel of the Resurrection, 1866 (and later editions).
A General View of the History of the English Bible, 1868.
Commentaries on St John, 1882, Epistles of St John, 1883, Epistle to the
    Hebrews, 1889.
Christus Consummator, 1886.
Social Aspects of Christianity, 1887.
    (Note: Westcott's intervention was mainly responsible for a just settle-
    ment to the great Durham coal-dispute of 1892.)
The Victory of the Cross, 1888.
Essays in the History of Religious Thought in the West, 1891.
The Gospel of Life, 1892,

and other works.

Life and Letters, by Arthur Westcott, 1903.

HORT, FENTON JOHN ANTHONY (1828-92)

The Way, the Truth and the Life (Hulsean Lectures for 1871), 1893.
Judaistic Christianity, 1894.
Six Popular Lectures on the Ante-Nicene Fathers, 1895.
The Christian Ecclesia, 1897,

and sermons.

Life and Letters, by A. F. Hort, 1896.

D. THE LAST GENERATION

Three representatives only of the next generation of theologians shall be noted. The first, Tyrrell, is the clearest exponent of that 'modernism' which was officially condemned
by the Roman Church, and he was himself condemned. He
may be contrasted in his eager impatience with the second,
Baron Friedrich von Hügel, who was able to reconcile intellectual freedom and speculation with orthodoxy—at least, he
was not condemned. In pure thought Von Hügel is the
greatest of the three. The third is the Anglican Charles Gore:
though he was looked upon at first with suspicion as tainted
with modern critical heresies, he lived, without retreating
from his position, to be accepted by the orthodox and considered old-fashioned by the more advanced; his theological
influence was important, but was probably exceeded by his
influence as a prophet of social righteousness.

TYRRELL, GEORGE (1861-1909)

Nova et Vetera, 1897.
Hard Sayings, 1898.
External Religion, 1899.
The Faith of the Millions (coll. articles), 1901-02.
Oil and Wine, 1902.
Lex Orandi, 1903.
Lex Credendi, 1906.

This book showed his modernism unmistakably.

Through Scylla and Charybdis, 1907.
Mediaevalism, 1908.
Christianity at the Cross-roads, 1909.
Autobiography, and Life, by Maude D. Petre, 1912.

VON HÜGEL, BARON FRIEDRICH (1852-1925)

Von Hügel, 'that lay-bishop in the Church of God', was only half British by birth, and was not naturalized until ten years before his death; but he lived most of his life in England, wrote in English though sometimes with a German flavour in his style, and exercised so strong an influence upon the religious thought of all communions and of many people outside any communion that it would be absurd to ignore him.

The Mystical Element of Religion, 1908.
Eternal Life, 1912.
The German Soul, 1916 (a valiant protest against wholesale condemnation).
Essays and Addresses on the Philosophy of Religion, 1921; 2nd series, 1926.
The Reality of God, and Religion and Agnosticism, 1931.
Selected Letters, 1896-1924, with a memoir by Bernard Holland, 1927.
Letters to a Niece, 1928.

GORE, CHARLES (1853-1932)

ed. Lux Mundi, 1890, and contributed to it the essay on The Holy Spirit and Inspiration.

Lux Mundi comes midmost of the succession of collections of theological essays which show the gradual permeation of the Church of England with 'modern' critical ideas: *Essays and Reviews*, 1861, and *Foundations*, 1912, are the other two. In each there are phrases, and in the first and last contributions, which would hardly be accepted by sober theologians, however advanced, but in the main the opinions expressed there are now taken for granted.

co-editor, A New Commentary on Holy Scripture, 1928.
The Church and the Ministry, 1889.
The Sermon on the Mount, 1896.
The Body of Christ, 1901.
Christian Moral Principles, 1921.
Belief in God, 1921; The Deity of Christ, 1922; Belief in Christ, 1922;
    The Holy Spirit and the Church, 1924.
Christ and Society, 1928.
Jesus of Nazareth, 1929.
The Philosophy of the Good Life, 1930.
Life, by Leonard F. Prestige, 1935.

PHILOSOPHY

THERE is no attempt here to group the philosophers in 'schools'; they are put together rather according to their common interests and subjects, with some, but not too much, regard to chronology; and a general warning should be given that there was a great deal of cross-fertilization of thought, both between these sections and between philosophy and religion and philosophy and science.

Note 1: *Mind* originated in 1876 and was edited for the first sixteen years by G. Croom Robertson. The Aristotelian Society was founded in 1878 and its *Proceedings* were published from 1887 onwards.

Note 2: The clearest exposition of some of the problems which are exercising philosophers at the present day is in A. N. Whitehead's *Science and the Modern World* (1926); it may be thought that many of the writers noted in this bibliography were remote from them, but it is not impossible to see how they developed and how they are connected with other movements of thought and knowledge.

A. LOGIC.

> Whewell, Herschel, Venn, De Morgan, Boole, Jevons, W. K. Clifford, Bertrand Russell, A. N. Whitehead.

B. THE BEGINNINGS OF NINETEENTH-CENTURY PHILOSOPHY.

> James Mill, Sir William Hamilton, Mansel, Ferrier, Morell, J. Grote, G. H. Lewes, J. H. Stirling.

C. HEGEL, KANT AND SPINOZA; WITH A NOTE ON SOME PLATONISTS.

> 1. S. H. Hodgson, Edward Caird, T. H. Green, Nettleship, H. Sidgwick, W. Wallace, F. H. Bradley, Bosanquet, Seth (Pringle Pattison), Adamson, Romanes, James Martineau, Campbell

Fraser, Sorley, Balfour, R. B. Haldane, A. E. Taylor.

    II. Jowett, Inge, Lowes Dickinson.

D. PSYCHOLOGY AND PHILOSOPHY.

Bain, James Ward, G. F. Stout.

E. POLITICAL ECONOMY, SOCIOLOGY, ANTHROPOLOGY, CONNECTED WITH PHILOSOPHY.

John Stuart Mill, Herbert Spencer, Havelock Ellis, Westermarck, Hobhouse.

F. BIOLOGY AND THE PHYSICAL SCIENCES, CONNECTED WITH PHILOSOPHY.

Lloyd Morgan, J. S. Haldane.

G. MODERN PHILOSOPHERS.

G. E. Moore, F. C. S. Schiller, S. Alexander, McTaggart.

H. W. W. READE, S. BUTLER, E. CARPENTER.

See also under—

Science (A. R. Wallace, Huxley, Frazer, Karl Pearson).
Theology (Newman, W. G. Ward, Von Hügel).
Poetry (passim).
Novels ('George Eliot,' May Sinclair).
Criticism and Essays (John Sterling, Pater, Mallock, Myers).

A. LOGIC

WHEWELL, WILLIAM (1794-1866)

History of the Inductive Sciences, 1837.
Philosophy of the Inductive Sciences, 1840.
Of the Plurality of Worlds (first published anon.), 1853.
William Whewell: an Account of his Writings, Todhunter, 1876.
Life and Correspondence, Mrs Stair Douglas, 1881.

HERSCHEL, SIR JOHN FREDERICK WILLIAM (1792-1871)

Preliminary Discourse on the Study of Natural Philosophy, 1830. This was described by Whewell as 'an admirable comment on the Novum Organum'.

Essays, 1857.

Familiar Lectures on Scientific Subjects, 1867.

VENN, JOHN (1834-1923)

Symbolic Logic, 1881.

The Logic of Chance (3rd ed. 1888).

Empirical Logic (2nd ed. 1907).

Venn came of an interesting family, and his *Venn Family Annals*, 1904, is worth reading.

DE MORGAN, AUGUSTUS (1806-71)

Formal Logic: or The Calculus of Inference Necessary and Probable, 1847. This was partly superseded by Boole's work, see below.

Syllabus of a Proposed System of Logic, 1860.

De Morgan was a pleasant writer on less technical matters, and his *Budget of Paradoxes*, 1872, contains excellent reading.

BOOLE, GEORGE (1815-64)

The Mathematical Analysis of Logic, 1847. This lays down the leading principles of—

An Analysis of the Laws of Thought on which are founded the Mathematical Theories of Logic and Probabilities, 1854.

Boole laid the foundations of modern logical calculus, and his work leads on to Jevons.

JEVONS, WILLIAM STANLEY (1835-82)

Remarks on the Australian Goldfields, 1859.

Pure Logic, 1864. The Coal Question, 1864.

The Substitution of Similars, 1869.

Elementary Lessons in Logic, 1870.

Primer of Logic, 1876.

Studies in Deductive Logic, 1880.

Principles of Science, 1874.

Theory of Political Economy, 1871.

Primer of Political Economy, 1878.

The State in Relation to Labour, 1882.

Methods of Social Reform, and other Papers, 1883.

Investigations in Currency and Finance, 1884.

Letters and Journal, edited by his Wife, 1886.

Jevons was, it will be noticed, as much a political economist as a logician, but he is put here because of his connection with Boole.

CLIFFORD, WILLIAM KINGDON (1845-79)

Lectures and Essays, ed. by F. Pollock and L. Stephen, with a Life by F. Pollock, 1879.
Mathematical Papers, ed. R. Tucker, 1882.
Common Sense of the Exact Senses, ed. and partly written by Karl Pearson, 1885.

Clifford, who was much admired by Huxley, was an illuminating lecturer and his essays are models in prose of their kind.

RUSSELL, BERTRAND ARTHUR WILLIAM (1872-)

(with Alfred North Whitehead) Principia Mathematica, Vol. I, 1910; Vol. II, 1912; Vol. III, 1912.
Principles of Mathematics, Vol. I, 1903.
Philosophical Essays, 1910.
Problems of Philosophy, 1911.
Our Knowledge of the External World, 1914.
Principles of Social Reconstruction, 1917.
Mysticism and Logic, 1918. Roads to Freedom, 1918.
Introduction to Mathematical Philosophy, 1919.
Education and the Social Order, 1938.
Power, 1938.
History of Western Philosophy, 1946.
My Philosophical Development, 1959,

and other works.

A good study is Alan Wood's Bertrand Russell: The Passionate Sceptic.

WHITEHEAD, ALFRED NORTH (1861-1948)

A Treatise on Universal Algebra, 1898.
(with Bertrand Russell) Principia Mathematica, 1910-12.
Science and the Modern World, 1926.
The Aims of Education, 1929.
Adventures of Ideas, 1933.
Nature and Life, 1934.
Modes of Thought, 1938.

Most of the work of A. N. Whitehead falls outside our period, but *Science and the Modern World* should be specially noted as providing an introduction to some of the problems which are most exercising philosophers at the present day. He represents the turning of some scientists away from determinism to a sort of vaguely apprehended mysticism. Their God is really not much unlike Matthew Arnold's (see Introduction).

(John Stuart Mill might be thought to belong to this company of logicians, but he will be found among the political economists.)

B. THE BEGINNINGS OF NINETEENTH-CENTURY PHILOSOPHY

MILL, JAMES (1773-1836)

Analysis of the Phenomena of the Human Mind, 1829.

Mill continued in the Benthamite tradition of Utilitarianism and the Associationist school.

James Mill: a Biography, A. Bain, 1882.

HAMILTON, SIR WILLIAM (1788-1856)

Philosophy of the Unconditioned, 1829.

In this book Hamilton widened the field of inquiry in English philosophy and helped to break down the provincialism of English thought.

Discussions, 1836.

Hamilton is further important, especially in this book, for his obstructionist attitude to the recognition of Kant and Hegel, whom he misinterpreted.

Lectures, on Metaphysics, 1859; on Logic, 1861.

MANSEL, HENRY LONGUEVILLE (1820-71)

The Limits of Religious Thought (Bampton Lectures), 1858.
The Philosophy of the Conditioned, 1866.
Letters, Lectures and Reviews, ed. Chandler, 1873.

Mansel took over Hamilton's doctrine of the relativity of knowledge, and worked out its theological implications.

FERRIER, JAMES FREDERICK (1808-64)

An Introduction to the Philosophy of Consciousness (*Blackwood's Magazine*, 1838-39, reprinted in *Remains*).
The Institutes of Metaphysic, 1854.
Lectures on Greek Philosophy and other Philosophical Remains, 1866.
Philosophical Works, 1875.

Ferrier gives the first sympathetic account of Hegel and Schelling.

MORELL, JOHN DANIEL (1816-91)

Historical and Critical View of the Speculative Philosophy of Europe in the Nineteenth Century, 1846.

Morell pays attention to the German school, especially to Hegel. His is the first attempt to come to grips with Hegel's own philosophical position. He condemns it, mainly on theological grounds.

GROTE, JOHN (1813-66)

Exploratio Philosophica, Pt. I, 1865; Pt. II, 1900.
Examination of the Utilitarian Philosophy, 1870—an acute criticism.
A Treatise on the Moral Ideals, 1876.

He 'made a definite advance beyond his English predecessors of all schools in the clearness with which he apprehended the difference between psychology and philosophy' (*D.N.B.*).

LEWES, GEORGE HENRY (1817-78)

Biographical History of Philosophy, 1845-46.

This expresses the prevailing Positivism in its interpretations; it is essentially opposed to German Idealism.

Comte's Philosophy of the Sciences, 1853.

Lewes wrote also the best English *Life of Goethe*, 1855, and other books.

STIRLING, JAMES HUTCHISON (1820-1909)

The Secret of Hegel, 1865.

The importance of this book was recognized by all outstanding contemporary thinkers in England as marking decisively a new departure in British philosophy and the beginning of a new period.

Analysis of Sir William Hamilton's Philosophy, 1865.
Lectures on the Philosophy of Law, 1871.
Complete Text-Book to Kant, 1881.
Philosophy and Theology, 1890.
What is Thought? or the Problem of Philosophy, 1900.
The Categories, 1903.

C. HEGEL, KANT AND SPINOZA;
WITH A NOTE ON SOME PLATONISTS

I

HODGSON, SHADWORTH HOLLOWAY (1832-1912)

Metaphysic of Experience, 1898—shows an early phase of empirical reaction against nineteenth-century post-Hegelian Idealism.

CAIRD, EDWARD (1835-1908)

A Critical Account of the Philosophy of Kant, 1877, 1889 (2nd ed. 1909).
Hegel, 1883.
The Social Philosophy and Religion of Comte, 1885.
Essays on Literature and Philosophy, 1892.
The Evolution of Religion, 1893.
The Evolution of Theology in the Greek Philosophy, 1904.
Lay Sermons and Addresses, 1907.

GREEN, THOMAS HILL (1836-82)

Introduction to Hume's Treatise on Human Nature, 1874.
Prolegomena to Ethics (incomplete at his death, ed. A. C. Bradley), 1883.
Works, with Memoir, ed. R. L. Nettleship, 1885-88.
An Estimate of the Value and Influence of Works of Fiction in Modern
    Times, ed. F. N. Scott, 1911.

The influence of Green's idealism upon the life as well as upon the thought of the last three decades of the nineteenth century was reinforced by his personal character and example as a strenuous worker in the cause of education and political and social reform. He was a tutor and lecturer at Balliol, and it was largely due to him that the empiricist logic of Mill lost its authority at Oxford in favour of a philosophy inspired by the great German thinkers, Kant and Hegel, as well as by the reviving study of Platonism. As in his lectures on Ethics Green is one of the most effective early critics of Utilitarian hedonism, so in his political theory he presents a philosophy of democracy based indeed upon the supreme value of personality but hostile to the *laisser faire* individualism taught by Herbert Spencer, and better fitted for a generation which was beginning to recognize the need for positive interventions by the State in the life of the community.

NETTLESHIP, RICHARD LEWIS (1846-92)

—who was equally influential as a tutor and lecturer, but published nothing but the memoir of Green and an essay on *The Theory of Education in Plato's Republic* (contributed to *Hellenica*, ed. Evelyn Abbot, 1880).

SIDGWICK, HENRY (1838-1900)

Sidgwick shows an advance on the Hedonism of Mill and Bentham. His chief work was in the fields of Ethics and Social Philosophy, to which he brought great knowledge, wide sympathies and an exceptional power of recognizing the value in opposing theories. In Ethics he developed a form of Utilitarianism, far less open to criticism than that of J. S. Mill, which did better justice to the position of the 'Intuitionist' school (e.g., Martineau). Sidgwick was one of the first philosophers to treat with respect the claims advanced by the new study of 'Psychical Research', of which his friend, F. W. H. Myers, was one of the pioneers.

The Methods of Ethics, 1874.
The Principles of Political Economy, 1883.
Outlines of the History of Ethics, 1886.
The Elements of Politics, 1891.
Practical Ethics, 1898.
Lectures on the Ethics of T. H. Green, Herbert Spencer and James
    Martineau, 1902.
Miscellaneous Essays and Addresses, 1904.
Lectures on Kant, 1905, ed. J. Ward.
Memoir, by Arthur Sidgwick and Mrs. E. M. Sidgwick, 1906.

WALLACE, WILLIAM (1844-97)

The Logic of Hegel (trans. from Hegel's *Encyclopaedia of Philosophical
    Sciences*), 1873.
Life of Arthur Schopenhauer, 1890.
Hegel's Philosophy of Mind (trans.), 1890.

Wallace begins the second Hegelian generation.

BRADLEY, FRANCIS HERBERT (1846-1924)

Bradley influenced the whole of idealistic and, by reaction, realistic thought.

The Presuppositions of Critical History, 1874.
Ethical Studies, 1876.
Principles of Logic, 1883 (revised with Commentary and Terminal
    Essays, 1922).
Appearance and Reality, 1893.
Essays on Truth and Reality, 1914.

To many laymen Bradley seems the most important philosopher of the last century. *Appearance and Reality* has achieved some popularity, and the prose of its kind is masterly.

See below under Bosanquet and John Stuart Mill.

BOSANQUET, BERNARD (1848-1923)

Logic, 1888.
Essentials of Logic, 1895.
Essays and Addresses, 1889.
History of Æsthetic, 1892.

Knowledge and Reality, 1892.
The Civilisation of Christendom, 1893.
The Psychology of the Moral Self, 1897.
The Philosophical Theory of the State, 1899, 1910.
Individuality and Destiny (Gifford Lectures, 1911-12; 2nd series, 1912-1913).
Three Lectures on Æsthetic, 1915.
Implication and Linnear Influences, 1919.
The Meeting of Extremes in Contemporary Philosophy, 1921.

F. H. Bradley and Bernard Bosanquet can hardly be thought of apart. They are the Castor and Pollux of 'Absolute' Idealism in England. Bradley's *Appearance and Reality*, characteristically put forward by the author as a 'metaphysical essay', is in fact an imposing presentation of an Absolutism in which every 'reality' is displayed as relatively unreal short of the total Real (Bosanquet's absolute Individual), but in which (as distinct from the Hegelian absolutism) thought itself is shown to be ultimately inadequate because inevitably abstract. Bradley is largely concerned to expose the insufficiency of empiricism (whether in Logic, Psychology or Metaphysics) and the shallowness of all forms of positivism. Bosanquet's most impressive work was in relation to the rather later movements of thought that began with the next century, in which the type of Idealism for which he stood became more and more on the defensive. With great vigour and freshness he seizes upon salient points for counter-attack in the anti-intellectualist movement (e.g., Bergson) and in the neo-Idealist doctrines which give to Time, Process and finite 'individuality' a reality and importance which he cannot allow to them. The philosophical influence of G. E. Moore and Bertrand Russell has become very great, perhaps even dominant, in this country in the period after 1914. It represents, though in different ways, a reaction against systematic speculation and a growing preoccupation with questions of logical and epistemological analysis.

SETH, ANDREW, afterwards PRINGLE PATTISON (1856-1931)

The Development from Kant to Hegel (Hibbert Lectures), 1882.

The first *informed* criticism of Hegelianism.

Essays in Philosophical Criticism, ed. A. Seth and R. B. Haldane, 1883.

Essays contributed by A. Seth, R. B. and J. S. Haldane, Bosanquet, Sorley, D. G. Ritchie, W. P. Ker, Henry Jones, James Bonar, T. B. Kilpatrick. It was a manifesto of the younger generation of neo-Kantians in England, its purpose 'to show how the principles of an idealistic philosophy may be brought to bear on the various problems of science, ethics and religion'.

Hegelianism and Personality (Balfour Lectures), 1887.

This marks the beginning of a reaction, within the lines of a general acceptance of Kant's work, against the neo-Kantian interpretation—a kind of 'back to Kant' movement. It shows the influence of Lotze.

Man's Place in the Cosmos, 1897 (enlarged, 1902).
The Philosophical Radicals, and other Essays, 1907.
The Idea of God in the Light of Recent Philosophy, 1917.
The Idea of Immortality, 1922.
Studies in the Philosophy of Religion, 1930.

ADAMSON, ROBERT (1852-1902)

On the Philosophy of Kant, 1879.
The Development of Modern Philosophy, ed. W. R. Sorley, 1903.

This expresses the characteristic beginnings of the empirical reaction against Idealism.

The Development of Greek Philosophy, ed. W. R. Sorley and R. P. Hardie, 1908.
A short History of Logic, ed. W. R. Sorley, 1911.

ROMANES, GEORGE JOHN (1848-94)

A Candid Examination of Theism by Physicus, 1878.
Animal Intelligence, 1881.
Scientific Evidences of Organic Evolution, 1882.
Mental Evolution in Animals, 1883.
Mental Evolution in Man, 1888.
Darwin and after Darwin, I, 1893; II, 1895.
Thoughts on Religion, 1895 (posthumous, ed. C. Gore).
Mind and Motion, 1895.
Essays, 1896.
Life and Letters, by Mrs Romanes, 1896.

Romanes came back to the problems of philosophy and religion through the problems raised by scientific investigation, as the titles of his books show.

MARTINEAU, JAMES (1805-1900)

A Study of Spinoza, 1882.
Types of Ethical Theory, 1885.

A Study of Religion, 1888.
The Seat of Authority in Religion, 1890.
Essays, Reviews and Addresses, 1890-91.
Life and Letters, by James Drummond and C. B. Upton, 1902.

FRASER, ALEXANDER CAMPBELL (1819-1914)

Campbell Fraser was concerned primarily with the nature and limits of knowledge. He was a theistic philosopher, insisting on a faith that is ultimately a moral faith and not only faith in reason but in the goodness as well as the rationality of ultimate power; and holding that divine veracity was the natural presupposition of the validity of human knowledge.

ed. Berkeley, 1871.
The Philosophy of Theism, 1895-96.
Berkeley and Spiritual Realism, 1908.
Biographia Philosophica, 1904. (Reminiscences.)

SORLEY, WILLIAM RITCHIE (1855-1935)

Sorley starts from the problems set by evolutionistic theory in ethical thought.

On the Ethics of Naturalism, 1885.
Recent Tendencies in Ethics, 1904.
The Interpretation of Evolution, 1909-10.
The Moral Life, 1911.
Moral Values and the Idea of God, 1918.
A History of English Philosophy, 1920.

BALFOUR, ARTHUR JAMES, LORD (1848-1930)

A Defence of Philosophic Doubt, 1879.
Essays and Addresses, 1893 (enlarged edition, 1905).
The Foundations of Belief, 1895.
Theism and Humanism, 1915.
Essays, Speculative and Political, 1920.
Theism and Thought, 1923.
Opinions and Argument, 1927.

Lord Balfour, by Ian Malcolm, is a personal study rather than a biography; the full biography by Blanche Dugdale, 1936, deals with the man and the statesman more than with the philosopher, but there is an Appendix on the philosophy of Balfour by Pringle-Pattison.

Balfour's style is charming and witty, and the delicacy of his prose is excellently suited to express his scepticism.

HALDANE, RICHARD BURDON, LORD (1856-1928)

Education and Empire, 1902.
The Pathway to Reality, 1903.
The Reign of Relativity, 1921.
The Philosophy of Humanism, 1922.
Human Experience, 1926.

See also under Seth.

Life, by Sir Frederick Maurice, 1937.

TAYLOR, ALFRED EDWARD (1869-1945)

The Problem of Conduct, 1901.
Elements of Metaphysics, 1903.
St Thomas Aquinas as a Philosopher, 1924.
Plato, the Man and his Work, 1927.
The Faith of a Moralist, 1930.
The Christian Hope of Immortality, 1938.

Taylor's work is written in a good, close, hard style. It can be read with pleasure by the layman.

II

The revival of Platonic studies in the nineteenth century was largely due in the first place to Jowett, the great Master of Balliol. Of the two others who follow him here, the first is at least as much theologian as philosopher, and the second was perhaps rather a popularizer—the word is not used in a derogatory sense—than, strictly speaking, a philosopher.

JOWETT, BENJAMIN (1817-93)

The Dialogues of Plato, trans. with Analyses and Introduction, 1871.
    (The Republic followed in 1888, and there was an edition of the original text with notes in coll. with Lewis Campbell, in 1894.)
Thucydides, 1881.
Aristotle's Politics, trans. with Introduction, etc., 1885.
College Sermons, 1895 (and other volumes of sermons).

'In philosophy he was content to be critical. . . . He had almost a horror of falling under one set of ideas to the exclusion of others' (D.N.B.). It should be noted that he stimulated T. H. Green to the study of Hegel, and his influence on the Balliol men of his time and so on later generations is immeasurable. He was one of the great minor figures of the Victorian age. His *Plato* is occasionally first-rate English prose.

There is a biographical study by Geoffrey Faber.

INGE, WILLIAM RALPH (1860-1954)

Christian Mysticism, 1899.
Studies of English Mystics, 1906.
Truth and Falsehood in Religion, 1906.
Personal Idealism and Mysticism, 1907.
The Philosophy of Plotinus, 1918.
Outspoken Essays, 1919, 1922.
Personal Religion and the Life of Devotion, 1924.
The Platonic Tradition in English Religious Thought, 1926,

and other works.

Vale, 1934—a brief autobiography.

Dean Inge's works on neo-Platonism are extremely valuable. As a publicist he is frequently deplorable in both thought and style.

Life, by Adam Fox.

DICKINSON, GOLDSWORTHY LOWES (1861-1932)

The Greek View of Life, 1896.
The Meaning of Good, 1901.
A Modern Symposium, 1905.
Justice and Liberty, 1908.
Religion and Immortality, 1911.
Appearances, 1914.
The European Anarchy, 1916.
The Magic Flute, 1920.
War: Its Nature, Cause and Cure, 1923.
The International Anarchy, 1904-14, 1926.
After Two Thousand Years; a dialogue between Plato and a modern young man, 1930.
John McTaggart Ellis McTaggart, 1931.
Life, by E. M. Forster, 1934.

D. PSYCHOLOGY AND PHILOSOPHY

See John Grote above.

BAIN, ALEXANDER (1818-1903)

The Senses and the Intellect, 1855.
The Emotions and the Will, 1859.

These two treatises form the connecting link between the Associationism of the Mills and the evolutionary philosophy of Herbert Spencer. Both John Stuart Mill and Spencer acknowledged their importance.

Mental and Moral Science: a Compendium of Psychology and Ethics, 1868.
Mind and Body, 1872.

Bain also edited the *Philosophical Remains* of G. Croom Robertson.

Autobiography, 1904.

WARD, JAMES (1843-1925)

Psychology (article in the *Encyclopaedia Britannica*, 1886).
Naturalism and Agnosticism, 1899.
The Realm of Ends, or Pluralism and Theism, 1911.
Heredity and Memory, 1913.
Psychological Principles, 1918.
A Study of Kant, 1922.

James Ward's article on *Psychology* in the *Encyclopaedia Britannica* (1886) marked the beginning of a new scientific spirit in psychology and the end of the reign of the dominant Associationism (e.g., Bain). His *Naturalism and Agnosticism* similarly exposed—though here Ward was not so early in the field—the attempts to erect an evolutionary agnostic science into a satisfying philosophy. (Ward was chiefly attacking the philosophy of Spencer.) His own constructive views were developed in *The Realm of Ends*, where he expounds a sort of personal idealism more akin to the spirit of Kant than of Hegel.

STOUT, GEORGE FREDERICK (1860-1944)

Analytic Psychology, 1896.
Manual of Psychology, Groundwork of Psychology, 1899.
Studies in Philosophy and Psychology, 1930.
Mind and Matter, 1931.
God and Nature, ed. with a memoir by his son, 1952.

E. POLITICAL ECONOMY, SOCIOLOGY, ANTHROPOLOGY, CONNECTED WITH PHILOSOPHY

MILL, JOHN STUART (1806-73)

Logic, 1843.
Principles of Political Economy, 1848.
On Liberty, 1859.
Representative Government, 1861.
Utilitarianism, 1863.

Examination of Sir William Hamilton's Philosophy, 1865.
The Subjection of Women, 1869.
Autobiography, 1873.

There is a good life by M. St John Parke, and an interesting introduction by F. R. Leavis to a selection, *Mill on Bentham and Coleridge*. See also Dorothea Krook's *Three Traditions of Moral Thought*—those of Mill, Matthew Arnold and F. H. Bradley.

John Stuart Mill, if not the most profound, was certainly the most influential nineteenth-century British philosopher, and he more than any other stimulated the Victorian general reader to an interest in philosophical discussion. In the judgment of continental critics he stood, and indeed still stands, as the representative thinker of his generation, and the exponent *par excellence* of nineteenth-century British empiricism. Though in the main faithful to the tenets of this school, positivist in its views of science, associationist in psychology, agnostic in religion, Mill had a mind of singular candour and breadth of sympathy. These characteristics, already exhibited in his essays on Bentham and Coleridge, were most strikingly shown in the development of his social philosophy from a narrow individualism to something very like a liberal socialism. In all his writings Mill laid himself open to damaging criticism, but in nearly all his work has been significant beyond his own day. Characteristic in both respects was his *Logic*, riddled with just criticism by his Idealist opponents, but, especially in his treatment of inductive method, breaking new ground in ways to which logicians of today confess their debt.

SPENCER, HERBERT (1820-1903)

Social Statics, 1851.
Principles of Psychology, 1855.
Education, 1861.
First Principles, 1862; recast in 1870, 1872.
The Principles of Biology, 1864 and 1867.
The Study of Sociology, 1873.
The Principles of Sociology, 1876-96.
The Principles of Ethics, 1879-93.
The Man versus the State, 1884.
Autobiography, 1904.
Life and Letters, D. Duncan, 1903.

There is an *Epitome of the Synthetic Philosophy* (i.e., of all Spencer's philosophical system) in one volume, by F. Howard Collins.

To his Victorian devotees Herbert Spencer stood out as the

supreme philosopher of the age. Today he looms much less large, but he remains an important figure, impressive for the breadth of his intellectual survey rather than for philosophical penetration or depth. To Spencer more than to any of his contemporaries the notion of evolution came as a master clue with which to interpret every department of experience, and over a long life he worked out his interpretation not only with assiduity but with a system and constructiveness unusual in an English thinker. His ignorance of nearly all preceding philosophy, his strong prejudices and a sort of mental deafness that made him unwilling to correct them, prevented the imposing structure of the Synthetic Philosophy from withstanding criticism enduringly. But his work in special fields, especially in Ethics, Psychology and Sociology, not only was an important influence on the development of these studies but contains matter of permanent value.

ELLIS, HENRY HAVELOCK (1859-1939)

The New Spirit, 1890.
The Criminal, 1890.
Man and Woman, 1894 (and other volumes of Studies in the Psychology of Sex, 1897, 1898, 1903, 1905, 1906, 1910, 1928).
Affirmations, 1897.
A Study of British Genius, 1904 (revised and enlarged, 1926).
Impressions and Comments, 1914, 1921, 1924.
Essays in War-Time, 1916.
The Philosophy of Conflict, 1919.
Little Essays of Love and Virtue, 1922.
The Dance of Life, 1923.
More Essays of Love and Virtue, 1931.
The Psychology of Sex: a Manual for Students, 1933.
From Rousseau to Proust, 1936.
Questions of our Day, 1936.

Two lives, A. Calder-Marshall's *Havelock Ellis* and J. S. Collis's *An Artist of Life*, are equally good in different ways.

Havelock Ellis began as a critic of literature and an editor of the older dramatists; indeed, it is possible that his work on some of the Elizabethans encouraged him in that sane study of sexual psychology in which he was a pioneer and with which his name is chiefly associated. His literary criticism and general essays show distinctive grace and charm, and both these and his psychological studies have had more influence on the reading public than the work of greater specialists.

WESTERMARCK, EDWARD ALEXANDER (1862-1939)

The History of Human Marriage, 1891 (5th ed. rewritten, 1921).
Marriage Ceremonies in Morocco, 1914.
Ritual and Belief in Morocco, 1926.
A Short History of Marriage, 1926.
The Origin and Development of the Moral Ideas, 1906, 1908.
The Goodness of Gods, 1926.
Ethical Relativity, 1932.
Early Beliefs and their Social Influence, 1932,

and other books.

Memories of My Life (Swedish, 1927; English, 1929).

(Most of Westermarck's work is in English, although he was a Swede by birth.)

Westermarck ranks perhaps as an anthropologist, a sociologist, a psychologist, rather than as a pure philosopher. His works on marriage are classic and need no introduction here.

HOBHOUSE, LEONARD TRELAWNEY (1864-1929)

The Theory of Knowledge, 1896.
Mind in Evolution, 1901.
Morals in Evolution, 1906.
Development and Purpose, 1913.
Metaphysical Theory of the State, 1918.
The Labour Movement, 1893.
Democracy and Reaction, 1904.

F. BIOLOGY AND THE PHYSICAL SCIENCES, CONNECTED WITH PHILOSOPHY

The scientific thought of the last hundred years, particularly that which grew out of the Darwinian hypothesis and the discoveries in the physical sciences, raised philosophical problems of which scientists themselves are becoming increasingly conscious. Something has already been noted concerning the mathematicians (see above under LOGIC), and here are representatives of other branches of learning:

MORGAN, CONWY LLOYD (1852-1936)

Animal Life and Intelligence, 1890.
Habit and Instinct, 1896.
Animal Behaviour, 1900.
The Interpretation of Nature, 1905.

Instinct and Experience, 1912.
Emergent Evolution, 1923.
Life, Mind and Spirit, 1926.
Mind at the Crossways, 1929.
The Animal Mind, 1930.
The Emergence of Novelty, 1933.

HALDANE, JOHN SCOTT (1860-1936)

See Seth, Essays in Philosophical Criticism, 1883.
Mechanism, Life and Personality, 1913.
The Philosophical Basis of Biology, 1931.
Materialism, 1932.
The Philosophy of a Biologist, 1935.

G. MODERN PHILOSOPHERS

MOORE, GEORGE EDWARD (1873-1958)

Principia Ethica, 1903.
Ethics, 1912.
Philosophical Studies, 1922.
The Philosophy of G. E. Moore, 1943.
Philosophical Papers, 1959.

Moore stands with Russell as being the most influential philosopher of the day as far as the layman is concerned. He wrote in an admirably clear and incisive style, with the clarity and coolness of the Cambridge atmosphere.

SCHILLER, FERDINAND CANNING SCOTT (1864-1937)

Riddles of the Sphinx, 1891 (revised 1910).
Humanism, 1903 (2nd ed. enlarged, 1912).
Studies in Humanism, 1907.
Plato or Protagoras?, 1908.
Formal Logic, 1912.
Problems of Belief, 1924,

and other works.

He may be taken with Moore as being anti-systematic.

ALEXANDER, SAMUEL (1859-1938)

Moral Order and Progress, 1889.
Locke, 1908.
The Basis of Realism, 1914.
Space, Time and Deity, 1920.
Spinoza and Time, 1921.
Art and Material, 1925.
Beauty and other Forms of Value, 1933.

McTAGGART, JOHN McTAGGART ELLIS (1866-1925)

Studies in the Hegelian Dialectic, 1896.
Studies in Hegelian Cosmology, 1901.
Some Dogmas of Religion, 1906.
A Commentary on Hegel's Logic, 1910.
The Nature of Existence, Vol. I, 1921; II, 1927.
Philosophical Studies, ed. S. V. Keeling, 1934.
Life, by G. L. Dickinson, 1931.
C. D. Broad, Examination of McTaggart's Philosophy, 1933.

McTaggart, who was one of the 'systematic' philosophers of the present century, might also have been included among the Hegelians, for his whole thought was influenced by his prolonged and intimate study of the Hegelian system. He represents, as a continental critic has put it, the extreme Hegelian 'left' in England: he stands, that is (unlike, for instance, Green or Caird), for an Idealism free from any close relation with or sympathy for Christian theology and the Christian traditions, non-religious in temper, and pluralistic rather than monistic. In the latter respect McTaggart's system is in striking contrast to those of Bradley or Bosanquet, the absolutists of their day. All his working life was passed at Cambridge.

H

Three writers who have different claims to be included in this part of the bibliography may be grouped together here, though they have little in common. Two of them had original minds, and yet they were rather popularizers than profound original thinkers.

READE, WILLIAM WINWOOD (1838-75)

The Martyrdom of Man, 1872—the most vigorous expression of 'anti-God' opinion in the nineteenth century.

Reade is, however, a much less considerable person than the other two.

BUTLER, SAMUEL (1835-1902)

PHILOSOPHICAL AND SCIENTIFIC WRITINGS:
The Fair Haven, 1873.
Life and Habit, 1877.
Evolution, Old and New, 1879.

Unconscious Memory, 1880.
Luck or Cunning, 1886.
ESSAYS AND CRITICISM:
Alps and Sanctuaries, 1881.
Ex Voto, 1887.
The Authoress of the Odyssey, 1897.
Essays on Life, Art and Science, 1903.
Selection from Notebooks, 1912.
NOVELS:
Erewhon, 1872.
Erewhon Revisited, 1901.
The Way of All Flesh, 1903.
Life, by H. Festing Jones, 1920: this has been modified by Philip Hender-
    son's Samuel Butler: The Incarnate Bachelor and S. B. Harkness's
    The Career of Samuel Butler.

Butler's own account of his family, in *The Way of All Flesh* and
elsewhere, is severely handled by Mrs R. S. Garnett, in *Samuel
Butler and his Family Relations*, 1926. There is a general critical
study by Gilbert Cannan, 1915; and C. E. M. Joad's *Samuel Butler*,
1925, gives a critical exposition by a philosopher of Butler's
beliefs and theories. There is a good selection with an able introduction by G. D. H. Cole, *The Essential Samuel Butler*. See also
under Darwin.

Samuel Butler's wit and ingenuity are as undeniable as his
crankiness, and he had a style which gave an appearance of
brilliance or wisdom to what was sometimes merely silly or wil-
fully perverse. Yet there was wisdom mingled with the crankiness
and perversity, and the *Notebooks* and novels particularly have
set many other minds working.

CARPENTER, EDWARD (1844-1929)

Narcissus and other papers, 1873.
Towards Democracy, 1883; complete edition, 1913.
England's Ideal and other papers, 1887.
Civilisation, its Cause and Cure, 1889; enlarged, 1921.
Angels' Wings, 1898.
Love's Coming of Age, 1903.
The Art of Creation, 1904.
The Drama of Love and Death, 1912.
The Headling of Nations, 1915.
Towards Industrial Freedom, 1917.
Pagan and Christian Creeds, 1920.
My Days and Dreams: autobiographical notes, 1916.
E. Lewis—Edward Carpenter: an exposition and an appreciation, 1915.
A. H. Sime—Edward Carpenter: his ideas and ideals, 1916.
T. Swan—Edward Carpenter, the man and his message, 1922.

Carpenter's attitude was a queer mixture of Whitman and D. H. Lawrence, with sunny gods, however, instead of dark ones. His socialism was communistic, anti-property; government in its decay was to be replaced by the reign of love; here a mixture of Whitman and Henry George, the American who wrote the once famous *Progress and Poverty*.

POETRY

AN excellent guide to the work especially of the lesser poets of the periods is Alfred H. Miles: *Poets and Poetry of the Century*, which was published first in the nineties and afterwards in a new edition in 1905-06 (12 volumes). This is an anthology with introductory biographical notes and critical essays, many of which are of great value. For the latest poets mentioned here, see the four volumes of *Georgian Poetry*, published from 1912 onwards. Other anthologies which may be noted are *The Oxford Book of Victorian Verse* and—in part— *The Oxford Book of English Verse*, *Victorian Narrative Verse* (ed. Charles Williams), *Lyra Heroica* (ed. W. E. Henley), and the two series of *Poems of To-day*. The most famous Victorian Anthology, *The Golden Treasury of English Songs and Lyrics* (ed. F. Palgrave), in its original form contained nothing by Victorian poets, but Palgrave afterwards added a Second Series and there are varying supplements by other hands in some later editions published after the copyright expired. *Chambers's Cyclopaedia of English Literature* may be mentioned again here (see general introduction to this bibliography). There are also the later volumes of Ward's *English Poets*. One or other of these anthologies is likely to provide further examples of the work of poets whose books are not now easily obtainable.

To the critical essays in Miles, Chambers and Ward mentioned above may be added the last chapter in O. Elton's *The English Muse*, and the special critical works noted below under the names of their subjects. Lascelles Abercrombie's *Poetry, Its Music and Meaning*, may be consulted as an introduction to Prosody.

For convenience this section of the bibliography is divided into five, and the poets are arranged roughly in order of birth.

A. THE OLDER GENERATION.

W. S. Landor, R. E. Landor, Mrs Hemans, Hood,
W. M. Praed, Martin Tupper.

B. THE EARLY AND MID-VICTORIANS.

Ebenezer Elliott, Thomas Cooper, Gerald Massey,
W. Barnes, Beddoes, R. H. Horne, R. S. Hawker,
Tennyson, F. Tennyson, Charles Tennyson
Turner, FitzGerald, E. B. Browning, R. Browning,
Ferguson, de Vere, P. J. Bailey, A. H. Clough, M.
Arnold, Jean Ingelow, W. Cory, T. E. Brown,
Dobell, Alexander Smith.

C. THE PRE-RAPHAELITES AND AFTER.

William Allingham, D. G. Rossetti, C. Rossetti,
R. W. Dixon, W. Morris, Swinburne, Watts-
Dunton, P. B. Marston, W. B. Scott, T. Woolner.

D. THE LATE VICTORIANS.

I. Locker-Lampson, A. Dobson, A. Lang, W. E.
Henley, Newbolt.
II. Dolben, G. M. Hopkins, Coventry Patmore, F.
Thompson, L. Johnson, Alice Meynell.
III. James Thomson ('B.V.'), W. S. Blunt, R. Bridges,
W. Sharp, John Davidson, W. Watson, A. E.
Housman, H. Trench, L. Binyon, Lord Alfred
Douglas, W. B. Yeats, 'Æ.', E. Dowson.

E. THE GEORGIANS.

T. Sturge Moore, W. H. Davies, Ralph Hodgson,
De la Mare, G. Bottomley, W. W. Gibson, Mase-
field, E. Thomas, H. Monro, J. Freeman, A.
Noyes, L. Abercrombie, Drinkwater, J. Stephens,
Flecker, Squire, Brooke.

See also under
History (Macaulay).
Travel (Doughty).

Theology (Keble, I. Williams, Newman, Neale, Bright).
Philosophy (E. Carpenter).
Drama (Talfourd, Henry Taylor, Tom Taylor, Wilde,
   S. Phillips, L. Housman, J. M. Synge).
Novels (Peacock, C. Kingsley, G. Eliot, the Brontës,
   Thackeray, Lover, Hewlett, Hardy, Meredith, Steven-
   son, Kipling, Moore, Galsworthy, Sinclair, Middle-
   ton, Mackenzie, Cannan.
Children's Books (Rands, Macdonald, E. Nesbit).
Criticism and Essays (Leigh Hunt, Ruskin, 'Vernon Lee',
   Symons, Traill, Myers, Gosse, 'Q.', Belloc, Chester-
   ton, Baring).
Nonsense and Parody, Humour and Light Verse (passim).

A. THE OLDER GENERATION

LANDOR, WALTER SAVAGE (1775-1864)

Gebir, 1798 (revised 1803).
Count Julian, 1812.
Imaginary Conversations, 1824-29 (and later, see below).
Citation and Examination of William Shakespeare, 1834 (another
   imaginary conversation, based on the legend of Shakespeare's deer-
   stealing).
Pericles and Aspasia, 1836.
The Pentameron, 1837 (more imaginary conversations).
Works, 1846.
Hellenics, 1847 (revised 1859).
Last Fruit off an Old Tree, 1853.
Dry Sticks Faggoted, 1858.
Imaginary Conversations (in *The Athenaeum*), 1861-62.
Heroic Idylls, 1863.
Last Poems, 1863.
Letters and Unpublished Writings, ed. S. Wheeler, 1897-99.
Walter Savage Landor, Last Days, Letters and Conversations, ed. H. S.
   Minchin, 1934.

There is no absolutely complete edition of Landor, but the
edition of 1927-36, edited first by T. Earle Welby and later by
S. Wheeler, contains all his works with a few insignificant exceptions. It is, however, very expensive. There is a reasonably
full edition in the *Life and Works*, ed. Forster, 1876, and another
by C. G. Crump, 1891-92. There are Selections from the Poetry
in the *Golden Treasury* Series, and from the *Imaginary Conversations*

in the *World's Classics*, with excellent critical introductions by Colvin and E. de Selincourt respectively.

Forster's *Life* (1869) has been described as a life of Boythorn written by Podsnap. There are better critical studies by Sidney Colvin (1881), Malcolm Elwin (1941—and, based on this, *Landor: A Replevin*, 1958) and R. H. Super (1954).

Landor's poetry has been discussed in the previous volume, and his prose in the introduction to this volume. For first reading *Pericles and Aspasia* may be particularly recommended and some of the *Imaginary Conversations*, e.g., those which typify the tender, romantic element in him (*Aesop and Rhodope, Tiberius and Vipsania*), the easy argument between friendly equals of the conversation between *William Penn and Peterborough*, and the critical conversations between *Southey and Landor* on Milton and between *Southey and Porson* on Wordsworth.

LANDOR, ROBERT EYRES (1781-1869)

Count Arezzi, 1823. (Verse Drama.)
The Earl of Brecon, Faith's Fraud, The Ferryman, 1841. (Verse Dramas.)
The Impious Feast (i.e., Belshazzar's), 1828.
The Fawn of Sertorius, 1846. (Prose.)
The Fountain of Arethusa, 1848. (Prose.)

Robert Eyres Landor has been unjustly overshadowed by his elder brother. There is a volume of selections from his prose and verse, with a biographical and critical introduction by Eric Partridge, 1927. This will serve the student very well, since there is no collected edition, and the separate volumes are not easy to obtain. R. E. Landor had considerable gifts as a closet dramatist (his plays were not written to be acted), and as poet and prose-writer, and much of his brother's discipline; but the lyrical grace and the epigrammatic power are not so fully developed.

The Fawn of Sertorius is a charmingly told tale, much of it in dialogue form, but with good passages of narrative and description.

HEMANS, FELICIA DOROTHEA (1793-1835)

The Forest Sanctuary, 1825.
Records of Women, 1828.
Songs of the Affections, 1830.
Collected Works, 1839.

Mrs Hemans barely comes into the period, but her poetry is characteristic of the rather unregulated sensibility and enthusiasm of the minor literature of the thirties and forties. She had a genuine poetic gift, and her own writing is seldom weak, but she had a dangerous facility. Her personal charm is best seen in the letters printed in the *Memorials of Mrs Hemans*, by H. F. Chorley, 1836. There is also an edition of her poetical works, with a memoir, by W. M. Rossetti, 1873. Her most famous poems, *Casabianca*, *The Graves of a Household*, and *The Better Land*, hardly give a fair account of her work; better examples are *Despondency and Aspiration*, *The Treasures of the Deep*, and *The Hour of Death*.

HOOD, THOMAS (1799-1845)

The only poet except Beddoes (see pp. 214–15) with real quality between Keats and Tennyson, and with an unusual combination of comic and serious genius. Too much of his time was necessarily spent on hack-work, but even of this there is little which is entirely without value. His serious poetry has, on the whole, been ousted by his comic, but the *Ode to Autumn* is a fine piece of work. *The Song of the Shirt*, a bitter protest against sweated labour, first appeared in *Punch* in 1843. Of his other graver poems, *Eugene Aram* is perhaps the best known.

Odes and Addresses (with John Hamilton Reynolds), 1825.
The Plea of the Midsummer Fairies, 1827.
Whims and Oddities, 1826, 1827.
Comic Annuals, 1830-39 (re-issued as *Hood's Own*).
Up the Rhine, 1839.
Complete Works, 1862, 1869, 1882-84; in one volume, 1912.

Much of Hood's work appeared in *The London Magazine*, of which he was sub-editor 1821-23, *The New Monthly Magazine*, of which he was editor 1841-43, *Hood's Monthly Magazine* and *Punch*.

Memorials (not good) by his son and daughter was published in 1860. The biographical and critical sketch by Canon Ainger, published as preface to a selection of the humorous poems in 1897, is good. Walter Jerrold, *Thomas Hood. His Life and Times*, 1907, adds some letters, and these have been further added to by Leslie A. Marchand, *Letters of Thomas Hood*, 1945.

PRAED, WINTHROP MACKWORTH (1802-39)

Collected Poems, edited by Derwent Coleridge, 1864.
Political and Occasional Poems, ed. Sir George Young, 1888.

Praed was the first and perhaps the most brilliant writer of light verse and *vers de société* in the period, the master of Locker-Lampson, Lang, Dobson, Calverley, Seaman and others. It is not only as a comic versifier, however, that he is important in the poetic tradition, for his experiments in metre did much to break the old prosodic fetters.

There is a biography, *A Poet in Parliament*, by Derek Hudson, 1939, and a good selection, with introduction and commentary, by Kenneth Allott, 1953.

TUPPER, MARTIN (1810-89)

Proverbial Philosophy, 1838 (expanded into four series, 1839-76).
My Life as an Author, 1886.

Tupper was not a poet, but his flat lines have become proverbial in more than one sense, and he deserves to be recorded as one of the remarkable phenomena of the nineteenth century. Andrew Lang dealt fairly and wittily with him in his *Letters to Dead Authors*. A specimen of his rhymed verse, with comments, may be found in Thackeray's essay *On Alexandrines*, in *Roundabout Papers*. The following extract will serve as an example of his usual manner, which has the sententiousness of Polonius without his share of wisdom.

> To aim at thine own happiness, is an end idolatrous and evil,
> In earth—yea, in heaven, if thou seek it for itself, seeking thou shalt not find.
> Happiness is a roadside flower, growing on the highways of Usefulness,
> Plucked, it shall wither in thy hand; passed by, it is fragrance to thy spirit.

(Contrast Blake's *He that bends to himself a joy*.)

B. THE EARLY AND MID-VICTORIANS

ELLIOTT, EBENEZER (1781-1849)

Corn-law Rhymes, 1831.
Collected Works, 1876.

Elliott expressed with passion the emotions and convictions which were behind the Chartist movement. He was of it, soul and body. Two other poets who were definitely but less centrally in that movement should be mentioned with him, though they were younger men and the best work of one was not in poetry but in his autobiography: Thomas Cooper and Gerald Massey.

COOPER, THOMAS (1805-92)

The Purgatory of Suicides, 1845.
The Paradise of Martyrs, 1873.
Poetical Works, 1877.

Cooper also wrote tales and sermons, but his most memorable book is none of these nor of his poems, but *The Life of Thomas Cooper written by himself*, 1872, one of the best of nineteenth-century autobiographies.

MASSEY, GERALD (1828-1907)

was consciously a kind of Alton Locke (see Charles Kingsley) in real life. His poems are sometimes too poetical, and his later work is vaguely mystical and unsatisfactory, but he had a touch of the true fire.

Poems and Chansons, 1848.
Voices of Freedom and Lyrics of Love, 1850.
The Ballad of Babe Christabel, 1854.
Complete Poetical Works, with memoir by Samuel Smiles, 1861.
My Lyrical Life (i.e., his chief poems, collected by his daughter Christabel), 1899,

and many other books.

BARNES, WILLIAM (1801-86)

Poems of Rural Life in the Dorset Dialect, 1844; 2nd collection (Hwomely Rhymes), 1859; 3rd collection, 1863; three collections with a glossary, 1879.
Poems of Rural Life in common English, 1868.

Barnes's exquisite lyrics are almost the only poems in English dialect which are worthy to be set beside the numerous Scottish poems of the same kind. There is a good essay on him in Sir Arthur Quiller Couch's *The Poet as Citizen*. A selection of his poems, with an introduction by Thomas Hardy, appeared in 1908, and another, edited by Geoffrey Grigson, in 1950. *Life* by G. Dugdale, 1953.

BEDDOES, THOMAS LOVELL (1803-49)

The Brides' Tragedy, 1822.
Death's Jest-Book (begun in 1825, published 1850-51, with memoir by T. F. Kelsall).

Poems, ed. Gosse, 1890 (and new edition, 1928).
Letters, ed. Gosse, 1894.
Complete Poetical Works, ed. H. W. Donner, 1935.

In spite of the dramatic form and the date of most of Beddoes's work, his place seems to be here. His life and works are exhaustively studied in the two volumes by H. W. Donner—*The Browning Box* and *Thomas Lovell Beddoes*. Lytton Strachey's chapter in *Books and Characters—The Last Elizabethan*—and the volume of selections with a critical preface by F. L. Lucas in the *Poets in Brief* series, 1932, may be recommended as an introduction. He was addicted to the macabre, and he has more than a touch of Webster.

HORNE, RICHARD HENRY OR HENGIST (1803-84)

Cosmo de Medici, The Death of Marlowe (plays), 1837.
Orion, 1843. (An epic in ten books.)
A New Spirit of the Age, 1844. (Critical studies of contemporaries; note that Elizabeth Barrett had a hand in the book),

and other works. Horne is a 'poetical' poet, with little originality or force, and his plays illustrate that dead imitation of old forms which paralysed playwriting at this period.

HAWKER, ROBERT STEPHEN (1803-75)

Records of the Western Shore, 1832 and 1836.
The Quest of the Sangraal, 1864.
Collected Poems, 1879 and 1899.
Footprints of Former Men in Far Cornwall, 1870 (prose articles), 1903.
Stones Broken from the Rocks (extracts from his notebooks), ed. Appleton and Byles, 1922.
Life and Letters, by G. E. Byles, his son-in-law, 1905; and a study by M. F. Burrows, 1926.

Hawker was a character as well as a poet. His life, by S. Baring-Gould—*Hawker of Morwenstow*—was first published in 1875 (this is the standard life, afterwards much corrected and revised), and there was also a life by F. G. Lee, 1876. One of his poems, *And shall Trelawney die?*, deceived Macaulay and others into supposing it to be a traditional song.

TENNYSON, ALFRED, LORD (1809-92)

Poems by Two Brothers (really three—Alfred, Charles and Frederick), 1827.
Poems, chiefly Lyrical, 1830.

Poems, 1833.
Poems, 1842.
The Princess, 1847.
In Memoriam, 1850.
Maud, 1855.
Idylls of the King, 1859, 1869, 1872, 1885.
Enoch Arden, 1864.
Ballads and Poems, 1880.
Tiresias, 1885.
Locksley Hall Sixty Years After, 1886.
Demeter, 1889.
The Death of Oenone, 1892.

Tennyson also wrote plays which, like those of Browning, are interesting rather because he wrote them than for their intrinsic value; they belong to the class of usually undramatic poetic plays, of which the nineteenth century produced many. The early and spirited *The Devil and the Lady* was edited by Sir Charles Tennyson in 1930. *The Cup*, 1881, and *Becket*, 1884, were both successful on the stage, but their success was mainly due to Irving's acting.

The official life by Hallam, Lord Tennyson, is unsatisfactory because of its smoothness and should be corrected by Sir Charles Tennyson's *Alfred Tennyson* (1950) and *Six Tennyson Essays* (1953). Sir Harold Nicolson's study is readable and stimulating, but in parts facile.

There is a good edition of the 1842 *Poems* by A. M. D. Hughes and a valuable commentary on *In Memoriam* by A. C. Bradley. T. S. Eliot's Introduction to the *Everyman* Tennyson (reprinted in his *Essays Ancient and Modern*) is also of value, and so is W. P. Ker's in his *Collected Essays*, Vol. I.

A note should be added on the two brothers of Tennyson, mentioned above: Charles wrote some lovely sonnets, and Frederick would stand much higher in popular estimation if he had possessed a different surname.

Frederick Tennyson (1807-98) published *Days and Hours* (1854); *The Isles of Greece* (1890—part published in 1870); *Daphne and Other Poems* (1891); *Poems of the Day and Year* (1895, including some of *Days and Hours*).

Charles Tennyson—who took the additional name of Turner —(1808-79) is best represented in the *Collected Sonnets* published in 1880, which has also a biographical sketch by his nephew and a critical introduction by James Spedding.

FITZGERALD, EDWARD (1809-83)

Euphranor, 1851 (afterwards much enlarged)—a dialogue on education and life, exquisitely written.
Salaman and Absal, 1856 (translated from the Persian); edited with a literal translation and an introduction by A. J. Arberry, 1957.
Rubáiyát of Omar Khayyám, 1859.

The *Rubáiyát* stanzas are by no means a literal translation; the version by A. J. Arberry (1952) as well as Arberry's *The Romance of the Rubáiyát* (1959) may be consulted on this point. There were four editions, continually revised and added to, usually for the worse, though on the whole the first edition is not the best. Under the influence of his age FitzGerald tried to make the thought profounder, and wished to clear up what he feared might be obscurities, and in so doing a little injured the atmosphere and the mood, removing the suggestion of mystery and remoteness. At the same time his *Rubáiyát* appealed to the moral weariness fashionable in some circles in the second half of the century, and it consequently obtained and still retains a popular reputation higher than that of his noble versions of some of the plays of Calderon, of which *Such Stuff as Dreams are made of* (*La Vida es Sueno*) should be especially noted. *Six Dramas of Calderon* (not including this) appeared in 1853, and it would perhaps be true to say of them, as of his better known work, that they are re-creations rather than literal renderings. He was also one of the greatest of English letter-writers; see especially—

Letters and Literary Remains (ed. W. Aldis Wright), 1902-03.
Letters to Fanny Kemble, 1895.
More Letters, 1901.
Letters, ed. J. M. Cohen, 1960.

BROWNING, ELIZABETH BARRETT (1806-61)

The Seraphim and other Poems, 1838.
Poems, 1844.
Sonnets from the Portuguese, 1850.
Casa Guidi Windows, 1851.
Aurora Leigh, 1857.
Poems before Congress, 1860.
Last Poems, 1862.
Poetical Works (6 vols.), 1890.

BROWNING, ROBERT (1812-89)

Pauline, 1833.
Paracelsus, 1835.

Strafford (play), 1837.
Sordello, 1840.
A Blot in the Scutcheon (play), 1843.
Colombe's Birthday (play), 1844.
Bells and Pomegranates, 1841-46 and 1848.
Christmas Eve and Easter Day, 1850.
Men and Women, 1855.
Dramatis Personae, 1864.
The Ring and the Book, 1868-69.
Balaustion's Adventure, Prince Hohenstiel-Schwangau, 1871.
Fifine at the Fair, 1872.
Aristophanes' Apology, 1875.
Dramatic Idylls, 1879, 1880.
Asolando, 1889,

and other volumes.

There was a 6-volume collected edition in 1868, and a 17-volume edition in 1888-90. The best edition is that in two volumes, with a few explanatory notes by Sir Frederic Kenyon, published now by Macmillan.

It is impossible to separate the biographies of the Brownings; no full critical study of Mrs Browning can be selected for mention, but there is some incidental criticism of her work in some of the books mentioned below:

BIOGRAPHY AND CRITICISM:

Mrs Sutherland Orr, Life and Letters of Robert Browning, 1891 (new ed. 1908).
Letters of Elizabeth Barrett Browning, ed. Kenyon, 1897.
The Love-Letters of Robert Browning and Elizabeth Barrett, ed. Kenyon, 1899.
Letters of Elizabeth Barrett Browning to her Sister, ed. L. Huxley, 1929.
From Robert and Elizabeth Browning, ed. W. R. Benét, 1936.
Letters between Robert Browning and Julia Wedgewood, ed. Richard Curle, 1937.
Elizabeth Barrett to Miss Mitford, ed. Betty Miller, 1954.
New Letters of Robert Browning, ed. W. C. DeVane and K. L. Knickerbocker, 1951.
Robert Browning's Letters to Isabella Blagden, ed. E. C. McAleer, 1951.
G. K. Chesterton: Browning, 1903.
H. C. Minchin and W. Hall Griffin: Browning, 1910; rev. ed. 1938.
Osbert Burdett: The Brownings, 1928.
Betty Miller: Robert Browning, 1952—a not altogether sympathetic study.
J. M. Cohen: Robert Browning, 1952.
Paul de Reul: L'art et la pensée de Browning, 1929.
Mrs Sutherland Orr: A Handbook to Browning, 1885 (and later revised editions).

This is still obtainable, but it has been largely superseded by a recent very full commentary—

W. C. DeVane: A Browning Handbook, 1935; revised and enlarged, 1955.

Both these handbooks are trustworthy, and contain biographical information as well as critical explanation and comment on individual poems.

FERGUSON, SIR SAMUEL (1810-86)

Lays of the Western Gael, 1865.
Congal, 1872.
Poems, 1880.
Hibernian Nights' Entertainments, 1887 (prose tales based on early Irish history).

Ferguson's enthusiasm for Irish antiquity, as well as the quality of his poetry, makes him one of the forerunners of the Gaelic renaissance of the end of the century. There is a certain spirit and vigour in his poems, often reconstructions of the bardic tales, but to the modern reader the style smacks too much of that false antique ('Wardour Street') which makes so much Victorian verse, and sometimes even prose, tedious—in Tennyson, Morris and in Butcher and Lang's *Odyssey*.

DE VERE, AUBREY (1814-1902)

POETRY:
The Waldenses and other Poems, 1842.
The Search after Proserpine and other Poems, 1843.
Inisfail, a Lyrical Chronicle of Ireland, 1862.
The Legends of St. Patrick, 1872.
Poetical Works, 1884.
Legends and Records of the Church and Empire, 1887.
Mediaeval Records and Sonnets, 1893.
PROSE:
English Misrule and Irish Misdeeds, 1848.
Essays, chiefly on Poetry, 1887.
Essays, chiefly Literary and Ethical, 1889.

De Vere was a graceful poet and a discerning critic. He also wrote his *Recollections* (1897), which have great value for literary biography. There is a memoir by Wilfrid Ward, 1904. That he was considerably read is proved by a new edition of his *Poetical Works* (5 vols.) in 1897, together with his dramas, *Mary Tudor*, *Julian the Apostate*, and *The Duke of Mercia*, and another of his sonnets, with three volumes of prose, 11 volumes in all. His poems are grouped under such titles as *Poems Classical and Meditative*, *The Legends of Ireland's Heroic Age*, *Legends of the Saxon Saints*.

BAILEY, PHILIP JAMES (1816-1902)

Festus, 1839 (recast and enlarged until in the 11th edition, 1889, it stretched to 40,000 words).
The Angel World and other Poems, 1850.
The Mystic and other Poems, 1855.
The Universal Hymn, 1867.

Bailey wrote other works, of which only *The Age*, a colloquial satire (1858), need by mentioned here.

The early *Festus* was extremely popular: it was a long poem even then, justifying the ways of God to man on the basis of universalism and using the Faust legend for its purpose. Tennyson's recommendation of it to FitzGerald in 1846 is worth quoting: 'Order it and read: you will most likely find it a great bore, but there are really very grand things in *Festus*.' The later poems were not well received, and Bailey crammed great blocks of them into successive editions of *Festus*, which grew to twice its original size and became unreadable.

CLOUGH, ARTHUR HUGH (1819-61)

The Bothie of Tober-na-Vuolich, 1848.
Amours de Voyage, 1849.
Ambarvalia (with Thomas Burbridge), 1849.
Dipsychus, 1850.
Poems, with memoir by F. T. Palgrave, 1862.
Poems and Prose Remains, with Life by Mrs Clough, 1869.

The definitive edition of the poems is that by H. F. Lowry, A. L. P. Norrington, and F. L. Mulhauser, 1951, and of the correspondence that by F. L. Mulhauser, 1957.

Clough's introspective conscientiousness, encouraged first by his training under Arnold at Rugby and later by his temporary connection with the Oxford Movement, led to an uncertainty about the meaning and purpose of the universe which combines strangely in his poetry with sharp wit and observation. Some of his different moods may be seen in *The Bothie*, *The New Decalogue* and *Say not the Struggle naught Availeth*.

ARNOLD, MATTHEW (1822-88)

POETRY:
The Strayed Reveller, and other Poems (by 'A.'), 1849.
Empedocles on Etna, and other Poems (by 'A.'), 1852.

Poems, 1853.
Poems, 1855.
Merope (a tragedy in Greek form), 1858.
New Poems, 1867.
Collected Poems, 1869, 1877, 1885, 1890.

PROSE:

Arnold's critical writings appeared from about 1862 onwards. The theological volumes may be passed over, though *Literature and Dogma*, 1873, was influential in its time (on this point see Dorothea Krook's *Three Traditions of Moral Thought*): they were always superficial and now they are out of date; but the literary and social criticism should always retain its value. Most of the literary criticism will be found in the two series of *Essays in Criticism*, 1865 and 1888. There is historical interest, too, in the amateurish *On the Study of Celtic Literature*, 1867. The social criticism is at its best in—

Culture and Anarchy, 1869.
Friendship's Garland, 1871.
Mixed Essays, 1879.

Much of his thought may also be seen in the *Letters* (ed. G. W. E. Russell, 1895), *Letters to Arthur Hugh Clough* (ed. H. F. Lowry, 1933) and *Notebooks* (1902, and edited by H. F. Lowry, K. Young and W. H. Dunn, 1952).

There is no complete biography. The edition of the *Poems* in the Oxford edition of *Standard Poets* contains also his exposition of his ideas on poetry, and is to be recommended. A most useful commentary by C. B. Tinker and H. F. Lowry was published in 1940, and the same scholars produced a complete edition of the poems and prefaces with valuable critical apparatus in 1950. The essays, letters and reviews were collected and edited by F. Neiman in 1960.

INGELOW, JEAN (1820-97)
Poems, 1863, 1876, 1885.

Jean Ingelow is remembered by a few poems and, perhaps unfairly, by Calverley's parody. She also wrote novels which contain wit and poetic feeling, but are not well constructed: *Off the Skelligs*, 1872, and *Don John*, 1881, are the best. *High Tide on the Coast of Lincolnshire* is not only one of the best-known but also one of the best of her poems.

CORY, WILLIAM JOHNSON (1823-92)

Ionica, 1858 (enlarged 1891).
Extracts from Letters and Journals, selected and arranged by F. W. Cornish, 1897.

Cory's own lyric gift was exquisite, and as a schoolmaster he fostered poetry where he found it in his pupils. His *Heraclitus* is condemned by some modern critics, but it is a characteristic poem.

BROWN, THOMAS EDWARD (1830-97)

Fo'c'sle Yarns, 1881.
The Doctor, and other Poems, 1887.
The Manx Witch, and other Poems, 1889.
Old John, 1893.
Collected Poems, 1900.
Letters, with memoir by S. T. Irwin, 1900.
Collected Works (Poems and Letters), 1952.

T. E. Brown has become unfashionable, but if he was not very profound nor very skilful, he had a gift of lyric utterance, an acute perception of nature, and a certain courage of outlook. He is sometimes, perhaps, a little blatant, but if he deserves a high place among the second-rate poets of the period, it is precisely because he had rather more robustness than they.

DOBELL, SYDNEY THOMPSON (1824-74)

The Roman, 1850 (under the pseudonym of 'Sydney Yendys').
Balder, 1854.
England in Time of War, 1856.
Collected Poetical Works, 1875.
Collected Prose Works, 1876.
Life and Letters, 1878.

The tendency of Dobell and Alexander Smith (v. infra) to an exaggerated style provoked Aytoun's brilliant parody *Firmilian* (see under HUMOUR), but there is much beauty in their verse, especially the lyrics.

SMITH, ALEXANDER (1830-67)

A Life Drama, 1853.
City Poems, 1857.
Edwin of Deira, 1861.
Dreamthorpe, 1863 (essays).
Last Leaves, 1868 (miscellanies).

Smith has excellent descriptive passages in good middle prose in his essays.

C. THE PRE-RAPHAELITES AND AFTER

ALLINGHAM, WILLIAM (1824-89)

Day and Night Songs, 1854 (2nd ed. with additions, 1855).
Laurence Bloomfield in Ireland, 1864—'the epic of Irish philanthropic landlordism' (D.N.B.).
Complete Poetical Works, 1888-93.
Varieties in Prose, 1893.

Allingham was in the Rossetti circle, and was also intimate with Carlyle. His best-known poem is *Up the Airy Mountain*.

ROSSETTI, DANTE GABRIEL (Gabriel Charles Dante) (1828-82)

The Early Italian Poets, 1861. (Translations.)
Poems, 1870.
Dante and his Circle, 1874.
Ballads and Sonnets, 1881.

The best edition of the poems is that by Edmund G. Gardner, and Oswald Doughty's *A Victorian Romantic* is probably the definitive biography. See also—

W. M. Rossetti: Family Letters and Memoir, 1895.
Rossetti as Designer and Writer, 1889.
Ruskin, Rossetti and Pre-raphaelitism, 1899.
Pre-raphaelite Diaries and Letters, 1900.
Rossetti Papers, 1903.
Rossetti's Letters to William Allingham, 1897.
Rossetti's Letters to his Publisher, ed. O. Doughty, 1928.
R. D. Waller: The Rossetti Family, 1824-54, 1932.
Sir Max Beerbohm: Rossetti and his Circle, 1922. (Cartoons which are in themselves witty criticisms.)
Ford Madox Ford: Ancient Lights (and other books of reminiscence. F. M. Ford's grandfather, Ford Madox Brown, was himself one of the pre-Raphaelites and there is a good deal of not wholly trustworthy family tradition and recollection in these books).

The biographies of Rossetti's friends, especially William Morris, Burne-Jones and Swinburne, should be consulted.

The best recent study is by L. Wolff, 1934, in *Les grands écrivains étrangers*. This also contains a useful bibliography.

ROSSETTI, CHRISTINA (1830-94)

Goblin Market and other Poems, 1862.
The Prince's Progress, 1866.
A Pageant, 1881.

Verses, 1893.
New Poems, 1896.
Complete Poetical Works, 1904.

Also prose stories and devotional prose: note especially—

Time Flies, 1885.
The Face of the Deep, 1892.
Life by Mackenzie Bell, 1898; critical and biographical study by
   Dorothy Margaret Stuart, 1930, and study by Margaret Sawtell, 1954.

DIXON, RICHARD WATSON (1833-1900)

Christ's Company, 1861.
Historical Odes, 1863.
Mano, 1883.
Odes and Eclogues, 1884.
Lyrical Poems, 1886.
Selected Poems, edited by Robert Bridges, 1896.

Dixon was also an historian whose *History of the Church of England from the Abolition of the Roman Jurisdiction* (1877-1900) is a recognized authority. His singularly beautiful character and critical power are revealed in his correspondence with Gerard Manley Hopkins, ed. C. C. Abbot, 1935. He was never a popular poet, and is not much read now, but it seems likely that there will be a revival of interest in his work, though he will never be enthusiastically acclaimed. He was a member of William Morris's circle at Oxford, and was afterwards the friend also of Robert Bridges, who wrote a memoir for a collection of his poems in 1909.

MORRIS, WILLIAM (1834-96)

POETRY:

The Defence of Guenevere, and other Poems, 1858.
The Life and Death of Jason, 1867.
The Earthly Paradise, 1868-70.
Love is Enough, 1872.
Sigurd the Volsung, 1876.
Poems by the Way, 1891.

PROSE TALES AND ROMANCES:

The tales which appeared in *The Oxford and Cambridge Magazine* in 1856
   are included in The Early Romances of William Morris (Everyman
   Library).
A Dream of John Ball, 1888.
News from Nowhere, 1890 (in book form, 1891).
The House of the Wolfings, 1889.
The Roots of the Mountains, 1890.
The Story of the Glittering Plain, 1890.

The Wood beyond the World, 1894.
Child Christopher and Goldilind the Fair, 1895.
The Well at the World's End, 1896.
The Water of the Wondrous Isles, 1897.
The Sundering Flood, 1898.

CRITICAL AND POLITICAL PAPERS AND SPEECHES:
The Aims of Art, 1887.
Signs of Change, 1888.

Morris's translations, especially those from the Icelandic, should also be mentioned.

Complete edition, with introductions by his daughter, in 24 volumes, 1910-15; two additional volumes, 1936, particularly interesting for the reminiscences by Mr Bernard Shaw included. These 26 volumes include much which is otherwise unobtainable, e.g., other Socialist papers and the *Journals* of his visits to Iceland.

The standard life is by J. W. Mackail, 1899. There is also a study by Paul Bloomfield which may be recommended, and others by A. C. Benson, Clutton Brock, Bruce Glasier, M. Weekley and E. P. Thompson. See also *Memorials of Edward Burne-Jones*, by Lady Burne-Jones.

On the Kelmscott Press see—

H. Buxton Forman: The Books of William Morris, 1897.
S. C. Cockerell: A Description of the Kelmscott Press, 1898.
H. Halliday Sparling: The Kelmscott Press and William Morris, Master-Craftsman, 1924.

SWINBURNE, ALGERNON CHARLES (1837-1909)

POEMS AND PLAYS:
The Queen Mother, and Rosamund, 1860. (Plays.)
Atalanta in Calydon, 1865. (Play in Greek form.)
Chastelard, 1865. Bothwell, 1874. Mary Stuart, 1881. (A trilogy of plays.)
Poems and Ballads, 1866; 2nd series, 1878; 3rd series, 1889.
A Song of Italy, 1867.
Songs before Sunrise, 1871.
Songs of Two Nations, 1875.
Erechtheus, 1876. (Play in Greek form.)
Songs of the Springtides, 1880.
Studies in Song, 1880.
The Heptalogia, 1880. (Parodies.)
Tristram of Lyonesse, 1882.
A Century of Roundels, 1883.
A Midsummer Holiday, 1884.
Marino Faliero, 1885. (Play.)

Locrine, 1887. (Play.)
The Sisters, 1892. (Play.)
Astrophel, 1894.
The Tale of Balen, 1896.
Rosamund, Queen of the Lombards, 1899. (Play.)
A Channel Passage, 1904.
Collected Poems, 1904.

There is a good selection of the poems by Edward Shanks, 1950.

NOVEL:
A Year's Letters, 1877 (rep. as Love's Cross-Currents, 1905).

CRITICAL ESSAYS AND STUDIES:
William Blake: a Critical Essay, 1868.
George Chapman: a Critical Essay, 1874.
Essays and Studies, 1875.
A Note on Charlotte Brontë, 1877.
A Study of Shakespeare, 1880.
Miscellanies, 1886.
A Study of Victor Hugo, 1886.
A Study of Ben Jonson, 1889.
Studies in Prose and Poetry, 1894.
The Age of Shakespeare, 1908.
Shakespeare, 1909.
Contemporaries of Shakespeare, 1919.
Letters, ed. E. Gosse and T. Wise, 1918 (much censored); a new and complete edition is now appearing, ed. by C. Y. Lang.

Swinburne's critical essays show an enthusiastic appreciation of almost everything that he touched upon. His comparative judgments are always brilliant, but his essays on individuals, taken separately, would make every goose a swan or else a cormorant. Nevertheless he is an invaluable critic, and his poetic intuition enabled him to put his finger on what was essential and characteristic in every person whom he wrote about. His prose style has all the fervour and abundance, the command of word and phrase, the rushing vigour of his poetry, and he was a master of vituperation. His highly individual manner sometimes gives readers, when they read his work in long stretches, the effect of eating honey without bread, though this is not to imply that he erred on the side of sweetness.

The *Life* by Sir Edmund Gosse (1917), though not false, is too guarded; the best studies are the two (the earlier in French, the later, 1932, in English) by Georges Lafourcade. See also T. Earle Welby, *Swinburne*, 1914; Harold Nicolson in *English Men of Letters*

(1926) and Paul de Reul, *L'Œuvre de Swinburne* (1922); though the last is largely superseded by Lafourcade. Sir Max Beerbohm's *No. 2 The Pines*, in *And Even Now*, throws an amusing and typically Maxian sidelight on Swinburne and Watts-Dunton; and see again Sir Max Beerbohm's *Rossetti and his Circle*.

WATTS-DUNTON, THEODORE (1832-1914)
The Coming of Love, 1897.

An over-rated poem, as his novel *Aylwin*, 1898, was also over-rated—perhaps because both of them took so long to compose. Although he was a person of importance in his time, especially as a critic in *The Athenaeum*, Watts-Dunton would probably be forgotten altogether if his friendship for Swinburne, whom he undoubtedly kept alive, had not given him a reflected and not altogether enviable immortality. There is some valuable matter in his memories, *Old Familiar Faces*, 1916.

Life and Letters, by T. St E. Hake and A. Compton-Rickett, 1916.

Three minor poets who were in the pre-Raphaelite group may be included here:

MARSTON, PHILIP BOURKE (1850-87)
—son of John Westland Marston, 1819-90, the writer of poetic plays which were collected in 1876:
Song-Tide and other Poems, 1871,
and other volumes.
Collected Poems, with biographical sketch by Mrs Louise Chandler Moulton, 1892.

SCOTT, WILLIAM BELL (1811-90)
Hades, and The Progress of the Mind, 1838.
The Year of the World, 1846.
Poems, 1854.
Poems, 1875.
A Poet's Harvest Home, 1882 and 1893.

William Bell Scott was a painter and wrote books on art, but though these are not without value he is likely to be remembered by a few spirited poems and by the *Autobiographical Notes*, edited by W. Minto in 1892, which tell of his connection with Rossetti.

WOOLNER, THOMAS (1825-92)

Unlike William Bell Scott, Woolner is more likely to be remembered by his sculpture—especially the fine, passionate bust and medallion of Tennyson—than by his poetry, yet this too is characteristic. *My Beautiful Lady* appeared first, in a short form, in *The Germ* in 1850 and afterwards much enlarged in 1863. It is pre-Raphaelite poetry. Woolner's other volumes include *Pygmalion*, 1881; *Silenus*, 1884; and *Poems*, 1887; he is at his best in parts of *My Beautiful Lady*, of which the extracts quoted in the introduction here do not give a just notion, but even his best is only the same sort of thing better done.

D. THE LATE VICTORIANS

I

Certain poets and men of letters may be considered together here, not because they form a real school or group, but because they have certain characteristics in common: (*a*) a strong interest in the technicalities of verse, particularly in such Old French forms as the ballade and the rondeau; (*b*) critical discernment, enjoyment and scholarship which produced essays and editorial work often of permanent value. In one sense they may be called descendants of W. M. Praed (q.v.), and they have affinities with the pre-Raphaelites, but they are more scholarly than any of these and lighter in touch. The last two differ from the others and agree between themselves by being in a sense representatives of the imperialist sentiment of the end of the century.

LOCKER-LAMPSON, FREDERICK (1821-95)

London Lyrics, 1857 and later.
London Rhymes, 1882.
Rowfant Rhymes, 1895.
(ed.) Lyra Elegantiarum, 1867; enlarged edition in 1891.
Patchwork, 1879.
My Confidences, 1896 (ed. A. Birrell).

Locker-Lampson is the most like Praed of these poets, the most elegant and least substantial.

DOBSON, HENRY AUSTIN (1840-1921)

POETRY:
Vignettes in Rhyme, 1873.
Proverbs in Porcelain, 1877.
At the Sign of the Lyre, 1885.
Collected Poems, 1897 and 1913.

PROSE:
Lives of Hogarth, 1879, enlarged, 1891, Fielding, 1883, Steele, 1886, Goldsmith, 1888, Horace Walpole, 1890, Richardson, 1902, Fanny Burney, 1903.
Eighteenth-Century Vignettes (three series), 1892, 1894, 1896.
Side-Walk Studies, 1902.
De Libris, 1908.
Old Kensington Palace, 1910.
A Bookman's Budget, 1917.
Later Essays, 1921,

and other volumes and editorial work.

Dobson's poetry is scarcely more than pleasantly graceful, but his equally graceful prose covers a profound knowledge of eighteenth-century literature and social history.

LANG, ANDREW (1844-1912)

POETRY:
Ballads and Lyrics of Old France, 1872.
Ballades in Blue China, 1880, 1881.
Helen of Troy, 1882.
Rhymes à la Mode, 1884.
Grass of Parnassus, 1888.
Ban and Arrière Ban, 1894.
Collected Poems, 1923.

ESSAYS:
Letters to Dead Authors, 1886.
Books and Bookmen, 1887.
Old Friends (epistolary parody; e.g., Harold Skimpole and the Rev. Charles Honeyman correspond, Mrs Proudie tells Mrs Quiverful of Becky Sharp's behaviour in Barchester, Barry Lyndon tells of a meeting with Alan Breck), 1890.
Essays in Little, 1891 (and other collections of essays).
Adventures Among Books, 1905.
The World of Homer, 1910.
(Note that the translations of the *Iliad*, 1883, by Lang, Leaf and Myers, and the *Odyssey*, 1879, by Butcher and Lang, are perhaps the most satisfactory prose translations of Homer, in spite of their unfashionable 'Wardour Street' archaism of language.)

ANTHROPOLOGY:
Custom and Myth, 1884.

Myth, Ritual and Religion, 1887 (revised, 1899).
The Making of Religion, 1898.

HISTORY:
Pickle the Spy, 1897.
The Companions of Pickle, 1898.
Prince Charles Edward, 1900.
History of Scotland, 1900-07 (and monographs).
The Maid of France, 1908.

BIOGRAPHY:
Life, Letters and Diaries of Sir Stafford Northcote, First Earl of
    Iddesleigh, 1890.
Life and Letters of John Gibson Lockhart, 1896.

NOVELS:
The Mark of Cain, 1886.
The Disentanglers, 1902.

Besides much periodical and editorial work, among which his
multi-coloured series of fairy and other books for children should
be gratefully commemorated.

Lang's extraordinary variety and quantity of production gives
an unjust impression of superficiality. He was in fact a serious
anthropologist whose theories and arguments have considerably
modified the views of professional anthropologists. His knowledge
finds lighter expression in the two novels mentioned above: he
was a serious historian and biographer who did much original
research: and he was a poet who perhaps missed greatness
through shyness of his own emotions.

Biographical and critical study, by R. L. Green, 1946.

HENLEY, WILLIAM ERNEST (1849-1903)

POETRY:
A Book of Verses, 1888.
The Song of the Sword and other Verses, 1892; a second edition with
    additions appeared as London Voluntaries, 1893.
Poems, 1898 (a revision of the earlier volumes).
For England's Sake, 1900.
Hawthorn and Lavender, 1901.
A Song of Speed, 1903.

PROSE:
Much of Henley's prose grew out of editorial work—he was editor of
    The National Review and in that position encouraged his younger con-
    temporaries, and he had a main hand in the series of republications of
    Tudor Translations. His edition of Burns, with T. F. Henderson, 1896-
    1897, should also be mentioned; it contains an essay on Burns which

was also published separately. Views and Reviews (1890) contains some of his periodical work and his introductions are included in the—Collected Works (6 vols.), 1908.

Henley's violence contrasts strongly with the delicacy of Austin Dobson and often suggests weakness, but there is sometimes lyric beauty in his verse and there is real gusto in his prose criticism. And, as a set-off to his violence, he has the distinction of being one of the few of his time to see that Gilbert was vulgar.

NEWBOLT, SIR HENRY JOHN (1862-1938)

POETRY:
Admirals All, 1897.
The Island Race, 1898.
The Sailing of the Long Ships, 1902.
Poems New and Old, 1912.

NOVELS:
The Old Country, 1906.
The New June, 1909.

CRITICISM:
A New Study of English Poetry, 1917.
Studies Green and Gray, 1926.
New Paths on Helicon, 1927,

and many other books.

My World as in My Time, 1932.
Later Life and Letters, 1942.

Some of his verse contains the extreme of imperialist sentiment, but there is a good side to it, a passionate love of his own country, which is reflected in the two novels noted here.

II

A second group of mid and late Victorian poets is connected by their religion, which profoundly affected their poetry, different though they were in many other respects. The austere restraint of Alice Meynell in both prose and poetry makes her more akin to Christina Rossetti than to Francis Thompson in his exuberance, or to Coventry Patmore in some of his moods both of human and of ecstatic divine love; yet there is a religious kinship as well as a personal tie uniting these three. Lionel Johnson and Dolben, though he had not been formally received into the Roman Church at the time of his death, find their most natural place in the same company. A note on Gerard Manley Hopkins is added for the sake of completeness, but the peculiar circumstances of the publication of his work, as well as his tortured individuality of style, make it more convenient to consider him fully in the next volume of this series.

DOLBEN, DIGBY MACKWORTH (1848-67)

Poems, ed. with a Memoir by Robert Bridges, 1911. (A few are quoted in Bridges's anthology *The Spirit of Man*.)

Dolben was a poet of promise, whom the piety of his friend Bridges has saved from oblivion. See also *Three Friends*, by Robert Bridges, 1932.

HOPKINS, GERARD MANLEY (1844-89)

The poems of Hopkins, like those of Dolben, were published through the pious care of Bridges, who introduced them gradually to the knowledge of the public, first through Miles's *Poets and Poetry of the Century* (1893), then through his own anthology, *The Spirit of Man* (1916), and then in a fairly complete edition with notes (1918), which was enlarged in 1930 with an introduction by Charles Williams.

The *Letters* of Hopkins to Bridges and R. W. Dixon, containing his critical opinions and his explanation of his practice, were published in 1935, ed. by C. C. Abbott. His correspondence with Coventry Patmore followed (2nd ed. revised and enlarged, 1956). The *Journals and Papers*, ed. Humphrey House, completed by G. Strong, reached a revised edition in 1959, and the *Sermons and Devotional Writings* were edited by Christopher Devlin in 1959. There have been several recent studies, e.g., those by Lahey, Peck and Gardner, but the *Letters* remain the best commentary.

PATMORE, COVENTRY KERSEY DIGHTON (1823-1896)

POETRY:

Angel in the House: The Betrothal, 1854; The Espousals, 1856; Faithful for Ever, 1860. In the collected edition this last part was amalgamated with the poem of bereavement, The Victories of Love, 1862.

The Unknown Eros and other Odes, 1877.

Amelia, with a Study of English Metrical Law, 1878. The Study was enlarged from an earlier essay and was later included in the collected *Poetical Works*, 1886.

PROSE:
Principle in Art, 1889.
Religio Poetae, 1893.
Rod, Root and Flower, 1895.
Courage in Politics, and other essays, 1921.

The standard *Memoirs and Correspondence* by Basil Champneys, 1900, is trustworthy but rather heavy; more readable studies are in Derek Patmore's *Portrait of my Family*, 1935 and E. J. Oliver's *Coventry Patmore*, 1956. Frederick Page's *Patmore, a Study in Poetry*, 1933, is a good piece of criticism.

THOMPSON, FRANCIS (1859-1907)

Poems, 1893.
Sister Songs, 1895.
New Poems, 1897.
Health and Holiness, 1905. (Prose.)
Selected Poems, with Memoir by Wilfrid Meynell, 1908.
Essay on Shelley, 1909.
Works (Vols. I and II, Poems; Vol. III, Prose), 1913.

The standard *Life* is by Everard Meynell, 1913. See also the *Life* of Alice Meynell, Viola Meynell's *Francis Thompson and Wilfrid Meynell, a Memoir*, 1952, and J. C. Reid's *Francis Thompson: Man and Poet*, 1959.

Francis Thompson seems at present to be suffering in opinion from a reaction against what was perhaps an overestimate of his powers by some of his contemporaries, who were swept off their feet by his rhythms and the richness of his vocabulary. In both of these he rivalled Swinburne; but it is fair to say that he differed from Swinburne in that there was nearly always a fullness of emotional content, sometimes of intellectual content, to match the fullness of his verse. At the same time it is doubtful whether, if comparisons must be made, he is the equal of Patmore in profundity, and he certainly falls short of both Patmore and Alice Meynell in discipline. But for the restraining force of his religious convictions he would probably have run entirely to wordiness and waste. His prose criticism shares the qualities of his poetry.

JOHNSON, LIONEL PIGOT (1867-1902)

Poems, 1895.
Ireland, with other Poems, 1897.
Selected Poems, with a Memoir by Clement K. Shorter, 1908.
Poetical Works, 1915.

The Art of Thomas Hardy, 1894. (Still one of the best studies of Hardy.)
Post Liminium (critical essays), 1911.
Complete Poems, ed. Iain Fletcher, 1953.

MEYNELL, ALICE (1847-1922)

POETRY:
Preludes, 1875.
Poems, 1893.
Later Poems, 1901.
A Father of Women, 1917.
Collected Poems, 1913, 1923.

PROSE:
The Rhythm of Life, 1893.
The Colour of Life, The Children, 1896.
The Spirit of Place, 1898.
Ceres' Runaway, 1910.
Selected Essays, 1914.
Hearts of Controversy, 1917.
The Second Person Singular, 1921.
Life, by Viola Meynell, 1929.

Mrs Meynell's exquisite fastidiousness and reticence should not be mistaken for a strained and over-subtilized refinement. Her poetry and her prose alike have backbone, and the reasoned strength of her critical preferences may be seen, e.g., in the essays in *Hearts of Controversy* on Dickens, in whom she rejoiced, and Swinburne, whom she disliked as positively as she admired Dickens. Her best known poems are the early sonnet *Renouncement* and the lyric *She walks, the lady of my delight*; but her strength and delicacy and critical acuteness may be better seen in such poems as *Christ in the Universe, Easter Night, Length of Days*, and the half-humorous poem on *The English Metres*.

III

THOMSON, JAMES (1834-82)

The City of Dreadful Night, with some other poems, 1880. (The title poem appeared in *The National Reformer* in 1874.)
Vane's Story, Weddah and Om-el-Bouain, and other Poems, 1881.
Essays and Phantasies, 1881.
A Voice from the Nile and other Poems, 1884; Satires and Profanities, 1884.
Shelley, A Poem, 1885.
Poems, Essays and Fragments, 1892.
Poetical Works, 1895.
Biographical and Critical Studies, 1896.

The City of Dreadful Night, together with poems selected by H. S. Salt, was republished in 1933.
Life, by H. S. Salt, 1889; revised, 1898.

Thomson wrote under the pseudonym of B.V., i.e., Bysshe Vanolis; Bysshe being taken from Shelley's second name, and Vanolis being an anagram from the name of the German poet and mystic Novalis. His admiration for them does not indicate any similarity between their work and his, which is perhaps the most powerful poetry of despair in English, his possible rival in this respect being John Davidson (see below).

BLUNT, WILFRID SCAWEN (1840-1922)

Love Sonnets of Proteus, 1880.
Poetical Works, 1914.

Mention should also be made of his versification of the translations from Arabic, made by Lady Anne Blunt—

The Stealing of the Mare, 1892, and The Seven Golden Odes of Pagan Arabia, 1903.

W. S. Blunt belonged to that not uncommon type of Englishman whose jealousy for his country's honour leads him to suspect her good faith in her relations with other countries. His political activities in Ireland and Egypt led to imprisonment, to the production of some of his best sonnets, and to the writing of diaries and other books which, though no less biased than those of a Government official, are of historical value.

My Diaries, 1919-20. Secret History of the English Occupation of Egypt, 1907; India under Ripon, 1909; Gordon at Khartoum, 1911; The Land War in Ireland, 1912.

BRIDGES, ROBERT (1844-1930)

POETRY:
Poems, 1873, 1879, 1880.
The Growth of Love (sonnet sequence: XXIV Sonnets, 1876; LXXIX Sonnets, 1889; LXIX Sonnets in the 1898 and 1912 collected editions).
Poetical Dramas, 1885-93.
Eros and Psyche, 1885, revised 1894.
Shorter Poems, 1890.
Poetical Works (6 vols.), 1898-1905.
Poetical Works, excluding the dramas, 1912.
October and other Poems, 1920.
New Verse, 1925.
The Testament of Beauty, 1929.

CRITICISM:
Milton's Prosody, 1893.
John Keats, 1895.
The Spirit of Man (an anthology which contains much incidental
    criticism), 1916.
The Necessity of Poetry, 1918.
Collected Essays, Papers, etc., 1927, and later.

Bridges was one of the most learned English poets, and, like his
friend Gerard Manley Hopkins, he not merely took a critical
interest in the technical problems of poetry, but also discussed
them and made experiments in metre which may considerably
affect the practice of later poets. The study by F. E. Brett Young
(1914) was written too early to take account of his use of quanti-
tative verse, but some remarks on this as well as an exposition of
his later thought will be found in the study of *The Testament of
Beauty* by Oliver Elton (1933). There is also an excellent study by
Edward Thompson, 1945.
See also Dolben and Gerard Manley Hopkins.

SHARP, WILLIAM—'FIONA MACLEOD' (1855-1905)

This curious double personality wrote, as William Sharp,
Romantic Ballads and Poems of Fantasy, 1888—and many other
poems, articles and novels.

As Fiona Macleod he wrote stories, sketches and poems of a
misty imaginative quality which he and others believed to be
Celtic.

Pharais, 1894.
The Mountain Lovers, 1895. The Sin Eater, 1895.
The Washer of the Ford, 1896. Green Fire, 1896.
From the Hills of Dream, 1896.
The Dominion of Dreams, 1899.
The Immortal Hour (play), 1900.
Uniform edition of Fiona Macleod, 1910.
Memoir of William Sharp, by his wife, 1910.

DAVIDSON, JOHN (1857-1909)

PLAYS:
Bruce, 1886.
Scaramouche in Naxos, 1889,

and other plays; special mention should be made of—

Godfrida, 1878, with a notable preface.
The Triumph of Mammon, 1907; and

Mammon and his Message, 1908, which were intended to be part of a trilogy, God and Mammon.

POETRY:
In a Music Hall and other Poems, 1891.
Fleet Street Eclogues, 1893, 1896.
Ballads and Songs, 1894.
New Ballads, 1897.
The Last Ballad, 1899.
Selected Poems, 1904.

PROSE:
Testament of a Vivisector, 1901.
Testament of a Man Forbid, 1901.
Testament of an Empire Builder, 1902.
Testament of John Davidson, 1908.

These *Testaments* and the two *Mammon* plays explain Davidson's philosophy of life. He wrote many other books besides.

Poems and Ballads (a selection with a biographical introduction by R. D. Macleod), 1959.

WATSON, SIR WILLIAM (1858-1935)

The Prince's Quest, 1880.
Epigrams of Art, Life and Nature, 1884.
Wordsworth's Grave, 1890.
Collected Poems, 1898, 1906.
New Poems, 1909.
Poems Brief and New, 1925.
Selected Poems, with notes by the Author, 1928,

and other volumes of poetry.

Watson's poetry is always dignified and often has lofty or delicate beauty, though it sometimes seems derivative rather than original. He was not a great enough poet ever to write badly, but he never received the appreciation which he deserved and desired.

HOUSMAN, ALBERT EDWARD (1858-1936)

A Shropshire Lad, 1896.
Last Poems, 1922.
The Name and Nature of Poetry, 1933. (Lecture.)
More Poems, 1936.

Though they may seem to have no connection with the poems, Housman's editions of Manilus (1903-30), Juvenal (1905) and Lucan (1926) should be mentioned. They show, in fact, the disciplined sense of form which gives the lyrics part of their peculiar quality, and the introduction to the Juvenal sets out memorably

I

the principles of scholarly critical editing. The preface to Manilius contains passages of masterly invective, and should by no means be missed by those who enjoy that kind of writing. All Housman's prose is admirable.

The *Life*, by A. F. S. Gow, an excellent study, has a bibliography. See also Percy Withers, *A Buried Life: Personal Recollections of A. E. Housman*, 1940.

Bibliography: An Annotated Hand-List, by John Carter and John Sparrow, 1952.

TRENCH, HERBERT (1865-1923)

Deirdre Wed and other Poems, 1901.
New Poems, 1907.
Lyrics and narrative poems, 1911.
Poems with Fables in Prose, 1917.
Collected Works, 1924.
Selected Poems, edited with an introduction by Harold Williams, 1924.

A dignified traditional poet, who also attempted the poetic drama with a handling of the Napoleonic theme—*Napoleon*, 1918.

BINYON, ROBERT LAURENCE (1869-1943)

Lyric Poems, 1894.
Poems, 1895.
London Visions, 1895, 1898 (collected, 1908).
The Sirens: an Ode, 1925.
Collected Poems, 1931,

and also books of art criticism, particularly on William Blake and on Oriental art.

His best-known poem is *For the Fallen*, which illustrates his qualities.

DOUGLAS, LORD ALFRED (1870-1945)

The City of the Soul, 1899.
Sonnets, 1909.
Collected Poems, 1919.
Complete Poems, 1928.
Collected Satires, 1927,

and other volumes.

Oscar Wilde and Myself, 1914.
Autobiography, 1929.

The sonnets are the most notable of his writings.

YEATS, WILLIAM BUTLER (1865-1939)

The Wanderings of Oisin, 1889.
The Countess Kathleen, 1892 (and later plays).
The Celtic Twilight, 1893.
Poems, 1895, 1899, 1901.
The Secret Rose, 1897.
The Wind among the Reeds, 1899.
Collected Plays and Poems (8 vols.), 1908.
New collected edition (first 6 vols.), 1923-26.
Collected Poems, 1933.
Collected Plays, 1934.
A Vision, 1937.
Essays 1931-36, 1938.
The Herne's Eggs, 1938.
New Poems, 1938.
Last Poems, 1939.
Letters on Poetry from W. B. Yeats to Dorothy Wellesley, 1940.
Collected Plays, 1952.
Letters, ed. Allan Wade, 1954.
Variorum Edition of the Poems, ed. Peter Allt and R. K. Alspach, 1958.

The greatest of those who made the Irish renaissance, Yeats
drew his inspiration from legend and the ideals of a united
Ireland, but his poetry always transcended any narrow interpretation of nationalism. Both in lyric poetry and in drama his
recent work shows a heightening and development of the mystical
philosophy present in it from the first: the 'escape' motive has
disappeared, and he has come to closer grips with a common
reality. His share in the history of the Abbey Theatre is noted
elsewhere (v. pp. 111-12). He will be critically considered in the
next volume.

There is a full life by J. Hone, 1942, and a useful *Reader's Guide
to W. B. Yeats* by John Unterecker, 1959.

RUSSELL, GEORGE WILLIAM—'Æ' (1867-1935)

Homeward: Songs by the Way, 1894.
The Earth Breath, 1897.
The Nuts of Knowledge, 1903.
The Divine Vision, 1904; The Mask of Apollo, 1904; New Poems, 1904.
Irish Essays, 1906; By Still Waters, 1906.
Deirdre, 1907.
The Hero in Man, 1909.
The Renewal of Youth, 1911.
Co-operation and Nationality, 1912.
Collected Poems, 1913.
Gods of War, 1915; Imaginations and Reveries, 1915.

The National Being, some thoughts on an Irish Policy, 1917.
The Candle of Vision, 1919.
The Interpreters, 1922.
Midsummer Eve, 1928.
Vale and other Poems, 1931.
Song and its Fountains, 1932.
The Avatars, 1933.

The titles of 'Æ's' books indicate the double strain in him of a seer with a philosophy and religion as peculiar as Blake's, and a practical statesman whose work for co-operation was perhaps itself the pursuit of a vision of ideal good. He was an organic member of the Irish literary revival.

DOWSON, ERNEST (?1867-1900)

Dilemmas. Stories and studies in sentiment, 1895.
Verses, 1896.
The Pierrot of the Minute, 1897.
Decorations: in verse and prose, 1899.

The poems were collected with a critical essay and memoir by Arthur Symons in 1904, but the edition by Desmond Flower of 1934 is more complete.

Dowson was perhaps the most characteristically 'decadent' of the poets of the nineties. See the sketch by Frank Harris in *Contemporary Portraits*, 2nd series, the less favourable estimate by A. R. Orage in *Readers and Writers*, John Gawsworth's *The Dowson Legend*, and the study by V. G. Plarr. The fullest biography and study is that by J. M. Longaker, 1944.

E. THE GEORGIANS

See the general Introduction for general criticism.

MOORE, THOMAS STURGE (1870-1944)

The Vinedresser and other Poems, 1899.
Collected Poems, 1932-33.
Art and Life, 1910.

and other books of literary and artistic criticism.

DAVIES, WILLIAM HENRY (1871-1940)

The Soul's Destroyer, 1907. New Poems, 1907.
Nature Poems, 1908.
Collected Poems, 1916, 1928, 1934.

Love Poems, 1935.
The Autobiography of a Super-Tramp, 1908.
Later Days, 1925.

HODGSON, RALPH (1871-   )

The Last Blackbird, 1907.
Poems, 1917.
The Skylark and Other Poems, 1958.

DE LA MARE, WALTER (1873-1956)

Songs of Childhood, 1902.
*Henry Brocken, 1904.
Poems, 1906.
*The Three Mulla-Mulgars, 1910; *The Return, 1910.
The Listeners, 1912. A Child's Day, 1912.
Peacock Pie, 1913.
Motley, 1918. Flora, 1919.
Collected Poems 1901-18, 1920.
*The Veil, 1921; *Crossings, 1921; *Memoirs of a Midget, 1921.
Down-adown-Derry, 1922.
*The Riddle, 1923.
Come Hither (an anthology with comments), 1923.
*Ding Dong Bell, 1924.
*Broomsticks, 1925.
*The Connoisseur, 1926.
*Told Again, 1927; Stuff and Nonsense, 1927.
*Desert Islands, 1930.
*On the Edge, 1930.
Poems for Children, 1930.
The Fleeting and other Poems, 1933.
*The Lord Fish, 1933.
*A Froward Child, 1934.
*Early One Morning, 1935.
*Poetry in Prose, 1936.
The Wind Blows Over (anthology), 1936.
This Year, Next Year, 1937.
Memory and Other Poems, 1938.
Behold, this Dreamer (anthology), 1939.
*Pleasures and Speculations, 1940.
Bells and Grass, 1941.
Collected Poems, 1942.
Love (anthology), 1943.

The books marked * are stories, novels, plays, criticism, essays, but so shot through with the magical quality of the poetry, and often interspersed with poems, that it has seemed better not to make unreal classifications. A selection, *Stories, Essays and Poems*, was published in *Everyman's Library* in 1938. For a sketch of the quality of the man see Sir Russell Brain's *Tea with Walter de la Mare*, 1957.

BOTTOMLEY, GORDON (1874-1948)

Chambers of Imagery, 1907, 1912.
Poems of Thirty Years, 1925.
King Lear's Wife and other Plays (coll. 1920).
Gruach and Britain's Daughter (plays), 1921.
Lyric Plays, 1932.
The Acts of St Peter, 1933.
Choric Plays, 1939.
Kate Kennedy, 1945.
Plays and Poems (a selection) with an introduction by C. C. Abbott, 1953.

Gordon Bottomley, besides being one of the most considerable poets in this group in other forms, is one of the few who have written poetic drama which is dramatic: *The Riding to Lithend* (in the *King Lear's Wife* volume) takes one of the most heroic stories in the sagas and handles it with fidelity and passionate imagination—it is a good acting play if the actors know how to speak poetry. *The Acts of St Peter* is interesting as an example of the religious drama which is now being attempted in various places.

GIBSON, WILFRED WILSON (1878-1962)

Stonefolds, 1907,

and other volumes to 1926.

Collected Poems (1905-25), 1926.
The Golden Room, 1928.
Hazards, 1930.
Highland Dawn, 1932. Islands, 1932.
Fuel, 1934.

MASEFIELD, JOHN, (1878-   )

POEMS:
Salt-Water Ballads, 1902. (Some of his best lyrics are here.)
Mainsail Haul, 1905.
The Everlasting Mercy, 1911.
The Widow in the Bye Street, 1912.

These two are perhaps his best long poems before *Reynard the Fox*.

The Daffodil Fields (a mishandling in modern terms of the old Icelandic tragic story of Gunnlaug and Helga, further spoilt by the introduction of a theme from the story of Gudrun of Laxdale), 1913; Dauber, 1913.

Sonnets and Poems, 1916.
Lollingdon Downs, 1918.
Reynard the Fox, 1919.

One of the most spirited poems of hunting, by a man who does not hunt. The sympathy is as much with the fox as with hounds and men.

King Cole, 1923.
Collected Poems, 1923,

and other volumes.

PLAYS:
The Tragedy of Nan, 1909.
Pompey the Great, 1910.
Philip the King, 1914 and 1926.
The Faithful, 1915.
Good Friday, 1917.
The Trial of Jesus, 1925,

and others.

NOVELS:
Captain Margaret, 1908.
Multitude and Solitude, 1909.
Sard Harker, 1924.
Odtaa, 1926,

and others among which *Basilissa*, 1940, and *Conquer*, 1941, may be especially mentioned as giving an amusingly contrasted interpretation of a period of Byzantine history to the *Count Belisarius* of Robert Graves. There are also two excellent children's books, *The Midnight Folk*, 1927, and *The Box of Delights*, 1935.

Mainsail Hail, 1905.
Gallipoli, 1916.
The Conway, 1933.
Shakespeare (in the *Home University Library*: a good introduction).
The Nine Days Wonder, 1941 (the story of the Dunkirk evacuation).
In the Mill, 1941 (autobiography).
A Macbeth Production, 1945.
Thanks before Going, 1946.
So Long to Learn, 1952.
Study by Muriel Spark, 1953.

THOMAS, EDWARD (1878-1917)

POETRY:
Poems, 1917.
Last Poems, 1918.
Collected Poems, 1922.

ESSAYS:
Cloud Castle and other Papers, 1922.
The Last Sheaf, 1928.
A Literary Pilgrim in England, 1928.

His life is told by his wife Helen Thomas in *World Without End*, 1931, and *As It Was*, 1935. See also *Edward Thomas: The Last Four Years*, by Eleanor Farjeon, 1958.

MONRO, HAROLD (1879-1932)

Poems, 1906.
Judas, 1908.
Before Dawn, 1911.
Children of Love, 1914.
Trees, 1915.
Strange Meetings, 1917.
Real Property, 1922.
The Earth for Sale, 1928.
Some Contemporary Poets, 1920.
Collected Poems, edited by A. Monro, with a biographical sketch by
   F. S. Flint and a critical note by T. S. Eliot, 1933.

Monro's generous appreciation of the work of others, particularly of young and struggling poets, found practical expression in the opening of the Poetry Bookshop, where readings and discussions of poetry were given by himself and others of the younger poets. He himself had a searching mind, and a quality of discipline in his verse which might have set an example to the weaker among the Georgian Poets.

FREEMAN, JOHN (1880-1929)

POETRY:
Twenty Poems, 1909.
Fifty Poems, Stone Trees, Presage of Victory, 1916.
Memories of Childhood, 1918.
Memories and other Poems, 1919.
Poems New and Old, 1920.
Music, Two Poems, 1921.
The Grove, Prince Absalom, 1925.
Solomon and Balkis, 1926.
Collected Poems, 1928.
Last Poems, 1930.

ESSAYS AND CRITICISM:
The Moderns, 1916.
Portrait of George Moore, 1922.
Punch and Holy Water, 1923.
English Portraits and Essays, 1924.
Herman Melville, 1926.

Freeman's disciplined verse was matched by his fine and discriminating criticism—he was, e.g., among the early admirers of C. M. Doughty. His letters (ed. Gertrude Freeman and J. C. Squire, 1936) contain a pleasant mixture of friendship and incidental criticism, never forced or self-conscious.

NOYES, ALFRED (1880-1958)

The Loom of Years, 1902.
The Flower of Old Japan, 1903.
Poems, 1904.
Forty Singing Seamen, 1907.
Drake, 1908.
The Enchanted Island, 1909.
Collected Poems, 1910; 3rd vol., 1920; 4th, 1927.
Tales of the Mermaid Tavern, 1912.
The Elfin Artist, 1920.
The Torchbearers (an Epic of Scientific Discovery), 1922, 1925, 1930.
Ballads and Poems, 1928,

and novels and criticism.

The Unknown God (spiritual autobiography), 1934.
Voltaire, 1936.

ABERCROMBIE, LASCELLES (1881-1938)

POETRY:
Interludes and Poems, 1908.
Emblems of Love, 1912; Deborah, 1912.
Four Short Plays, 1922.
Phoenix, 1923.
Twelve Idylls, 1928.
Collected Poems, 1930.
The Sale of St Thomas, 1931 (first part, 1911).

CRITICISM:
Thomas Hardy, 1912.
Speculative Dialogues, 1913.
The Epic, 1914.
Towards a Theory of Art, 1922.
Principles of English Prosody, 1923.
The Theory of Poetry, 1924.
The Idea of Great Poetry, 1925.
Romanticism, 1926.
Progress in Literature, 1929.
Poetry—Its Music and Meaning, 1932.

Of the poems *The Sale of St Thomas* contains the greatest and the most subtle poetry. The critical works may be read with enjoyment by the lover of literature as well as the specialist. His poetic dramas have met with deserved success in repertory theatres, and his poems have qualities not usually shared by his fellow-Georgian poets.

DRINKWATER, JOHN (1882-1937)

POETRY:
Poems of Men and Hours, 1911.
Poems of Love and Earth, 1912.
Cromwell and other Poems, 1913.
Swords and Ploughshares, 1915.
Olton Pools, 1916.
Tides, 1917; Poems 1908-14, 1917.
Seeds of Time, 1921.
Preludes, 1922.
Collected Poems, 1923,

and others.

PLAYS:
Abraham Lincoln, 1918.
Mary Stuart, 1921.
Oliver Cromwell, 1921.
Robert E. Lee, 1923.
Collected Plays, 1925.

AUTOBIOGRAPHY:
Inheritance, 1931.
Discovery, 1932.

and other works, especially historical studies.

STEPHENS, JAMES (1882-1950)

POETRY:
Insurrections, 1909.
The Hill of Vision, 1912.
Adventures of Seumas Beg, Songs from the Clay, 1915.
Green Branches, 1916.
Reincarnations, 1918.
Deirdre, 1923.
In the Land of Youth, 1924.
A Poetry Recital, 1925.
Collected Poems, 1926.
Etched in Moonlight, 1928.
Poems, 1931.

NOVELS AND STORIES:
The Crock of Gold, 1912; The Charwoman's Daughter, 1912.
Here are Ladies, 1913.

Stephens belongs to the Irish revival, in which he is an important figure of the second order.

FLECKER, JAMES ELROY (1884-1915)

POETRY:
The Bridge of Fire, 1907.
Thirty-Six Poems, 1910.
Forty-two Poems, 1911.
The Golden Journey to Samarkand, 1913.
The Old Ships, 1915.
The Burial in England, 1915.
Collected Poems, 1916, with introduction by Sir J. C. Squire.

PROSE:
The King of Alsander, 1914.
Collected Prose, 1920 (and 1922).

PLAYS:
Hassan, 1922.
Don Juan, 1925.
Letters of James Elroy Flecker to Frank Savery, 1926.
Some Letters from Abroad, 1930.
Life, by Geraldine Hodgson, 1925.

SQUIRE, SIR JOHN COLLINGS (1884-1959)

POETRY:
The Three Hills, and other Poems, 1913.
The Lily of Malud, 1917.
Poems, 1918, 1922.
The Birds and other Poems, 1919.
Poems in One Volume, 1926,

and other volumes.

PROSE:
Books in General, 1918, 1920, 1921.
Essays at Large, 1922,

and other essays and criticism.

Grub Street Nights (stories), 1924.
Collected Parodies (verse and prose), 1921.
Collected Poems with a preface by John Betjeman, 1959.

BROOKE, RUPERT (1887-1915)

POETRY:
Poems, 1911.
1914 and other Poems, 1915.
Collected Poems, with memoir by Edward Marsh, 1916.
Poetical Works, ed. Geoffrey Keynes, 1960.

PROSE:

John Webster and Elizabethan Drama, 1916.
Letters from America, with a preface by Henry James, 1916.

It is appropriate to end with the poet whose death symbolized to his contemporaries the destruction caused by the Great War.

DRAMA

THE course of drama during the period is reviewed in the Introduction, where also the more significant figures are considered. See also—

ALLARDYCE NICOLL—Nineteenth-Century Drama, 1800-59.
ERNEST REYNOLDS—Early Victorian Drama.
GEORGE ROWELL (ed.)—Nineteenth-Century Plays.
J. BRANDON-THOMAS—Charley's Aunt's Father.
CAMILLO PELLIZZI—English Drama: the last great phase.
E. A. BOYD—The Contemporary Drama of Ireland.
GERARD FAY—The Abbey Theatre.
HERBERT HOWARTH—The Irish Winters.
UNA ELLIS-FERMOR—The Irish Dramatic Movement.

For convenience there are three divisions in this section:

A. THE EARLY VICTORIANS.

 Sheridan Knowles, Talfourd, Sir Henry Taylor.

B. THE MID-VICTORIANS.

 Douglas Jerrold, J. M. Morton, H. J. Byron, Dion Boucicault, Tom Taylor, T. W. Robertson.

C. THE LATE VICTORIANS AND THEIR SUCCESSORS.

 I. Henry Arthur Jones, Arthur Wing Pinero, Oscar Wilde, Stephen Phillips.

 II. H. Granville-Barker, Allan Monkhouse, Elizabeth Baker, Githa Sowerby, Cicely Hamilton, Stanley Houghton, St John Hankin, Laurence Housman, George Bernard Shaw, Lady Gregory, J. M. Synge, William Archer, St John Ervine.

See also under:
 Poetry (Beddoes, Horne, Tennyson, FitzGerald, Browning, de Vere, Swinburne, Marston, Davidson,

Binyon, Trench, Yeats, Bottomley, Masefield, Abercrombie, Drinkwater, Flecker).
Novels (Mitford, Lytton, Lover, Reade, Hardy, Zangwill, Jacobs, Jerome, Galsworthy, Bennett, Cannan).
Nonsense and Parody: (Burnand, Gilbert, Anstey).

A. THE EARLY VICTORIANS

KNOWLES, JAMES SHERIDAN (1784-1862)

Virginius, 1820.
William Tell, 1825.
The Hunchback, 1832.
The Love Chase, 1837.
Dramatic Works, 1843.
Life, by his son, revised and edited by Francis Hervey, 1872.

Knowles made serious attempts to rehabilitate the drama of
his day, but finding this impossible forsook the stage for the
Baptist pulpit and published two anti-Romanist polemical works.
The Love Chase is still a readable play. He was looked on as a
candidate for the Laureateship in 1850.

TALFOURD, SIR THOMAS NOON (1795-1854)

Ion, 1835.

Talfourd's verse is workmanlike, if not very moving, and at
least he has no sham archaisms. His collected plays are easily
obtained, but he is remembered not for *Ion* and his other successful tragedies in verse, but as the author of the first Copyright Act
(1842) and as the friend and literary executor of Charles Lamb.

Letters of Charles Lamb, 1837.
Final Memorials of Charles Lamb, 1848.

These were republished in one volume in 1875 and 1892.

TAYLOR, SIR HENRY (1800-86)

Isaac Comnenus, 1827.
Philip van Artevelde, 1834.
Edwin the Fair, 1842.
St Clement's Eve, 1862.
Plays and Poems, 1863. Works, 1877-78.

These poetic dramas, especially *Philip van Artevelde*, have much
fine poetry of a sort in them and some of Taylor's observation
of men, but are hardly fitted for the stage. A contrast to them

is the worldly-wise *The Statesman*, 1836, a volume of essays for which Taylor said that *Pragmatic Precepts* would have been a better title. The *Autobiography*, 1885, and *Correspondence*, 1888, have individual as well as historic value.

B. THE MID-VICTORIANS

JERROLD, DOUGLAS WILLIAM (1803-57)

Jerrold was a typical hard-working man of letters, a prolific dramatist and journalist, best remembered by his contributions to *Punch*, especially—

Mrs Caudle's Curtain Lectures, 1846.
Collected Works, 1851-54.
Life and Remains, by his son W. Blanchard Jerrold, 1859.

MORTON, JOHN MADDISON (1811-91)

Box and Cox, 1847.

Morton was the author of some forty-five plays, mostly farces, and his work is typical of what the audience in his day enjoyed. The only one of his plays that has survived is *Box and Cox*, based on a French farce, *Une Chambre à deux lits*.

• BYRON, HENRY JAMES (1834-84)

Our Boys, 1875. (This held the Victorian record for a long run, from Jan. 16, 1875, to April 18, 1879.)

And many other comedies, burlesques, farces and extravaganzas, as well as more serious plays.

BOUCICAULT, DIONYSUS LARDNER (?1820-90)

London Assurance, 1841.
The Corsican Brothers, 1852.
The Colleen Bawn, 1860.
The Octoroon, 1861.
Arragh-na-Pogue, 1865.
The Shaughraun, 1875,

and many other plays, of which *Old Heads and Young Hearts*, 1844, *The Poor of New York*, *The Willow Copse* and *After Dark*, 1868, may be noted.

Dion Boucicault was the author of some hundred and twenty-four plays, most of them failures, but some of them startling successes. His first great success, *London Assurance*, was described by Poe as 'that despicable mass of inanity', and by Archer as 'probably the shallowest and flashiest production that ever passed for serious comedy'. But it reappears sporadically. Boucicault had no ideas to impart, there is very little literary merit in his plays, but he had every trick of the stage readily at his disposal. His latest plays were failures, but his group of Irish melodramas, relieved by a certain amount of passable comedy, deserved, in that age, the applause that greeted them. In this group, notably in *The Colleen Bawn*, *Arragh-na-Pogue* and *The Shaughraun*, he broke away from the old type character which had been his stock-in-trade and the stilted stage-speech he had previously employed, and produced something fresh. It can be said, therefore, that he did something towards liberating the stage for the emergence of that revival which he lived to see, but in which he did not share. *After Dark* has been revived with success in America.

There is a *Life* by Townshend Walsh. See also William Archer in *The Old Drama and the New*.

TAYLOR, TOM (1817-80)

Masks and Faces (with Charles Reade), 1854 (acted in 1852).
Still Waters Run Deep, 1855.
Our American Cousin, 1858. (This play contains Taylor's best known character, Lord Dundreary, but it is fair to add that the part was written up by the actor, E. A. Sothern.)
Lady Clancarty, 1874,

and many other plays, about seventy in all.

The early plays were collected in 1854, the historical dramas in 1877.

Taylor in his prose dramas, such as *The Contested Election*, 1859, and *The Ticket-of-Leave Man*, 1863, did his best to deal with contemporary life, and the plays are still readable. Less so, but not disagreeable, are his historical dramas in verse, *Anne Boleyn*, 1875, and *Joan of Arc*, 1871. *Arkwright's Wife*, 1873, in prose, shows that he realized something important to humanity had happened in the last fifty years. His verse goes well, and is not pseudo-Elizabethan pastiche; and his prose is good colloquial English. As befitted an editor of *Punch* (1874-80), his most successful plays were social comedy.

Taylor did much other work, of which his *Life of B. R. Haydon*, 1853, and his edition of Haydon's *Autobiography and Memoirs* are of special value. A rather remarkable and very pleasant achievement is his *Ballads and Songs of Brittany*, 1868, translations in good workmanlike vein of Breton songs.

ROBERTSON, THOMAS WILLIAM (1829-71)

David Garrick, 1864.
Society, 1865.
Ours, 1866.
Caste, 1867.
School, 1869,

and other plays.

Principal Dramatic Works, with a Memoir by his son, 1889.

C. THE LATE VICTORIANS AND THEIR SUCCESSORS

I

JONES, HENRY ARTHUR (1851-1929)

A Clerical Error, 1879.
The Silver King, 1882 (with Henry Herman).
The Case of Rebellious Susan, 1894.
The Liars, 1897,

and many other plays, of which *The Dancing Girl*, 1891, *The Tempter*, 1893, *The Physician*, 1897, *Carnac Sahib*, 1899, and *Mrs Dane's Defence*, 1900, may be specially noted.

Life, by his daughter Mrs. Thorne.

His dramatic criticism is also interesting, e.g.—

The Renascence of the English Drama, 1895.
The Foundation of a National Drama, 1913.
The Theatre of Ideas, 1915.

PINERO, SIR ARTHUR WING (1855-1934)

Sweet Lavender, 1888.
The Second Mrs Tanqueray, 1893.
The Notorious Mrs Ebbsmith, 1895.
Trelawney of the Wells, 1899.
The Gay Lord Quex, 1899.
Iris, 1901.
Letty, 1903.
His House in Order, 1906.
Mid-Channel, 1909,

and many others, including some farces.

WILDE, OSCAR (1856-1900)

PLAYS:
Lady Windermere's Fan, 1892.
A Woman of No Importance, 1893.
Salome (originally written in French; the English version was by Lord
    Alfred Douglas), 1893-94.
The Ideal Husband, 1895.
The Importance of being Earnest, 1895.

OTHER WRITINGS:
The Happy Prince, 1888.
Lord Arthur Savile's Crime, 1891.
The Picture of Dorian Gray, 1891.
Intentions, 1891.
A House of Pomegranates, 1892.
De Profundis (written 1897), 1905.
The Ballad of Reading Gaol, 1898.
Uniform edition, excluding Dorian Gray, 1908.
Collected edition with some additions, 1909.

There is a good chapter on Wilde in Janko Lavrin's *Phases of Modern Literature*. Of the many studies, those by Arthur Ransome, *Oscar Wilde*, 1912, and Hesketh Pearson, 1946, as well as a less favourable one by St John Ervine, 1952, may be specially mentioned. See also Vyvyan Holland, *Son of Oscar Wilde*, 1954, and *Oscar Wilde, a Pictorial Biography*.

Wilde's general work is treated in the Introduction. It is unlikely that any of his plays will survive except *The Importance of being Earnest* and, perhaps, *Lady Windermere's Fan*. *The Importance of being Earnest*, with its paradoxical wit, its verging on farce, its unrealistic quality and its admirable phrasing, can be related to Restoration comedy; but though undoubtedly amusing, it lacks the depths of either satirical or tender feeling characteristic of the best of the earlier writers, while the social criticism implied is shallow.

PHILLIPS, STEPHEN (1864-1915)

PLAYS:
Herod, 1901 (performed 1900).
Paolo and Francesca, 1900 (performed 1902).
Ulysses, 1902.
The Sin of David, 1904 (revised 1912).
Nero, 1906,

and others.

POEMS:
Poems, 1898.
New Poems, 1908.
Lyrics and Dramas, 1913,
and others.

Stephen Phillips enjoyed a great vogue in his day, *Paolo and Francesca* being acclaimed as a great work. It still has a certain faded charm, but Phillips's writing now appears to us to be false and merely decorative His plays can be classed with the other failures during our period to revive the poetic drama, attempts in which the authors seem to have thought that to plaster inferior derivative poetry on to mediocre plays would produce the required effect. The only exception to this general statement seems to be John Davidson (see under POETRY), who tried to integrate modern thought with the poetic forms of his time—forms themselves decrepit and certainly not to the taste of Edwardian audiences accustomed to realistic social drama.

II

GRANVILLE-BARKER, HARLEY GRANVILLE
(1877-1946)

PLAYS:
The Marrying of Anne Leete, 1901.
The Voysey Inheritance, 1905.
Waste, 1907.
(These were published together as *Three Plays* in 1909.)
Prunella, 1906 (with L. Housman).
The Madras House, 1910.
Three Short Plays, 1917. (Rococo, Vote by Ballot, Farewell to the Theatre.)

CRITICISM:
A National Theatre, 1907 (with W. Archer).
The Harlequinade, 1918 (with Dion Clayton Calthrop).
Prefaces to Shakespeare, 1923 onwards; collected as Prefaces to Shakespeare, series 1, 1927; 2, 1929; 3, 1936.
On Dramatic Method, 1931.
The Study of Drama, 1934.

The place of Granville-Barker is mentioned in the Introduction, but a little more may be said here about his work. The main conflict in his dramas, from the delicious *Anne Leete* to *The Madras House*, is that between man's moral responsibility to himself and his public moral responsibility. *The Voysey Inheritance* is still a striking play. There is enough metaphysical background to his work to make it likely that it will last longer than, at least, Galsworthy's. He never forgets he is an artist. Hardly second to his plays in importance are his *Prefaces to Shakespeare*, which are illuminating not only as to the way in which the plays of Shakespeare should be produced, but also as to their structure. The *Prefaces* also contain a considerable amount of interpretation, and constitute a healthy antidote to the 'profounder' interpretations of certain recent men of letters. Himself a playwright and producer, Granville-Barker in his approach to Shakespeare's plays is essentially different from esoteric philosophers, making his *Prefaces* essays which should be studied side by side with the works of scholars and philosophers.

MONKHOUSE, ALLAN NOBLE (1858-1936)

NOVELS:
A Deliverance, 1898.
Love in a Life, 1903.
Dying Fires, 1912.
Men and Ghosts, 1918.
My Daughter Helen, 1922.
Marmaduke, 1924.
Suburb, 1925.
Alfred the Great, 1927.
Farewell Manchester, 1931,

and others.

PLAYS:
Mary Broome, 1912.
War Plays, 1916.
The Conquering Hero, 1923.
Sons and Fathers, 1925,

and others.

CRITICISM:
Books and Plays, 1894.

Monkhouse's plays and novels deserve respect, and are much appreciated by a small but enthusiastic following. *Mary Broome* was one of the great standard plays of the immediately pre-War period, and must always be regarded as such.

HAMILTON, CICELY (1872-1953)

Diana of Dobson's, 1908.
The Old Adam (a post-War play),

and other plays.

Diana of Dobson's, Elizabeth Baker's *Chains*, 1909, and Githa Sowerby's *Rutherford and Son*, 1912, are all three standard plays of their period, especially in relation to the 'suffragette' movement. *The Old Adam* is a powerful and interesting play about war in the future which ought to be better known.

Also novels:

William, an Englishman, 1919.
Theodore Savage, 1922. One of the earliest and most memorable of the novels which contemplate a future breakdown of our civilization,

and other essays and studies.

Autobiography—Life Errant, 1935.

HOUGHTON, WILLIAM STANLEY (1881-1913)

The Younger Generation, 1910.
Hindle Wakes, 1912.
Works, with introduction by Harold Brighouse, 1914 (3 vols.).

HANKIN, ST JOHN EMILE CLAVERING (1869-1909)

The Two Mr Wetherbys, 1903.
The Return of the Prodigal, 1905.
The Charity that Began at Home, 1906.
The Cassilis Engagement, 1907.
The Last of the De Mullins, 1908.
The Burglar who Failed (1 Act), 1908.
The Constant Lover (1 Act), 1912.

The Return of the Prodigal, *The Charity that Began at Home* and *The Cassilis Engagement* were published together as *Three Plays with Happy Endings* in 1907, with a preface. Hankin also wrote two witty volumes of parody—

Mr Punch's Dramatic Sequels, 1901.
Lost Masterpieces, 1904.

Hankin is probably the 'purest' artist among the playwrights of his day. George Calderon referred to 'the fine, dry, Hankin flavour', but perhaps cool is a better adjective to apply to him. He was a real writer of comedy, who dealt with certain absurd idealisms in mankind which do not belong to any particular period. He moved with unruffled and sympathetic ease among his characters, with their kindness, stupidity and snobbery; most of his people belong to 'the county' which he realized was disappearing. He is witty, detached and tender. His weakness was his fragility, but he was an artist in words and, alone among his contemporaries' except Shaw, understood phrasing. But he was never successful.

HOUSMAN, LAURENCE (1865-1959)

PLAYS:
Prunella, 1906 (with Granville-Barker).
Angels and Ministers, 1921.
Little Plays of St Francis, 1922 (and later series).
Followers of St Francis, 1925.
The Comments of Juniper, 1926.
Cornered Poets, 1929.
Victoria Regina, 1934.
The Golden Sovereign, 1937.
Palestine Plays, 1942,

and others.

OTHER WRITINGS:
An Englishwoman's Love-Letters, 1900.
Selected Poems, 1909. Collected poems, 1938.
Trimblerigg, 1924 (a political satire in novel form),

and other novels, tales, poems and satires.

Laurence Housman's plays are charming examples of closet dramas, but few of them are adapted to production on a large stage, though *Victoria Regina* has been a success. They are admirably written within the limits of their intention. The merciless satire of *Trimblerigg* is in them subdued and mellowed, but its flavour is still perceptible.

Of his later works some deserve special mention:

The Unexpected Years (autobiography), 1937.
Back Words and Fore Words: An Author's Year Book, 1893-1945.

SHAW, GEORGE BERNARD (1856-1950)

PLAYS:
Plays, Pleasant and Unpleasant, 1898.
Three Plays for Puritans, 1900.
Man and Superman, 1903.
John Bull's Other Island, 1904.
Major Barbara, 1905.
The Doctor's Dilemma, 1906.
Getting Married, 1908.
The Showing-up of Blanco Posnet, 1909.
The Dark Lady of the Sonnets, 1910.
Misalliance, 1910.
Fanny's First Play, 1911.

Androcles, Pygmalion, and Overruled, 1912.
Great Catherine, 1913.
Heartbreak House, 1917.
Back to Methuselah, 1921.
Saint Joan, 1923.
The Apple Cart, 1929.
Too True to be Good, 1932.
A Village Wooing and On the Rocks, 1933.
The Six of Calais, The Simpleton of the Unexpected Isles, and The
    Millionairess, 1934.
Complete Plays, 1931.
Geneva, 1938.
In Good King Charles's Golden Days, 1939.

CRITICAL AND OTHER WRITINGS:
The Quintessence of Ibsenism, 1891 and 1913.
The Perfect Wagnerite, 1898.
Our Theatres in the Nineties (coll. articles), 1931.
Music in London, 1890-94 (coll. articles), 1931.
The Intelligent Woman's Guide to Socialism and Capitalism, 1928.
Major Critical Essays, 1932.
Prefaces, 1934.
Everybody's Political What's What, 1944.
Novels, tracts on Socialism, etc.

There are many studies of Shaw, of which St John Ervine's
and Stephen Winsten's *Jesting Apostle* may be particularly
mentioned.

GREGORY, AUGUSTA, LADY (1852-1932)

Gods and Fighting Men, 1906.
Seven Short Plays, 1909.
New Comedies, 1913.
Three Last Plays, 1928.
Life, by Elizabeth Coxhead.

SYNGE, JOHN MILLINGTON (1871-1909)

The Shadow of the Glen; and Riders to the Sea, 1905; The Well of the
    Saints, 1905.
The Playboy of the Western World, 1907.
Aran Islands, 1907.
The Tinkers' Wedding, 1907.
Poems and Translations, 1909.
Deirdre of the Sorrows, 1910.
Works (4 vols.), 1910.
There is a volume of selections in Everyman's Library.
Biography, by David H. Greene and Edward M. Stephens, 1959.

ARCHER, WILLIAM (1856-1924)

CRITICISM:
Masks or Faces: a Study in the Psychology of Acting, 1888.
The Theatrical World, 1893-97 (5 vols.).
Play-Making, 1912.
The Old Drama and the New, 1923.
(With H. Granville-Barker) A National Theatre Scheme and Estimates, 1907.
C. Archer, William Archer, 1931.

Archer surprised himself, towards the end of his life, by writing a dramatic thriller which was a success—*The Green Goddess*, 1921; the incongruity of the situation lying mainly in the seriousness of his dramatic criticism, and for the rest in his having been one of the first and most valiant champions of Ibsen. He edited, and partly translated, Ibsen's *Prose Dramas* and the *Collected Works* of Ibsen. His book on *Play-Making* is an admirable technical manual for the fabrication of 'well-made' plays, in which he shows himself as the descendant of Scribe and Sardou. His views on the new drama are stimulating, but his opinions of the old are nothing less than deplorable.

ERVINE, ST JOHN GREER (1883-   )

Mixed Marriage, 1910-11.
Jane Clegg, 1911-12.
John Ferguson, 1914.

Since the First War St John Ervine's plays have been comedies, unlike his earlier grim studies of conflict. He has also written much dramatic criticism and published volumes of essays, novels and biographies of General Booth—*God's Soldier*, 1935—Oscar Wilde, Shaw, and others.

NOVELS AND SHORT STORIES

FOR convenience there are four main divisions here:

A. THE EARLY AND MID-VICTORIANS
B. THE LATE VICTORIANS—

    the dividing date being about 1880.

C. THE EDWARDIANS AND SOME GEORGIANS.
D. A NOTE ON SOME BEST SELLERS.

But it should be emphasized that these, like other divisions, are merely for convenience. It is easier to pin Henry James down to a period than Thomas Hardy, and—to take an opposite example—William De Morgan insisted on removing himself from his actual to his spiritual date when the list was made. Within the periods the arrangement is usually by age, except that certain writers are grouped together because of their common interests or characteristics, e.g., the 'social' novelists in (A), the followers of R. L. Stevenson in (B).

A. THE EARLY AND MID-VICTORIANS.

    I. Some older writers:
        Peacock, Marmion Savage, Frances Trollope, Mary Russell Mitford, Emily Eden.
    II. Historical novelists:
        G. P. R. James, Harrison Ainsworth, Meadows Taylor.
    III. Bulwer Lytton, Disraeli.
    IV. Dickens, Wilkie Collins, the Brontës, Thackeray, Anne Thackeray Ritchie, William De Morgan.
    V. Marryat, Lever, Lover, 'Cuthbert Bede', Surtees, Whyte-Melville, Anthony Trollope, T. Adolphus Trollope, R. D. Blackmore, Somerville and Ross.

VI. The 'Social' novel:
Harriet Martineau, Mrs Gaskell, Charles Kingsley, Henry Kingsley, T. Hughes, Charles Reade, 'George Eliot'.

VII. The background of religious life and thought:
C. M. Yonge, J. H. Shorthouse, Mrs. Oliphant, 'Mark Rutherford', Mrs. Humphry Ward.

B. THE LATE VICTORIANS.

I. George Meredith, Thomas Hardy, Henry James, Rhoda Broughton.

II. Novelists of middle- and lower-class London life:
Besant, Gissing, Arthur Morrison, Whiteing, Pett Ridge, Zangwill, W. W. Jacobs, J. K. Jerome.

III. Bohemia and Society at the turn of the century:
George Du Maurier, Henry Harland, R. S. Hichens, 'Anthony Hope', E. F. Benson, 'Baron Corvo', Leonard Merrick, 'John Oliver Hobbes', Richard Garnett.

IV. Romance: Stevenson and others:
R. L. Stevenson, Stanley Weyman, Rider Haggard, 'H. S. Merriman', Conan Doyle, Maurice Hewlett.

V. Some masters of terror:
Le Fanu, M. R. James, Arthur Machen.

VI. Kipling, F. A. Steel.

C. EDWARDIANS AND SOME GEORGIANS.
Conrad, George Moore, H. G. Wells, Galsworthy, Bennett, G. D. Brown, 'Saki', J. D. Beresford, E. M. Forster, May Sinclair, Richard Middleton, Compton Mackenzie, Gilbert Cannan, F. A. Swinnerton, Hugh Walpole.

D. SOME BEST SELLERS.
Mrs Henry Wood, Miss Mulock, George Lawrence, Miss Braddon, 'Ouida', Marie Corelli, Hall Caine.

There is a real difficulty in deciding whether to include
Meredith, Hardy, Kipling and others here or elsewhere, and
the actual classification has been made merely on the ground
that probably their prose has more readers than their
poetry.

See also under—

History (J. A. Froude, 'George Bourn').
Travel (Borrow, Trelawney, Johnston).
Theology (Newman, Neale).
Poetry (Ingelow, W. Morris, Swinburne, Watts-Dunton,
Lang, Newbolt, W. Sharp, De la Mare, Masefield,
J. Stephens, Flecker, Squire).
Drama (Jerrold, Wilde, Monkhouse, L. Housman, G. B.
Shaw, Lady Gregory, Ervine).
Children's Books (*passim*).
Criticism and Essays (Pater, 'Vernon Lee', A. Symons,
Mallock, 'Q', Jefferies, Hudson, Cunninghame
Graham, Beerbohm, Lucas, Belloc, Chesterton,
Baring).
Nonsense and Parody ('Lewis Carroll', Burnand, Gros-
smith, 'F. Anstey', Bentley).

Certain general books of criticism and history may be
suggested here for study, in addition to those (e.g., Sadleir's
Trollope) which are noted later under their subject.

GENERAL CRITICISM:

E. M. FORSTER—*Aspects of the Novel.*
T. H. GREEN—*An Estimate of the Value and Influence of Works
of Fiction in Modern Times*, ed. F. N. Scott.
HENRY JAMES—*The Art of the Novel*; and *Notes on Novelists.*
H. W. LEGGETT—*The Idea in Fiction.*
PERCY LUBBOCK—*The Craft of Fiction.*
EDWIN MUIR—*The Structure of the Novel.*
A. T. SHEPPARD—*The Art and Practice of Historical Fiction.*
WILFRID WARD—*Last Lectures* (one is *On the Methods of
depicting Character in Fiction and Biography*).

LITERARY HISTORY AND THE VICTORIAN NOVELISTS:

E. A. BAKER—*History of the English Novel*, Vols. VII, VIII, IX and X; these cover the whole of the period.

MICHAEL SADLEIR—*Excursions in Victorian Bibliography*. (Essays on, as well as bibliographies of, Trollope, Marryat, Disraeli, Collins, Reade, Whyte-Melville, Mrs Gaskell.)

L. CAZAMIAN—*Le roman social en Angleterre (1830-50)*. (This considers especially Dickens, Disraeli, Mrs Gaskell, C. Kingsley.)

MADELEINE L. CAZAMIAN—*Le roman et les idées en Angleterre, L'influence de la science, 1860-90*.

M. E. SPEARE—*The Political Novel*. (Special reference to Disraeli.)

JOSEPH ELLIS BAKER—*The Novel and the Oxford Movement*.

W. C. BROWNELL—*Victorian Prose Masters*. (Thackeray, Carlyle, G. Eliot, Matthew Arnold, Ruskin, Meredith.)

LORD DAVID CECIL—*Victorian Novelists*. (Dickens, Thackeray, the Brontës, Mrs Gaskell, G. Eliot, Trollope.)

HOLBROOK JACKSON—*Great English Novelists*. (Lytton, Dickens, Disraeli, Thackeray, Meredith.)

A. QUILLER-COUCH—*Charles Dickens and other Victorians*. (Dickens, Thackeray, Disraeli, Mrs Gaskell, Trollope, The Victorian Background.)

KATHLEEN TILLOTSON—*Novels of the Eighteen Forties*.

PATRICIA THOMSON—*The Victorian Heroine: A Changing Ideal*.

The following deal more especially with the later novelists, from Henry James to E. M. Forster, particularly Bennett, Wells, Conrad and Kipling:

G. K. CHESTERTON—*Heretics*.

ABEL CHEVALLEY—*Le roman anglais de notre temps*.

ANDRE CHEVRILLON—*Nouvelles études anglaises*.

BONAMY DOBRÉE—*The Lamp and the Lute*.

RAMON FERNANDEZ—*Messages*.

JOHN FREEMAN—*English Portraits and Essays*; and *The Moderns*.

EDWARD GARNETT—*Friday Nights*.

EDMUND GOSSE—*Aspects and Impressions*.

R. BRIMLEY-JOHNSON—*Some Contemporary Novelists (Men)*; and *The Women Novelists.*

ROBERT LYND—*Books and Authors*; and *Old and New Masters.*

DESMOND MACCARTHY—*Portraits.*

ANDRÉ MAUROIS—*Poets and Prophets (Logiciens et magiciens.)*

DIXON SCOTT—*Men and Books.*

ORLO WILLIAMS—*Some great English Novels.*

GILBERT PHELPS—*The Russian Novel in English Fiction.*

A. THE EARLY AND MID-VICTORIANS

1. Some Older Writers

PEACOCK, THOMAS LOVE (1785-1866)

Headlong Hall, 1816.
Melincourt, 1817.
Nightmare Abbey, 1818.
Maid Marian, 1822.
The Misfortunes of Elphin, 1829.
Crotchet Castle, 1831.
Gryll Grange, 1860.

'Little tales of a heady and bewildering nature, interspersed with unusual songs'—Kipling's description of Peacock's novels, in *Stalky & Co.*, may be supplemented with J. B. Priestley's 'Aristophanic fiction . . . creating fantastic personages out of their opinions.'

Yet the personages exist, or at least his sybaritic, scholarly parsons, Doctors Opimian and Folliott, have an air of immortality about them. Peacock is entertainingly reactionary: he intensely disliked 'the march of mind' and the pretensions of the early optimists who so touchingly believed in an immediate Utopia. He is more fully dealt with in the previous volume, where his only half serious *Four Ages of Poetry* is considered.

The best edition of Peacock's works is the Halliford edition, in 10 vols., ed. H. F. B. Brett-Smith and C. E. Jones, 1924-34, but there are others easily accessible. The tales can be obtained in a single volume.

Peacock's best poetry is in the songs of the novels and in *Rhododaphne* (1818). His witty and paradoxical *Four Ages of Poetry* (1820) provoked Shelley's *Defence of Poetry*, and a convenient edition of the two, with Browning's *Essay on Shelley* thrown in, was brought out by H. F. B. Brett-Smith in 1929.

The 1875 edition of the collected works contains a Memoir; but the *Life* by Carl Van Doren, 1911, and the studies by J. B. Priestley, 1927, and Olwen Campbell, 1953, are more satisfactory.

SAVAGE, MARMION (1803-72)

The Falcon Family; or Young Ireland, 1845.
The Bachelor of the Albany, 1847.
Reuben Medlicott; or the Coming Man, 1852.

When Marmion Savage died *The Athenaeum* declared that he was worthy of being held in kindly remembrance 'if only for his wholesome wit and airy vivacity'. He had these and something more—scholarship, a sense of criticism and a knowledge of affairs. He derives from Peacock, and has all his dislike of cranks, but he is, perhaps, especially noticeable for his heroines, who, most unlike the Amelia Sedley of Thackeray, or the Agnes Wickfield of Dickens, have minds of their own and suggest rather George Meredith's Clara Middleton. In *The Falcon Family*, a 'caustic and brilliant skit' on the physical force party in Ireland, he especially ridiculed the Celtic men. *Reuben Medlicott* is a kindly joke at the self delusions of youth, whereas *The Bachelor of the Albany* has the Oxford Movement as its chief butt. The book is well constructed and extremely entertaining throughout.

• TROLLOPE, FRANCES (1780-1863)

Domestic Manners of the Americans, 1832.

One of the first, liveliest and most unflattering accounts of a residence in the United States. It may be compared with Harriet Martineau's more sympathetic *Society in America* (1837) and *A Retrospect of Western Travel* (1838).

The Vicar of Wrexhill, 1837.
The Widow Barnaby, 1838.
The Widow Married, 1840.

Mrs Trollope wrote many other novels, and though most of them were pot-boilers there is plenty of wit and observation in them. She deserves to be remembered for her own sake, not merely as the mother of Anthony Trollope. Her daughter-in-law, Frances Eleanor Trollope, published a study of her life and work in 1895. Her work is discussed in the previous volume.

MITFORD, MARY RUSSELL (1787-1855)

Mary Russell Mitford wrote many successful plays, poetic tragedies of a kind which is now dead—*Rienzi*, 1828, is the best—but she is remembered for her stories and sketches of village life.

Our Village, 1824-32 (published in *The Lady's Magazine* from 1819).

Most of the later one-volume editions are made by selection from the original five volumes.

Recollections of a Literary Life, 1852.
Life, related in a selection from her letters, ed. by A. G. L'Estrange and H. F. Chorley, 1869-72.
Correspondence with Charles Boner and John Ruskin, ed. Elizabeth Lee, 1914.

The best biographer of Miss Mitford is Miss Mitford in her letters; but see also A. G. L'Estrange, *The Friendships of Mary Russell Mitford*, 1882, and Vera Watson's *Mary Russell Mitford*, 1950.

EDEN, EMILY (1797-1869)

Portraits of the People, 1844.
Up the Country, 1866.

The above books are on India, where Miss Eden had lived with her brother, the Governor General, Lord Auckland, from 1835 to 1842. These books were widely read, and give a good idea of the attitude of the governing class towards India in those days.

The Semi-detached House, 1859.
The Semi-attached Couple, 1860.

The later book was written thirty years before its publication and is fresher than its predecessor in the press. It seems to owe a good deal to *Pride and Prejudice*, but exists in its own virtue as the result of a humorous and trained mind, directed by the education young women of good family were provided with before Victorian ideas relegated them to homelier spheres of action. Miss Eden knew the high social and political world of her day and treated it in the manner of amiable comedy in what Lord Houghton called 'pure and facile English'.

II. Historical Novelists

JAMES, GEORGE PAYNE RAINSFORD (1799-1860)

James's historical novels have become proverbial for their

solitary horsemen—he was parodied by Thackeray in *Barbazure*—
but he was a not contemptible follower of Scott. He wrote over a
hundred novels, of which a few may be named as an indication
of his range.

Richelieu, 1829.
Philip Augustus, 1831.
Mary of Burgundy, 1833.
Darnley, 1833.
There is a study of James by S. M. Ellis—The Solitary Horseman, 1927.

AINSWORTH, WILLIAM HARRISON (1805-82)

Ainsworth is, on the whole, a more spirited writer than James,
though he was apt to cumber the movement of his stories with
chunks of information from his antiquarian and historical sources.
He also was a voluminous producer, and only a few of his books
need be named.

Rookwood, 1834.
Jack Sheppard, 1839.
The Tower of London, 1840.
Old St Paul's, 1841.
Windsor Castle, 1843.
The Lancashire Witches, 1848.

These and other books, with their lurid historical atmosphere,
may be wholly recommended to children, but they also appeal to
what is left of the childish in adults.

S. M. Ellis—William Harrison Ainsworth and His Friends, 1911; M.
Elwin—Victorian Wallflowers, 1934.

TAYLOR, PHILIP MEADOWS (1808-76)

The Confessions of a Thug, 1839.
Tippoo Sultaun, 1840.
Tara, 1863.
Ralph Darnell, 1865.
Seeta, 1872.
A Noble Queen, 1878.

Meadows Taylor's novels deal with Indian history and life, of
both of which he had a deep knowledge and understanding, from
the sixteenth to the nineteenth century. He had a large share in
the suppression of Thuggery, and *The Confessions of a Thug* contains more fact than fiction. His *Story of My Life* (1877) is an
admirable, simple and unaffected autobiography. In every
respect he is better than James or Ainsworth, though he receives
far less attention than they do in most histories of literature.

III

LYTTON, EDWARD BULWER, LORD (1803-73)

Lytton as a novelist tried every fashionable kind in turn. From *Pelham* (1828), a novel of society, he passed to the interpretation —his enemies said glorification—of the murderer *Eugene Aram* (1832). Then came historical novels in the Scott tradition—

The Last Days of Pompeii, 1834.
Rienzi, 1835.
The Last of the Barons, 1843.
Harold, 1848.

Then he tried the domestic novel—

The Caxtons, 1850.
My Novel, 1853.
What will he do with it?, 1858.

And he wrote at least two good uncanny stories—

The Haunted and the Haunters, 1859.
A Strange Story, 1862.

These are only about half his novels; he wrote also poetry which is of little value and plays which can still hold the stage—

The Lady of Lyons, and Richelieu, 1838.
Money, 1840.

None of his novels is exactly worthless, and most of them have a marked individual quality, but in literature and in life he just missed the first rank.

There was a library edition of the novels in 1859-63, and the poetic and dramatic works were collected in 1852-54.

Life, Letters and Literary Remains, by his son, 1883; this comes down only to 1832, but may be supplemented by the *Memoir* prefixed to his *Speeches,* 1874, and by the later lives by his grandson, 1913, and T. H. S. Escott, 1910.

Michael Sadleir's *Bulwer, a Panorama, Edward and Rosina* (1931; since republished under the second half of the title) should be read; it again covers only the earlier part of the life. There is a critical study of the writings by E. G. Bell; *Introductions to the Prose Remains, Plays and Comedies of Edward Bulwer, Lord Lytton,* 1914. On the plays see also *Bulwer and Macready,* ed. by C. H. Shattuck, 1958.

K

DISRAELI, BENJAMIN, LORD BEACONSFIELD
(1804-81)

Disraeli's early novels of society have the brilliance of Lytton's, with an extra touch of gaudiness, but also something more permanent—perhaps the definite personality, sure of itself, in which Lytton was lacking.

Vivian Grey, 1826.
The Young Duke, 1831.
Contarini Fleming, 1832.
Alroy, 1833.

There is also a group of witty and satiric extravaganzas:
Ixion in Heaven, The Infernal Marriage, Popanilla, 1828. But it is the political novels which show the real difference between Disraeli and Lytton.

Coningsby, 1844 ('the best novel of politics ever written').
Sybil, or The Two Nations, 1845: a book which owes something to
    Carlyle's Past and Present, but at the same time is the work of a states-
    man who sees for himself the dangers of social cleavage.
Tancred, 1847: another side of Disraeli's political thought is here.
Lothair, 1870, and Endymion, 1880, have the same wit and knowledge
    of the world and the political game, with increased experience but loss
    of freshness.

The Political Biography of Lord George Bentinck, 1852, is a complement to the novels and even a kind of commentary on them. It is an interesting experiment in being a biography in terms of politics rather than in terms of personality. Disraeli's poetry is negligible.

The standard life is that by Monypenny and Buckle, 1910-20. See also *Dizzy* by Hesketh Pearson, 1951, and *Peacocks and Primroses,* by Muriel Masefield, 1953.

The *Disraeli* of André Maurois has the interest of a life seen through foreign eyes, and perhaps the insight which one Jew can have into the mind of another. A not too friendly sketch of Disraeli ('Mr Daubeny') is drawn by Trollope in his *Phineas Finn* series (see p. 279).

IV

DICKENS, CHARLES (1812-70)

The novels of Dickens stretch from *Sketches by Boz* (1833 onwards serially, 1835-36 in book-form) to the unfinished *Edwin Drood.* They are so easily accessible that it is not necessary to note even collected editions here; most of them appeared in monthly numbers or in one of the magazines which Dickens edited, and they followed in rapid succession:

Posthumous Papers of the Pickwick Club, 1836-37.
Oliver Twist, 1838.
Nicholas Nickleby, 1839.
Master Humphrey's Clerk (The Old Curiosity Shop, Barnaby Rudge), 1840-41.
A Christmas Carol 1843. (Other Christmas tales, 1844-47).
Martin Chuzzlewit, 1844.
Dombey and Son, 1848.
David Copperfield, 1850.
Bleak House, 1853.
Hard Times, 1854.
Little Dorrit, 1857.
A Tale of Two Cities, 1859.
Great Expectations, 1861.
Our Mutual Friend, 1865.
The Mystery of Edwin Drood, 1870.

Also the volumes of sketches: *American Notes*, 1842; *Pictures from Italy*, 1846; *The Uncommercial Traveller*, 1860.

The standard life remains that by John Forster, first published in 1872; the best editions of this are those by B. W. Matz, 1911, and J. W. T. Ley, 1928. The *Letters* were published in 1880-82, and the *Letters to Wilkie Collins, 1851-70*, in 1892.

There are many good studies and essays, among the best Alice Meynell's essay in *Hearts of Controversy*, G. K. Chesterton's study (first published in 1906: see also his *Appreciations and Criticisms of the Works of Charles Dickens*, 1911); Stephen Leacock's *Charles Dickens* (1933); Oliver Elton's *Dickens and Thackeray*, 1930; Bernard Darwin's *Dickens*, 1933; the critique by George Santayana in his *Soliloquies in England*; the study by Edmund Wilson in *The Wound and the Bow*, 1941; and the *Charles Dickens* of Dame Una Pope-Hennessey, 1945. See also *Dickens at Work*, by John Butt and Kathleen Tillotson, 1957; *Charles Dickens: The World of his Novels*, by J. Hillis Miller, 1958; and Humphrey House's *The Dickens World*.

COLLINS, WILLIAM WILKIE (1824-89)

Wilkie Collins's twenty-odd novels are all workmanlike, well constructed and not without character-drawing. Among the best are—

The Woman in White, 1860.
No Name, 1862.

Armadale, 1866.
The Moonstone, 1868—one of the best detective stories ever written. This and *The Woman in White* are his best novels, but many others, e.g., *Poor Miss Finch*, 1872, are also good.

Collins is still very readable. His chief importance in the history of the novel lies in the fact that he attempted to impart some form to it, and that he influenced Dickens in the same direction towards the end of his life.

There is a good study by S. M. Ellis in *Wilkie Collins, Le Fanu and others*, 1931; and T. S. Eliot's introduction to *The Moonstone* in the *World's Classics* should be read. The best life is that by N. P. Davis, 1956.

BRONTË, CHARLOTTE (1816-55)

The Professor (written first, not published until 1857).
Jane Eyre, 1847.
Shirley, 1849.
Villette, 1853.

BRONTË, EMILY (1818-48)

Wuthering Heights, 1848.

See also *Gondal's Queen*, by Fannie E. Ratchford, 1955.

BRONTË, ANNE (1820-49)

Agnes Grey, 1848 (published with *Wuthering Heights*).
The Tenant of Wildfell Hall, 1848.

The three sisters joined in the *Poems by Currer, Ellis and Acton Bell*, 1846.

An edition of Emily Brontë's poems, ed. Clement Shorter, was published in 1923 but the best edition is the *Complete Poems*, edited by C. W. Hatfield, 1941 (new ed. 1954).

The most complete edition of the works of the Brontë sisters is the Shakespeare Head, 1931-34, including the *Letters* and the *Life* by T. J. Wise and J. Alexander Symington. There is an interesting collected edition of Charlotte Brontë with introductions by Mrs Humphrey Ward, 1899-1900, and another edited by Clement Shorter, 1903, and the Heather edition, 1949.

The earliest and still in some ways the standard biography —a classic in its own right—was Mrs Gaskell's *Life of Charlotte Brontë*, 1857, but this should be corrected and supplemented by

Margaret Lane's admirable *The Brontë Story*, which reconsiders it in the light of such later books as—

A. C. Swinburne—A Note on Charlotte Brontë, 1877.
Clement Shorter—The Brontës and their Circle, 1896.
The Brontës, Life and Letters, 1908.
May Sinclair—The Three Brontës, 1914.
Ernest Dimnet—Les Soeurs Brontë, 1910, trs. L. N. Gill, The Brontë Sisters, 1927.
E. F. Benson—Charlotte Brontë, 1932.
E. M. Delafield—The Brontës: their lives recorded by their contemporaries, 1935.
Herbert E. Wroot—Persons and Places, Sources of Charlotte Brontë's Novels, 1935.
G. Elsie Harrison—Methodist Good Companions, 1935. (The Brontë originals.)
A good introductory study with a useful bibliography is—
K. A. R. Sugden—A Short History of the Brontës, 1929.

See also the two recent lives of Anne Brontë, one by Winifred Gérin, the other by A. M. Harrison and Derek Hudson; the studies of Branwell Brontë by Daphne Du Maurier (*The Infernal World of Branwell Brontë*) and Winifred Gérin; the *Emily Brontë* of Muriel Spark and Derek Hudson, and Margaret Crompton's *Passionate Search: a Life of Charlotte Brontë*.

THACKERAY, WILLIAM MAKEPEACE (1811-63)

There are so many editions available that it is hardly necessary to give a full list of Thackeray's works, but it may be noted that though the *Paris Sketch-Book* appeared in 1840 and the next eight years were full of activity, it was not until 1848, when *Vanity Fair* and *The Book of Snobs* appeared, that he made much impression on the public. After that the dates of his chief works are—

Pendennis, 1848-50.
The History of Henry Esmond, 1852.
The English Humorists of the Eighteenth Century, 1853.
The Newcomes, 1854-55.
The Rose and the Ring, 1854.
Miscellanies (including Barry Lyndon), 1855.
The Virginians, 1858-59. (A continuation of Esmond.)
The Four Georges, 1861.
The Adventures of Philip, 1862.
Roundabout Papers, 1863.

The great works are *Vanity Fair*, *Esmond*, *Pendennis* and *The Newcomes*. *The English Humorists* is a disappointing and impercipient work: *The Four Georges* is thoroughly bad, and has been more responsible than any other work for disseminating false views of the early Hanoverian monarchs. *The Rose and the Ring* is a permanently delightful book for children. The book most characteristic of Thackeray himself, who sometimes seems to be an essayist who was a novelist only by accident, is the *Roundabout Papers*.

Thackeray's early ambition to be a painter left its mark on his books, many of which contained his own illustrations when they were published. In modern editions these are usually omitted or replaced by the work of others, but the books have more of their true flavour if they have their author's pictures, as in the biographical edition of 1898-99. The introductions to this edition are by his daughter, Lady Ritchie, and contain as much biographical material as Thackeray himself would have wished to be published: he did not wish a formal biography to be written. This has however been done, to the great increase of our understanding, by Gordon N. Ray in *Thackeray: The Buried Life*, 1952; *Thackeray: The Uses of Adversity*, 1955, and *Thackeray: The Age of Wisdom*, 1958.

The study by Anthony Trollope is surprisingly disappointing; those by Saintsbury, 1931, and G. K. Chesterton, 1909, should be read, and so should A. A. Jack, *Thackeray*, 1895, Oliver Elton, *Dickens and Thackeray*, 1930, Malcolm Elwin's biographical study, 1932, and the critical studies by J. Y. T. Greig, 1950, and Geoffrey Tillotson, 1954.

Percy Lubbock's *The Craft of Fiction* contains an admirable analysis of *Vanity Fair*.

See also—*Some Family Letters of William Makepeace Thackeray, together with recollections by his Kinswoman, Blanche Warre Cornish*, 1911. *Thackeray's Letters to an American Family*, with an introduction by Lucy W. Baxter, 1904. *The Letters and Private Papers of W. M. Thackeray*, ed. Gordon N. Ray, 1946.

THACKERAY, ANNE ISABELLA (Lady Ritchie) (1837-1919)

Thackeray's daughter had a touch of her father's genius, and her delicate novels and essays are written in a cadenced prose which possesses a half-melancholy charm not unlike his. Out of them may be selected—

The Story of Elizabeth, 1863.
The Village on the Cliff, 1867.

Old Kensington, 1873.
Miss Angel, 1875.
A Book of Sibyls, 1883. (Critical essays.)
Records of Tennyson, Ruskin and Browning, 1892.
Chapters from some Memoirs, 1894.

See also *Thackeray's Daughter: Some Reminiscences* compiled by
H. T. Fuller and V. Hammersley, 1952—a study of her youth.
Trollope's comment on Rhoda Broughton (see below, pp 291-2)
and Anne Thackeray is illuminating. He implies that Anne
Thackeray's characters are a little insipid, and that Rhoda
Broughton gives too much life to her figures, 'making them speak
as men and women do speak'.

DE MORGAN, WILLIAM FREND (1839-1917)

Joseph Vance, 1906.
Alice-for-Short, 1907.
Somehow Good, 1908.
It never can Happen again, 1909.
An Affair of Dishonour, 1910.
A Likely Story, 1911.
When Ghost meets Ghost, 1914.

The Old Madhouse, 1919; *The Old Man's Youth*, 1921: these were
left unfinished and published posthumously; the second contains
a good deal of autobiography, and De Morgan also put a good
deal of himself into Charles Heath in *Alice-for-Short*.

De Morgan's active life was spent in the designing and making
of pottery which is treasured by museums and private owners;
he was in the Burne Jones–Morris circle. It was only after he had
had to give that up that he began, almost by accident, to write
novels; and they are, not unnaturally, novels of the kind that he
enjoyed as a young man before his energies were directed to art.
They are not imitative, but they are of a pattern nearer that of
1860 than that of their date; it may be noted that *Joseph Vance*
and Galsworthy's *The Man of Property* appeared in the same year.
De Morgan is a kind of counterpart to Gerard Manley Hopkins,
whose poems belong to the date of their publication rather than
the time of their composition, and the two men may serve as a
warning against laying undue emphasis on dates and tendencies,
De Morgan being thirty years behind his time, Hopkins fifty
years ahead. De Morgan had an unusual power of following the
illogical processes of his characters, and of giving their conversation in all its ungrammatical, slipshod significance; his working

men are Shakespearian, and his representation of the middle-class professional and artistic society which he knew is as faithful as it is humorous and sometimes touching. The first two and the last of his completed novels are the best, but *The Old Man's Youth* might have excelled them: it contains passages of tragic intensity to which there are some, but few, parallels in them. On the whole, he was inclined to look at life through rose-coloured spectacles, but at least there is this to be said, that he did not begin writing about life until he knew something about it.

A. M. W. Stirling—William De Morgan and his Wife, 1922.

V

Marryat's and Lever's stories of lively adventure have something in common with the hunting literature of Surtees and, with some modification, Whyte-Melville; and Whyte-Melville in turn with Trollope and Blackmore and with 'Somerville and Ross'; but the links of connection should not be strained. 'Cuthbert Bede' and Lover show a lower level of the Lever type.

MARRYAT, FREDERICK (1792-1848)

The King's Own, 1830.
Peter Simple, 1834.
Jacob Faithful, 1834.
Mr Midshipman Easy, 1836.
Japhet in Search of a Father, 1836.
The Dog Fiend, or Snarleyow, 1837.
Masterman Ready, 1841.

These seven books give a full picture of 'the old navy' after Smollett and at the beginning of the nineteenth century. To them should be added one of the best historical tales for children—*The Children of the New Forest*, 1847—and his *Diary in America*, not published until 1960.

Marryat, who wrote good straightforward narrative in good straightforward prose, is still very readable, and his novels still have a sense of reality and freshness.

Life and Letters by his daughter, Florence Marryat, 1872. The best life is that by Oliver Warner, 1953. There is also a bio-graphical essay by Michael Sadleir in an edition of *Peter Simple*, published in 1929, and a commentary on the novels in *Captain Marryat and the Old Navy* by Christopher Lloyd, 1939.

LEVER, CHARLES JAMES (1806-72)

Harry Lorrequer, 1837.
Charles O'Malley, 1840,

and many other novels with a good deal of horse-play and irresponsible adventure in them. He is now difficult to read: his novels date, and now seem rather faded, but in their day they were regarded as lively.

● LOVER, SAMUEL (1797-1868)

Lover was in his day a well-known song-writer, whose best-known song was *Rory O'More*, 1826, as well as a novelist and dramatist.

Legends and Stories of Ireland, 1831.
Rory O'More—a novel suggested by his song, out of which he subsequently made a play also—1837.
Songs and Ballads, 1839.
Handy Andy, his best-known and perhaps his best book, 1842.

and other books.

The verdict of the *Dictionary of National Biography* may be accepted without injustice: 'his contributions to literature are only those of a second-rate Lever and a third-rate Moore'.

'CUTHBERT BEDE' (Edward Bradley) (1827-89)

'Cuthbert Bede' wrote many books, most of which he himself illustrated, and one of them retains a pale reputation: *Adventures of Mr Verdant Green*, of which the three parts appeared in 1853, 1854 and 1856. As the *D.N.B.* biographer remarks, 'Verdant Green himself is a kind of undergraduate Pickwick, and the book is full of harmless fun.'

SURTEES, ROBERT SMITH (1803-64)

Jorrocks's Jaunts and Jollities, 1838 (published from 1831 to 1834 in *The New Sporting Magazine*).
Handley Cross, 1843, expanded 1854.
Hillingdon Hall, 1845.
Hawbuck Grange, 1847.
Mr Sponge's Sporting Tour, 1853.

Ask Mamma, 1858.
Plain or Ringlets, 1860.
Mr Facey Romford's Hounds, 1865.
Frederick Watson: Robert Smith Surtees: a critical study, 1933.
Leonard Cooper: R. S. Surtees, 1952.
Anthony Steel: Jorrocks's England, 1932.

See also the essay by Bonamy Dobrée in *Essays of the Year,
1929-30*, and the introduction by Joyce Cary to *Mr Sponge's
Sporting Tour* in The World's Classics.

'It was a foul world into which he peeped for the first time
—a heavy-eating, hard-drinking hell of horse-copers, swind-
lers, match-making mothers, economically dependent virgins
selling themselves blushingly for cash and lands: Jews, trades-
men, and an ill-considered spawn of Dickens-and-horsedung
characters (I give Midmore's own criticism), but he read on,
fascinated, and behold, from the pages leaped, as it were,
the brother to the red-eyed man of the brook, bellowing at a
landlord (here Midmore realized that *he* was that very animal)
for new barns; and another man who, like himself again,
objected to hoof-marks on gravel. Outrageous as thought and
conception were, the stuff seemed to have the rudiments of
observation. . . . [Midmore's neighbours] lied, except about
horses, grudgingly and of necessity, not for art's sake; and,
men and women alike, they expressed themselves along their
chosen lines with the serene indifference of the larger animals.
Then Midmore would go home and identify them, one by
one, out of the natural-history books by Mr Surtees.'

KIPLING, *My Son's Wife.*

In Siegfried Sassoon's *Memoirs of a Fox-hunting Man*, Sherston
and Colwood 'adopted and matured a specialized jargon, drawn
almost exclusively from characters in the novels of Surtees; since
we knew these almost by heart they provided us with something
like a dialect of our own, and in our care-free moments we ex-
changed remarks in the mid-Victorian language of such character-
parts as Mr Romford, Major Yammerton and Sir Moses Main-
chance, while Mr Jorrocks was an all-pervading influence.' That
'adaptation of the Ringwell Hunt to the world created by that
observant novelist was simplified by the fact that a large proportion of the Ringwell subscribers might have stepped straight out
of his pages'.

WHYTE-MELVILLE, GEORGE JOHN (1821-78)

Captain Digby Grand, 1853.
Kate Coventry, 1856.
Market Harborough, 1861,

and others.

Collected Edition, ed. Sir Herbert Maxwell, 1898.

Whyte-Melville has not the robustness of Surtees and he has no characters equal to Jorrocks and James Pigg or a dozen others. But he gives a pleasant picture of the hunting life of his day, which he knew intimately: it was hunting and not people that interested him: his manual on riding still has some value, though the style of horsemanship has changed.

TROLLOPE, ANTHONY (1815-82)

Trollope wrote about fifty novels, of which the *Phineas Finn* series are notable in the difficult kind of the political novel: they are perhaps excelled only by Disraeli's. Others are not negligible but are less likely to endure than the Barsetshire novels—

The Warden, 1855.
Barchester Towers, 1857.
Doctor Thorne, 1858.
Framley Parsonage, 1861.
The Small House at Allington, 1864.
The Last Chronicle of Barset, 1867.

Collected Oxford edition of the novels, 1952; the introduction by Mgr R. Knox to *The Warden* is in effect a discerning introduction to the whole Barsetshire series.

Trollope also wrote his *Autobiography*, which was published in 1883 just after his death, and did some harm to his reputation among the sentimental by its exceedingly unsentimental account of his habits of work.

Letters, ed. B. A. Booth, 1951. Michael Sadleir's *Trollope, A Commentary*, 1927, rev. ed. 1945, considers the Victorian background—there is a useful and suggestive division of the reign into three periods—as well as the novels themselves. See also Hugh Walpole's *Trollope* in the *English Men of Letters* series and B. A. Booth's *Anthony Trollope: Aspects of his Life and Art*, 1958.

TROLLOPE, THOMAS ADOLPHUS (1810-92)

—was the brother of Anthony, whom he provided with the plot

of *Dr Thorne*, and he wrote tolerable novels and miscellaneous books, mainly on Italian subjects, such as—

La Beata, 1861.
Marietta, 1862.
Giulio Malatesta, 1863.

These three were novels. Of his books of historical and topographical gossip and more serious historical studies, two may be specially mentioned—

Philippo Strozzi, 1860.
Paul V the Pope and Paul the Friar, 1860.

BLACKMORE, RICHARD DODDRIDGE (1825-1900)

Blackmore is remembered almost solely as the author of

Lorna Doone, 1869,

but others of his novels deserve reading, especially—

The Maid of Sker, 1872.
Cripps the Carrier, 1876.
Springhaven, 1887.

The shapelessness of many of Blackmore's books illustrates the dangers of serial publication more clearly than the faulty construction of many of the greater Victorian novels.

There is a critical study by Q. G. Burris: *Richard Doddridge Blackmore*, 1930, and one by K. Budd: *The Last Victorian*, 1960.

• EDITH ŒNONE SOMERVILLE (1858-1949) AND 'MARTIN ROSS' (Violet Florence Martin, 1862-1915)

The Real Charlotte, 1894.
Some Experiences of an Irish R.M., 1899.
Further Experiences of an Irish R.M., 1908.
In Mr Knox's Country, 1915.

and other stories of the Irish hunting countryside.

Hitchcock edition of the *Sporting Works*, 1927.

'Martin Ross' wrote two volumes of essays, mainly autobiographical: *Some Irish Yesterdays*, 1906, and *Strayaways*, 1920.

Nobody can pretend that the novels written by the ladies known as 'Somerville and Ross' are great literature, but they are written in a very clear and delightful style, the best form of ordinary English, with a respect for language, and no affectation whatever. The stories, moreover, present a sympathetic picture of a state of Irish society that has now passed away, observed with great accuracy and a very high sense of humour. The characters they portray seem to be permanent enough.

VI. The 'Social' Novel

Disraeli's novels dealing with social conditions and political questions have already been noted, and some of Dickens's fall into the same category—especially *Oliver Twist, Bleak House* and *Hard Times*. The social conscience is, however, most marked in some of the novelists who are grouped here, particularly Mrs Gaskell, Charles Kingsley and Charles Reade. There are reasons for including also Thomas Hughes and Henry Kingsley; and the intense seriousness of George Eliot gives an excuse for adding her to the list, even though *Felix Holt the Radical* is by no means her best book.

MARTINEAU, HARRIET (1802-76)

Harriet Martineau is the least attractive of the 'social' novelists, the most of a theorist and propagandist, writing tales simply with the object of inculcating sound notions of political economy, according to James Mill and Ricardo. It is surprising that there should be any life at all in her tales, and more surprising that she should have written some for children, e.g., *Feats on the Fiord*, which children still enjoy.

Illustrations of Political Economy (9 vols.), 1832-34.
Poor Laws and Paupers Illustrated, 1833.
Illustrations of Taxation, 1834.

These are all volumes of tales, though their titles may be misleading.

Deerbrook, 1839.
The Hour and the Man, 1841 (a novel on Toussaint L'Ouverture).
The Playfellow, 1841. (The Settlers at Home, The Peasant and the Prince, Feats on the Fiord, The Crofton Boys.)
Forest and Game Law Tales, 1845,

and other tales and novels.

She wrote also a useful *History of England during the Thirty Years' Peace*, 1849.

Society in America, 1837.
Retrospect of Western Travel, 1838.

These two books deal with her American experiences, and may be compared with Mrs Trollope's and Charles Dickens's.

Autobiography, with Memorials by Maria Weston Chapman, 1877.
Theodora Bosanquet: Harriet Martineau, 1927, with useful bibliographies.
Vera Wheatley: The Life and Work of Harriet Martineau, 1957.
R. K. Webb: Harriet Martineau: a radical Victorian, 1960.

GASKELL, ELIZABETH CLEGHORN (STEVENSON) (1810-65)

Mary Barton, 1848.
North and South, 1855.

Novels of the industrial north, with descriptions (especially in the first) of conditions of life and labour so sympathetic to the 'artisans' that they were considered dangerous and subversive by many of her contemporaries.

Ruth, 1853, again deals with a problem of morality in a way which shocked the rigidity of many of her contemporaries.
Cranford, 1851-53: the best-known, because the most charming and least disturbing of her books.
Sylvia's Lovers (a tragic novel), 1863. Cousin Phyllis (a pathetic idyll—the most perfect of her short stories), 1863-64.
Wives and Daughters, 1864-66. (Unfinished, but the most perfect of her longer books.)

Many short stories and sketches.

Life of Charlotte Brontë, 1857.

Complete edition of novels and tales, 1872-73; most of them are also available in modern cheap editions.

Elizabeth S. Haldane: Mrs Gaskell and her Friends, 1930.

KINGSLEY, CHARLES (1819-75)

The Saint's Tragedy, 1848,

and other poems.

Alton Locke, Tailor and Poet, 1850.
Yeast, 1851.

Two novels which show the motives behind the Chartist movement, with which Kingsley was in strong and active sympathy. As 'Parson Lot' he wrote a succession of tracts, Politics for the People, in 1848, in the second of which occurs a phrase which was taken up and used with a different intention by Karl Marx: 'We have used the Bible as if it was a mere special constable's handbook—an opium-dose for keeping beasts of burden patient while they were being overloaded—a mere book to keep the poor in order. . . . Instead of being a book to keep the poor in order, it is a book, from beginning to end, written *to keep the rich in order.*' The whole passage is characteristic of his onslaught on social evils. His close connection with F. D. Maurice should be noted, cf. the Introduction to *Theology*, here.

Hypatia, 1853.
Westward Ho! 1855.
Hereward the Wake, 1866.

These three historical novels are marred by the introduction of Kingsley's prejudices, especially his religious prejudices, and his tendency to glorify physical strength, but they are full of vigour and good story-telling.

Two Years Ago, 1857, has something in common with the Chartist novels in its exposure of the consequences of bad housing conditions. There is also a good deal of social propaganda, well managed, in The Water Babies, 1863.
The Heroes, 1856, tells Greek stories for children.
At Last, 1870 (a voyage to the West Indies).

Kingsley also wrote sermons and historical essays, and did much useful work as a popularizer of science, particularly geology. His *Glaucus*, 1855, and *Madam How and Lady Why*, 1869, which were intended for children, should be specially noted. He would repay detailed study: he had an interesting streak of fantasy, shown not only in *The Water Babies*, 1863, but in the chapter in *Alton Locke* describing Locke's delirium. He was hampered by believing that an English gentleman was the finest of God's creatures, but he also held other, sometimes contradictory, values.

Collected edition, 1879-81. The introduction, or rather prefatory memoir, by Thomas Hughes to *Alton Locke* in this edition should be read.
Letters and Memories of His Life, by his widow, 1877.
Life and Works, 1901-03.
C. W. Stubbs: Charles Kingsley and the Christian Social Movement, 1899.
C. E. Vulliamy: Charles Kingsley and Christian Socialism, 1914.
R. D. Martin: The Dust of Conflict, 1960.

KINGSLEY, HENRY (1830-76)

Henry Kingsley has been overshadowed by his brother, but he is a novelist of greater achievement in some ways; the construction of his novels is often chaotic, but the characters are alive as few of Charles Kingsley's are, and there is a pervading generosity of temper and expression. He wrote too much, and not all his books are noted here. The first and the fourth mentioned have a special interest as being the earliest, and for a long time the only, good novels of which the scene is laid in Australia. The slum scenes in *The Hillyars and the Burtons* and in *Ravenshoe* give the excuse for the inclusion of Henry Kingsley here.

The Recollections of Geoffrey Hamlyn, 1859.
Ravenshoe, 1861.
Austin Elliot, 1863.
The Hillyars and the Burtons, 1865.
Mademoiselle Mathilde, 1868. (One of the few good novels about the French Revolution.)
Stretton, 1869.
The Boy in Grey, 1871. (An odd, confused, half-prophetic political allegory, nominally a children's story.)

HUGHES, THOMAS (1822-96)

Hughes showed his interest in social conditions by his life, not by writing novels with a purpose; but the two *Tom Brown* books show the training which produced such men as Hughes himself.

Tom Brown's Schooldays, 1857.
Tom Brown At Oxford, 1861 (not so good, but illuminating on class distinctions and the position of women).
The Scouring of the White Horse, 1859. A delightful and too-little known book, full of the spirit of the Berkshire downs and the life of their people.
Life, by E. C. Mack and W. H. G. Armytage, 1953.

READE, CHARLES (1814-84)

Reade made many of his novels documents, e.g., *It is Never too Late to Mend*, 1856, exposes abuses of the penal system, and *Hard Cash*, 1863, those of private lunatic asylums; his power of telling a story comes out in these as well as in his best book—

The Cloister and the Hearth, 1861. This was first published as *A Good Fight*, 1859, and had a happy ending in that form. It is a fine picaresque novel about Europe in the late fifteenth century, owing a good deal to the writings of Erasmus, the story of whose parents it purports to tell.

Other novels which may be mentioned are—

Peg Woffington, 1853. At one time, if not now, as famous as *The Cloister and the Hearth*, but a poor book. Reade had a hand in a good many stage productions, but his picture of Garrick is disappointing.

Christie Johnstone, 1853.
Griffith Gaunt, 1866.
Life and critical study, by Malcolm Elwin, 1934.

'GEORGE ELIOT' (Mary Ann Evans) (1819-80)

Scenes of Clerical Life, 1858.
Adam Bede, 1859.
The Mill on the Floss, 1860.
Silas Marner, 1861.
Romola, 1863.
Felix Holt, the Radical, 1866.
Middlemarch, 1871-72.
Daniel Deronda, 1876,

and minor writings, especially theological and philosophical.
Her verse is pedestrian, but *O may I join the choir invisible* is well
known.

J. W. Cross: George Eliot's Life as related in her Letters and Journals,
    1884. A full edition of the Letters is in progress, ed. Gordon S. Haight.
O. Browning: Life of George Eliot, 1890.
Elizabeth S. Haldane: George Eliot and her Times, 1927.
A. H. Paterson: George Eliot's Family Life and Letters, 1928.
J. Lewis May: George Eliot, 1930.

There is a good article by R. H. Hutton in Chambers's
Cyclopaedia of English Literature, Vol. III, and an interesting
study by P. Bourl'honne: *George Eliot. Essai de biographie intel-
lectuelle et morale*, 1933.

See also—

Marjory A. Bald: Women Writers of the Nineteenth Century, 1923.
Muriel Masefield: Women Novelists from Fanny Burney to George
    Eliot, 1934.
Lawrence and Elizabeth Hanson: Marian Evans and George Eliot, 1952.
Barbara Hardy: The Novels of George Eliot, 1959.
J. Thale: The Novels of George Eliot, 1959.

vii. Religious Life and Thought

Certain writers, deliberately or half-consciously, show the
movement of religious thought through the nineteenth
century.

YONGE, CHARLOTTE MARY (1823-1901)

Miss Yonge's novels have both individual and historic value,
since more than any other writer she shows the effect of one of

the most far-reaching movements of the century, the Oxford Movement, on ordinary men and women of gentle breeding. Her novels fall into two groups: domestic stories such as *The Daisy Chain*, 1856, and its successors, in which she anticipates the twentieth-century fashion of family chronicles; and historical tales such as *The Chaplet of Pearls*, 1868, and *Unknown to History*, 1882—by no means as mild fare as is often supposed. She had a real sense of character and of history, and she wrote some historical sketches and biographies of value. On the other side of her work the most significant of her books is perhaps *The Heir of Redclyffe*, 1853, which, with its high, if not strained, sense of dedication and discipline, was extraordinarily influential: see, e.g., Mackail's *Life of William Morris* for its effect on Morris and his friends at Oxford. Careful reading of her novels will provide a good deal of understanding of certain sides of Victorian life, by no means the least admirable, and even throw amusing light on some of the changing ideals of her age. A woman of wide and deep reading, almost a scholar, she approved of the education of women, but she felt nothing but horror for most forms of feminism.

A collected, but not complete, edition of her novels was published in 1888-89. There is a *Life* by Christabel Coleridge, a good study by Geraldine Battiscombe, 1943, and another in *Victorian Best-Seller: The World of Charlotte Mary Yonge*, by Margaret L. Mare and Alicia Percival, 1947.

SHORTHOUSE, JOSEPH HENRY (1834-1903)
John Inglesant, 1881.

A book of strange and rare quality, unreadable by some people, to others one of major importance: in a sense an historical novel, since the story is laid in England and Italy in the seventeenth century, but better described by its author's term, 'a philosophical romance', the outward experiences of the hero being a kind of shadow of his search for a reconciliation 'between the noblest parts of man's nature arrayed against each other. On the one side obedience and faith, on the other, freedom and the reason.' The book is steeped in the sacramental thought of the Oxford Movement, as Miss Yonge's are in its sober, self-distrustful piety.

Shorthouse's other books are no great matter.

OLIPHANT, MARGARET (1828-97)

Passages in the Life of Mrs Margaret Maitland, 1849,
and other stories of Scottish life.

Chronicles of Carlingford, 1862-76.
  Salem Chapel, in this series, may be compared with the novels of
  'Mark Rutherford' for its picture of provincial Nonconformity. In the
  others there are sidelights on movements in the Church of England.
A Beleaguered City, 1880. An excellent story of the supernatural.

Mrs Oliphant had to write for her living and produced,
besides many other novels, guide-books, etc., of which *The
Makers of Florence*, 1874, is the best. Another valuable work is
her *Annals of a Publishing House*, 1897, the history of the Blackwood firm.

Autobiography and Letters, 1899.

'MARK RUTHERFORD' (William Hale White) (1831-1913)

The Autobiography of Mark Rutherford, 1881.
Mark Rutherford's Deliverance, 1885.
The Revolution in Tanner's Lane, 1887.
Miriam's Schooling, 1890.
Catharine Furze, 1893.
Clara Hopgood, 1896.
The Early Life of Mark Rutherford by Himself, 1913.

Besides these half-autobiographical books Hale White also
wrote essays and criticism—

An Examination of the Charge of Apostasy against Wordsworth, 1898.
Pages from a Journal, 1901.
John Bunyan, 1905.
More Pages from a Journal, 1910.
Last Pages from a Journal, 1915,

and other books.

The best life is *Mark Rutherford*, by Catherine MacLean, 1955,
and there are good studies by Wilfred Stone (*The Religion and
Art of William Hale White*, 1954) and Irvin Stock (with a foreword
by Lionel Trilling), 1956. The life and spiritual history are
however best understood from his own works, his *Letters to Three
Friends*, 1924, and *The Groombridge Diary*, by his wife, 1924.

The 'Mark Rutherford' novels are in effect an historical document, a record of provincial Nonconformity, not at its best, in
the mid-nineteenth century, and of the pain suffered by souls

such as Hale White's, who rebelled against its narrowness while retaining their deep religious sense. White himself had wished to be a minister, but being unable to give the required answer to the question 'Do you believe a thing because it is in the Bible or because it is true?' was asked to leave the theological college where he was training.

WARD, MRS HUMPHRY (Mary Augusta) (1851-1920)

Robert Elsmere, 1888. A study of the agnosticism which resulted in many minds from scientific discovery and the critical discussion of Biblical texts; for years a book that 'everybody' read.

Of Mrs Humphry Ward's novels some others may be mentioned—

Sir George Tressady, 1896.
Helbeck of Bannisdale, 1898.
Eleanor, 1900.
Lady Rose's Daughter, 1903.
The Marriage of William Ashe, 1905. (This was in fact a working up of the story of Lord Melbourne's marriage, and Fenwick's Career, 1906, has also a biographical basis. In her political novels, such as Marcella, 1894, Mrs Humphry Ward may be compared with 'John Oliver Hobbes', see below (p. 298).
A Writer's Recollections, 1918.
J. P. Trevelyan (daughter)—Life of Mrs Humphry Ward, 1923.

B. THE LATE VICTORIANS

I

MEREDITH, GEORGE (1828-1909)

POETRY:
Poems, 1851.
Modern Love, 1862.
Poems and Lyrics of the Joy of Earth, 1883.
Ballads and Poems of Tragic Life, 1887.
A Reading of Earth, 1888.

CRITICISM:
The Idea of Comedy and the Uses of the Comic Spirit (lecture, 1877; reprinted separately, 1897).

NOVELS:
The Shaving of Shagpat, 1855.
The Ordeal of Richard Feverel, 1859.
Evan Harrington, 1861.
Sandra Belloni (Emilia in England), 1864.
Rhoda Fleming, 1865.

Vittoria, 1866.
The Adventures of Harry Richmond, 1871.
Beauchamp's Career, 1875.
The Egoist, 1879.
The Tragic Comedians, 1880.
Diana of the Crossways, 1885.
One of our Conquerors, 1891.
Lord Ormont and his Aminta, 1894.
The Amazing Marriage, 1895.
Celt and Saxon (unfinished: published in the *Fortnightly* in 1910 and in the memorial edition).
Collected edition of all works in 36 vols. begun in 1896, completed in 1910-11. Surrey edition, 1912.
Collected Letters, 1912.

The best critical studies are G. M. Trevelyan: *The Poetry and Philosophy of George Meredith*, 1906; J. W. Beach: *The Comic Spirit in George Meredith*, 1911; René Galland: *George Meredith*, 1923; L. Wolff: *George Meredith, poète et romancier*, 1924; the essay by Ramon Fernandez in *Messages*, and that by Bonamy Dobrée in *The English Novelists* (ed. D. Verschoyle). Galland and Wolff deal to some extent with Meredith's life, which is covered more closely by Mary Sturge Henderson: *Writings and Life of George Meredith*, 1926, and R. E. Sencourt: *Life of George Meredith*, 1929. The biography by J. B. Priestley in the *English Men of Letters* series is informative and that by S. M. Ellis is of general value. See also *Art and Substance in George Meredith* by Walter F. Wright, 1953 (a study of the novels), and Jack Lindsay's *George Meredith: His Life and Work*, 1956.

HARDY, THOMAS (1840-1928)

POETRY:
Wessex Poems, 1898 (written 1865 onwards).
Poems of the Past and the Present, 1901.
The Dynasts, Pt. I, 1903; Pt. II, 1906; Pt. III, 1908 (drama).
Time's Laughing-Stocks, 1909.
Satires of Circumstances, 1911; with Lyrics and Reveries, 1914.
Moments of Vision, 1917.
Late Lyrics, 1922.
The Queen of Cornwall, 1923 (drama).
Human Shows, 1925.

NOVELS:
Desperate Remedies, 1871.
Under the Greenwood Tree, 1872.
A Pair of Blue Eyes, 1872-73.
Far from the Madding Crowd, 1874.

The Hand of Ethelberta, 1876.
The Return of the Native, 1878.
The Trumpet-Major, 1879.
A Laodicean, 1880-81.
Two on a Tower, 1882.
The Mayor of Casterbridge, 1884-85.
The Woodlanders, 1886-87.
Wessex Tales, 1888.
A Group of Noble Dames, 1891.
Tess of the d'Urbervilles, 1891.
Life's Little Ironies, 1894.
Jude the Obscure, 1895.
The Well-Beloved, 1897 (revised from 1892 serial).
A Changed Man, 1913.
Our Exploits at West Poley, 1925—a boys' story.
Wessex edition of works in prose and verse with new prefaces and notes, 1912-22.
Complete poetical works, 1919.
Mellstock edition of works, 1920.

There are many critical studies of Hardy, of which those by Lionel Johnson 1894 (best edition, 1923), and Lascelles Abercrombie, 1912, should be specially noted, as well as F. A. Hedgecock's *Thomas Hardy, penseur et artiste*, 1910, the essay by Bonamy Dobrée in *The Lamp and the Lute*, Edmund Blunden's *Hardy*, 1942, and Lord David Cecil's *Hardy the Novelist*, 1943. See also—

Florence Emily Hardy: The Later Years of Thomas Hardy, 1930.
Carl J. Weber: Hardy of Wessex, 1940; this is the fullest biography yet published.

JAMES, HENRY (1843-1916)

The facts that James lived most of his mature life in England and was naturalized in 1915 justify his inclusion here, though many of his novels deal with American society.

Roderick Hudson, 1876.
The American, 1877.
Daisy Miller, 1879.
The Europeans, 1879.
The Madonna of the Future, 1879.
The Portrait of a Lady, 1881.
Tales of Three Cities, 1884.
The Bostonians, 1886.
The Princess Casamassima, 1886.
The Reverberator, 1888.
Partial Portraits, 1888.
The Tragic Muse, 1890.

The Private Life, 1893.
The Reprobate, 1895.
Embarrassments, 1896.
The Other House, 1896.
The Spoils of Poyeton, 1897.
What Maisie Knew, 1897.
In the Cage, 1898.
The Two Magics, 1898.
The Awkward Age, 1899.
The Soft Side, 1900.
The Sacred Fount, 1901.
The Wings of the Dove, 1902.
The Ambassadors, and The Better Sort, 1903.
The Golden Bowl, 1904.
The Finer Grain, 1910.
The Outcry, 1911.
The Ivory Tower, and The Sense of the Past, 1917.

Revised and collected edition of novels and tales, with prefaces, New York, 1907-09 (24 vols.); there is also the uniform edition, 1915-18 (13 vols.); and the novels and stories, 1921-23 (35 vols.).

James's critical theory is seen in his *Hawthorne*, 1879; *Views and Reviews* (ed. Le Roy Phillips), 1908; *Notes on Novelists*, 1914; and *The Art of the Novel*, critical prefaces, 1935. For a criticism on his own practice, see Percy Lubbock, *The Craft of Fiction*, 1926; Rebecca West, *Henry James*, 1916; and J. W. Beach, *The Method of Henry James*, 1918; as well as Theodora Bosanquet's *Henry James at Work*, 1924, which gives the direct observations of his secretary. See also Stephen Spender, *The Destructive Element*, and the essay by Graham Greene in *The English Novelists* (ed. D. Verschoyle).

James's biography may be made out from his own books:

A Small Boy and Others, 1913.
Notes of a Son and Brother, 1914.
The Middle Years, 1917,

and his *Letters*, 1920, *Letters to A. C. Benson and Auguste Monod*, 1930, and *Henry James and H. G. Wells*, letters edited with an introduction by Leon Edel and Gordon N. Ray. The definitive biography by L. Edel began to appear in 1953.

BROUGHTON, RHODA (1840-1920)

Rhoda Broughton, in her own phrase, began as Zola and ended as Charlotte Mary Yonge: in other words, her acute, unembarrassed novels were looked upon as dangerous and indelicate in her early days and as fairly mild and certainly inoffensive at the end of her long life. One of her best books is *Belinda*, in which there is a portrait of Mark Pattison (Professor Forth) as unfriendly as that by George Eliot in *Middlemarch*, but she never wrote anything unworthy, and her place is here after Meredith and Henry James though a good deal below them. She has one trick which disturbs some readers, that of the persistent use of the present tense—but at least she is persistent in it.

See also the note on Anne Thackeray.

Cometh Up as a Flower, 1867.
Not Wisely but too Well, 1867.
Red as a Rose is She, 1870.
Goodbye, Sweetheart, Goodbye, 1872.
Nancy, 1873.
Joan, 1876.
Second Thoughts, 1880.
Belinda, 1883.
Dr Cupid, 1886.
Alas, 1890.
Mrs Bligh, 1892.
A Beginner, 1894.
Scylla or Charybdis?, 1895.
Dear Faustina, 1897.
The Game and the Candle, 1899.
Foes in Law, 1900.
Lavinia, 1902.
The Devil and the Deep Sea, 1910.
Between Two Stools, 1912.

11. Novelists of middle- and lower-class London life

BESANT, SIR WALTER (1836-1901)

Besant lived a life of terrifying activity: he wrote much on the history of London, was secretary of the Palestine Exploration Fund and wrote on its work, was first chairman of the Society of Authors and did much to prevent the exploitation of authors by unscrupulous publishers, and wrote some literary criticism and biography and scores of novels. Of these *All Sorts and Conditions of Men*, 1882, ought to be singled out, as it led to the establishment of The People's Palace in Whitechapel. *Children of Gibeon*, 1886, is another study, in the main, of East End life.

Besant's earlier novels, up to 1881, were written in collaboration with James Rice, but it is not easy to distinguish them in style from those he wrote alone. Among them may be noted:

Ready-Money Mortiboy, 1872.
The Golden Butterfly, 1876.
By Celia's Arbour, 1878.
The Chaplain of the Fleet, 1879 (i.e., the Fleet Liberties in London; Besant knew the eighteenth century well, and several of his best stories are laid in it).
Autobiography, 1902.

GISSING, GEORGE ROBERT (1857-1903)

The Unclassed, 1884.
Thyrza, 1887.
The Town Traveller, 1898.
New Grub Street, 1891.
Born in Exile, 1892. This seems to be the first novel in which the hero is from a 'modern' university. It is almost as good as—
The Odd Women, 1893, which faces the problem of ageing unmarried ladies without money or trained minds. This is probably Gissing's best book. Of the others the most important is—
The Private Papers of Henry Ryecroft, 1903, an essay-like book which reflects Gissing's relief at escaping to the country after the sordid experiences of poverty in London which produced his dismal realistic novels.

Gissing wrote other novels, stories and sketches, and also a study of Charles Dickens, 1898, and introductions to the Rochester edition of Dickens, 1900 and later.

The House of Cobwebs and other Stories, with an introductory survey by T. Seccombe, 1906.
Letters to members of his Family, collected and arranged by A. and E. Gissing, 1927.

There is a critical study by Frank Swinnerton, 1912, and one by Mabel Collins Donnelly, 1954; and Morley Roberts's *The Private Life of Henry Maitland*, 1912, though ostensibly a novel, is in fact a biography of Gissing. A selection from his works, with biographical and critical notes by his son and an introduction by Virginia Woolf, appeared in 1929.

Two minor writers of the same kind are—

MORRISON, ARTHUR (1863-1946)

Tales of Mean Streets, 1894.
A Child of the Jago, 1896.
The Hole in the Wall, 1902,
and other books, including a study of *The Painters of Japan*, 1911.

WHITEING, RICHARD (1840-1928)

No. 5 John Street, 1899.
The Yellow Van, 1903,

and others.

RIDGE, WILLIAM PETT (d. 1930)

A kindly and humorous painter of lower middle-class life, especially of small shopkeepers and office-workers, between 1890 and 1930.

His work is very readable, and he is now underestimated as a humorist and sympathetic observer.

Mord Emly, 1898.
A Son of the State, 1899.
A Breaker of Laws, 1900.
Mrs Galer's Business, 1905.
The Wickhamses, 1906.
Name of Garland, 1907.
69 Birnam Road, 1908.
The Kennedy People, 1915.
Madam Prince, 1916,

and many others.

A Story-Teller Forty Years in London, 1923.
I Like to Remember, 1924.

ZANGWILL, ISRAEL (1864-1926)

Zangwill's studies of Jewish life began with London Jews.

Children of the Ghetto, 1892.
Ghetto Tragedies, 1893.
The King of Schnorrers, 1894.
Dreamers of the Ghetto, 1898,

and other novels, most of them on Jewish subjects, and plays.

These are quite competent works, but do not probe very deep into humanity.

Two other writers fall into natural association with Pett Ridge and Zangwill; in fact, in the nineties they were grouped together as representatives of 'the new humour': W. W. Jacobs and J. K. Jerome.

JACOBS, WILLIAM WYMARK (1863-1943)

Many Cargoes, 1896.
The Skipper's Wooing, 1897.

Sea Urchins, 1898.
A Master of Craft, 1900.
Light Freights, 1901.
At Sunwich Port, The Lady of the Barge, 1902.
Odd Craft, 1903.
Dialstone Lane, 1904.
Captains All, 1905.
Short Cruises, 1907.
Salthaven, 1908.
Sailors' Knots, 1909.
Ship's Company, 1911.
Night Watches, 1914.
The Castaways, 1916.
Deep Waters, 1919.
Sea Whispers, 1926.

Jacobs may have learnt part of his technique from Kipling, but he is an original artist, and many of his stories are certainly very amusing. His types—longshoremen, sailors of coasting vessels, etc.—are few in number, and he is apt to repeat his characters, but he is no mean craftsman in the art of short-story telling. His humour is human and entertaining, but he seldom rises to the really comic. *The Monkey's Paw* is a classic of horror, and has been adapted for the stage.

JEROME, JEROME KLAPKA (1859-1927)

Idle Thoughts of an Idle Fellow, 1889.
Three Men in a Boat, 1889.
Paul Kelver, 1902.
The Passing of the Third Floor Back, 1907,

and other tales, novels and plays.

My Life and Times, 1926.

Jerome was mainly 'funny', and nothing dates more than the funny. *Three Men in a Boat*, a very successful work, is perhaps just readable now. *The Passing of the Third Floor Back*, which was a fairly successful play, is a kind of allegory which most will find tiresome and sentimental.

III. Bohemia and Society at the Turn of the Century

Certain writers reflect artistic society and 'Society' at the turn of the century.

DU MAURIER, GEORGE LOUIS PALMELLA BUSSON (1834-96)

Peter Ibbetson, 1892.
Trilby, 1894.
The Martian, 1897.

Half the charm of Du Maurier's books is in the illustrations, but there is a dream quality of imagination in *Peter Ibbetson*, and something of the same in *The Martian*. *Trilby* is less good, though it has been more popular.

He represents a slightly older generation than—

HARLAND, HENRY (1861-1905)

Editor of *The Yellow Book*, 1894-97.

Harland's own stories and sketches show the sometimes strained elegance of much of *The Yellow Book*. He was a conscious stylist with not much substance behind.

Grey Roses, 1895.
Comedies and Errors, 1898.
The Cardinal's Snuff Box, 1900.
The Lady Paramount, 1902.
My Friend Prospero, 1904.
The Royal End, 1909.

Aestheticism, rather that of Oscar Wilde than that of *The Yellow Book*, was neatly parodied by ROBERT SMYTHE HICHENS (1864-1950) in *The Green Carnation*, 1894; his later novels show the same neatness of construction, but are valueless as regards matter. *Bella Donna* was a great popular success.

'ANTHONY HOPE' (Sir Anthony Hope Hawkins) (1863-1933)

The Dolly Dialogues, 1894, were considered by their contemporaries light, neat, witty, the prose equivalents of *vers de société*; the same qualities appear in the style, especially the dialogue, of the romantic stories—something in the manner of Stevenson—which won such popularity as to add an adjective, Ruritanian, to the language.

The Prisoner of Zenda, 1894.
Rupert of Hentzau, 1898.

Of the other novels, *The King's Mirror*, 1899, is perhaps the best, but none are really poor.

Life, by Sir Charles Mallet, 1935.

BENSON, EDWARD FREDERIC (1867-1940)

Dodo, 1893, covers one side of the society of the nineties—the frothy but not unintellectual. It was famous in its day, and has recently been reprinted. Its psychological level is about that of Ouida, but though the representation of 'high society' is more accurate than hers, it lacks her gusto,

and many other novels.

As We Were, 1930, an interesting volume of reminiscences.
Charlotte Brontë, 1932—one of the best balanced studies of the Brontës.

'BARON CORVO' (Frederick William Serafino Austin Lewis Mary Rolfe) (1860-1913)

Stories Toto Told Me, 1897.
In His Own Image, 1901; reprinted, 1924.
Chronicles of the House of Borgia, 1901.
Hadrian the Seventh, 1904.
Don Tarquinio, a kataleptic phantasmatic romance, 1905.
The Weird of the Wanderer, 1912.

He also published in 1903 a translation from the French of J. B. Nicolas's version of Omar Khayyám.

Posthumously published—

The Desire and Pursuit of the Whole, 1934.
Hubert's Arthur, 1935.

The only large-scale study of him is—

The Quest for Corvo, by A. J. A. Symons, 1934.

Rolfe was an extraordinary and fantastic person, who might have been a saint, and was, in fact, very much the reverse. His writings have a peculiar quality, and he was certainly an artist in words, and one who could use strange ones with effect. Many of the 'Toto' stories, and some of those in *In His Own Image*, appeared in *The Yellow Book*, where they attracted attention as much by the charm of the stories themselves, which retell Italian Christian folk-legends, as by their style, which was more developed in his curious spiritual 'biography', *Hadrian the Seventh*. *Hubert's Arthur*, which gives a version of the 'blinding' of Arthur, is too 'Wardour Street' to be inviting, but *The Desire and Pursuit of the Whole* is a brilliantly told and unlikely Venetian romance, with streaks of libellous satire.

MERRICK, LEONARD (1864-1939)

Leonard Merrick's mastery of construction in his short stories has scarcely received its due of appreciation, but some amends

have been made by the introductions by his peers to the collected
edition of his novels and stories which appeared in 1918.

Conrad in Quest of his Youth.
When Love Flies out of the Window.
The Position of Peggy Harper.
The Man who understood Women.
The Quaint Companions.
The Man who was Good.
One Man's View.
The House of Lynch.
To Tell you the Truth.
Cynthia.
A Chair on the Boulevard.
The Worldlings.
The Actor-Manager.
While Paris Laughed.

Since then *The Little Dog Laughed*, 1930, has been added to the
list.

Merrick has always been better liked by his fellow-craftsmen
than by the general public. There is nothing striking either about
his subdued prose or in what he has to say: he has, indeed, points
to make, but he makes them too quietly for the casual reader.

'JOHN OLIVER HOBBES' (Pearl Mary Teresa Craigie) (1867-1906)

Some Emotions and a Moral, 1891.
The Sinner's Comedy, 1892.
The School for Saints, 1897.
The Serious Wooing, 1901.
Love and the Soul Hunters, 1902.
Robert Orange, 1902.
The Vineyard, 1904.
The Dream and the Business, 1906.
Life told in her Correspondence, with a Biographical Sketch by her
    father, John Morgan Richards, 1911.

John Oliver Hobbes's novels are neat in construction, sensitive
in style, and show understanding of political life especially in its
interactions with religious convictions. *Robert Orange* contains in
the hero an idealized portrait of Disraeli, who appears also under
his own name in the book.

GARNETT, RICHARD (1835-1906)

The Twilight of the Gods, 1888 (republished 1903).

There is something independent of its date about this collection

of ironies, but its exquisitely careful writing perhaps puts it into
this group.

iv. Stevenson and Others

STEVENSON, ROBERT LOUIS (1850-94)

Especially in his essays, and to some extent in his tales and
novels, Stevenson has a close kinship to the careful stylists of the
eighties and nineties, and in construction he is indubitably an
artist. His sometimes artificial prose is responsible for a great deal
of bad, imitative, self-conscious writing among his successors;
but on the other hand he is also at least partly responsible for the
revival of the romantic tale of adventure and for a great deal of
spirited story-telling. His own long-short stories are exquisite.
His verse is pleasant but has not any remarkable distinction.
His letters, when they are not touched with artificiality, are
excellent, but they have been considerably edited

ESSAYS AND CRITICISM:
An Inland Voyage, 1878.
Travels with a Donkey, 1879.
Virginibus Puerisque, 1881.
Familiar Studies of Men and Books, 1882.
The Silverado Squatters, 1883.
Memories and Portraits, 1887.
Across the Plains, 1892.

TALES AND NOVELS:
Treasure Island, New Arabian Nights, 1882.
More New Arabian Nights, 1885.
The Dynamiter, 1885; Prince Otto, 1885.
The Strange Case of Dr Jekell and Mr Hyde, 1886.
Kidnapped, 1886.
The Merry Men, 1886.
The Black Arrow, 1888.
The Master of Ballantrae, 1889.
Catriona, Island Nights' Entertainments, 1893.
The Ebb-Tide, 1894.
Weir of Hermiston (unfinished), 1896.
St Ives (completed by 'Q'), 1897.
(With Lloyd Osbourne)—
The Wrong Box, 1888.
The Wrecker, 1892.

POETRY:
The Child's Garden of Verses, 1885.
Underwoods, 1887.

Ballads, 1890.
Songs of Travel, 1896.
Collected Poems, ed. Janet Adam Smith, 1951.

There are several complete or almost complete editions, notably the Edinburgh edition of 1894-98, in 28 volumes, and the Pentland edition of 1905-07, in 20 volumes.

Vailima Letters, 1895.
Letters to his Family and Friends, ed. S. Colvin, 1899.
Our Samoan Adventure, by Fanny and Robert Louis Stevenson, ed. by Charles Neidor, 1956.
Life, by Graham Balfour, 1901.
Frank A. Swinnerton: Robert Louis Stevenson: a critical study, 1914.
Life, by Rosaline Masson, 1923.
J. A. Steuart: Robert Louis Stevenson: Man and Writer, 1924.

This contains a good deal of biographical matter which was ignored or minimized by earlier writers.

Janet Adam Smith: R. L. Stevenson, 1937.

WEYMAN, STANLEY JOHN (1855-1928)

The House of the Wolf, 1890.
A Gentleman of France, 1893.
Under the Red Robe, 1894.
The Long Night, 1903,

and many other stories of merit, most of them historical, of the cloak-and-sword variety.

HAGGARD, SIR HENRY RIDER (1856-1925)

King Solomon's Mines, 1885.
Allan Quatermain, She, 1887.
Eric Brighteyes, 1891.
Nada the Lily, 1892.
Ayesha, or The Return of She, 1905,

and many other tales of adventure, of which the best deal with the surprising experiences of Allan Quatermain and give a romantic account of the Zulus.

Haggard was also a serious student of agricultural problems, v. esp. *A Farmer's Year*, 1899, and *Rural England*, 1902.

His life was full, varied and interesting, and is well described in *The Days of my Life*, 1926. There are also lives by his daughter, Lilias Haggard (*The Cloak that I Left*) and by M. N. Cohen.

'HENRY SETON MERRIMAN' (Hugh Stowell Scott) (1862-1903)

The Slave of the Lamp, 1892.
From One Generation to Another, 1892.
With Edged Tools, 1894.
The Sowers, 1896.
In Kedar's Tents, 1897.
Roden's Corner, 1898.
The Velvet Glove, 1901.
Barlasch of the Guard, 1902,

and many others.

Seton Merriman's books are always honestly constructed; he has little variety of character, but his few types are credible, and in Barlasch of the Guard he succeeded in creating an unmistakable person.

DOYLE, SIR ARTHUR CONAN (1859-1930)

Conan Doyle invented that almost mythological figure, Sherlock Holmes, and is the father of all modern detective novelists; but he also deserves to be remembered as an historical novelist and as a serious historian; his *Great Boer War*, 1900, is an authoritative work.

(*a*) DETECTIVE NOVELS AND STORIES:
A Study in Scarlet, 1887.
The Sign of Four, 1889.
Adventures of Sherlock Holmes, 1891.
The Memoirs of Sherlock Holmes, 1893.
The Hound of the Baskervilles, 1902.
The Return of Sherlock Holmes, 1904.
His Last Bow, 1918.
The Case-Book of Sherlock Holmes, 1927.

(*b*) HISTORICAL NOVELS:
Micah Clark, 1888.
The White Company, 1890.
The Refugees, 1891.
The Exploits of Brigadier Gerard, 1896.
Rodney Stone, 1896.
Adventures of Gerard, 1903.
Sir Nigel, 1906,

and other works.

Memories and Adventures (autobiography), 1924.

Conan Doyle is the first of the English line of writers of detective fiction where a detective character is created: Wilkie

L

Collins in *The Moonstone* wrote a good detective novel, but of a different kind. Gaboriau, in France, preceded Doyle in his creation of Lecoq, who is, however, more ordinary than Holmes. There is, besides, no Watson. Doyle had no outstanding imitators within our period: Edgar Wallace was close on his heels, but soon degenerated into the 'thriller', and Chesterton's Father Brown belongs to another species. Doyle's talents in other directions are overshadowed by his Holmes creation, but *Rodney Stone* at least attains a very high level as a romance of action, depicting the days of the prize-ring at its height.

There is a study by Hesketh Pearson, 1941, and two books which would have delighted Conan Doyle himself: *Prolegomena to the study of a biographical problem, with a bibliography of Sherlock Holmes*, by S. C. Roberts, 1931 (research into the biography of Dr Watson); and *The Private Life of Sherlock Holmes*, by Vincent Starrett, 1934.

These four writers are not of the highest class, but they give excellent and sterling entertainment. Hewlett, though he has something in common with them, was a serious and even ambitious artist.

HEWLETT, MAURICE HENRY (1861-1923)

Hewlett was a voluminous novelist (a few characteristic novels are named below), and he is best known as a novelist, but his finest work was in poetry, essays and letter-writing.

NOVELS:
The Forest Lovers, 1898.
Little Novels of Italy, 1899.
Richard Yea-and-Nay, 1900.
The Queen's Quair, 1904.
The Stooping Lady, 1907,

and others.

POETRY:
Artemision, 1909.
The Agonists: a Trilogy of God and Man, 1911.
The Song of the Plow, 1916,

and other volumes.

ESSAYS:
Earthwork out of Tuscany, 1895.
In a Green Shade, 1920.

Wiltshire Essays, 1922.
Extemporary Essays, 1922.
Last Essays, 1924.

and other volumes.

Letters, ed. L. Binyon, 1926.

Hewlett was a writer of quality, who never quite enough fined down his style to be of the first rank in prose. His essays are not negligible even now. *Little Novels of Italy* are probably his best fiction, over-decorated as all his work is. *The Forest Lovers* is a little sugary in its romance of the Middle Ages—a watery copy of Morris—and his account of Richard I is in nearly every respect better. *The Queen's Quair*, about Mary Queen of Scots, is undoubtedly moving, but the prose is tiresome.

As a poet he has been too readily forgotten owing to the trend poetry has taken since his day, but it had qualities of firmness very welcome in the Georgian era, added to those of thought, and a certain precision of emotion. *The Agonists* is a trilogy in play form on classical themes; *The Song of the Plow* is a kind of history of England as concerning the country labourer, and displays an admirable indignation at the oppression and neglect of 'Hodge'.

v. Some Masters of Terror

LE FANU, JOSEPH SHERIDAN (1814-73)

The House by the Churchyard, 1863.
Uncle Silas, 1864.
In a Glass Darkly, 1872.

Undoubtedly the greatest writer of creepy stories in his generation.

S. M. Ellis—Wilkie Collins, Le Fanu and others, 1931.

JAMES, MONTAGUE RHODES (1862-1936)

Ghost Stories of an Antiquary, 1904.
More Ghost Stories of an Antiquary, 1911.
A Thin Ghost and Others, 1919.
The Five Jars, 1922.
A Warning to the Curious, 1925.
Collected Ghost Stories, 1931.

Dr James's editorial work on ancient MSS. does not come within our scope. His *Norfolk and Suffolk* is an admirable guide-book, but it is as a writer of excellent ghost-stories that he is known to the public. His construction and style are scholarly.

MACHEN, ARTHUR (1863-1947)

TALES:
The Great God Pan, 1894.
The Three Impostors, 1895.
The House of Souls, 1906.
The Hill of Dreams, 1907.
The Bowmen, 1914. (This has the distinction of having created a modern myth; it is the source of the legend of the angels of Mons.)

AUTOBIOGRAPHY, ESSAYS, ETC.:
Far Off Things, 1922.
Things Near and Far, 1923.
The London Adventure, 1924,

and many other books. It is surprising that the quality of their imagination and their prose style should be so little recognized.

Works, Caerleon edition, 1923.

VI

KIPLING, RUDYARD (1865-1936)

POETRY:
Departmental Ditties, 1886.
Barrack-Room Ballads, 1892.
The Seven Seas, 1896.
The Five Nations, 1903.
Songs from Books, 1913.
The Years Between, 1918.
Collected Verse, 1912, 1919, 1921, 1927, 1933.

NOVELS AND TALES:
Plain Tales from the Hills, 1887.
Soldiers Three, 1888-89.
Life's Handicap, 1890.
The Light that Failed, 1891.
Many Inventions, 1893.
The Jungle Book, 1894.
The Second Jungle Book, 1895.
Captains Courageous, 1897.
The Day's Work, 1898.
Stalky and Co., 1899.
Kim, 1901.
Just So Stories, 1902.
Traffics and Discoveries, 1904.
Puck of Pook's Hill, 1906.
Actions and Reactions, 1909.
Rewards and Fairies, 1910.
A Diversity of Creatures, 1917.
Land and Sea Tales, 1923.

Debits and Credits, 1926.
Thy Servant a Dog, 1930.
Limits and Renewals, 1932.

ARTICLES, ETC.:
From Sea to Sea, 1899.
The New Armies in Training, 1914.
The Fringes of the Fleet, France at War, 1915.
Sea Warfare, 1916.
Letters of Travel, 1920.
A Book of Words (speeches), 1928.
Something of Myself (autobiographical notes), 1936.

It may be too soon to get Kipling into true perspective, but it may safely be stated that he was a writer of immense natural force, who would have created even if he had been born into an unliterary world; that he was a most cunning artist in the construction of his stories and in the selection of detail; that he gave his contemporaries brilliant pictures of unfamiliar ways of life, and to many of them a grave sense of imperial responsibility and service (in spite of a common accusation, there is very little jingoism in him); and that to the last he kept his quick eye for new discoveries and his power of turning them to artistic use.

An excellent estimate by Katharine Fullerton Gerould appeared in *Harper's Magazine*, April 1936. Of other studies, one of the best is by André Maurois in *Logiciens et Magiciens* (translated as *Poets and Prophets*). See also the essay by Bonamy Dobrée in *The Lamp and the Lute*, the preface by T. S. Eliot to *A Choice of Kipling's Verse*, Noel Annan's *Kipling's Place in the History of Ideas* (in *Victorian Studies*, June 1960), and F. Léaud's *La Poétique de Rudyard Kipling*. The first full study which deserves consideration, by Edward Shanks, appeared in 1940, the second, by Hilton Brown, in 1945, and the best, by J. M. S. Tompkins, *The Art of Rudyard Kipling*, in 1959. The facts of the life are given by C. Carrington in his *Rudyard Kipling, his Life and Work*, 1955.

STEEL, FLORA ANNIE (1847-1929)

Mrs Steel's work, in comparison with Kipling's, shows the difference between ability and genius; but the ability was great.

From the Five Rivers, 1893.
Tales from the Punjab, The Potter's Thumb, 1894.
On the Face of the Waters, In the Tideway, 1896.
In the Permanent Way, 1897.
Voices in the Night, The Hosts of the Lord, 1900.

A Prince of Dreamers, 1908.
The Gift of the Gods, 1911.
King Errant, 1912.
The Adventures of Akbar, 1913.
The Mercy of the Lord, 1914.
Tales of the Tides, 1923.
The Law of the Threshold, 1924.
The Builder, 1928.

AUTOBIOGRAPHY:
The Garden of Fidelity, 1929.

C. THE EDWARDIANS AND SOME GEORGIANS

CONRAD, JOSEPH (Teodor Josef Konrad Korzeniowski) (1857-1924)

Almayer's Folly, 1895.
Am Outcast of the Islands, 1896.
The Nigger of the Narcissus, 1897.
Tales of Unrest, 1898.
Lord Jim, 1900.
Youth and Other Tales, 1902.
Typhoon, 1903.
Nostromo, 1904.
The Mirror of the Sea, 1906.
The Secret Agent, 1907.
A Set of Six, 1908.
Under Western Eyes, 1911.
'Twixt Land and Sea, 1912.
Chance, 1914.
Within the Tides, 1915.
Victory, 1915.
The Shadow-Line, 1917.
The Arrow of Gold, 1919.
Rescue, 1920.
The Rover, 1923.
With F. M. Hueffer, Romance, 1903.
Uniform edition, 1923-28 (22 vols.).
Some Reminiscences, 1912.
Notes on Life and Letters, 1921.

Most of the things which mattered in the life of this Polish master-mariner who became one of the greatest masters of modern English prose style and fiction are recorded in his own *Reminiscences*. *Joseph Conrad*, by Mrs Conrad, 1935, contains some additional information, and so do the studies by Richard Curle, 1914, and the reminiscences by F. M. Ford, 1924. The full *Life and*

Letters, by G. Jean-Aubrey, appeared in 1927; see also *Conrad to a Friend*, selected Letters to R. Curle, 1928; and *Letters*, 1895-1924, ed. E. Garnett, 1928. *Joseph Conrad: Some Aspects of the Art of the Novel*, by Edward Crankshaw, 1936, is a good technical study, and may be supplemented by E. H. Visiak's *The Mirror of Conrad*, 1955; Albert J. Guerard's *Conrad the Novelist*, 1958; and J. Baines, *Joseph Conrad, a critical biography*, 1959. He is especially noteworthy as an experimentalist in construction: in the end his craftsmanship somewhat overshadowed his creative impulse and his exciting vision.

MOORE, GEORGE (1857-1933)

POETRY, ESSAYS, ETC.:
Flowers of Passion, 1877.
Pagan Poems, 1881.
Literature at Nurse, 1885.
Parnell and his Island, 1887.
Confessions of a Young Man, 1888.
Spring Days, 1888.
Impressions and Opinions, 1890.
Modern Painting, 1893.
The Bending of the Bough, 1900.
Memoirs of my Dead Life, 1906.
Hail and Farewell, I, Ave, 1911; II, Salve, 1912; III, Vale, 1914.

NOVELS:
A Modern Lover, 1883.
A Mummer's Wife, 1884.
A Drama in Muslin, 1886.
A Mere Accident, 1887.
Mike Fletcher, 1889.
Vain Fortune, 1890.
The Strike at Arlingford, 1893.
Esther Waters, 1894, revised ed., 1920.
Celibates, 1895.
Evelyn Innes, 1898.
Sister Teresa, 1901.
The Untilled Field, 1903.
The Lake, 1905.
The Brook Kerith, 1916.
A Story-Teller's Holiday, 1921.
Heloise and Abelard, 1921.
In Single Strictness, 1922.
Ulick and Soracha, 1926.
Aphrodite in Aulis, 1931.

George Moore's quest for a perfect style—which induced him in his later years to rewrite some of his early books—has the effect to some tastes of rendering his books marmoreally cold and un-readable; but it is right to add that to some good judges he is one of the greatest writers, if not the greatest, of the last fifty years. *Hail and Farewell* is a most entertaining and extremely useful book of reminiscences, in its way a masterpiece of autobiography.

The authorized biography is by Joseph Hone, 1936. See also the *Letters to Lady Cunard*, ed. R. Hart-Davis, 1957.

Four critical books should be especially noted—

John Freeman—A Portrait of George Moore, 1922.
G. Goodwin—Conversations with George Moore, 1929.
Charles Morgan—Epitaph on George Moore, 1935.
Malcolm Brown—George Moore, A Reconsideration, 1956.

WELLS, HERBERT GEORGE (1866-1946)

NOVELS AND TALES:
The Time Machine, 1895; The Stolen Bacillus, 1895.
The Wonderful Visit, 1895.
The Island of Dr Moreau, The Wheels of Chance, 1896.
The Plattner Story, The Invisible Man, 1897.
The War of the Worlds, 1898.
When the Sleeper Wakes, 1899. (The Sleeper Awakes, 1911.)
Tales of Space and Time, 1899.
Love and Mr Lewisham, 1900.
The First Men in the Moon, 1901.
The Sea Lady, 1902.
Twelve Stories and a Dream, 1903.
The Food of the Gods, 1904.
Kipps, 1905.
In the Days of the Comet, 1906.
The War in the Air, 1908.
Tono-Bungay, 1909; Ann Veronica, 1909.
The History of Mr Polly, 1910.
The New Machiavelli, 1911.
Marriage, 1912.
The Passionate Friends, 1913.
The Wife of Sir Isaac Harman, 1914.
Mr Britling Sees it Through, 1916,

and many others.

OTHER WORKS:
Anticipations, 1901.
Mankind in the Making, 1903.
A Modern Utopia, 1905.
New Worlds for Old, 1908.
First and Last Things, 1908 (revised, 1917).
An Englishman looks at the World, 1914.

The World Set Free, 1914.
The Outline of History, 1920.
The Book of Catherine Wells, 1928.
The Open Conspiracy, 1928.
The King who was a King, 1929.
The Work, Wealth and Happiness of Mankind, 1932.
The Shape of Things to Come, 1933.
Experiment in Autobiography, 1934,

and many others.

Collected Works (Atlantic edition), 1925. The scientific romances and the short stories may be obtained in omnibus volumes.

See also James, Henry.

GALSWORTHY, JOHN (1867-1933)

NOVELS, ESSAYS, POEMS AND TALES:
Jocelyn, 1898.
The Island Pharisees, 1904.
The Man of Property, 1906.
The Country House, 1907.
A Commentary, 1908.
Fraternity, 1909.
A Motley, 1910.
The Patrician, 1911.
The Inn of Tranquillity, 1912.
The Dark Flower, 1913.
The Little Man, 1915; The Freelands, 1915.
Five Tales, 1918.
The Saint's Progress, 1919.
In Chancery, 1920; Awakening, 1920.
To Let, 1921.
The Forsyte Saga, 1922.
Captures, 1923.
The White Monkey, 1924.
The Silver Spoon, 1926.
Swan Song, 1928.
A Modern Comedy, 1929.
On Forsyte Change, 1930.
Maid in Waiting, 1931.
Over the River, 1933.
Flowering Wilderness, 1934,

and others.

PLAYS:
The Silver Box, 1906.
Strife, 1909.
Justice, 1910.

The Skin Game, 1920.
Loyalties, 1922.
Old English, 1924,

and others.

Collected Plays, completed in 1930.

Galsworthy's novels will be treated in the next volume: whatever their artistic merit may be—and it is not of the first order—they give an excellent picture of one section of the middle class, and for that at least will prove of enormous value to future historians. His plays are discussed in the Introduction, p. 110.

Letters, ed. E. Garnett, 1934.
Life and Letters, H. V. Marrot, 1935.
For Some We have Loved, a portrait of Galsworthy and his wife, R. H. Mottram, 1956.

There is an excellent study by Edouard Guyot, of which only the first volume (*John Galsworthy. I. Le Romancier*, 1933) has yet appeared.

BENNETT, ENOCH ARNOLD (1867-1931)

NOVELS:
A Man from the North, 1898.
The Grand Babylon Hotel, 1902.
Anna of the Five Towns, 1902.
The Grim Smile of the Five Towns, 1907.
Buried Alive, 1908.
The Old Wives' Tale, 1908.
Clayhanger, 1910.
The Card, Hilda Lessways, 1911.
The Matador of the Five Towns, 1912.
The Pretty Lady, 1918.
Riceyman Steps, 1923.
Elsie and the Child, 1925.
Imperial Palace, 1930,

and others.

PLAYS:
Milestones (with E. Knoblauch), 1912.
The Great Adventure (dramatized from Buried Alive), 1913.
Things that have Interested Me, 1921, 1923, 1925.

JOURNALS, ETC.:
Journals, 1896-1928, ed. Newman Flower.
Dorothy Cheston Bennett: Arnold Bennett, 1935.
Letters to his Nephew, 1936.
Pauline Smith: 'A.B.', a minor marginal note, 1933.

Arnold Bennett was, and perhaps still is, an over-rated writer. There is plenty of vivacity about his works, but they are, for the most part, no more than good journalism. By far his best book is *The Old Wives' Tale*, which is very nearly a good book. *The Pretty Lady* has form, and *Riceyman Steps* has a certain power. The criticism which he wrote in *The New Age* during Orage's editorship, under the name of Jacob Tonson, had the merit of blowing away a few cobwebs.

BROWN, GEORGE DOUGLAS (1869-1902)
The House with the Green Shutters, 1901.

A powerful and gloomy book, interesting in itself and as a sign of revolt against the more amiable, sometimes sentimental, pictures of Scottish life in the novels of Sir James Barrie and such lesser men as 'Ian Maclaren' and S. R. Crockett.

It might be looked upon as one of the precursors of those startlingly realistic novels of the country which, in their turn, provoked the satire of Stella Gibbons's *Cold Comfort Farm* (1932). In the main, however, these novels descend from Hardy.

'SAKI' (Hector Hugh Munro) (1870-1916)
Reginald, 1904.
Reginald in Russia, 1910.
The Chronicles of Clovis, 1911.
The Unbearable Bassington, 1912.
When William Came, 1913.
Beasts and Super-Beasts, 1914.

Up to this date, with the exception of *When William Came*, Saki's brilliant sketches had a certain irresponsibility. The two later books, published posthumously, have more bite and seriousness in their satire.

The Toys of Peace, 1919.
The Square Egg (with a biography), 1924.

'Saki' also wrote plays. *The Watched Pot* has the easy, not very penetrative note of the novels.

BERESFORD, JOHN DAVYS (1873-1947)
Jacob Stahl, 1911.
The Hampdenshire Wonder, 1911.
A Candidate for Truth, 1912.
Goslings, 1913.

The House in Demetrius Road, 1914.
The Invisible Event, 1915.
God's Counterpoint, 1918.
An Imperfect Mother, 1920,

and later novels.

Beresford, whose *Jacob Stahl* trilogy has considerable imaginative power, ranks with Zangwill, Cannan and others as a good,
competent writer, typical of the time in which he wrote. Unlike
the romancers, this group of novelists wrote of the things which
were occupying men's minds at the time, with no special lucidity
of vision or originality of style, but as good craftsmen doing their
job honestly and well.

FORSTER, EDWARD MORGAN (1879-   )

NOVELS:
Where Angels Fear to Tread, 1905.
The Longest Journey, 1907.
A Room with a View, 1908.
Howard's End, 1910.
The Celestial Omnibus, 1911.
A Passage to India, 1924.
The Eternal Moment, 1928.

OTHER WORKS:
Pharos and Pharillon, 1923.
Aspects of the Novel, 1927.
A Letter to Madan Blanchard, 1931.
Goldsworthy Lowes Dickinson, 1934.
Abinger Harvest (essays, etc.), 1936.
What I Believe, 1939.
England's Pleasant Land, 1940.
Virginia Woolf, 1942.

Forster's novels have been discussed in the Introduction. His
'other works' are equally delightful, detached, clean-cut, impish,
but always clear as to the set of values for which he stands.
Pharos and Pharillon is a brilliant series of imaginative essays on
Egyptian history, an offshoot, apparently, of *Alexandria, a History
and a Guide*, 1922, which, excellent as a guide-book, contains some
literary surprises.

There is an admirable study by Rose Macaulay, 1938. See also
H. J. Oliver's *The Art of E. M. Forster*, 1960.

SINCLAIR, MAY (1879-1946)

NOVELS:
The Divine Fire, 1904.

The Helpmate, 1910.
The Combined Maze, 1913.
The Three Sisters, 1914.
The Tree of Heaven, 1917.
Mary Oliver, 1919.
The Romantic, 1920.
Mr Waddington of Wyck, 1921.
The Life and Death of Harriet Frean, 1922.
Anne Severn and the Fieldings, 1922.
Uncanny Stories, 1923; A Cure of Souls, 1923.
The Dark Night, 1924.
The Rector of Wyck, 1925.
Far End, 1926.
The Allinghams, 1926; The History of Anthony Waring, 1927.
Fame, 1929.
Tales told by Simpson, 1930.
The Intercessor and other Stories, 1931.

Also poetry and literary and philosophical criticism. Note especially—

The Three Brontës, 1914.
A Defence of Idealism, 1917.
The New Idealism, 1922.

There is good and sincere craftsmanship in all her work, and a richer and more solid intellectual background than is possessed by many of the contemporary novelists.

MIDDLETON, RICHARD (1882-1911)

The Day before Yesterday, 1912.
The Ghost-ship and other Stories, introduction by Arthur Machen, 1912.
    This volume contains his most perfect work, the story which gives it
    its title.
Poems and Songs, introduction by Henry Savage, 1912.
Monologues, 1913. (Prose.)
The Pantomime Man, 1933. (Prose.)
Letters to Henry Savage, 1929.
Richard Middleton, the Man and his Work, Henry Savage, 1922.

MACKENZIE, SIR COMPTON (1883-   )

NOVELS:
The Passionate Elopement, 1911.
Carnival, 1912.
Sinister Street, I, 1913; II, 1914.
Guy and Pauline, 1915.
Sylvia Scarlett, 1918.
Sylvia and Michael, 1919.
Poor Relations, 1919.

Rich Relatives, 1921.
The Altar Steps, 1922.
The Parson's Progress, 1923.
The Heavenly Ladder, 1924.
The Four Winds of Love, 1937-1945,

and other novels.

OTHER WORKS:
Poems, 1907.
Gallipoli Memories, 1929.
First Athenian Memories, 1931.
More Athenian Memories, 1932.
Aegean Memories, 1940.
Greece in my Life, 1960.

Sinister Street was an extremely promising work, with plenty of dash and a fine, if undisciplined, sense of words, and contained one of the best descriptions of Oxford life ever done, as well as an extremely interesting account of a conversion to Roman Catholicism. *Guy and Pauline* was also interesting, and contained some fine, if overloaded, descriptions. But since then Mackenzie has aimed at the general taste, and his work has become unimportant though often highly amusing.

The *Memories* are well written and extremely interesting. The character sketches are admirable.

CANNAN, GILBERT (1884-1955)

NOVELS:
Old Mole, 1914.
Young Earnest, 1915.
Three Pretty Men, Mendel, 1916.
Everybody's Husband, 1917.
Mummery, The Stucco House, 1918.
Pink Roses, 1919.
Pugs and Peacocks, 1921.
Old Maid's Love, Annette and Bennett, Noel, 1922,

and others.

PLAYS:
Miles Dixon, 1910.
James and John, 1911.
Mary's Wedding, 1912.
Wedding Presents, 1912.
The Perfect Widow, 1912.
The Arbour of Refuge, 1913.
The Release of the Soul, 1920,

and others. *Four Plays* appeared in 1913, and *Seven Plays* in 1923.

OTHER WORKS:
Windmills (poems), 1915.
Samuel Butler, 1915.

Cannan also translated Romain Rolland's *Jean Christophe*.
See the note to J. D. Beresford.

SWINNERTON, FRANK ARTHUR (1884-   )

NOVELS:
The Merry Heart, 1909.
The Young Idea, 1910.
The Casement, 1911.
The Happy Family, 1912.
The Chaste Wife, 1916.
Nocturne, 1917.
Shops and Houses, 1918.
September, 1919.
Coquette, 1921.
The Three Lovers, 1922.
The Elder Sister, 1925.
Summer Storm, 1926.
The Georgian House, 1932,

and other novels.

ESSAYS, REMINISCENCE AND CRITICISM:
George Gissing, 1912.
Robert Louis Stevenson, 1914.
Tokefield Papers, 1927.
A London Bookman, 1928.
A Brood of Ducklings, 1928.
The Georgian Literary Scene, 1935.
Swinnerton, 1937,

and others.

Nocturne is a very good book indeed, but nothing else Swinnerton
has written approaches it in quality or structure. *The Georgian
Literary Scene* is of no critical value whatever, but it contains
entertaining thumb-nail sketches of the leading personalities. As
gossip it can be recommended.

WALPOLE, SIR HUGH SEYMOUR (1884-1941)

The Wooden Horse, 1909.
Maradick at Forty, 1910.
Mr Perrin and Mr Traill, 1911.
The Prelude to Adventure, 1912.
Fortitude, 1913.

The Duchess of Wrexe, 1914.
The Golden Scarecrow, 1915.
The Dark Forest, 1916.
The Green Mirror, 1918.
The Secret City, 1919. Jeremy, 1919.
The Cathedral, 1922.
Jeremy and Hamlet, 1923.
The Old Ladies, 1924.
Portrait of a Man with Red Hair, 1925.
Jeremy at Crale, 1927.
Wintersmoon, The Silver Thorn, 1928.
Rogue Herries, 1930.
Judith Paris, 1931.
Vanessa, 1933.
The Fortress, 1932.
Captain Nicholas, 1934.
The Inquisitor, 1935.
The Bright Pavilions, 1940.
Roman Fountain, 1940,

and other books.

Walpole's work will be treated in the next volume. From a rigorist standpoint, *Mr Perrin and Mr Traill* is by far his best book, a very nearly perfect work of art, compressed, tense, well-constructed, aiming at a definite effect, and sticking throughout to one subject, the atmosphere existing among the masters in a school. From *The Duchess of Wrexe* onward, Walpole tended more and more to write novels of the Trollope school.

Life, by Rupert Hart-Davis, 1952.

D. SOME BEST-SELLERS

Some attention ought to be paid to those novelists who were best-sellers in their own generation and are now perhaps unjustly derided. They could all tell a story, most of them had imagination, though it was too often undisciplined and ran to excess, they were honest craftsmen, and their popularity throws light on the taste of the ordinary reading public. A few typical names are added here, and the reader may enlarge the list at pleasure.

WOOD, MRS HENRY (1814-87)

Danesbury House, 1860.
East Lynne, 1861 (successful later both as play and as film).

Mrs Halliburton's Troubles, 1862.
The Channings, 1862,

and many others.

MULOCK, DINAH MARIA (Mrs Craik) (1826-87)

John Halifax, Gentleman, 1857 (the middle-class Victorian ideal of a
gentleman, and not an unworthy one).
A Life for a Life, 1859,

and many others.

LAWRENCE, GEORGE (1827-76)

Guy Livingstone; or Thorough, 1857.

Lawrence wrote other books, and by some *Sword and Gown*,
1859, is considered his best; but *Guy Livingstone* is that by which he
is known. 'Its deification of strength and very questionable morality' (*D.N.B.*) mark it as the predecessor of much 'strong man'
and 'sheik' novel-writing of a later date. 'The author of *Guy
Livingstone*'—he never published under his own name—was a
best-seller in his time, and undoubtedly influenced 'Ouida'.

BRADDON, MARY ELIZABETH (Mrs Maxwell) (1837-1915)

Lady Audley's Secret, 1862; and about seventy other thrillers, up to—
The Green Curtain, 1911.

'OUIDA' (Marie Louise de la Ramée) (1839-1908)

Held in Bondage, 1863.
Strathmore, 1865.
Under Two Flags, 1867.
A Dog of Flanders, 1872.
Two Little Wooden Shoes, 1874.
Moths, 1880,

and many others.

A good study is Monica Stirling's *The Fine and the Wicked: The
Life and Times of Ouida*, 1958.

Everybody read Ouida, but her books were not allowed to lie
about on drawing-room tables: she was 'unwholesome', that is
to say she rebelled against rigid Victorian conventions, and
against current moral, religious, and domestic ideals, and did
much to free the novel from unhealthy restraint. Her naughtiness
seems very tame to us now. She is lavish, exuberant, preposter-
ously superabundant; but if her good people are too perfect,

adorned with every virtue, every grace and every human power, while her bad people are as superbly wicked, her values were the right ones, and she is above all supremely generous. She was called 'flashy', but the ideals against which she tilted were tawdry. Her style, too, is lavish, but she gives life and its glamour with both hands. 'Her every page,' Sir Max Beerbohm has said, 'is a riot of unpolished epigrams, and unpolished poetry of vision.' She was much laughed at for the mistakes she made in describing masculine activities, but if her work will not stand the test of actuality, it will stand that of an undisciplined imaginative truth. She wrote emotional thrillers which are rather better than the more pretentious stuff we get today, of which the type is rather the work of—

MARIE CORELLI (1864-1924)

A Romance of Two Worlds, 1886.
Thelma, 1887.
The Sorrows of Satan, 1895.
The Master Christian, 1900.
God's Good Man, 1904,

and many others.

There is a life by Eileen Bigland, *Marie Corelli: The Woman and the Legend*, 1953.

Marie Corelli wrote novels of great length and very wide scope, in which she tried to reflect the scientific learning of her day. By no means so good an imaginative writer as Ouida, she impressed her contemporaries by her evident earnestness and her power; and by making the stark truths of science more palatable she brought comfort to thousands of readers, especially to those somewhat deficient in critical and reasoning powers.

CAINE, SIR THOMAS HENRY HALL (1853-1931)

The Shadow of a Crime, 1885.
The Deemster, 1887.
The Bondman, 1890.
The Manxman, 1894,

and many other novels; collected edition, 1921.

Recollections of Rossetti, 1882.
My Story, 1908,

Hall Caine, too, was a great comforter. White was white and black was black, and it was very exciting to read about them when they struggled in the distant and picturesque scenery of the Isle of Man; it was better still when the story was also removed in time. Caine was a writer of considerable power, and he had a sense of literary values (he was one of the first to defend Rossetti), but though he was a competent craftsman, his own works cannot rank very high.

CHILDREN'S BOOKS

IT was one of the achievements of the nineteenth century
—anticipated to some degree by Maria Edgeworth, but
by hardly anyone else—that it provided children with books
which suited their minds and their tastes, with only incidental
care, or none at all, for their moral and spiritual improvement. This section of the bibliography is short only because
some of the best minds of the century turned to the writing
of children's books and have already been dealt with. R. L.
Green's *Tellers of Tales* (rev. ed. 1953) gives information
about writers of children's stories from Catherine Sinclair to
J. R. R. Tolkien.

Four magazines should be noted as of real value and
importance:

> *The Monthly Packet*, edited from 1851 to 1890 by Miss Yonge,
> and containing many of her stories and historical articles.
> *Aunt Judy's Magazine*, 1866-85, edited by Mrs Gatty and her
> daughter, H. K. F. Gatty, and containing most of the
> work of Mrs Gatty and her daughter Mrs Ewing.
> *Good Words for the Young*, 1869-72 (continued under other
> titles until 1877), containing work of the two Kingsleys,
> George Macdonald and other good writers.
> *The Boy's Own Paper*, founded in 1879 and still flourishing.

Mrs Gatty.
Mrs Ewing.
William Brighty Rands.
George Macdonald.
Kenneth Grahame.
'E. Nesbit.'

See also under—
   Theology (Neale).
   Poetry (Lang, De la Mare, Masefield).

Novels (Thackeray, Marryat, H. Martineau, C. Kingsley, H. Kingsley, T. Hughes, C. M. Yonge, Stevenson, Kipling).

Criticism and Essays (Belloc).

Nonsense and Parody (Lear, 'Lewis Carroll').

GATTY, MARGARET (1809-73)

Parables from Nature, 1855. (This was the first series; the fifth and last appeared in 1870.)

Aunt Judy's Tales, 1858.

Aunt Judy's Letters, 1862.

There is a memoir in the edition of *Parables from Nature* published in 1885.

'Her writings are conspicuous for truthfulness, cheerfulness, humour, and the absence of false sentiment'; the comment of the *D.N.B.* might be applied to all the writers mentioned after her, but particularly to her daughter—

EWING, JULIANA HORATIA (1841-85)

Mrs Ewing has her mother's qualities, but a more exquisite art in the construction and telling of her stories. Most of them appeared in *Aunt Judy's Magazine* first, and all deserve to be read.

Melchior's Dream and other Tales, 1862.

Mrs Overtheway's Remembrances, 1866-68.

A Flat-Iron for a Farthing, 1870-71.

Six to Sixteen, 1872.

Jan of the Windmill, 1872-73.

Lob Lie-by-the-Fire and other Tales, 1873.

A Great Emergency and other Tales, 1874.

Jackanapes, 1879 (published 1883).

Daddy Darwin's Dovecot, 1881.

The Story of a Short Life, 1882 (published 1885). This book had social consequences: it led to the foundation of what are now called the Heritage Craft Schools at Chailey.

Mary's Meadow, 1883-84.

Juliana Horatia Ewing and her Books, by Horatia K. F. Gatty, 1885.

See also *Mrs Gatty and Mrs Ewing*, by Christabel Maxwell, 1949, and *Mrs Ewing, Mrs Molesworth and Mrs Hodgson Burnett* by Marghanita Laski, 1950.

RANDS, WILLIAM BRIGHTY (1823-82)

Rands wrote also as Henry Holbeach and Matthew Browne.

Most of his best work appeared in *Good Words for the Young*; some of his poems seem to anticipate Stevenson's.

Lilliput Levee, 1864.
Lilliput Lectures, 1871-72.
Lilliput Revels, 1871.
Lilliput Legends, 1872.
Henry Holbeach, Student in Life and Philosophy, 1865.
Verses and Opinions, 1866 (by 'Matthew Browne').

MACDONALD, GEORGE (1824-1905)

George Macdonald has a strong claim to be included both among the poets and among the novelists in this bibliography, but as his poetic imagination and his story-telling faculty are found in his children's books, less drawn-out than in his other work, he may stay here.

Within and Without, 1855.
Poems, 1857.
Phantastes, 1858.

These may all count as poems, though the third is mainly in prose.

David Elginbrod, 1863.
Alec Forbes, 1865.
Robert Falconer, 1868,

and many other novels, of which the best have a Scottish background.

Ranald Bannerman's Boyhood, 1871.
At the Back of the North Wind, 1871.
The Princess and the Goblin, 1872.

These all first appeared in *Good Words for the Young* between 1867 and 1871; they are the best of his longer books for children, but he wrote also many short fairy-stories which were collected in 1904.

Works of Fancy and Imagination (prose and poetry, excluding novels)
(10 vols.), 1886.
Poetical Works, 1893.

GRAHAME, KENNETH (1859-1932)

Grahame's early work was done for *The National Review* and then for *The Yellow Book*, and his style always kept a touch of the artifice of *The Yellow Book*.

Pagan Papers, 1893 (some of these were included afterwards in The Golden Age).
The Headswoman, 1898.

Of the three books for children, the third alone is really a children's book, though the story of *The Reluctant Dragon* in *Dream Days* may be added to it; the others are rather recollections of childhood. It is significant that *The Wind in the Willows* grew out of a story told to a child.

The Golden Age, 1895.
Dream Days, 1898.
The Wind in the Willows, 1908.
Patrick R. Chalmers: Life, Letters and Unpublished Work of Kenneth Grahame, 1933.
Peter Green: Kenneth Grahame, 1959.

'EDITH NESBIT' (Mrs Hubert Bland) (1858-1924)

Edith Nesbit was very nearly, if not quite, perfect as a writer for children; she never condescended, she never preached—though there is excellent morality, good breeding and even a touch of socialist propaganda in her work—and she possessed the gift of making the impossible probable.

The Story of the Treasure Seekers, 1899.
The Wouldbegoods, 1901.
Five Children and It, 1902.
The New Treasure Seekers, 1904.
The Phoenix and the Carpet, 1904.
Oswald Bastable and Others, 1905.
The Railway Children, 1906.
The Enchanted Castle, 1906.
The House of Arden, 1908.
Harding's Luck, 1909.
The Wonderful Garden, 1911.
The Magic World, 1912.
Wet Magic, 1913,

and other books of fairy stories, poetry and novels. It may be the presence of the Bastable family that makes *The Red House*, 1903, stand out among these.

There is a *Life*—a sad book—by Doris Langley Moore, and a brief critical study by Noel Streatfeild, *Magic and the Magician*.

CRITICISM AND ESSAYS

THIS section is divided into five:

A. SOME EARLY AND MID-VICTORIAN CRITICS AND ESSAYISTS.
B. AESTHETIC CRITICISM, 1840-1900.
C. LITERATURE AND POLITICS.
D. ACADEMIC CRITICS AND SOME OTHERS.
E. SOME GENERAL ESSAYISTS.

A. SOME EARLY AND MID-VICTORIAN CRITICS AND ESSAYISTS.

> Leigh Hunt, Robert Chambers, John Sterling, Dr John Brown, Samuel Smiles, Sir Arthur Helps, Augustus Hare.

B. AESTHETIC CRITICISM, 1840-1900.

> Anna Jameson, Ruskin, Eneas Sweetland Dallas, Walter Pater, John Addington Symonds, 'Vernon Lee', Arthur Symons.

C. LITERATURE AND POLITICS.

> Walter Bagehot, R. H. Hutton, John Morley, H. D. Traill, W. H. Mallock, F. W. H. Myers, Augustine Birrell, Charles Whibley.

D. ACADEMIC CRITICS AND SOME OTHERS.

> Mark Pattison, Edward Dowden, Sidney Colvin, George Saintsbury, Gosse, A. C. Bradley, C. H. Herford, W. P. Ker, J. W. Mackail, Oliver Elton, Raleigh, 'Q', E. K. Chambers, H. J. C. Grierson.

E. SOME GENERAL ESSAYISTS.

> I. Richard Jefferies, W. H. Hudson, R. B. Cunninghame Graham.
> II. Max Beerbohm.

III. E. V. Lucas, Hilaire Belloc, G. K. Chesterton, Maurice Baring.

See also under—

History (Sir J. Stephen, Carlyle, Macaulay, Froude, G. M. Trevelyan, Leslie Stephen, Dicey).

Science (Huxley, Frazer).

Theology (Keble, R. W. Church, F. W. Robertson).

Philosophy (A. De Morgan, W. K. Clifford, Caird, Bosanquet, Romanes, Balfour, Inge, G. L. Dickinson, Havelock Ellis, Butler).

Poetry (W. S. Landor, Horne, de Vere, M. Arnold, Swinburne, Dobson, Lang, Henley, Patmore, F. Thompson, L. Johnson, A. Meynell, James Thomson, Bridges, Davidson, A. E. Housman, 'Æ.', De la Mare, Masefield, E. Thomas, H. Monro, J. Freeman, Abercrombie, Squire).

Drama (Sir H. Taylor, Wilde, Granville-Barker, Monkhouse, Shaw, Archer, Ervine).

Novels (Peacock, Thackeray, Anne Thackeray Ritchie, T. Adolphus Trollope, 'Mark Rutherford', Meredith, H. James, Gissing, Stevenson, Hewlett, Machen, Conrad, George Moore, E. M. Forster, May Sinclair, R. Middleton, Compton Mackenzie, Cannan, Swinnerton).

Nonsense and Parody (*passim*).

A. SOME EARLY AND MID-VICTORIAN CRITICS AND ESSAYISTS

LEIGH HUNT, JAMES HENRY (1784-1859)

Most of Leigh Hunt's work, especially his poetry, lies in an earlier period, but he may be looked upon as the predecessor of many of those pleasant writers whose essays have a flavour of literary allusion and a touch of scholarship. His poetry is not considered here.

The Companion, 1828.
Leigh Hunt's London Journal, 1834-35.

Imagination and Fancy (anthology with critical remarks and an essay on the Nature of Poetry), 1844.
Wit and Humour selected from the English Poets, with an essay, 1846.
Men, Women and Books (collected papers), 1847.
A Jar of Honey from Mount Hybla, 1848 (as essays, 1844).
The Town, 1848.
Table-Talk, 1851.
The Old Court Suburb, 1855.
Autobiography, 1850; revised edition, 1860.
Edmund Blunden: Leigh Hunt, 1930.

CHAMBERS, ROBERT (1802-71)

Robert Chambers and his brother William (1800-83) hold an honourable place in the history of popular education. They were responsible, among much else, for *Chambers's Journal* (1832 onwards), *Chambers's Cyclopaedia of English Literature* 1844; (the new edition, 1901-03, is a most valuable work of reference, quotation and criticism), and *Chambers's Encyclopaedia* (first edition, 1859-68).

Traditions of Edinburgh, 1823.
Vestiges of Creation (first pub. anon.), 1844.
W. Chambers: Memoir of William and Robert Chambers, 1872. 13th edition with supplementary chapter, 1884.

STERLING, JOHN (1806-44)

Essays and Tales, ed. Julius Hare with memoir, 1848.

The memoir seemed to Carlyle to misrepresent Sterling, though unintentionally, and he accordingly wrote his *Life of Sterling*, published in 1851. It is by this *Life* that Sterling himself survives.

BROWN, DR JOHN (1810-82)

Horae Subsecivae, 1858, 1861, 1882.
Rab and his Friends, 1859.
Marjorie Fleming, 1863.
Letters, with Letters from Ruskin, Thackeray and others, ed. by his son and D. W. Forrest, with a biographical introduction by E. T. McLaren, 1907.

Of all the essayists considered in this section, Dr John Brown 'dates' least—less even than Leigh Hunt. He had a warm heart and an independent mind, humour, a real sense of pathos, and a style which expressed himself.

In contrast to Dr John Brown, the three writers who follow

almost succeed in filling the conventional picture of 'the Victorian'. Smiles had the respect for the less attractive virtues and, if not smug himself, was certainly the cause of smugness in others ; Helps, though less aggressively respectable, has a touch of the same qualities; Augustus Hare gives in his best books a picture of the sheltered life of certain religious circles which did not neglect their minds in cultivating their souls.

SMILES, SAMUEL (1812-1904)

Self-Help, 1859. In spite of its somewhat forbidding title, this contains some rattling good stories for boys, like Smiles's other books.

Lives of the Engineers, 1861-62 (much enlarged, 1874). This is a really useful set of biographies, none the worse for its emphasis on the characteristics which led to the success of its heroes.

Character, 1871.

Thrift, 1875.

The Huguenots in France, 1878, an excellent popular study.

Duty, 1880.

Life and Labour, 1887.

Smiles wrote also a valuable history of the publishing house of Murray—*A Publisher and his Friends*, 1891.

Autobiography, 1905.

HELPS, SIR ARTHUR (1813-75)

Friends in Council, 1847-59 (several series).

Helps wrote other volumes of essays, plays and novels, and two histories of the Spanish conquest of America; and he prepared for the press the *Speeches of Prince Albert* (1862) and Queen Victoria's *Leaves from the Journal of our Life in the Highlands* (1868) and *Mountain, Loch and Glen* (1869).

HARE, AUGUSTUS JOHN CUTHBERT (1834-1903)

Memorials of a Quiet Life, 1872-76.

The Gurneys of Earlham, 1895,

and many other biographical sketches and books of travel, of which *Walks in Rome*, 1871, is typical.

The Story of My Life, 1886-1900, is not as good as his stories of other lives, but has been well abridged by Malcolm Barnes in *The Years with Mother* and *In my Solitary Life*.

B. AESTHETIC CRITICISM, 1840-1900

JAMESON, ANNA BROWNELL (1794-1860)

Mrs Jameson's art criticism is old-fashioned, but the first four books named below, which form a history of Christian art up to the seventeenth century, have still some value and the charm of enthusiasm.

Legends of the Saints, 1848.
Legends of the Monastic Orders, 1850.
Legends of the Madonna, 1852.
The History of Our Lord (completed by Lady Eastlake), 1860.

These volumes are grouped together under the title *Sacred and Legendary Art*.

Characteristics of Women, 1832 (essays on Shakespeare's female characters).
Essays, 1846.
A Commonplace Book, 1854.
Life, by her niece Gerardine Macpherson, 1878.

RUSKIN, JOHN (1819-1900)

The chronological succession of Ruskin's works shows his progress from the criticism of art to political economy.

Modern Painters, 1843, 1846, 1856, 1860.
The Seven Lamps of Architecture, 1849.
The Stones of Venice, 1851, 1853.
The Political Economy of Art, 1857.
The Two Paths, 1859.
Unto this Last, 1862.
The Crown of Wild Olive, 1865.
Sesame and Lilies, 1865.
Fors Clavigera, 1871-84 (published at irregular intervals).
Munera Pulveris, 1872.
Praeterita, 1885-89,

and many others.

Like most artists in words, Ruskin attempted poetry in his youth. His verse may be read in his collected works, but he was no exception to the rule that few writers of the Prize Poem at Oxford ever write any later poetry of value. His poetic feeling showed itself in other forms.

Collected works, 1903-09, ed. E. T. Cook and Alexander Wedderburn.
Diaries, selected and edited by Joan Evans and J. H. Whitehouse, 1956-1959.
Letters from Venice, ed. J. L. Bradley, 1955.

For the early part of Ruskin's life, his own *Praeterita* is the best authority. The standard life is that by E. T. Cook, 1911; another good one, and shorter, is by W. G. Collingwood, first published in 1893 and revised after Ruskin's death. Wilenski in his study, 1933, gives a more modern, if too 'psycho-analytic', view of Ruskin and his artistic criticism. The study by Joan Evans, 1954, is good.

DALLAS, ENEAS SWEETLAND (1828-79)

Poetics, 1852.
The Gay Science, 1866.

The work of Dallas on aesthetic theory is now receiving more attention than it has done since his death. In his own time he was a critic of considerable influence, and he ought not to be omitted from the history of criticism in the period.

The other names in this section are connected in greater or less degree with the 'aesthetic movement' of the eighties and nineties. Pater had the most direct effect upon it, because of his teaching of the essential value of beauty for its own sake; he was also one of those who revived the study of Plato in the last quarter of the century. John Addington Symonds and 'Vernon Lee' show the preoccupation with the Italian art and life of the Renaissance, but 'Vernon Lee' had more originality than any of her companions here except Pater. Her analytical work on English prose is extremely valuable. Arthur Symons comes later and really belongs to the nineties —to the time of Beardsley and after.

PATER, WALTER HORATIO (1839-94)

Studies in the History of the Renaissance, 1873.
Marius the Epicurean, 1885. A novel of shadowy characters and a vague, melancholy beauty.
Imaginary Portraits, 1887.
Appreciations, with an Essay on Style, 1889.
Plato and Platonism, 1893.
The Child in the House, 1894 (written in 1878).
Greek Studies, 1895.
Miscellaneous Studies, 1895.
Essays from *The Guardian*, 1901.
Collected works (10 vols.), 1910.

Besides the study by A. C. Benson in the *English Men of Letters* series, there is one by Arthur Symons, 1932. Symons wrote earlier critical essays on Pater, which are in *The Savoy* and his volumes of essays, and there is, among many other essays and books, one which deserves mention, by T. Earle Welby in *Revaluations*.

SYMONDS, JOHN ADDINGTON (1840-93)

The Renaissance in Italy, 1875-86.
Shakespeare's Predecessors in the English Drama, 1874,

and other books of criticism and translation.

Life, compiled from his Letters, by Horatio F. Brown, 1895.

'VERNON LEE' (Violet Paget) (1856-1935)

'Vernon Lee' wrote studies of art and life (especially in Italy), essays, sketches and stories, and the different kinds of writing sometimes fade into each other. Her style would be too careful if it were not strengthened with knowledge and original thought.

Studies of the Eighteenth Century in Italy, 1880.
Belcaro, essays, 1881.
Ottilie, 1883.
Euphorion, essays on the Renaissance, 1884; Miss Brown, 1884.
Baldwin, philosophical dialogues, 1886.
A Phantom Lover, 1886.
Juvenilia, essays, 1887.
Hauntings, 1890.
Vanitas, 1892.
Althea, philosophical dialogues, 1893.
Renaissance Fancies and Studies, 1895.
Limbo, essays, 1897.
Hortus Vitae, essays, 1903.
Genius Loci, Pope Jacynth, The Enchanted Woods, 1905.
Sister Benvenuta, 1906.
The Sentimental Traveller, 1907.
Gospels of Anarchy, 1908.
Laurus Nobilis, 1909.
The Tower of Mirrors, essays, 1914.
Louis Norbert, novel, 1914.
Satan the Waster, 1920.
The Handling of Words, 1923.
The Golden Keys, 1925.
Music and its Lovers, 1932.

SYMONS, ARTHUR (1865-1945)

Days and Nights, 1889.
Silhouettes, 1892.
London Nights, 1895.
Studies in Two Literatures, 1897.
The Symbolist Movement in Literature, 1899.
Images of Good and Evil, 1900.
Collected Poems, 1901.
Cities, 1903.
Studies in Prose and Verse, 1904.
Spiritual Adventures, 1905; A Book of Twenty Songs, 1905.
The Fool of the World, 1906; Studies in Seven Arts, 1906.
William Blake, 1907; Cities of Italy, 1907.
The Romantic Movement in English Poetry, 1909.
Figures of Several Centuries, 1915.
Tragedies, 1916.
Studies in Elizabethan Drama, 1920.
Charles Baudelaire, 1921.
Dramatis Personae, 1926.
A Study of Thomas Hardy, 1927.
Studies in Strange Souls, 1929.
Confessions, 1930.
Wanderings, 1931.
Jezebel Mort and other Poems, 1931.
Collected Works (16 vols.), 1924 onwards.

A little 'aesthetic' and 'ninetyish', but with many good things: the student cannot afford to neglect him. In 1896 he edited a noteworthy magazine, *The Savoy* (see p. 137). There is a study of him by T. Earle Welby, 1925, and Ruth Z. Temple's *The Critic's Alchemy* (1953) brings out his particular importance as helping to 'domesticate' French symbolist poetry in England.

C. LITERATURE AND POLITICS

BAGEHOT, WALTER (1826-77)

Bagehot was one of the most original and prescient critics of the century. His *English Constitution*, 1867, shows his power of political thought and analysis and, in spite of the changes of the last seventy years, is not entirely out of date; and his understanding of political economy and finance is evident in *Lombard Street*, 1873. His *Literary Studies*, *Economic Studies*, and *Biographical Studies* have suffered less from the passage of time. They appeared first as articles in reviews but were collected after his death and published with a memoir by R. H. Hutton in 1879-81. His essay on Sterne and Thackeray 'dates' him: but the brilliant essay on Dickens is remarkably free from prejudice; and there are few pieces of nineteenth-century criticism better than the two essays on Wordsworth, Tennyson and Browning (*Pure, Ornate and Grotesque Art*) and on *Shakespeare the Man*.

There is a good biography by William Irvine, 1939, and studies by Norman St John Stevas, 1959, and Alastair Buchan (*The Spare Chancellor*), 1959.

HUTTON, RICHARD HOLT (1826-97)

Studies in Parliament, 1866.
Essays, Theological and Literary, 1871, largely recast 1877, 1888.
Aspects of Religious and Scientific Thought (contributions to *The Spectator*), 1899.

R. H. Hutton might almost stand as a type of the best Victorian reviewer: a man of strong and independent judgment, deeply affected by the great problems of his day, and expressing his convictions with gravity and a sense of responsibility. His essays are guides to contemporary opinion, and also contain much general and literary criticism of permanent value.

MORLEY, JOHN, LORD MORLEY OF BLACK-BURN (1838-1923)

Morley's political interests combined, not always for good, with his literary interests. Perhaps his best critical work was done on the eighteenth-century French thinkers, whose temper had something congenial to a certain clear rigidity in his. He ranks highest as a biographer.

Critical Miscellanies, 1871; 2nd series, 1877.
Voltaire, 1871.
Rousseau, 1873.
Diderot and the Encyclopaedists, 1878.
Studies in Literature, 1891.
Life of Gladstone, 1903.
Recollections, 1917.
J. H. Morgan—John, Viscount Morley, 1924.
F. W. Hirst—Early Life and Letters of Lord Morley, 1927.

TRAILL, HENRY DUFF (1842-1900)

Traill's political and literary criticism are alike witty. He wrote also a *Life of Sir John Franklin*, 1896, and edited a history of *Social*

England (1893-97), as well as editing the centenary edition (1896-1901) of Carlyle's works with introductions.

Recaptured Rhymes, 1882.
Saturday Songs, 1890.
The New Lucian, 1884, expanded 1900.
Number Twenty, 1892.
The New Fiction, 1897.

MALLOCK, WILLIAM HURRELL (1849-1923)

The New Republic, 1877.

A 'Platonic symposium' in which the characters, easily recognizable as satirical portraits of great figures of the day (e.g., Pater, Jowett) discuss questions of politics, philosophy and religion. In form a novel, it is in fact rather of the nature of a succession of essays. His other novels are bad.

MYERS, FREDERICK WILLIAM HENRY (1843-1901)

Wordsworth, 1881.
Essays, Classical and Modern, 1883.

Myers was in fact less interested in politics than the others in this group, but he joins them by reason of his literary interests. He wrote at least one poem of memorable quality—*St Paul*, 1867—and *Fragments of Prose and Poetry* were published in 1904.

He was much interested in the question of human survival, and in all those problems which are classed as psychical. He was a very interesting personality, and his philosophy is by no means considered negligible by professional philosophers.

Phantasms of the Living, 1886 (joint author).
Science and a Future Life, 1893.
Human Personality and its Survival of Bodily Death, 1903.

BIRRELL, AUGUSTINE (1850-1933)

Obiter Dicta, 1884.
Life of Charlotte Brontë, 1885.
Res Judicatae, 1892.
Men, Women and Books, 1894.
Collected Essays, 1900.
Miscellanies, 1901.
William Hazlitt, 1902.
Andrew Marvell, 1905.
In the Name of the Bodleian, 1905.
Frederick Locker Lampson, 1920.

M

More Obiter Dicta, 1924.
Et Cetera, 1930.
Things Past Redress, autobiography, 1937.

Birrell was of the same political complexion as Morley, but politics come very little into his essays; he was a lighter figure than either Morley or Myers.

WHIBLEY, CHARLES (1859-1930)

Thackeray, 1903.
Literary Portraits, 1904.
William Pitt, 1906.
Essays in Biography, 1913.
Jonathan Swift, 1917.
Political Portraits, 1917; 2nd series, 1923.
Literary Studies, 1919.
Lord John Manners and his Friends, 1925,

and other books, as well as introductions to several volumes of the *Tudor Translations* series. Whibley was in the Henley tradition and a stout Tory. His political views, like those of Morley, sometimes affected his literary criticism. He wrote good, clear, direct prose, and his work is all very readable, if a little too 'downright' in manner.

D. ACADEMIC CRITICS AND SOME OTHERS

Most of those whose names follow speak with recognized authority.

PATTISON, MARK (1813-84)

Casaubon, 1875.
Milton, 1879 (revised in 1880 and later).
College and University Sermons, 1885.
Essays, 1889.
Memoirs (down to 1860—dictated in 1883), 1885.

Mark Pattison is almost the conventional type of the scholar. He was not an altogether likeable person—George Eliot's Mr Casaubon in *Middlemarch* is an unkind portrait, and Rhoda Broughton's Professor Forte in *Belinda* is another—but almost infallible within his limits. His memoirs are of interest as giving some account of the Oxford Movement by one who was first attracted by it and then repelled.

V. H. H. Green: Oxford Common Room. A Study of Lincoln College and Mark Pattison.

DOWDEN, EDWARD (1843-1913)

Shakespeare, his Mind and Art, 1875.
Shakespere Primer, 1877.
Introduction to Shakespere, 1893.

Dowden's Shakespearian criticism is of great importance historically, and has not lost its influence, though modern criticism differs from it and has modified his conclusions in many ways. He wrote many other volumes and articles of literary history and criticism. His *Life of Shelley*, 1886, was the standard life, in spite of deficiencies, until it was at least in part superseded by the work of Peck and Ingpen.

Letters of E. Dowden and his Correspondents, ed. E. D. and H. M. Dowden, 1914.

COLVIN, SIR SIDNEY (1845-1927)

Landor, 1881.
Keats, 1887.
John Keats, his Life and Poetry, 1917.
Edinburgh edition of the works of Robert Louis Stevenson, 1894-97, and his Letters, 1899 and 1911.

Colvin would have desired to be remembered chiefly as the friend of Stevenson, but he was a critic in his own right. His own *Memories and Notes*, 1921, should be supplemented by E. V. Lucas, *The Colvins and their Friends*, 1928. His work is solid and to be trusted, and his writing reaches a high, but not inspired, standard.

SAINTSBURY, GEORGE EDWARD BATEMAN (1845-1933)

Primer of French Literature, 1880.
Dryden, 1881.
Short History of French Literature, 1882.
Nineteenth-Century Literature, 1896.
A Short History of English Literature, 1898.
History of Criticism, I, 1900; II, 1902; III, 1904.
History of English Prosody, I, 1906; II, 1908; III, 1910.
The Later Nineteenth Century, 1908.
Historical Manual of English Prosody, 1910.
History of English Criticism, 1911.
History of English Prose Rhythm, 1912.
The English Novel, 1913.
The Peace of the Augustans, 1915.

History of the French Novel, I, 1917; II, 1919.
Collected Essays and Papers (4 vols.), 1924.
A Consideration of Thackeray, 1931.

Saintsbury was an omnivorous reader and sometimes appears omniscient. He had immense gusto in life and literature, which may be enjoyed also in certain books of a mixed and indescribable kind.

Notes on a Cellar Book, 1920.
A Scrap Book, 1922.
A Second Scrap Book, 1923.
A Last Scrap Book, 1924.

He is invaluable as a literary historian, especially when prosody is in question; he wrote with great vigour, and never lacked for critical ideas.

A Last Vintage, 1950, with personal portraits by friends and a bibliography by W. M. Parker.

GOSSE, SIR EDMUND (1849-1928)

Gosse was less of a scholar than his companions here, though his *Northern Studies*, 1879, had much to do with the beginning of the study of Ibsen in this country. He is not always to be trusted for his facts, and he is often irritating. His best book is the subtle, autobiographical study of the relations between two temperaments, *Father and Son*, 1907. Of his other books—essays, literary criticism, biographies, etc., may be noted:

Seventeenth Century Studies, 1883.
Congreve, 1888.
Collected Poems, 1911.
Collected Essays (5 vols.), 1913.
Books on the Table, 1921.
Aspects and Impressions, 1922.

BRADLEY, ANDREW CECIL (1851-1935)

Shakesperian Tragedy, 1904.

The most influential book of Shakespearian criticism which appeared in England in the first quarter of the twentieth century. With it goes—

Oxford Lectures on Poetry, 1909.
A Miscellany, 1929 (essays and lectures).

Bradley must certainly rank very high as a critic. It is claimed by some that he completed Coleridge's theory of poetry: but he was not himself a poet, and though he felt poetry profoundly, he was inclined to feel it a little heavily.

HERFORD, CHARLES HAROLD (1853-1931)

Studies in the Literary Relations of England and Germany in the Sixteenth Century, 1886.
The Age of Wordsworth, 1897.
Browning, 1904.
Shakespeare, 1912.
Goethe, 1913.
Shakespeare's Treatment of Love and Marriage, and other Essays, 1916.
The Post-War Mind of Germany, and other European Essays, 1927.
Wordsworth, 1929.

Sound and conscientious, informative and clear, but without Bradley's occasional flashes of imagination.

KER, WILLIAM PATON (1855-1923)

Epic and Romance, 1897 (a book which revolutionized European criticism of epic).
The Dark Ages, 1904.
Essays on Mediaeval Literature, 1905.
English Literature: Medieval 1912.
The Art of Poetry, 1923.
Collected Essays, ed. with an introduction by Charles Whibley, 1925.
Form and Style (lectures, ed. R. W. Chambers) 1928.

See also under *History*—J. A. Doyle, and *Philosophy*—Seth.

Bibliography by J. H. P. Pafford, 1950.

Ker's knowledge and imaginative comprehension of classical, medieval and modern literature was both wider and more profound than that of almost any other scholar named in this section, and he could convey it without pedantry in a style that is both easy and disciplined. He was himself of heroic temper, and spoke nobly of heroic things.

MACKAIL, JOHN WILLIAM (1859-1945)

Latin Literature, 1895.
Select Epigrams from the Greek Anthology, 1890 (translations; revised ed. 1906).
The Springs of Helicon, 1909.
Lectures on Poetry, 1911.
Studies of English Poets, 1926.
The Approach to Shakespeare, 1930.
The Life of William Morris, 1899—the standard life.
Life of George Wyndham, 1925.

Mackail may be looked upon as an offshoot of the pre-Raphael-ites, and exhibits their best tendencies without their diffuseness. His work is full of charm.

ELTON, OLIVER (1861-1945)

The Augustan Ages, 1899.
Life, Letters and Occasional Writings of Frederick York Powell, 1906.
Modern Studies, 1907.
Survey of English Literature from 1780-1830, 1912; from 1830-1880, 1920; from 1730-1780, 1928.
A Sheaf of Papers, 1922.
Dickens and Thackeray, 1930.
The Testament of Beauty, 1933. (A criticism of Bridges's poem.)
The English Muse, 1933.
Essays and Addresses, 1939.

The *Surveys* are the most trustworthy guides for anyone who wishes to go further into the literary history of the eighteenth and nineteenth centuries, and *The English Muse* for anyone who wishes to learn something of the history of English poetry without losing delight in the poetry. It was characteristic of Elton's energy and enjoyment of literature that, after his retirement from academic teaching, he took up the study of Slavonic languages, and in the last ten years of his life produced some of the best English trans-lations of Slavonic poetry—

Verse from Pushkin and Others, 1935.
Pushkin's Evgeny Onegin in English Verse, 1938.
Lyrics from Polish and Serbian (*Slavonic Review*, 1940-44).

RALEIGH, SIR WALTER (1861-1922)

The English Novel, 1894.
Style, 1897.
Milton, 1900.
Wordsworth, 1903.
Shakespeare, 1907.
Six Essays on Johnson, 1910.
Some Authors, 1923.
The War in the Air, I, 1922. (It was while collecting the material for this history that Raleigh contracted his fatal illness.)
Laughter from a Cloud (miscellanies), 1923.
Letters, ed. Lady Raleigh, with a preface by D. Nichol Smith, 1926.

Raleigh was temperamentally a man of action, and never made the mistake of divorcing literature from life. His criticism makes no pretence to be eternal, but it is always stimulating and fresh, and will probably outlast that of most of his contemporaries.

QUILLER-COUCH, SIR ARTHUR THOMAS (1863-1944)

It is possible that 'Q' will be remembered chiefly for his poems and novels, but Sir Arthur Quiller-Couch, as a professor, published criticism which is valuable for its stimulating qualities and its wide humanism; at times 'Q' can bite. All students of literature should read at least *On the Art of Writing* and *On the Art of Reading*.

NOVELS:
Dead Man's Rock, 1887.
Hetty Wesley, 1903—the best and the best-constructed of his novels, though the more rigorous prefer *Hocken and Hunken*, 1912,

and others, the scene usually set in Cornwall.

POETRY:
Verses and Parodies, 1893.
Poems and Ballads, 1896.
The Vigil of Venus, and other poems, 1912.

CRITICISM:
Adventures in Criticism, 1896.
On the Art of Writing, 1916.
Shakespeare's Workmanship, 1918.
Studies in Literature, 1918; 2nd series, 1922; 3rd series, 1929.
On the Art of Reading, 1920.
Charles Dickens and other Victorians, 1925.
The Poet as Citizen, 1934.

A fragment of autobiography was published shortly after his death.

CHAMBERS, SIR EDMUND KERCHEVER (1866-1954)

The Mediaeval Stage, 1903.
The Elizabethan Stage, 1923.
Shakespeare, a Survey, 1925.
Arthur of Britain, 1927.
William Shakespeare, 1930.
Samuel Taylor Coleridge, 1938.
English Literature at the Close of the Middle Ages, 1945,

and other books.

Sir E. K. Chambers and Granville-Barker (see under DRAMA) should be read together by anyone who wishes to get understanding of the conditions of the Elizabethan stage.

GRIERSON, SIR HERBERT JOHN CLIFFORD (1866-1960)

The First Half of the Seventeenth Century, 1906.
The Background of English Literature, and other collected essays, 1925.
Cross-Currents in the Literature of the Seventeenth Century, 1929,

and other books.

Most of Sir Herbert Grierson's books fall outside the period, but he is included here as belonging to the same great generation of humane scholars: his prose is 'nourished' and delightful.

E. SOME GENERAL ESSAYISTS

I

JEFFERIES, JOHN RICHARD (1848-87)

The Gamekeeper at Home, 1877.
Wild Life in a Southern County, 1879.
The Amateur Poacher, 1880.
Wood Magic, 1881.
Round about a Great Estate, 1881.
Bevis, 1882.
Nature near London, 1883.
The Life of the Fields, 1884.
Red Deer, 1884.
The Open Air, 1885.
After London, 1885,

and other books.

Some of these are nominally novels, but differ little from essays in their nature.

The Story of My Heart, 1883, is a kind of autobiography. There is also a life by H. S. Salt, 1894.

Jefferies had an intimate knowledge and real love of the countryside, but his feeling, like his prose, seems a little self-conscious.

HUDSON, WILLIAM HENRY (1841-1922)

In all Hudson's books, as in Jefferies's, whether they are supposed to be novels, like *The Purple Land* or *A Crystal Age*, or autobiography, like *Far Away and Long Ago*, the interest is in the background of plant and animal life to which the writer feels himself closer than to men.

The Purple Land, 1885. (2 v⸰1)
The Naturalist in La Plata, 1892.
Birds in a Village, 1893.
Nature in Downland, 1900.
El Ombù, 1902.
Green Mansions, 1904.
A Crystal Age, 1906.
Far Away and Long Ago, 1918,

and others.

Collected works (24 vols.), 1923.
Letters, ed. E. Garnett, 1923.
Morley Roberts—W. H. Hudson: A Portrait, 1924.

Hudson's prose is much admired by those who follow 'the middle style'. It is, others will think, a little monotonous.

CUNNINGHAME GRAHAM, ROBERT BONTINE
(1852-1936)

Cunninghame Graham's stories, essays and biographies show, like Hudson's, a love of nature, especially at its wildest, but an even greater love of the heroic in man. He was romantic, preposterous, lovable, aristocratic, humane, a *hidalgo* of literature, and 'the uncrowned king of Scotland'.

Mogreb el Acksa, 1898 and 1921.
The Ipané, 1899.
Thirteen Stories, 1900.
A Vanished Arcadia, 1901.
Success, 1902.
Life of Hernando de Soto, 1903.
Progress, 1905.
His People, 1906.
A Hatchment, 1913.
Life of Bernal Diaz del Castillo, 1915.
Brought Forward, 1916.
The Conquest of New Granada, 1922.
The Conquest of the River Plate, 1924.
Doughty Deeds, 1925.
Pedro de Valdivia, 1926.
The Horses of the Conquest, 1930.
Writ in Sand, 1932.
Portrait of a Dictator, 1933.
Rodeo, a collection of the tales and sketches, selected by A. F. Tschiffely, 1936.

A study by Herbert Faulkner West, containing much correspondence from Cunninghame Graham's friends, was published in 1932. A. F. Tschiffely's *Don Roberto*, 1937, is a more complete biography.

II

BEERBOHM, SIR MAX (1872-1956)

Contributed to *The Yellow Book*.
The Works of Max Beerbohm, 1896.
The Happy Hypocrite, 1897.
More, 1899.
The Poets' Corner, 1904 (cartoons with annotations).
Yet Again, 1909.
Zuleika Dobson, 1911.
A Christmas Garland, 1912. (Parodies.)
Seven Men, 1919.
And Even Now, 1920.
Rossetti and his Circle, 1922. (Cartoons with annotations.)
Things New and Old, 1923.
Observations, 1925.
Lytton Strachey (Rede Lecture), 1943.

Max Beerbohm's mingled pictorial and verbal satire and more gentle criticism is unique. It is strange that he should live at the same time as H. G. Wells, and equally strange that so great a master of subtle prose should have proved himself a master of the technique of broadcast speaking.

S. N. Behrman—Conversations with Max, 1960.

III

LUCAS, EDWARD VERRALL (1868-1938)

The Open Road, 1899,
and other anthologies.

Highways and Byways in Sussex, 1904.
A Wanderer in Holland, 1905.
A Wanderer in London, 1906.
A Wanderer in Paris, 1909.
A Wanderer in Florence, 1912.
A Wanderer in Venice, 1914.
One Day and Another, 1909.
Loiterer's Harvest, 1913.
Landmarks, 1914.
A Boswell of Baghdad, 1917,
and other volumes of essays.

Listener's Lure, 1906.
Over Bemerton's, 1908.
Mr. Ingleside, 1910.
London Lavender, 1912,

and other essay-like novels.

The Colvins and their Friends, 1928.
The Life of Charles Lamb, 1905—a standard work. Ed. The Works of
    Charles and Mary Lamb, 1903-05; The Letters of Charles and Mary
    Lamb, 1935. These are standard editions.

Outside this work of scholarship, E. V. Lucas was an extremely
competent writer of the best sort of journalism, flavoured with
sentiment which may or may not appeal to the reader. His book
of reminiscences, *Reading, Writing and Remembering*, 1932, has a
drier savour.

BELLOC, HILAIRE (1870-1953)

POETRY:
Verses and Sonnets, 1895.
Verses, 1910.
Verses and Sonnets, 1924.
HISTORY:
Danton, 1899.
Robespierre, 1901,

and other biographies and longer histories.

BOOKS FOR CHILDREN:
The Bad Child's Book of Beasts, 1896.
More Beasts for Worse Children, 1897.
The Moral Alphabet, 1899.
Cautionary Tales, 1907.

ESSAYS AND SATIRES:
The Path to Rome, 1902.
Caliban's Guide to Letters, 1903.
Mr Burden, 1904.
The Old Road, 1905.
The Hills and the Sea, 1906.
Mr Clutterbuck's Election, 1908.
On Nothing, 1908.
The Pyrenees, 1909.
On Everything, 1909.
On Anything, 1910.
On Something, 1911.
First and Last, 1911.
The Four Men, 1912.
The Stane Street, 1913.

This and That, 1913.
On, 1923.
The Cruise of the 'Nona', 1925,

and other volumes.

Belloc's history is tendentious, though not more so than that of historians who are less frank about their beliefs, but his essays are brilliant journalism and something more, and his prose is usually excellent. His satire of the financial basis of our civilization is altogether well-grounded and admirably achieved.

Memoir, by J. B. Morton, 1955.
Testimony to Hilaire Belloc, by Eleanor and Reginald Jebb, 1956.

The official *Life* by Robert Speaight appeared in 1957.

CHESTERTON, GILBERT KEITH (1874-1936)

POETRY:
The Ballad of the White Horse, 1911.
Poems, 1915.
Collected and New Poems, 1927.

NOVELS:
The Napoleon of Notting Hill, 1904.
The Club of Queer Trades, 1905.
The Man who was Thursday, 1908.
The Ball and the Cross, 1910.
The Innocence of Father Brown, 1911 (The Wisdom of Father Brown, 1914; The Incredulity of Father Brown, 1926; The Secret of Father Brown, 1927; The Scandal of Father Brown, 1935).
Manalive, 1911.
The Flying Inn, 1914.
Tales of the Long Bow, 1925.
The Four Faultless Felons, 1930.

ESSAYS AND CRITICISM:
Heretics, 1905.
Dickens, 1906—one of the best books on Dickens.
Orthodoxy, 1908.
All Things Considered, 1908.
Tremendous Trifles, 1909.
What's Wrong with the World, 1910.
Alarms and Discursions, 1911.
The Victorian Age in Literature, 1913.
The Uses of Diversity, 1921.
St Francis of Assisi, 1925.
The Everlasting Man, 1925.
Generally Speaking, 1928.

The Thing, 1929.
The Resurrection of Rome, 1930.
Chaucer, 1932.

and other volumes.

Autobiography, 1936. This is much more revealing than the bulky and too controversial life by Maisie Ward.

Chesterton was perhaps the only writer of fantasy in the later part of the period who made the fantasy symbolic of anything. In the same way, though the Father Brown stories are first-rate detective fiction, no one can fail to see that the values are Christian values and sometimes distinctively Roman Catholic.

BARING, MAURICE (1874-1945)

POETRY:
Sonnets and Short Poems, 1906.
Collected Poems, 1911.
Poems 1914-17, 1918.
Poems 1914-19, 1921.
Collected Poems, 1925.

SATIRE AND PARODY:
Dead Letters, 1910.
Diminutive Dramas, 1910, 1919.
Lost Diaries, 1913.
(Diminutive Dramas and Lost Diaries were published together under the apt title of *Unreliable History* in 1935.)

ESSAYS, CRITICISM AND SHORT STORIES:
A Year in Russia, 1907.
Russian Essays and Stories, 1909.
Landmarks in Russian Literature, 1910.
Half a Minute's Silence, 1925.

NOVELS:
Cat's Cradle, 1925,

and others.

The Puppet Show of Memory, 1922 (reminiscences).

NONSENSE AND PARODY; HUMOUR AND LIGHT VERSE

IT should be noted that much 'nonsense' and parody is wisdom and acute criticism, and should be treated with respect, as much as is due to inspired nonsense. See especially below, for parody which is literary criticism, 'Bon Gaultier', Calverley, 'Lewis Carroll', Hilton, J. K. Stephen, Leaman.

R. H. Barham.
Edward Lear.
'Bon Gaultier'.
C. S. Calverley.
'Lewis Carroll'.
F. C. Burnand.
W. S. Gilbert.
George and W. Grossmith.
'F. Anstey'.
A. C. Hilton.
J. K. Stephen.
Owen Seaman.
E. C. Bentley.
See also under—
Poetry (Hood, Praed, Lang, Squire).
Criticism and Essays (Traill, Quiller-Couch, Beerbohm, Belloc, Chesterton, Baring).
Drama (Hankin).

BARHAM, RICHARD HARRIS (1788-1845)

The Ingoldsby Legends, 1840 (2nd and 3rd series, 1847, the 3rd with a brief memoir by his son).

Some of the riotous humour is out of date, but it is not likely that *The Ingoldsby Legends* will ever fall out completely.

LEAR, EDWARD (1812-88)

The Book of Nonsense, 1846.
Nonsense Songs and Stories, 1871.

More Nonsense Songs, Pictures, etc., 1871.
Laughable Lyrics, 1877.
Nonsense Botany and Nonsense Alphabets, 1877.
Teapots and Quails, 1953.

Lear's deliberately serious books of travel and landscape paintings were neglected for many years, but have been appreciated by Lawrence Durrell and others. His other books are inspired nonsense and sometimes reach heights of poetic suggestion. Now that the subconscious is coming to the fore in criticism, Lear is receiving a good deal of attention and is hailed by some as a surrealist. As 'pure poetry' his work is acclaimed by poets.

A good selection from his *Journals* was edited by Herbert Van Thal in 1952, and his *Indian Journals* by Ray Murphy in 1953. There is a full life by Angus Davidson, 1950.

'BON GAULTIER' (i.e., WILLIAM EDMON-STOUNE AYTOUN, 1813-65, and THEODORE MARTIN, 1816-1909)

Bon Gaultier Ballads, 1855 (written before 1844).

Brilliant parody of contemporary poets, mock-heroic and topical satire.

Aytoun wrote an even better parody, *Firmilian*, 1854, which shows up the weaknesses of Dobell and Alexander Smith ('the Spasmodic school of poets'). He also wrote the spirited *Lays of the Scottish Cavaliers*, 1848.

Both partners were adequate translators from the German, and Martin wrote a very different book from *Bon Gaultier*—the official *Life of the Prince Cons*⌐⌐ 18⌐⌐-80.

'LEWIS CARROLL' (Charles Lutwidge Dodgson) (1832-98)

Alice's Adventures in Wonderland, 1865.
Through the Looking Glass, 1871.
Phantasmagoria and other Poems, 1876.
The Hunting of the Snark, 1876.
Rhyme? or Reason?, 1883.
Sylvie and Bruno, 1889.
Sylvie and Bruno Concluded, 1893.

The mathematical works of the Rev. C. L. Dodgson, including the puzzles in which he collaborated with Lewis Carroll, need not concern us, except as they emphasize the logical basis of Lewis Carroll's nonsense.

Life and Letters, S. D. Collingwood, 1898—a dull book. Derek Hudson's biography, 1954, is more useful, and so is R. L. Green's, 1960, and Green's edition of the *Diaries*, 1953, but when the divine inspiration of nonsense was not in Carroll, there was only an amiable but not very interesting man.

Carroll also is claimed as a surrealist, and also as a predecessor of James Joyce. There is, however, a logical and even mathematical basis to the dream-world of the *Alice* books and *The Hunting of the Snark*, which are to the grown-up extremely witty, as well as being amusing to most, though not all, children.

A. L. Taylor—The White Knight, 1952.
Elizabeth Sewell—The Field of Nonsense, 1952, deals mainly with Carroll and Lear.

BURNAND, SIR FRANCIS COWLEY (1836-1917)

Happy Thoughts, 1866,

and many other h............................now old-fashio..........

Plays (including many other plays) were printed at dates from 1876 to 1911: *Original Comic Operas* in 1890.

Songs of a Savoyard, 1890.

Whether Gilbert or Sullivan was more responsible for the success of the operas is a question which they themselves could not decide; the story of their relations is told in Hesketh Pearson's *Gilbert and Sullivan*, 1935, and *Gilbert*, 1957. At least Gilbert's topsy-turvy wit has enriched the language with the word Gilbertian. He had a miraculous facility in rhyming, and much of his work is worth reading for its own sake for that reason. But he had a commonplace and rather vulgar mind.

W. A. Darlington, *The World of Gilbert and Sullivan*, 1952, deals with the operas and their background.

GROSSMITH, GEORGE (1847-1912) and WALTER WEEDON (1854-1919)

Diary of a Nobody, 1894.

By some good judges considered a classic.

'F. ANSTEY' (Thomas Anstey Guthrie) (1856-1933)

Vice Versa, 1882.
The Giant's Robe, 1883.
The Black Poodle, 1884,

and other tales and essays, rather satiric than humorous. There is much more in him than meets the schoolboy eye. *Voces Populi* shows keen observation.

The Man from Blankley's, 1901, was a successful play which satirized a certain kind of nineteenth-century snobbery and has become almost a social document.

A Long Retrospect, 1936—an autobiography which confirms the impression that he was rather a satirist than a humorist.

HILTON, ARTHUR CLEMENT (1851-77)

The Light Green, 1872.
Works, together with his Life and Letters, ed. R. P. Edgcumbe, 1904.

Hilton's poem in the manner of Swinburne, addressed to the Octopus in the Crystal Palace Aquarium, is the most complete and final criticism ever written of Swinburne in his mood of weak violence. Hilton, J. K. Stephen and Owen Seaman stand together in the next generation as the right heirs of Calverley in the highest kind of parodic criticism.

STEPHEN, JAMES KENNETH (1859-92)

Lapsus Calami, 1891.
Quo Musa Tendis, 1891.

Calverley's peer in parody and implied criticism.

SEAMAN, SIR OWEN (1861-1936)

The Battle of the Bays, 1896.

Parody of contemporary poets, and some satire.

In Cap and Bells, 1899.
Borrowed Plumes, 1902.

Parody, in the main, of prose-writers.

A Harvest of Chaff, 1904.
Salvage, 1908.
War Time, 1915.
Made in England, 1916.
From the Home Front, 1918.
Interludes of an Editor, 1929.

Seaman, as became the editor of *Punch* from 1906 to 1932, had a gift of dignified as well as pointedly satiric verse.

BENTLEY, EDWARD CLERIHEW (1875-1956)

Biography for Beginners, 1905.

Inspired nonsense which is often indistinguishable from wisdom. The illustrations are by G. K. Chesterton.

Baseless Biography, 1939, is of the same type.

Bentley also wrote some of the best modern detective stories; *Trent's Last Case*, 1912; *Trent's Own Case*, 1936; and *Trent Intervenes*, 1938.

Those Days (autobiography), 1940.

SPORT

A CONSTANT though perhaps minor literary activity during the period is the writing on sporting matters, especially foxhunting. The existence of the Badminton series indicates the interest taken in such matters. The best sporting writer of the period, apart from the novelists, is:

'NIMROD' (Charles James Apperley) (1779-1843)
Nimrod's Hunting Tours, 1835.
Memoirs of the Life of the late John Mytton, 1837.
The Life of a Sportsman, 1842.

Mytton's was a fantastic life (there is a convenient essay by Virginia Woolf in *The Common Reader II*); and in connection with this sort of existence, much entertainment and social sidelight may be obtained from the autobiography of GEORGE OSBALDESTON (1787-1866), the great Squire, edited and published by Ed. Cuming.

Another popular writer was William Knightley Horlock, who wrote under the name of 'SCRUTATOR'. Apart from some poor novels, of which *The Squire of Beechwood* was the best known, he wrote such works as *Lessons on the Management of Hounds*, 1852; *The Master of Hounds*, 1859; *Practical Lessons on Hunting and Sporting*, 1865. His most agreeable work is probably *Recollections of a Foxhunter*, 1861. Scrutator, however, is not so accomplished a writer as Nimrod, who gives admirable little pictures of personalities and the countryside.

The interest continued through the century, and still continues. As a more recent example in our period, we might name *The Sport of Kings*, by Scarth Dixon, 1900.

See TRAVEL.

INDEX OF NAMES

Numbers in roman type refer to the Prefaces, in *italics* to the Bibliography. Separate entries have not been made for editors, biographers and critics who appear only in relation to their subjects; e.g., of four editors of Carlyle, Firth and Traill are indexed, but not Holland Rose and Lomas. The authors of books suggested for general reading and the study of special numbers (pp. 135–8, 140, 174–5, 187, 208, 249, 320,) are not indexed unless they are also noted elsewhere.

A

à Beckett, G., 107
Abercrombie, L., 33, 55n., 112, *208, 209, 245–6, 250, 290, 325*
Acton, Lord, *140, 149, 150*
Adamson, R., *187, 196*
Addison, J., xi
'Æ' (George Russell), 55n., *209, 239–240, 325*
Ainsworth, Harrison, *261, 268*
Aldington, R., 57
Alexander, S., *175, 188, 204–5*
Alison, Sir A., *140, 144*
Allingham, W., *209, 223*
Amiel, H. F., 93
Anson, Sir W., *141, 155*
'Anstey, F.' (T. Anstey Guthrie), *250, 263, 346, 349*
Arch, J., 124
Archer, W., *249, 252, 255, 260, 325*
Armstrong, Lord, 122
Arnold, M., xiii, 2, 5, 6, 11n., 18, 21, 25n., 35–7, 41, 52, 88, 89, 93–5, 97, 99, 100, 108, 114, 124, *171, 190, 209, 220–21, 325*
Arnold, T., 37, 70, *140, 142, 172, 220*
Augustine, St, 97
Austen, Jane, 72
Aytoun, W. E., *222, 347*

B

Bagehot, W., xix, 10n., 103, *138, 141, 324, 331–2*
Bailey, P. J., 23, *209, 220*
Bain, A., *188, 191, 199–200*
Baker, Elizabeth, 109, *249, 257*
Balfour, Arthur, Lord, *175, 188, 197, 325*

Barham, R. H., *346*
Baring, M., *137, 139, 210, 263, 325, 345, 346*
Barnes, W., *209, 214*
Barnett, Canon S., *174, 183*
Barrie, Sir J., *132, 311*
Bateson, F. W., 20n.
Beales, H. L., 126
Beardsley, A., 99, *137, 329*
Beddoes, T. L., *209, 212, 214–15, 249*
'Bede, Cuthbert' (E. Bradley), *261, 276, 277*
Beerbohm, Sir Max, x, 33, 103, *137, 223, 227, 263, 318, 324, 342*
Bellamy, E., *132*
Belloc, H., 3, 6, 85, 102, *141, 210, 263, 321, 325, 343–4*
Bennett, A., *250, 262, 310–11*
Benson, E. F., *262, 273, 297*
Benson, Archbishop E. W., *173*
Bentham, J., 2, 4, 7, 10, 89, 117, *119–120, 201*
Bentley, E. C., *263, 346, 350*
Beresford, J. D., *262, 311–12*
Berkeley, Bishop G., 98
Besant, Sir W., *262, 292–3*
Bessemer, Sir H., 122
Binyon, L., *209, 238, 250, 303*
Birrell, A., 102, *228, 324, 333–4*
Blackmore, Sir R., 19n.
Blackmore, R. D., *261, 276, 280*
Blake, W., 27, *42, 213, 240*
Blavatsky, Madame, 12
Blunt, W. S., 53, 54, *141, 159, 209, 235*
Boccaccio, xii
Bonar, J., *196*
'Bon Gaultier' (Aytoun and Martin), *346, 347*
Boole, G., *187, 189*
Booth, C., *141, 156*

Booth, W., *141, 156, 260*
Borrow, G., *139, 159–60, 263*
Bosanquet, B., *187, 194–5, 205, 325*
Bosch, Hieronymus, 91
Bottomley, G., *112, 209, 242, 250*
Boucicault, D., 106, 107, *249, 251–2*
'Bourn, George' (George Sturt), *139, 141, 156, 263*
Braddon, M. E., *262, 317*
Bradlaugh, C., 10
Bradley, A. C., 104, *193, 216, 324, 336–7*
Bradley, F. H., 22, *187, 194, 195, 205*
Brémond, Abbé, *177*
Breughel, P., 91
Bridges, R., *52–3, 162, 209, 224, 232, 235–6, 325, 338*
Bright, J., 119, *152*
Bright, W., *141, 175, 181, 210*
Brontë, A., 72, *210, 261, 272–3*
Brontë, C., 72, 82, *210, 261, 272–3*
Brontë, E., 18, 21, 39, 59, *72–3*, 75, *210, 261, 272–3*
Brooke, R., 56, *209, 247–8*
Broughton, R., 20, *262, 275, 291–2, 334*
Brown, G. D., *262, 311*
Brown, Dr J., *324, 326–7*
Brown, T. E., *209, 222*
Browne, Sir T., xvi
Browning, E. B., 11, 13, 33–5, *209, 215, 217–19*
Browning, R., 5, 6, 19, 29–33, 35, 41, 43, 65, 76, 107, *209, 217–19, 249, 265*
Bryce, Lord, *141, 152, 154, 157*
Buckle, H. T., *141, 153*
Bunyan, J., xvi
Burnand, Sir F., *250, 263, 346, 348*
Burton, J. H., *140, 147*
Burton, Sir R., *159, 162–3*
Bury, J. B., *140, 142–3*
Butcher, S. H., 95–6n., *219, 229*
Butler, S., 12, 101, 110, *166, 175, 188, 205–6, 325*
Byron, George, Lord, 38
Byron, H. J., *249, 251*

C

Caine, Sir T. Hall, *262, 318–19*
Caird, E., *145, 175, 187, 193, 205, 325*
Calverley, C. S., *213, 221, 346, 347*
Cannan, G., *206, 210, 250, 262, 312, 314–15, 325*
Carlyle, J. W., *145–6*

Carlyle, T., xii, xiv, 4, 5, 19, 88–92, 93, 94, 95, 97, 114, *138, 139, 140, 144–6, 151, 223, 270, 325, 326, 333*
Carpenter, E., 104, *137, 175, 188, 206–207, 210*
'Carroll, Lewis' (C. L. Dodgson), *263, 321, 346, 348*
Cecil, Lord D., 18, 59, *264, 290*
Chadwick, E., 120, 123
Chambers, Sir E. K., *324, 339*
Chambers, R., 10, 69n., *166, 324, 326*
Chapman, G., 19
Charles II, xvi
Chaucer, G., xii, xv, 48, 55
Chesterton, G. K., 6, 85, 102, *210, 218, 263, 264, 271, 274, 302, 325, 344–5, 350*
Church, R. W., 9n., *141, 175, 176, 180–1, 325*
Clapham, Professor, 122
Clifford, W. K., *187, 190, 325*
Clough, A. H., xix, 11, 37–8, *176, 209, 220, 221*
Cobbett, W., 6, 118, 129
Cobden, R., 119
Colenso, Bishop J. W., 11, *175, 182*
Coleridge, S. T., xii, 27, 100, 106–7, *174, 201, 336*
Collins, Wilkie, 59, 66, *261, 271–2, 301–2*
Colvin, Sir S., *211, 300, 324, 335*
Comte, A., *192, 193*
Congreve, W., 86
Conrad, J., 60, 80, *137, 139, 262, 306–7, 325*
Cooper, T., 117, *139, 209, 214*
Corelli Marie, *262, 318*
'Corvo, Baron' (F. Rolfe), *137, 262, 297*
Cory, W., *209, 222*
Crabbe, G., 49, 72
Craig, Gordon, 111
Creasy, Sir E., *141, 157*
Creighton, Bishop M., *140, 150*
Cunningham, W., *141, 156*
Curzon, Lord, *141, 150, 154, 157, 159*

D

Dale, R. W., *171, 175, 183*
Dallas, E. S., *324, 329*
Dante, xii, 19
Darwin, C., 10, 98, 122, *159, 166, 167*
Davidson, J., 54, 111, *137, 209, 235, 236–7, 249, 255, 325*

Davies, W. H., *139, 209, 240–1*
Davis, H. W. C., *141, 151*
Defoe, D., xi, xvi, 61
de Guérin, M., 93
de la Mare, W., 55n., *136, 209, 241–2, 263, 320, 325*
De Morgan, A., *187, 189, 325*
De Morgan, W., *261, 275–6*
d'Ennery, 108
Descartes, 98
de Vere, A., 14, *209, 219–220, 249, 325*
Dicey, A. V., *141, 154, 325*
Dickens, C., 18, 19, 20, 58, 59, 60, 61, 62, 64, 65–6, 67, 69, 71n., 72, 75, 76, 82, 120, *137, 159, 165, 171, 234, 261, 266, 270–1, 272, 281, 282, 293, 332*
Dickinson, G. L., 104–5, *141, 188, 199, 205, 325*
Disraeli, B. (Lord Beaconsfield), 61, 62, 69–70, 71n., 117, 124, *141, 261, 270, 281, 298*
Dixon, R. W., 9, *141, 175, 176, 209, 224, 232*
Dixon, Scarth, *351*
Dobell, S., *207, 222, 347*
Dobson, A., 53, *137, 209, 213, 229, 231, 325*
Dolben, D. M., *176, 209, 231, 232, 236*
Donne, J., ix, xvi, 27
Doughty, C. M., *132, 159, 162, 163–4, 209, 245*
Douglas, Lord A., 53, *209, 238, 254*
Dowden, E., 23, *103, 324, 335*
Dowson, E., 9, *137, 209, 240*
Doyle, Sir A. Conan, 82, *141, 262, 301–2*
Doyle, J. A., *141, 157–8, 337*
Drinkwater, J., *141, 209, 246, 250*
Dryden, J., x, 18, 86, 102
Dufferin, Lord, *159, 160*
Du Maurier, G., *262, 296*

E

Eden, E., *261, 267*
Edgeworth, M., *320*
'Eliot, George' (M. A. Evans), 21, 60, 61, 69, 73–5, 77, 78, 82, *137, 171, 188, 210, 262, 281, 285, 292, 334*
Eliot, T. S., *216, 244, 272, 305*
Elliott, E., 5, *209, 213–14*
Ellis, Havelock, 104, *137, 166, 188, 202, 325*
Elton, O., *208, 236, 271, 274, 324, 338*

Engels, F., 71n., 123
Ensor, R. C. K., 3n., *135*
Ervine, St John, 109, *156, 249, 259, 260, 263, 325*
Etherege, Sir G., x, 109
Evans, Sir A., *140, 143–4, 159*
Ewing, J. H., *320, 321*

F

Faldo, J., x, 19n.
Faraday, M., 10, *166, 167*
Farquhar, G., xvi, 110
Farrar, F. W., *175, 182*
Ferguson, Sir S., *209, 219*
Ferrier, J. F., *187, 191*
Fielding, H., 60, 61, 74
Finlay, G., *140, 142*
Firth, Sir C., *140, 145, 146, 148, 151*
Fisher, H. A. L., *141, 151–2, 154, 155*
FitzGerald, E., 39–40, *209, 217, 220, 249*
Flaubert, G., 78
Flecker, J. E., 56–7, *209, 247, 250, 263*
Flint, F. S., 57, *244*
Ford, F. M. (F. M. Hueffer), *223, 306*
Ford, R., *159, 160*
Forster, E. M., xvi, 60, 62, 83–4, *199, 262, 263, 312, 325*
Fraser, A. C., *175, 187–8, 197*
Frazer, Sir J. G., *166, 169, 175, 188, 325*
Frederick the Great, 90
Freeman, E. A., 6, *140, 148*
Freeman, John, *209, 244–5, 264, 308, 325*
Froude, J. A., 11, 103, *140, 145, 147–8, 154, 175, 176, 263, 325*
Froude, R. H., *148, 175, 177*

G

Galsworthy, J., 13, 85, 109, 110, 115, *210, 250, 256, 262, 275, 309–10*
Galton, Sir F., *166, 170*
Gardiner, S. R., *140, 148–9*
Garnett, R., *137, 262, 298–9*
Gaskell, Mrs, 62, 69, 71–2, 73, 92, 101, *137, 138, 171, 262, 281, 282*
Gatty, Mrs, *320, 321*
George H., 128, *132, 207*
Gibbon, E., xi, *143*
Gibbons, S., *311*
Gibson, W. W., *209, 242*
Gilbert, Sir W. S., *231, 250, 346, 348–6*

Gissing, G., 60, 80–1, 129, *262, 293, 325*

Gladstone, W. E., 98

Godwin, W., 7, 10

Goethe, 36, 89, 93, *146, 192*

Gore, Bishop C., 13, *173, 174, 175, 181, 184, 185–6, 196*

Goschen, 126

Gosse, Sir E., 49, *137, 139, 210, 215, 226, 264, 324, 336*

Graham, R. B. Cunninghame, 3, *141, 161, 263, 324, 341–2*

Grahame, K., *137, 320, 322–3*

Grant, 'Baron', 123

Granville-Barker, H., 109, 110–11, 115, *136, 249, 255–6, 260, 325*, 339

Green, J. R., 103, *140, 149*

Green, T. H., *175, 181, 187, 193, 194, 198, 205, 263*

Gregory, Lady, 111, *249, 259, 263*

Grierson, Sir H., *163, 324, 340*

Grossmith, G. and W., *263, 346, 349*

Grote, G., *140, 142*

Grote, J., *187, 192*

H

Haggard, Sir H. Rider, 82, *262, 300*

Haldane, J. S., *166, 188, 196, 204*

Haldane, Lord, *188, 195, 196, 198*

Halifax, Lord, xii

Hamilton, C., *139, 249, 256–7*

Hamilton, Sir W., 22, *187, 191*

Hankin, St John, 109, *249, 257–8*

Hardy, T., x, 12, 18, 21, 51–2, 58, 61, 75, 77, 78, *210, 214, 234, 250, 261, 262, 263, 289–90, 311*

Hare, A., *141, 324, 327*

Harland, H., *137, 262, 296*

Hartley, D., 98

Hawker, R. S., *138, 209, 215*

'H. D.' (Hilda Doolittle), 57

Hegel, *187, 191, 192, 193, 194, 195, 196, 198, 200, 205*

Heine, 94

Helps, Sir A., *141, 324, 327*

Hemans, F., *209, 211–12*

Henley, W. E., *208, 209, 230–1, 325, 334*

Herbert, G., 18, 44, *178*

Herford, C. H., *324, 337*

Herschel, Sir J. F. W., *166, 187, 188–9*

Hewlett, M., 54, 95–6n., *210, 262, 302–3, 325*

Hichens, R., *262, 296*

Hicks, T., x

Hilton, A. C., *346, 349*

Hitler, Adolf, 90

'Hobbes, John Oliver' (P. M. T. Craigie), *137, 262, 298*

Hobbes, T., xiii, 98

Hobhouse, L. T., *141, 188, 203*

Hodgkin, T., *140, 142*

Hodgson, R., 56, *209, 241*

Hodgson, S. H., *187, 192*

Hood, T., 13, *209, 212*

'Hope, Anthony' (Sir A. H. Hawkins), 82, *262, 296*

Hopkins, G. M., 12, 18, 21, 50, 57n., *175, 176, 209, 224, 232, 236, 275*

Horne, R. H., *209, 215, 249, 325*

Hort, F. A., *175, 183, 184*

Houghton, S., 109, 112, *249, 257*

Housman, A. E., *209, 237–8, 325*

Housman, L., *210, 249, 258, 263*

Hudson, W. H., *139, 161, 263, 324, 340–1*

Hughes, T., 70, *262, 281, 283, 284, 321*

Hulme, T. E., 55, 57

Hume D., 98, *168, 193*

Hunt, Leigh, *139, 210, 324, 325–6*

Hutton, R. H., *141, 285, 324, 331, 332*

Huxley, T., xiv, 11, 21, 97–9, 122, *159, 166, 167, 168, 175, 188, 190, 325*

I

Ibsen, H., 108, 109, 111, *260, 336*

Inge, W. R., *175, 188, 199, 325*

Ingelow, J., *209, 221, 263*

J

Jacobs, W. W., *250, 262, 294–5*

James, G. P. R., *261, 267–8*

James, Henry, 58, 59, 74, 78, 79–80, *137, 139, 248, 261, 262, 263, 290–1, 292, 309, 325*

James, M. R., *262, 303*

Jameson, Anna, *324, 328*

Jefferies, R., *263, 324, 340*

Jeremiah, 90

Jerome, J. K., *250, 262, 294, 295*

Jerrold, D., 107, *249, 251, 263*

Jessopp, A., *141, 155*

Jevons, Stanley, *187, 189*

Johnson, L., *137, 209, 231, 233–4, 290, 325*

Johnson, S., 18, 101

Johnston, Sir H., *141, 159, 164–5, 263*
Jones, H., *196*
Jones, H. A., 107–8, *249, 253*
Jonson, B., x
Jowett, B., 63, 100, *175, 188, 198, 333*
Joyce, J., *348*

K

Kant, *145, 181, 187, 191, 192, 193, 194, 195, 196,* 200
Keats, J., 28, 42, 63n., *212*
Keble, J., 9, *173, 175, 177, 178, 210, 325*
Ker, W. P., *158, 196, 216, 324, 337*
Kilpatrick, T. B., *196*
King, B., *174*
King, Bishop E., *173*
Kinglake, A. W., *141, 159, 160–1*
Kingsley, C., 5, 13, 68, 69, 70–1, 73, 92, 97, 101, 113, 124, *141, 159, 161, 166, 174, 210, 214, 262, 281, 282–3, 320, 321*
Kingsley, G., *159, 161*
Kingsley, H., 69, 73, *161, 262, 281, 283–4, 320, 321*
Kingsley, M., 63, *159, 161, 164*
Kipling, R., 3, 53–4, 82–4, 127, *159, 210, 262, 265, 278, 295, 304–5, 321*
Knowles, S., 107, *249, 250*
Knox, J., 89

L

Lamb, C., 102, *250, 343*
Landor, R. E., *209, 211*
Landor, W. S., 21, 23, 86–7, 90n., 100, *209, 210–11, 325*
Lane, E. W., *159, 162*
Lang, A., 53, 95–6n., *141, 166, 209, 213, 219, 229–30, 263, 320, 325*
Lankester, Sir R., *166, 168, 169*
Lawrence, D. H., 42, 55n., 62, 207
Lawrence, G. A., *262, 317*
Layard, Sir A., *141, 159, 162*
Lear, E., *321, 346–7*
Lecky, W. E. H., *141, 147, 154*
Lee, N., 90
'Lee, Vernon' (V. Paget), *210, 263, 324, 329, 330*
Le Fanu, J. S., *262, 303*
Lemon, M., 107
Lever, C., 68, *261, 276, 277*
Lewes, G. H., *187, 192*
Liddon, H. P., *172, 175, 180*

Lightfoot, Bishop J. B., *141, 175, 183*
Livingstone, D., *159, 164*
Lloyd George, D., 15
Locke, J., xiii
Locker-Lampson, F., *209, 213, 228*
Lodge, Sir R., 22
Lover, S., *210, 250, 261, 276, 277*
Lovett, W., 117
Lucas, E. W., *263, 325, 335, 342–3*
Lyell, Sir C., *166–7*
Lytton, B. (Lord Lytton), 106, 107, *250, 261, 269, 270*

M

Macaulay, Lord, 5, 22, 87–8, *140, 146–7, 151, 152, 209, 215, 325*
Macdonald, G., *210, 320, 322*
Machen, A., *139, 262, 304, 325*
Mackail, J. W., *138, 225, 286, 324, 337–8*
Mackenzie, C., *210, 262, 313–14, 325*
Maine, Sir H. J. S., *141, 153*
Maitland, F. W., *141, 151, 153, 155*
Mallock, W. H., *188, 263, 324, 333*
Malthus, T. R., 2, 4
Mansel, H. L., *175, 187, 191*
Marryat, F., *261, 276–7*
Marston, P. B., *209, 227, 249*
Martin, Sir T., *347*
Martineau, H., 10, *139, 141, 159, 262, 266, 281–2, 321*
Martineau, J., *171, 175, 187, 194, 196–197*
Marvell, A., 18
Marx, K., xi, 4, 6, 40, 96, *282–3*
Masefield, J., 25, 54–5, *141, 209, 242–3, 250, 263, 325*
Massey, G., *209, 214*
Maurice, F. D., 9, 13, 70, 71, *174, 175, 181–2, 283*
Maxwell, Sir J. C., *166, 167*
Mayhew, H., *141, 155–6*
McTaggart, J., *175, 188, 205*
Meredith, G., 12, 21, 50–1, 58, 59, 60, 61, 66, 69, 74, 75–7, 78, 124, *153, 210, 262, 263, 266, 288–9, 292, 325*
Merivale, C., *140, 142*
Merrick, L., *262, 297–8*
'Merriman, H. Seton' (H. S. Scott), 82, *262, 301*
Meynell, A., 9, 50n., 53, *176, 209, 231, 233, 234, 271, 325*
Middleton, R., *210, 262, 313, 325*
Mill, J., 10, 89, *187, 191, 199, 281*

Mill, J. S., 10, 89, 103, *139, 188, 190, 193, 194, 199, 200–1*
Miller, H., *139, 166, 167*
Milman, H. H., *140, 141*
Milton, J., x, xi, 18, 25, 28, *211*
Mitford, M. R., 72, *250, 261, 267*
Monkhouse, A., 109, 249, 256, 263, *325*
Monro, H., 55, *209, 244, 325*
Montaigne, xii
Moore, G., 59, 60, 62, 78–9, *137, 210, 262, 307–8, 325*
Moore, G. E., *175, 188, 195, 204*
Moore, T. S., 55n., *209, 240*
More, P. E., *132*
Morell, J. D., *175, 187, 191–2*
Morgan, C. Lloyd, *166, 188, 203–4*
Morley, John, Lord, 104, *138, 141, 324, 332, 334*
Morris, W., 4, 5, 6, 21n., 25n., 36n., 41, 48–9, 88, 89, 95–7, 114, 129, *137, 159, 160, 209, 219, 223, 224–5, 263, 275, 286*
Morrison, A., *262, 293*
Morton, J. M., 107, *249, 251*
Muggleton, x, 19n.
Mulock, D. (Mrs Craik), *262, 317*
Myers, F. W. H., *175, 188, 194, 210, 229, 324, 333, 334*

N

Napier, Sir W., *140, 144*
Neale, J. M., *141, 175, 180, 210, 263, 320*
'Nesbit, E.' (Mrs Hubert Bland), *137, 210, 320, 323*
Nettleship, R. L., *187, 193*
Newbolt, Sir H., 54, *209, 231, 263*
Newman, Cardinal, 7, 8, 9, 10, 18, 21, 22, 97–8, 99, 100, *173, 175, 176, 177, 178–9, 188, 210, 263*
Newton, Sir I., xi
Nightingale, F., 8n., 63, 71
'Nimrod' (C. J. Apperley), *351*
Novalis, 89, *235*
Noyes, A., *139, 166, 175, 209, 245*

O

O'Casey, S., 111
Oliphant, M., *171, 262, 287*
Oman, Sir C., *140, 141, 151*
Osbaldeston, G., *351*
Ossian, 6

'Ouida' (Louise de la Ramée), 45, 62, *262, 297, 317–18*
Owen, R., 3–4, 118

P

Paine, T., 4
Palgrave, Sir F., *140, 144*
Palmer, E. H., *159, 163*
Pascal, 97
Pater, W., 21, 99–100, *188, 263, 324, 329–30, 333*
Patmore, C., 9, 12, 41, 42, 49–50, *175, 176, 209, 231, 232–3, 325*
Pattison, M., 11, *139, 175, 176, 292, 324, 334–5*
Peacock, T. L., 101, 210, *261, 265–6, 325*
Pearson, K., *166, 170, 175, 188, 190*
Penn, W., x, 19n.
Petrie, Sir F., *140, 143, 159*
Pett Ridge, W., *262, 294*
Phillips S., 107, *210, 249, 254–5*
Pinero, Sir A. W., 108, *249, 253*
Planché, 107
Plato, *187, 192, 193, 198, 199, 329*
Plummer, C., *140, 150*
Pollard, A. F. *141, 152*
Pope, A., x
Pound E., 33, 57
Powell, F. York, *151, 338*
Praed, W. M., *209, 212–13, 228, 347*
Prynne, W., 19n.
Pugin, A., 6
Pusey, E. B., 6, 7, *172, 173, 175, 176, 179*

Q

'Q' (Sir A. T. Quiller-Couch), 60, 82, *210, 214, 263, 264, 299, 324, 339*

R

Raleigh, Sir W., 45, *324, 338*
Ramsay, Sir J., *140, 150*
Ramsay, Sir W. M., *140, 143, 159*
Rands, W. B., *210, 320, 321–2*
Reade, C., 71n., 106, 123, *137, 250, 252, 262, 281, 284–5*
Reade, W. W., *175, 188, 205*
Renan, E., 94
Rhodes, C., 3
Ricardo, D., 2, *281*
Ritchie, D. G., *196*

Robertson, F. W., *175*, *181*, *182–3*, *325*
Robertson, G. C., *187*, *200*
Robertson, J. M., 104
Robertson, T. W., 107, *249*, *253*
Rogers, J. T., *140*, *141*, *155*
Romanes, G., *166*, *175*, *187*, *196*, *325*
Rosebery, Lord, *140*, *150*, *154*, *157*
Rossetti, C., 9, 34, 39, 40–1, 44–5, 47, 49, *175*, *176*, *180*, *209*, *223–4*, *231*
Rossetti, D. G., 25n., 30, 40–4, 50, 99, *137*, *162*, *209*, *223*, *227*, *319*
Rossetti, W. M., 40, 43, *212*, *223*
Ruskin, J., 5, 6, 14, 21, 40, 50, 88, 89, 91–3, 95, 97, *139*, *210*, *324*, *328–9*
Russell, B., 22, 104, *187*, *190*, *195*, *204*
'Rutherford, Mark' (W. Hale White), *171*, *262*, *287–8*, *325*

S

Sadler, M., 12
Sainte Beuve, 68n.
Saintsbury, G., 23n., 35, *137*, *274*, *324*, *335–6*
'Saki' (H. H. Munro), *262*, *311*
Santayana, G., *132*, *271*
Sardou, 108, *260*
Savage, M., 9, *261*, *266*
Schiller, F. C. S., *175*, *188*, *204*
Scott, Sir W., 6, 73, *268*, *269*
Scott, W. B., *209*, *227*, *228*
Scribe, 108, *260*
'Scrutator' (W. K. Hurlock), *351*
Seaman, Sir O., *213*, *346*, *349*, *350*
Seeley, Sir J. R., *140*, *149*, *175*
Seth (Pringle Pattison), A., *175*, *187*, *195–6*, *197*, *198*, *337*
Shaftesbury, Lord, 12, 124, *135*, *171*
Shakespeare, W., xii, 23, 65, 111, *255*, *256*, *335*, *336*, *337*
Sharp, W. ('Fiona Macleod'), *209*, *236*, *263*
Shaw, G. B., xvi, 3, 12, 55, 101, 102, 108, 109, 110, 111, 113, *132*, *137*, *165*, *249*, *258–9*, *263*, *325*
Shelley, P. B., xiii, xvi, 31, *235*, *265*
Shorthouse, J. H., 9, *176*, *262*, *286*
Sidgwick, H., *187*, *193–4*
Siemens, Sir W., 122
Sinclair, M., *188*, *210*, *262*, *273*, *312–13*, *325*
Smart, C., 56
Smiles, S., xvi, 4, 126, *166*, *214*, *324*, *327*
Smith, Adam, xiv, 89

Smith, Alexander, *209*, *222*, *347*
Smith, G. Adam, *141*, *158*, *159*, *175*
Smith, Toulmin, 120
Somervell, D. C., 15, *136*, *164*
'Somerville and Ross', *261*, *276*, *280–281*
Somerville, M., *166*
Sophocles, 74
Sorley, W. R., *175*, *188*, *196*, *197*
Sowerby, G., 109, *249*, *257*
Speke, J. H., *159*, *164*
Spencer, H., 102, *141*, *188*, *193*, *194*, *199*, *200*, *201–2*
Spenser, E., xv
Spinoza, *187*
Squire, Sir J., *209*, *245*, *247*, *263*, *325*
Stanley, A. P., *138*, *140*, *142*, *147*, *159*
Stanley, Sir H. M., *159*, *164*
Stead, W. T., *141*, *156*
Steel, F. A., *139*, *262*, *305–6*
Steele, R., xi, xvi
Stephen, Sir J., 88, *140*, *144*, *325*
Stephen, Sir J. FitzJames, *141*, *144*, *153*
Stephen, J. K., *346*, *347*, *349*, *350*
Stephen, Sir L., 104, *138*, *141*, *153*, *190*, *325*
Stephens, J., *209*, *246*, *263*
Sterling, J., *188*, *324*, *326*
Sterne, L., *332*
Stevenson, R. L., 5, 21, 60, 81–2, *167*, *210*, *262*, *296*, *299–300*, *321*, *325*, *335*
Stirling, J. H., *175*, *187*, *192*
Stout, G. F., *188*, *200*
Stubbs, Bishop W., *140*, *148*
Surtees, R. S., 5, 67–8, 69, 119, *261*, *276*, *277–8*, *279*
Swedenborg, 42n.
Swift, J., 18, 102, 110
Swinburne, A. C., 12, 19, 29, 41, 43, 45–48, 49, 50, 51, 107, *209*, *223*, *225–7*, *233*, *234*, *249*, *263*, *273*, *325*, *349*
Swinnerton, F. A., *262*, *293*, *300*, *315*, *325*
Symonds, J. A., *141*, *324*, *329*, *330*
Symons, A., 53, 99, 101, *137*, *210*, *240*, *263*, *324*, *329*, *330*, *331*
Synge, J. M., 111, 112, *210*, *249*, *259*

T

Taine, 123
Talfourd, Sir T. N., 107, *210*, *249*, *250*
Tawney, R. H., xiii
Taylor, A. E., *188*, *198*

Taylor, Sir H., 107, *139*, *210*, *249*, *250-1*, *325*
Taylor, J., xvi, 21
Taylor, Meadows, *139*, *141*, *159*, *261*, *268*
Taylor, T., 107, *210*, *249*, *252-3*
Tennyson, Alfred, Lord, 5, 6, 11, 17, 18, 19, 24-9, 30, 33, 35, 41, 59, 107, 114, 121, *179*, *209*, *212*, *215-16*, *219*, *220*, *228*, *249*
Tennyson, F., *209*, *215*, *216*
Thackeray, A. I. (Lady Ritchie), 20, *261*, *274-5*, *325*
Thackeray, W. M., 20, 21, 58, 60, 61, 62, 64-5, 66, 67, 68, 69, 74, 75, 82, 93, 121, *137*, *141*, *171*, *210*, *213*, *261*, *266*, *268*, *273-4*, *321*, *325*, *332*
Thomas, E., *209*, *243-4*, *325*
Thomas, G., 122
Thompson, F., 9, 50n., 53, *176*, *209*, *231*, *233*, *325*
Thomson, J. ('B. V.'), 38-9, *209*, *234-235*, *325*
Tout, T. F., *140*, *151*
Toynbee, A., *141*, *156*, *174*
Traherne, T., 18
Traill, H. D., *137*, *141*, *145*, *210*, *324*, *332-3*
Trelawney, E. J., *139*, *159*, *160*, *263*
Trench, H., *209*, *238*, *250*
Trevelyan, G. M., *141*, *144*, *146*, *150*, *152-3*, *289*, *325*
Trevelyan, Sir G. O., *138*, *140*, *146*, *147*, *150*, *152*
Trollope, A., 5, 20, 21, 60, 61, 68, 69, 124, *137*, *171*, *261*, *266*, *270*, *274*, *275*, *276*, *279*, *316*
Trollope, F., *261*, *266*, *282*
Trollope, T. A., *141*, *261*, *279-80*, *325*
Tupper, J. L., 43
Tupper, M., 5, 23, *209*, *213*
Turner, C. Tennyson, *209*, *215*, *216*
Turner, J. M. W., 92
Turner, W. J., 55n.
Tylor, Sir E. B., *166*, *169*
Tyndall, J., *159*, *166*, *169*
Tyrrell, G., *175*, *184*, *185*

V

Venn, J., *187*, *189*
Victoria, Queen, xix, *135*, *327*
Vinogradoff, Sir P., *141*, *152*, *155*
Von Hügel, Baron F., *175*, *184*, *185*, *188*

W

Wallace, A. R., *159*, *166*, *167*, *168*, *175*, *188*
Wallace, E., *302*
Wallace, W., *187*, *194*
Walpole, Sir H., *262*, *279*, *315-16*
Ward, Mrs Humphry, *262*, *288*
Ward, J., *188*, *194*, *200*
Ward, W. G., *175*, *176*, *179*, *188*
Waterton, C., *159*, *161*
Watson, Sir W., 54, *137*, *209*, *237*
Watt, J., xiv
Watts-Dunton, T., 47n., *209*, *227*, *263*
Webb, B. and S., 3, 102, *139*, *141*, *157*
Wells, H. G., 3, 4, 54, 58, 84-5, 102, 110, 115, *139*, *141*, *166*, *262*, *291*, *308-9*, *342*
Wesley, C., *180*
Westcott, Bishop B. F., *141*, *174*, *175*, *183-4*
Westermarck, E., *141*, *166*, *175*, *188*, *203*
Weyman, S., 82, *262*, *300*
Whewell, W., *187*, *188*, *189*
Whibley, C., *141*, *324*, *334*, *337*
Whistler, J. McN., 92
Whitehead, A. N., *170*, *187*, *190*
Whiteing, R., *262*, *294*
Whitman, W., 104, *207*
Whitworth, 122
Whymper, E., *159*, *161*
Whyte-Melville, G. J., 68, *261*, *276*, *279*
Wilde, O., 22, 76, 100-1, 108-9, *210*, *249*, *254*, *263*, *296*, *325*
Williams, I., *139*, *175*, *176*, *177-8*, *210*
Wolff, J., *159*, *161-2*
Wood, Mrs Henry, *262*, *316-17*
Woolner, T., 41, 44, *209*, *228*
Wordsworth, W., 23, 25, 28, 33, 52, 100, *154*, *211*

Y

Yeats, W. B., 57, 111, 112, *137*, *209*, *239*, *250*
Yonge, C. M., 9, 58, 63n., *141*, *176*, *262*, *285-6*, *291*, *320*, *321*
Young, G. M., 14n., 78n., 121, *135*

Z

Zangwill, I., *250*, *262*, *294*, *312*
Zola, E., *291*